The Irish General

The Irish General

Thomas Francis Meagher

Paul R. Wylie

University of Oklahoma Press : Norman

Library of Congress Cataloging-in-Publication Data

Wylie, Paul R., 1936–
    The Irish general : Thomas Francis Meagher / Paul R. Wylie.
        p.   cm.
    Includes bibliographical references and index.
    ISBN 978-0-8061-3847-3 (cloth)
    ISBN 978-0-8061-4185-5 (paper)
    1. Meagher, Thomas Francis, 1823–1867.   2. Generals—United States—Biography.
3. United States. Army—Biography.   4. United States—History—Civil War, 1861–
1865—Biography.   5. Irish Americans—Biography.   6. Revolutionaries—Ireland—
Biography.   7. Ireland—History—1837–1901—Biography.   8. Pioneers—Montana—
Biography.   I. Title.
    E467.1.M4W95   2007
    355.0092—dc22
    [B]

                                                                        2007002881

3 4 5 6 7 8 9 10

Contents

Illustrations

Acknowledgments

Researching and writing this book was not an easy task, and it took many weekends and evenings, and the understanding of my family, to complete it. I would first like to thank my wife, Arlene, for her unfailing support for this work and her careful reading of its passages over a period of several years. I also had the support of my children, Lynne Catherine Wylie, John Wylie, and Thomas Wylie, and my brother-in-law Michael Klem, who all gave needed encouragement, each in their unique way, as did Alice Wylie, my 102-year-old mother, whose blindness will prevent her from ever reading the book, but there will be other ways to let her share in what is written here.

Pierce Mullen, now a retired history professor from Montana State University and my longtime friend, gave me invaluable guidance. If it were not for Pierce's support and enthusiasm for this project, it might have long since been discarded. While Pierce provided the assurance I needed, my friend Volney Steele, M.D., who became the author of several history books and articles after he retired from medicine, provided a role model.

After the manuscript was first assembled, Pierce put me in touch with historian Ursula Smith, who gave me some valuable writing advice and an introduction to Chuck Rankin, editor-in-chief at the University of Oklahoma Press. After looking over a couple of chapters and an out-line, Chuck suggested that I continue with the project. I needed someone with experience to review the manuscript and give me an evaluation, and

I asked my old grade-school friend, Ivan Doig, to suggest someone. Ivan directed me to Marianne Keddington-Lang, who looked at some of the writing and offered approval and some helpful comments. Marianne also suggested that I try to enlist the services of Martha Kohl in Helena to work with me to edit the manuscript, and I was lucky enough to find she had time to do the job. Martha and I had many meetings over a period of time, and at the end of our joint effort I had a manuscript ready to send to the University of Oklahoma Press for formal review. Before sending it, Wendy Zirngibl, a Montana State University graduate student in history, now in a doctoral program, worked hard with me to assure the endnotes were in order.

As part of the Press's evaluation, Professors David Emmons and Susannah U. Bruce reviewed the manuscript and gave heartening approval as well as constructive suggestions, which were passed on to me and resulted in a better book. As the editorial process continued, I received even more support from Chuck Rankin and Christi Madden, and then in turn from Alice Stanton, managing editor at the Press, and Kathy Burford Lewis, who did the copyediting.

During the research phase, I received much help from historians, archivists, librarians, and others. Time and space do not permit me to mention all of these people, but there are those who went out of their way to be helpful. If Brian Shovers hadn't shown the interest he did when I first walked into the Montana Historical Society Research Library, the project could have wilted. Also at the library, Ellie Arguimbau, Jody Foley, Angela Murray, and Charlene Porsild gave valuable advice and assistance. At the Huntington Library in San Marino, California, Romaine Ahlstom and her staff provided valuable information and an opportunity to review important archival materials. When it came time to decide on illustrations, Lory Morrow, Becca Kohl, and Katie Curey of the Montana Historical Society Photo Archives gave their expert assistance. Civil War author Joe Bilby helped me get in touch with Michael MacAfee and Jack McCormick, who both supplied hard-to-find photos of Thomas Francis Meagher. Reg Watson of Tasmania, a fellow Meagher biographer, graciously helped look for a photo taken there. Catherine Greene, the sculptor of the Meagher statue in Waterford, helped out by providing me with her own photos of the work.

While I did most of the archival research myself, Matt Treacy of Dublin obtained documents from the National Library of Ireland, Carrie Johnson helped in getting documents from the National Archives in Washington, and Keegan Sapp reviewed files and copied documents for me in the New York State Library in Albany. I would also like to thank court clerks Nancy Sweeney in Helena and Bundy Bailey in Virginia City, who worked with me to locate important court records. Kim Allen Scott, a fellow Oklahoma Press author and the head of the Montana State University Library Special Collections, helped me locate documents, and Dave Martinez of the Spain-Sedivy Resource Center at the MSU Library provided me with the knowledge and skill to conduct my review of what seemed to be endless microfilm.

While Arlene and I were collecting material on a tour of the Civil War battlefields where Meagher had fought, battlefield historians Robert Krick and Frank O'Reilly assisted me. Mike Gamble gave us a wonderful private tour of Antietam, and Tom White of the George Tyler Moore Center for the Study of the Civil War was most helpful while we were there. After returning from the tour I was able to consult with Professor Brian Burton on the identification of certain documents relating to Meagher's military career.

I would also like to thank the members of two groups to which I belong. The first is the venerable eighty-five-year-old QK Club of Bozeman. QK stands for "Quest for Knowledge," and this scholarly, talented, and eclectic group meets six times a year to hear its members give papers. They listened attentively one evening while I talked about Meagher, and the topic seemed to receive their approval, which gave me motivation to delve further into his fascinating history. The second group, the Boulder River Literary Society, is perhaps unknown to anyone other than its four members, who are, in addition to myself, architect George Mattson, English professor George Slanger, and attorney Steve Foster. We have known one another for decades, and we gather annually in good fellowship at a cabin on the river to discuss our projects and goad one another into taking on hard tasks. Mine was *The Irish General*.

The Irish General

Introduction

In Helena, Montana, an imposing equestrian statue of Thomas Francis Meagher stands in front of the State Capitol. One might assume that a prominent statue in that location would honor a famous person in the state, but that is not the Meagher legacy. He was indeed famous: in Ireland for his part in the 1848 Revolution; in New York City for his lectures, social contacts, and editorship of the *Irish News;* in the Civil War as the commanding general of the celebrated Irish Brigade. But he was not acclaimed for his deeds in Montana, despite service as both territorial secretary and acting territorial governor.

Meagher's story is told on the tablets at the base of the statue. Even they make no claim for greatness in Montana. Instead the inscriptions speak of the death sentence that Meagher received for treason against the British Crown. That punishment was not carried out, in favor of exile for life to the penal colony in Tasmania. Meagher found himself sentenced because, as a member of the "Young Ireland" group of well-educated Irish intellectuals, he had come to believe that the only way to Ireland's freedom from England was through the use of arms.

As one of the leaders of an aborted revolution in 1848, Meagher captured the imagination of the Irish and roused the ire of the English. Tried for high treason in October 1848, he was found guilty and sentenced to be drawn on a hurdle, hung, and quartered. He asked for no

The Meagher statue in Helena, Montana. In 1905 thousands attended the dedication of the famous Thomas Francis Meagher equestrian statue in front of the Capitol building in Helena. The statue was funded by Irish groups from around the state, and no public funds were used. (Courtesy Montana Historical Society, Helena)

mercy, instead choosing to become a martyr and defy the Crown to carry out the sentence. The punishment was reduced anyway to transportation for life to Tasmania, along with six other revolutionaries.

As the tablets on Meagher's statue in Montana tell, he made a perilous escape from Tasmania. Proceeding to New York, Meagher became the celebrity of the moment. He fit the mold perfectly—a young, handsome, and articulate Irishman, a revolutionary, and a brilliant orator. So gifted a speaker was Meagher, traveling to the far corners of the United States to deliver his orations, that he found himself on the same bill with the likes of Daniel Webster and William Makepeace Thackeray.

After stints as a lawyer, a newspaper editor, and a Central American adventurer, Meagher joined the Union army, ultimately rising to the rank of brigadier general. The choice to support the Union was not an easy one for Meagher, who had visited the South and knew many good Irish Catholics there. After deciding that the Union Army would serve well as a training ground for a future Irish revolutionary force, however, he joined the Irish 69th New York State Militia. With patriotic eagerness and typical flamboyance, he fought as a militia captain and then colonel in the first Battle of Bull Run.

A falling out with his superior officer, William Tecumseh Sherman, would have lasting effects; but in the short-term Meagher thrived, using his gift of oratory to recruit Irish troops to the Union cause. Soon he had assembled an entire brigade and was off to war once again as a brigadier general. On the eve of the brigade's first major engagement, Chaplain Father William Corby ominously predicted that most of Meagher's troops would die. As the volunteer Irish Brigade gained stature as a fighting unit and was thrown into the major battles of the Civil War, Corby's prophecy proved true. The ranks of the brigade were reduced from over a thousand men to only a few hundred after the battles of the Peninsula Campaign, Antietam, Fredericksburg, and Chancellorsville. The casualty numbers reflect the men's courage, and the Irish Brigade is still remembered for the vigor and dash of its members, their persistent suicidal attacks on the wall at Marye's Heights, and the stirring oratory of its leaders.

Meagher was not with the Irish Brigade during the last two years of the war, but the Irish general would be permanently linked to those legendary troops. He played an essential part in the creation and early reputation of the brigade, and its later brave deeds burnished Meagher's own reputation. It would still be referred to as "Meagher's Brigade" long after he had left the field as its commander.

Meagher's later Civil War career was less illustrious, and he ended his service amid rumors of incompetence and drunkenness, perhaps exacerbated by the horror of witnessing the slaughter of so many of the men he had recruited. In the end he was sent home to New York in disgrace, without the brevet promotion to major general that he had hoped for and with a court-martial pending. Meagher's relationship with the American Irish had soured as well, for the press had carried some unkind words that Meagher had written about his compatriots.

Out of a job and out of favor with the New York Irish, Meagher wandered into a lecture in New York given by Montana trailblazer James Liberty Fisk, touting an upcoming expedition soon departing from Minnesota for Montana. Meagher signed on to join him. Meagher had requested a territorial governorship from President Andrew Johnson. In St. Paul (departure point for the Fisk wagons) he received word that Johnson had appointed him territorial secretary of Montana. He arrived in Montana by stagecoach in September 1865 and immediately found himself acting governor, because the appointed governor, Sidney Edgerton, had left the territory for the East.

By the time Meagher reached Montana, the political tensions that were to dominate the last years of his life had already emerged. Radical Republicans, Confederates, Democrats, Copperheads, political opportunists, government-appointed judges, miners, highwaymen, Masons, Fenians, and vigilantes were already established there. The vigilantes had attained a hefty record of swift justice and hangings. These men, their few wives, and their clashing cultures had descended on the territory in a period of only a few years.

Meagher was no stranger to controversy when he reached Montana. He had conquered adversity before. As a bold and brash idealist in his twenties he had incited armed revolt against the English. In his early thirties he had arrived as an escaped prisoner in New York to the tumultuous welcome of tens of thousands and had become perhaps the best-known Irishman in the United States. In the Civil War he had become a brigadier general and led the famous Irish Brigade, renowned for its valor. He had also suffered the tragedy of the early death of his mother, incarceration, political defeat, the death of comrades, the death of a wife and a son, and, as a front-line commander in the Civil War, watching the suffering and killing of the men under his command. Despite his past resilience, in Montana he found that he could not straddle the wide political gulfs that existed there.

Although Meagher was only forty-two when he arrived in Montana Territory, time and circumstances had taken their toll. He had lost some of the respect he once had, and certainly he had been worn down by the events of his troubled life. What he had left when he reached Montana was his fame as an Irish revolutionary, his oratorical skills, the ability to work long and hard, and the respect due his military rank and combat service. What he had lost was his previously good relationship with the Irish leadership in the East, his ability to mingle with the politically powerful of the country, and any defense against his intemperate habits. He had been given an opportunity by President Johnson. Montana was his last chance to rebuild his reputation, but he would fail.

Mistaken for a Unionist Republican when he first arrived, Meagher soon became the symbolic leader of the Democrats and was taken to task by the territory's most prominent newspaper. A legislature he called was ruled illegal; and his political detractors hung the term "bogus" on it, even though its invalidity was debatable. Serving under two appointed governors, he was twice left for lengthy periods to run the territorial government as they flitted in and out of Montana to serve their own interests. For his trouble he earned from his detractors the derisive title "The Acting One."

As acting governor Meagher heeded the call of fearful local citizens of all political stripes and organized a militia to fight off expected attacks from the Indians. These efforts resulted in his being called a "Stampeder" by General William Tecumseh Sherman, who suddenly withdrew his support after the militia had been formed and was in the field. After Meagher's death, Sherman unfairly blamed him for the large debt that had been run up. Unfortunately, much of the blame stuck and has passed down through history as Meagher's legacy. While his detractors during his life viciously criticized his judgment, distinguished historians such as Hubert Howe Bancroft also have assailed his character: "As for Meagher he could be eloquent but he could not be honest," said Bancroft.[1] Yet it was lack of judgment and not dishonesty that Meagher had been accused of in his lifetime. Even his most vociferous political enemies found him a man of principle.

The tragedy of the last chapter in Meagher's life is recorded cryptically on yet another tablet on his statue in Helena: Meagher, last seen in Fort Benton on the night of July 1, 1867, was presumed drowned. Conflicting reports cite the cause of his disappearance as murder, suicide, and drunken accident. Although the circumstances of his death remain cloudy, Meagher had clearly reached a crisis point. He was out of a job and heavily in debt, thousands of miles away from New York, a continent and an ocean away from Ireland, and he had not been able to control his drinking for years.

Friend and foe alike produced polite eulogies after Meagher's death and memorialized his leadership and contributions. But these sentiments were only temporary. The calling of the "Bogus Legislature" and Sherman's indictment of him as a "Stampeder" obscured Meagher's earlier accomplishments. Even some Irish nationalists questioned his contributions. Yet, for the most part, Meagher retained a place of honor for his commitment to Irish freedom. He remained well enough known in the Irish world that in 1904 the loyal Irish of Montana commissioned the monument to him in front of the State Capitol in Helena from privately raised funds.

Meagher's record, then, remains blurred and polarized. Historians and commentators have settled on referring to him simply as "colorful"—and they may have it right. But perhaps a more apt single-word description of Meagher would be simply "orator," a tribute that was paid to him by the whole world. Indeed, his memory has been honored by his inclusion in various compendiums of the world's greatest orators of all times. As Claude Bowers said in his book containing biographical sketches of the nine greatest Irish orators of history:

> The passion of Meagher, his rapid-fire method of attack, his exceptional capacity for condensation, his extraordinary ability to paint a picture, to find an illuminating analogy, to draw an indictment, to run the gamut of emotions, to coin a phrase, to crucify with a characterization, make him unique even among the Irish orators. Added to this, his wonderful vocabulary, his mastery of the music of words, the exalted lyrical quality of his

finest passages, impart to his speeches a literary tone that is lacking in some of Ireland's more virile orators.[2]

But one word would never do Meagher justice, no matter how appropriate, and a true appraisal of the man can only be found in the details of his life. I have tried to report both Meagher's consistencies and his inconsistencies in this book, which tells the story of a young boy in Ireland, an assiduous student of the classics, a romantic, a realist, a revolutionary, an exile in Tasmania, a celebrity speaker, a newspaperman, a visitor to the California gold fields, a lawyer, an adventurer in Central America, an army recruiter, a Civil War general, and a governor of the Montana Territory.

This is a story of a man who possessed literary gifts and the ability to use them; a man capable of great leadership, symbolically expressed by the equestrian statue; a man daring enough to take to the seas to escape his exile; a man with both nerve and ability enough to mingle with the great American leaders of his age despite being a newly arrived Irishman; and a man with ambition enough to start his own newspaper in New York City.

It is also a story fraught with hard personal truths, including an improvident marriage; the birth of two sons he never saw; the death of his first wife while she was separated from him by an ocean; a second marriage into New York society; and a disastrous fascination with alcohol, which began as a romanticized conviviality and ended with bouts of intemperance that damaged his judgment and blemished his reputation.

Finally, this is the story of a devout Catholic who held an almost naive belief in a great brotherhood of gentlemen of superior status, regardless of their religion or political stance. Meagher's willingness to question the Catholic hierarchy caused him no end of political trouble. He remained committed to old friends and comrades, some of whom showed him little mercy as critics and lashed out at him with resentment and envy after he became famous in America.

Today Thomas Francis Meagher remains a fascinating and unresolved enigma. His admirers remember him first as an Irish patriot and second as the bold leader of the Irish Brigade in the Civil War. His name appears in almost all Irish histories, and he is mentioned prominently in many if not most of them. In New York he is still well remembered, as the Irish

Famous Irishmen. This is an 1850 lithograph of the most famous Irishmen of history. It shows Daniel O'Connell seated at the table in the first row, with Meagher standing in the second row between the first two gentlemen to the right of O'Connell. Also included are such famous historical figures as Theobold Wolfe Tone, Henry Grattan, Father Theobold Mathew, and Brian Boru. (Courtesy National Library of Ireland)

Brigade Association continues to march in the St. Patrick's Day parade. Yet in Montana, where the impressive Meagher statue watches over the State Capitol, it is still sometimes the fashion to deride him for his abuse of alcohol and his presumed mishandling of territorial government.

Ultimately, these polarized views of Thomas Francis Meagher cannot be reconciled, but we need to gain a better understanding of the man hailed by some as a hero and dismissed by others as a sot. It was this desire that first prompted me, as a Montanan raised in Meagher County, to begin my research. Using lifelong discipline in finding and marshaling facts, I set out to report in an unbiased way the definitive story of Meagher's life. In so doing, I hope that a truer picture has emerged of the ever fascinating "Meagher of the Sword."

CHAPTER ONE

The Making of an
Irish Revolutionary

As far as Ireland was concerned, they left us, like blind and crippled children, in the dark.

Thomas Francis Meagher

In Waterford, Ireland, on February 29, 1848, a fashionably attired young man stepped forward to address the assembled townspeople. Thomas Francis Meagher, twenty-four years old, announced: "Fellow Citizens:— I ask you to select me as the representative of your opinions, in the British Parliament." He stated his intent clearly: "I shall go to the English House of Commons, to insist upon the right of this country to be held, governed, and defended by its own citizens, and by them alone." These were brave words for Meagher, for many in the audience were satisfied to continue under British rule—including his own father, Thomas Meagher, Sr., who had been the first Catholic mayor of Waterford and was himself a member of the British Parliament. He was not a supporter of his fiery son's political philosophy.[1]

The citizens of Waterford knew that Thomas Francis Meagher had an active, independent mind. They had watched him grow up and lead the other boys of his age on hikes up a barren hill across the River Suir, called locally "Mount Misery." Belying the dismal name, the heights were dear to Meagher as a place to climb and glory in the view of the city and its wharves below. There he could watch the merchant ships sailing off to the greater world beyond the distant horizon.[2] As Meagher observed and listened to the patterns and sounds of Waterford, he became aware that many Irish were leaving Ireland. His life had started to take direction, and he dreamed of great things. Years later he recounted those sights from Mount Misery:

> There was one scene I witnessed in the morning of my boyhood which left upon my memory an impression that can never be effaced. That scene was the departure of an emigrant-ship from the quay of my native city of Waterford. . . . On the deck of the ship were huddled hundreds of men, women and children—the sons and daughters of Innisfail—sorrow-stricken, and yet hopeful and heroic fugitives from the island that gave them birth. . . . Young as I was . . . I had heard enough of the cruelty that had, for years and years, been done to Ireland, to know that her people were leaving her, not from choice, but from compulsion; that it was not the sterility of the soil, or any other unfavorable dispensation of nature, but the malignant hostility of laws and practices, devised and enforced for the political subjugation of the country, which compelled them to leave.[3]

The misery that Meagher witnessed was rooted in centuries-long dominance of Ireland by England. It began in the twelfth century, when Pope Adrian IV granted the king of England the title and right to be lord of Ireland. From that time on, England considered Ireland its own. "On the morning of the 18th of October, in the year 1172, upon the broad waters of our native Suir, the spears and banners of a royal pirate were glittering in the sun," Meagher informed the audience before him. "[A]s the pageant moved up the stream . . . the name of Strongbow was heard amid the storm of shouts that rocked the galleys to and fro. He was the first adventurer that set his heel on Irish soil in the name of England; and he—the sleek, the cautious, and the gallant Strongbow— was the type and herald of that plague with which this island has been cursed for seven desolating centuries." The invaders that Meagher spoke of were Anglo-Normans, and Strongbow was the name given to Richard fitz Gilbert de Clare, Earl of Pembroke. He had come across the Irish

Sea with a small force to invade Ireland and take Waterford and Dublin. "By force or fraud—by steel or gold—by threat or smile— . . . they have held this island ever since that morning in October, 1172—seducing those whom they could not terrify—slaying those whom they could neither allure nor intimidate," Meagher said.[4]

The rest of the story is told in Irish history. Soon after Strongbow, King Henry II of England came to start the rule of Ireland by the English. But English power was far from total; and by the fourteenth and fifteenth centuries it was limited to only a small area around Dublin known as the "Pale."[5] In Meagher's time, however, England was in total control, and the people of the Emerald Isle did not even have an Irish Parliament to pass their own laws. Instead they had been given a number of seats in the British Parliament, one of which Meagher was running for. But he left no doubt that he would not be content with the Parliament that he sought to enter making laws for his Ireland.

As early as 1297 England had given Ireland an ineffective legislative body of only Anglo-Norman members and had excluded the native Irish, and this is what rankled Meagher. At best that Parliament had from the start served only as a tool of the British to legitimize their control. When even the mock legislature came to threaten England, the English imposed Poynings Law of 1494, binding the Irish Parliament to legislate only if the Crown approved of its bills.[6] The British Parliament applied more control in 1720, when it passed the "Declaratory Act" and for the first time ever took unto itself the right to pass laws for Ireland.[7]

Thomas Francis Meagher and his ancestors were Catholics. Over the years the Meaghers had felt the sting of Anglican rule, which exacerbated the conflict with the English. The first attempt at suppression of Catholicism in Ireland came during the reign of Henry VIII, who had just founded the Church of England as an antipapist church with the king himself as its head. Thereafter, as the English tried to force Protestantism on all of Ireland, the Catholic "Old English"—those who had moved to Ireland before the founding of the Anglican Church—often joined with their Gaelic compatriots to resist.[8]

During Queen Elizabeth's reign, English determination to convert Ireland intensified. England's narrow escape from the Spanish Armada in 1588 had convinced the queen that an independent Catholic Ireland could unite with Catholic Spain to spell doom for England. The Tudor monarchs then set out in earnest to subjugate Ireland and achieved almost total English control of the Emerald Isle for the first time.[9]

English rule until the end of the sixteenth century was bad enough, but it became worse when a small number of landed Irish Catholics in the North took flight from the English. The English king, James I, seized the unclaimed land to start Ulster Plantation. Soon it was colonized with Presbyterians from Scotland, under English landowners.[10] Relations between English Protestants and Irish Catholics worsened even further during the English Civil War, after the Catholic-hating Oliver Cromwell gained control of England. Cromwell's English army invaded Ireland in 1649. In the space of only nine months he succeeded in slaughtering thousands of Irish as he swept through Drogheda and Wexford, fixing in the minds of the Irish (and Meagher's ancestors among them) the deepest hatred for the English. Meagher could take small pride that Cromwell had failed to take his native Waterford.[11]

The Restoration—after Cromwell's death in 1658—provided a brief era of religious tolerance, but anti-Catholicism was revived when the English-controlled Irish Parliament in Dublin commenced the passage of the "Penal Laws." Protestant political philosopher Edmund Burke described these laws in the eighteenth century as "a machine of wise and elaborate contrivance, as well fitted for the oppression, impoverishment and degradation of a people, and the debasement in them of human nature itself, as ever proceeded from the perverted ingenuity of man."[12]

The infamous laws controlled every aspect of Catholic life: all priests had to register their names and parishes under penalty of being branded on the cheek with a hot iron, and all Catholic bishops were banned from Ireland. Being hanged, drawn, and quartered was the penalty for staying. The laws ordered crosses used on Catholic churches or in Catholic services destroyed, and no Catholic chapel could have a belfry, tower, or steeple. Catholics were barred from being members of the Irish Parliament or voting for members of Parliament, excluded from grand juries, and forbidden to send their children abroad for education or to have their own schools. Catholics were prohibited from marrying Protestants; a death penalty for priests who married Protestants to Catholics was enacted; and all marriages not performed by a minister of the Protestant Church of Ireland were invalidated. Catholics were barred from the practice of law or from sitting as magistrates or judges, denied membership in municipal corporations, and prevented from holding commissions in the army or navy. Owning or carrying arms was prohibited for Catholics—including the wearing of a sword, which was considered the mark of gentlemen in the seventeenth century. Catholics were forbidden to own a horse with a value over five pounds; this was enforced by granting a Protestant the right to buy any horse owned by a Catholic for that amount. No Catholic could buy, receive as a gift, or inherit land from a Protestant. A Catholic fortunate enough to have land could not will it as a whole but had to divide it among his male heirs, unless the eldest son would turn Protestant, in which case he could inherit the whole estate. No Catholic could hold a lease longer than thirty-one years.[13]

As the insidious Penal Laws multiplied, their cruelty became so evident that even prominent Anglicans who were loyal to the Crown rose to question the British rule. These included Jonathan Swift, dean of St. Patrick's Church, who, although anti-Catholic himself, wrote anonymously in his *Drapier's Letters* in protest. Other well-known writers soon joined him, and the humanitarian movement against the British mistreatment of Ireland and its people began. While Swift's anti-British writings dealt with legislative independence, George Berkeley, the Episcopal bishop of Cloyne, writing in the mid-1730s, posed searching social questions about the living conditions of the Catholic peasants, asking "whether there be upon earth any Christian or civilized people as beggarly, wretched and destitute as the common Irish?"[14]

By the time Meagher was born on August 3, 1823, many of the Penal Laws had already been revoked; but their presence during a large part of the eighteenth century had caused inestimable damage to the Irish Catholics. Traditional Catholic families were broken up as they lost their lands. Only the very few upper-class Catholics had the option to leave the country. The poor peasants had few choices. Their religion made them outlaws, with no redress of the wrongs against them available from their landlords, the courts, or their Parliament, which did not represent them. They became suspicious of everything, especially all things English. Secret societies emerged as the "Oak Boys," "White Boys," and "Ribbon Men," who dispensed their own form of justice against their fellow Catholics if they became informers or supplanters of evicted tenants or were found to be on the side of the landlords.[15]

The Penal Laws also had a devastating effect on many Catholics of the landed or merchant class, who, unwilling to martyr themselves, converted to the Anglican Church of Ireland to avoid persecution and preserve their lands. Secrecy had become paramount in all phases of life, for the Catholic peasants had to protect their priests and their places of worship. During the period when the Penal Laws were in full force, education was conducted clandestinely. "Hedge schools"—so named because they were held outdoors, no buildings being considered safe—became prevalent and were supported by the peasants out of their meager earnings.[16]

Thomas Francis Meagher's family had escaped the worst consequences of the Penal Laws. Born into a family of little means in County Tipperary in the 1760s, Meagher's grandfather, also named Thomas, avoided the oppressive English laws by emigrating to Newfoundland, where the great fisheries were being harvested. As a young man, he apprenticed to a tailor and clothier named Crotty, who soon died, leaving Mary Crotty as a widow. Thomas Meagher married her and took over Crotty's business, which he expanded in the following years to include commercial shipping between St. John's, Newfoundland, and Waterford.

Thomas Francis Meagher's father, Thomas Francis Meagher, Sr., was born in Newfoundland in 1789, and an uncle, Henry Meagher, was born there in 1792. In 1816 his grandfather Thomas Meagher brought his two sons into business with him and sent Thomas Francis Meagher, Sr., to Ireland as his agent in Waterford. There he married Alicia Quan, the daughter of Thomas Quan of the venerable Wyse, Cashen and Quan, one of the largest trading companies in Waterford. The newlyweds first resided at No. 51 King Street in a house large enough for Henry Meagher to live with them. Then they acquired an interest in an impressive property across from the quay, which had been owned by the Quans. This site was so large that it later became the Commins Hotel and served as the transportation terminal for Charles Bianconi's Coach Service. Still later it became the Granville Hotel.[17]

This history placed young Thomas Francis in a privileged position, but it did not inure him to the social problems that surrounded him. As he learned more about Ireland's tortured past, he placed the blame for them squarely on the English. He also became enamored with earlier advocates for Irish freedom. Meagher was particularly impressed with the vision and courage that Henry Grattan had displayed toward the end of the eighteenth century. In an age when it had been neither popular nor safe to speak out in favor of Irish separation from England, Grattan, a Protestant member of the Irish Parliament in the 1770s, spoke loudly and often in favor of Ireland's total legislative independence. When the American Revolution caused redeployment of British forces out of Ireland, Grattan seized upon the opportunity to raise a volunteer force under the guise of defending Ireland against an invasion by the French but in reality to apply pressure on Britain. He soon ran into a problem when Catholic priests prohibited their parishioners from participating in his efforts. Nonetheless, by 1782 Grattan's labors had yielded some results, and the British Parliament for a time gave up its right to make Ireland's laws. In his speech in Waterford in February 1848 Meagher had said that the day Grattan's Parliament convened was "the one 'great day'—the only one—which Ireland has had." In 1793 Grattan obtained a major victory when the Catholic Relief Act was passed, giving Catholics in Ireland the right to be admitted to the practice of law.[18]

It was Grattan, the Protestant, who had started the first steps toward Catholic emancipation. It was Meagher, the Catholic, who stood before the group assembled in the Waterford on that day in 1848 and con-fronted the town's elders. "I tell you, Gentlemen—you, who are in that inconvenient corner there, and think you represent the city—I tell you this, that public men were more just and chivalrous in the days of Grattan than they are in yours; and if in the war of parties there might have been a keener enmity, there was assuredly less falsehood, and less cant."[19]

Young Thomas Francis Meagher came to have the greatest respect for Grattan's legislative accomplishments. But perhaps what impressed him even more were Grattan's incorruptible principles. When the British had sought to silence Grattan by offering him a post at Dublin Castle, the seat of British government in Ireland, he declined rather than subject himself to the subtle bribery and charge that he served for profit under the viceroy.[20] It was a point of honor that made a profound impression on Meagher, whose disdain for "place hunting" became a key part of his political philosophy and rhetoric. "Down with the place-beggar!" Meagher shouted at the crowd at the Waterford Court House in 1848. "He would traffic on a noble cause, and beg a bribe in the name of liberty. Down with the place-beggar!"[21] Grattan died in 1820, but his political achievements and personal honor became legend. In the 1840s Meagher proudly became president of the Grattan Club in Dublin.[22]

Grattan's legislative advances were followed in 1791 by Irish unrest; the Society of the United Irishmen was formed under Theobold Wolfe Tone and included both Protestants and Catholics as a militant anti-British group in Northern Ireland.[23] Their goal was independence for Ireland, but they also sought Catholic emancipation. With the success of the American Revolution, the Presbyterians of the North became more enamored with republican forms of government. When the Bastille fell in France on July 14, 1789, the news was greeted in Belfast with a joy that prompted an annual celebration of the event there for years after. When the United Irishmen seemed too strong, the British prime minister ordered them suppressed. The organization went underground and ultimately formed an alliance with the French for the overthrow of the British in Ireland by force. But just as it seemed that the interest of the Irish of both denominations had been joined, traditional religious persecution of the Catholics again broke out. In 1795 the Grand Orange Lodge of Ulster, which popularly became known as the Orange Order, was formed to combat Catholic Irish incursions on land traditionally worked by Presbyterian tenant farmers. A brief battle between the poorer classes of both denominations was followed by more brutal persecutions of Catholics. Many of them were driven south beyond the Shannon River, destroying the goal of the United Irishmen to unify a resistance against the British.[24]

Despite the bitter resentments that continue to this day between the Orangemen and the Catholics of Northern Ireland, Meagher always hoped the gulf could be bridged. In 1848 he declared before the crowd in Waterford: "I . . . have stretched out my hand to the Orangemen of Ulster, and from that spot, where the banner of King James was rent by the sword of William, have passionately prayed for the extinction of those feuds which have been transmitted to us through the rancorous blood of five generations."[25] Meagher always believed that Catholics and Protestants could get along in Northern Ireland, even though the resentments had seethed at the end of the eighteenth century. Even in the face of the presence of a large post–American Revolution British land force, the Irish Catholic peasants rose up in the Revolution of 1798. Although many of them were armed only with pitchforks and scythes, they achieved success for a short time at Wexford. They were aided by a small number of French troops, who were taken prisoner after a minor victory. The revolt was again condemned by the Catholic clergy and soon ground to an unsuccessful conclusion.[26] The Irish people did not mount another armed revolution for the next fifty years; but when they did, Thomas Francis Meagher was one of its leaders.

Subjugated even further to British will in 1800, a majority of the Irish Lords and Commons were bribed to pass the Act of Union, which put an end to any notion of Irish legislative independence by combining the Irish Parliament with the British Parliament in London. The Irish were given only a small minority of the seats, and Ireland was now firmly under the control of the British. They had taken over with the support of well-meaning but poorly informed Catholic bishops who became convinced that the Union would result in Catholic emancipation. Meagher read that Grattan had referred to them as "a band of prostituted men."[27] Nearly a half century later, having already attained oratorical fame in Ireland, Meagher echoed Grattan's denunciation of the Union in a speech at the Waterford Hustings on March 4, 1848: "I am an enemy of the Legislative Union—an enemy of that Union in every shape and form that it may assume—an enemy of that Union whatever blessing it may bring—an enemy of that Union whatever sacrifice its extinction may require. Maintain the Union, gentlemen, and maintain your beggary . . . your bankruptcy . . . your famine."[28]

Grattan was followed by a new Irish champion: Daniel O'Connell, one of the most effective advocates of Catholic emancipation the country would ever know. O'Connell came on the scene some twenty years before Meagher was born. Nevertheless, O'Connell lived long enough, and Meagher attained stature early enough, that the two clashed. O'Connell himself had been born in 1775, a descendant of an old Irish family, and had become a successful lawyer in Dublin, after Catholics were allowed to practice law. But O'Connell felt a burning resentment toward the British that drove him toward a much larger goal than just his personal success. A soldier, acting under the Penal Laws, had shot O'Connell's uncle, Arthur O'Leary, for refusing to sell his horse to a Protestant for five pounds, as required of a Catholic.[29]

In 1823, the year Meagher was born, O'Connell had become the leading voice in Ireland for Catholic emancipation and repeal of the

Act of Union. That year he founded the Catholic Relief Association to advocate the Catholic cause, with a flash of genius. An association membership could be bought for a penny a month, collected by the priests, thus bringing the masses, as well as the priests, to bear on Irish politics. In 1828 O'Connell stood for election to the British Parliament, from which Catholics were barred, and won by the sheer power of the newly mobilized Catholic majority. He was finally seated, and for the first time an Irish Catholic sat in the British Parliament. It was even more important to O'Connell that this had been accomplished without force, something unique in Europe at that time. O'Connell became the leading voice in Ireland for legislative independence, and his goal in the House of Commons was to repeal the Act of Union. He advocated peaceful means to accomplish that end, however, and was willing to accept a self-governing Ireland under the British Crown.[30]

During O'Connell's political career he was courted, and many times won over, by the British Whig government, which offered government positions for the Irish. While many viewed this "place hunting" as only a form of bribery, O'Connell felt assured that the placement of Irishmen in the government would lead to the right balance of independence.[31] Many disagreed with O'Connell, and his leadership did not go unchallenged in Ireland. Toward the end of his career, the independent-thinking Thomas Francis Meagher and his fellow revolutionaries would cause a tumult in the ranks of O'Connell's own organization as they effectively challenged his power.

Meagher was able to challenge O'Connell because of his own gifts of oratory but also with the benefits he accrued from his family. It could have been different. As his parents' second son, he thrived as a young boy; but some of his siblings did not, and the family was filled with tragedy. The Meagher family headstone at Faithlegg cemetery outside Waterford indicates that his older brother, also named Thomas, and a sister, Mary Josephine, died in infancy. A second sister, Alicia, who was four years younger than Meagher, died at the age of seven. Only Meagher and his year-older sister, Christine Mary, and younger brother, Henry, survived childhood.[32]

For Meagher, the cruelest loss was the death of his mother when he was only three and a half years old. The void that was left in his life could never be completely filled, but it was lessened by the efforts of his aunt Johanna Quan, who took over the challenging task of raising

Daniel O'Connell. (Courtesy National Library of Ireland)

her sister's children.[33] Another aunt, Christian Quan, with help from Meagher's father, had started the local Sisters of Charity convent in Waterford. That became a convenient place for little Thomas Francis to learn his letters and his catechism. Amid the nurturing Meagher and Quan families, the motherless child entered his boyhood with a "frank and happy nature," according to a childhood friend.[34]

Whatever his disadvantages, young Thomas Francis Meagher was to overcome them through the commitment to education and the economic means of his family. Following the upper-class tradition of strict boarding-school education, he was sent away in the spring when he was ten years old to the Jesuits at Clongowes College, an elementary and secondary boarding school set in the plains of Kildare some miles from Waterford. The school was near the center of an encirclement of ancient Irish villages with the gray River Liffey flowing past and presented a somber appearance when Meagher arrived in the drenching rain. The largest church near the school was Protestant, with a modest Catholic church and an unpretentious convent for three nuns nearby. Even during its establishment in 1814 Clongowes had endured the remnants of the Penal Laws, and Catholic education given by the Jesuit fathers had commenced on very tenuous grounds. From an early date, Clongowes had adopted the policy that children could not be removed from the school by their parents even for vacations during the eleven-month academic year, and they were encouraged to stay there even in the twelfth month.[35]

At Clongowes Meagher became fascinated with the classical writings he found in the library, where he spent many long hours in his studies. Nor was it all work. During his period at school, where "beer" was listed as one of the afternoon refreshments, Meagher also learned the mysteries of alcohol, as he delighted in the geniality of a variety of townspeople and clergy at the home of a local parish priest.[36] As the company sat on a hard clay floor, Meagher observed that "the sherry had gone round half a dozen times. . . . The port, too, had more than once circled." Then the order came from Father Kearney: "Jim, hand round the champagne."[37]

As described by his friend John Savage, Meagher's life at Clongowes was "distinguished for the heartiness with which he joined in all the freaks of student life, and the sudden impulses of study that enabled him to carry off the honors from those who had paled their brows in months of laborious scrutiny." It was Meagher's quickness of wit and mind that impressed Savage. "His mind was quick as gay, and retentive as playful."[38]

Even though he tended toward humor, young Meagher also had a questioning irreverence as he became aware of the Catholic Church's passivity in the face of English oppression. He had heard that the Irish Jesuits had sometimes been called conspirators against the stability of English rule—by the English, of course. But the charges seemed disingenuous to Meagher, because he viewed the Jesuits of Clongowes to be entirely content in their quarters as "hostages and aliens" rather than wanting to be "freemen and citizens."[39] Their lack of interest in seeking equality for their parishioners confused Meagher, for he thought surely in a God-fearing world there must be an answer to English dominance.

The inquiring young man soon found hope in a shabby-looking old book with miserable paper, print, and binding in the Clongowes library. In it was a speech by Daniel O'Connell, delivered in 1827. As Meagher read it, he was awakened to the global revolutionary movement and became fascinated with the words in front of him. "I look at home, and I am not disheartened," O'Connell had said. "I look abroad, and my spirit is exalted. From the coast of Labrador to where Cape Horn beholds two oceans commingle, Liberty is everywhere extending her dominion. Her voice comes to us across the Atlantic, is heard above the storm, and, like summer music in the heavens, gladdens the ear of seven millions of Irishmen."[40] The seed of revolution had fallen on fertile ground. Meagher was of the age to seek a cause, and he had found one. Ireland must be free from the English.

Despite his considerable talent and newfound revolutionary focus, Meagher's career at Clongowes did not end seriously. He finished up as part of a "historic episode" as leader of "The Gallant Seven"—a group of boys who one afternoon bolted from the supervision of Father Callan, the prefect of older students. The young men made their way in a rowboat for Dublin on the River Liffey; and soon Father John MacDonald, the master of rhetoric, followed in pursuit. He "found them in the height of enjoyment of a fine dinner" at a Dublin hotel. When MacDonald walked in, tradition has it that young Meagher, in a grand manner and with a display of gracious hospitality, ordered a place set for him and a chair drawn up, with the dinner going off amid the "utmost good humour." If Meagher received any punishment, it was not so severe as to discourage him and his fellow rhetoricians from presenting MacDonald with an engraved snuffbox as a sign of their respect.[41]

After Meagher had been at Clongowes for six years, his family decided that the gifted young man should seek further education. Although Trinity College in Dublin was a possibility, it was an institution founded by Queen Elizabeth I in 1592 to strengthen Protestant interests and had no great appeal for the devoutly Catholic Meagher family. And so, in the persistent rain, the sixteen-year-old Thomas Francis Meagher found himself in England at the Jesuit Stonyhurst College, a school even older than the collection of stone buildings that housed it on the south slope of Longridge Fell in Yorkshire. The college, which had moved there in 1794, originally had been founded in 1593 in St. Omer, France, to educate the children of English Catholics.[42] Many Irish sons had left their homes to study there before Meagher entered Stonyhurst in October 1839.[43] The school prided itself on academic discipline, and its curriculum was comprehensive and classical, with the philosophy of St. Thomas Aquinas added in. But even sterner order was practiced in the halls and dormitories, including constant monitoring by prefects, with "penance walks" of long duration as a punishment for minor infractions, and "birching" for major infractions. The spirited Meagher endured this regimen for four years, with breaks only in summer. The strict Jesuit fathers did not allow the school to recess at Christmas or Easter.[44]

In Meagher's droll mind, the principal object of his teachers at Stonyhurst was not to educate him but to eradicate his Irish brogue. One of his masters was the Reverend William Johnson, "an Englishman to the marrow . . . [who] couldn't bear the Irish brogue. It was to him a sickening vulgarism. . . . But the sweetest words . . . uttered with an Irish accent . . . was enough, and more than enough, to give hysterics of nausea to the Rev. William Johnson, Professor of Rhetoric. 'Meagher,' he used to say, coughing into his handkerchief, and looking as if the interposition of a basin would soothe him, 'that's a horrible brogue you have got.'"[45]

The devilish Meagher played up his Irish heritage and brogue to the limit. After having practiced his part for weeks in a clipped Saxon accent, he performed his full rehearsal performances as the Earl of Kent in Shakespeare's *King Lear* with the heaviest Munster Irish he could manage. His performance delighted the cast, which was put into hysterics, but it far from pleased the overwhelmed Reverend William Johnson, who demoted Meagher to a common soldier in the play. All of Meagher's antics were not as humorous as his performance as the Earl of Kent. As first clarinetist of the Stonyhurst band he refused to play in a musical offering honoring the anniversary of the English victory in the first battle of Waterloo, upsetting the whole performance.[46] Despite such resistance Meagher did not win the conflict over his accent. Instead his years at Stonyhurst changed his speech so much that many said he spoke in English tones. Meagher himself was never convinced that his speech had been changed permanently, and he was proud that he could speak, when it was convenient, with his original Munster tongue.[47]

During his time at Stonyhurst, Meagher became the friend of a most unusual student named Don Ramon Páez, the son of José Antonio Páez, who was then serving his second term as president of Venezuela. He had helped Venezuela to secede from Colombia in 1829, after allying himself with Simón Bolívar in the liberation of Colombia. The elder Páez was an accomplished revolutionary; and Ramon, who had great admiration for his father, may well have conveyed the romance of a successful revolution to his Irish friend.[48]

Despite—or perhaps because of—his time in England, Meagher arrived back in Waterford from Stonyhurst in 1843 with a growing passion for Irish independence. Waiting at the dock to meet him was Waterford's mayor: his own father. As the first Catholic to attain the position, Thomas Meagher, Sr., had benefited when the English Parliament passed an act authorizing the election of a city council by the people, giving Waterford Catholics a voice in their own city governance. The townspeople could see their own mayor going to mass, and it had been a long time coming. When Meagher had been only three years old, the Catholics of Waterford had won their first major victory with the election of William Villiers Stuart to the British Parliament. Although a Protestant, Stuart had challenged a formidable incumbent, Lord George Beresford, who was head of the Tory landlords' group around Waterford. Beresford was also leader of a ruthless army of Orangemen that included the police, tax gatherers, bailiffs, and sheriffs' deputies, all serving the English government.[49]

Meagher was far too young to remember the event with any clarity, but he had heard the story so often that it was firm in his memory. He had learned that a shrewd Roman Catholic bishop had mobilized patriotic Irish voters to elect Stuart. The Reverend Dr. Kelly, the Catholic bishop of Waterford, had chosen a dinner given in a local orphanage to expose statistically the relative voting strength of the Catholics—who could easily prevail in any relatively free election. As Meagher recalled, "In one huge mass the country rose against the Beresfords, and drove them from the haughty domination they had so long and with so much terror and prestige maintained."[50]

After returning to Waterford, Meagher could also see that the success in the Stuart election—and even in the election of his own father—had not helped the Catholics much. To him the victory proved hollow, because it gained nothing for the Irish as individuals. "One acre of land, good against all claims, ensured to him for ever, were better to the Irishman by a thousand times than a thousand of such triumphs," Meagher said. "With that one acre to take his stand on, a legion of Beresfords would be no more to him than a pyramid of mummies."[51] To his mind, more fundamental change was needed; and that change could only begin with separation from England.

In 1840, while Meagher was at Stonyhurst, Daniel O'Connell and his followers started the Loyal National Repeal Association (soon to be known simply as the Repeal Association). Its goal was the nullification of the Act of Union, which had now been on the books for forty years.[52] Settling into life in Waterford again, Meagher became aware of O'Connell's organization. But he also became aware of a broader, more loosely organized movement, which tapped thousands of people's desire for better lives. The movement had started out as merely a call for countrywide temperance, led by an Irish priest, Father Theobold Mathew. As more and more Irish joined in, Daniel O'Connell and his supporters recognized an opportunity to use the organization for political purposes. Taking the pledge of sobriety, O'Connell himself, who was not known to have displayed intemperate habits, joined the people. Soon patriotic activity and the moral and material welfare of the Irish also became goals of the temperance movement.[53]

O'Connell had often held large outdoor meetings, but now his followers started an ongoing series of "Monster Meetings," which far exceeded in size those held before. These impressive gatherings were held in all Catholic counties and were attended by almost all Irish

Catholic adult males. The largest of the meetings took place around the Hill of Tara in County Meath, a site of ancient Irish culture. At least one hundred thousand, and some say over a million, Irish men and women assembled there. The meetings were usually held on Sunday mornings, so the parish priests said a mass for their parishioners gathered around them. Working hand in hand with the temperance movement of Father Mathew, the organizers assured that sober order was well kept, thus depriving the British of the most natural excuse for interfering. The success of the monster meetings was due to O'Connell himself, whose voice and enthusiasm rang out on the still Sunday mornings over the huge throngs assembled.[54] With the power of the meetings behind him, O'Connell came out more strongly than ever against the Act of Union, and he had become the champion of repeal.

O'Connell had also been mayor of Dublin and brought the repeal issue before the Dublin Corporation in February 1843, with the debate lasting for three days. In the end he easily carried the vote to support repeal.[55] His speech had been powerful and was later reprinted as a manual for those advocating Irish independence. After learning of the new movements and O'Connell's stand at the Dublin Corporation, Meagher initially had nothing but praise for the man. In his own recollections, he described what he had heard of the deliberations. "Vivid eloquence on both sides of the house; a manly spirit of fair play; a chivalrous love of Ireland; intelligence, courtesy and patriotism characterised the event." The people had been "inert, sluggish, listless," but O'Connell had brought them to life. As Meagher said, "a tumultuous life leaped to the summons. . . . The first waves of the vast sea coming on, had struck the beach."[56]

On the day after Meagher's return to Waterford, however, he became immediately aware that another, more radical faction was also advocating Irish independence. The trade unions held a public meeting to petition Parliament for repeal of the Act of Union. It was there that Meagher observed an odd-looking and odd-acting man address the crowd. James Nash was a schoolmaster whose oratory condemned the threats of coercion uttered by the English government. As Meagher stood listening, he realized that Nash was obliquely speaking the words of armed resistance. "Let them come on," Nash shouted, "let them come on; let them draw the sword; and then woe to the conquered!—every potato field shall be a

Marathon, and every boreen a Thermopylae."[57] These words from the classics rang true to the young Meagher, and he started to believe that force might ultimately be used to achieve the ends of the Irish.

Even as he investigated the rising Irish nationalist movement, Meagher also began to take his place among the Waterford elite, being elected to the prestigious and exclusive Waterford Club. Three-fourths of the club's members were Conservatives or Tories; only two or three were Repealers (now including Meagher). Despite their opposing ideological beliefs, heated discussion of politics did not erupt amongst the members, because it was forbidden by club rules. Also excluded were any indicia of political leanings, and the umbrella stand in the hall held the saffron sashes of the Orangemen. Stripped of their political voices, Meagher found them to be cordial, respectful, and friendly. In fact he held a grudging respect for the English loyalist majority of the club, finding them to be "truthful, high-toned, [and] gallant."[58]

In the midst of this fraternally compatible group he developed a staunch adherence to the ideal of a congenial, nonpolitical, nondenominational Irish brotherhood. "They knew that in public, over and over again, I had prayed for that tolerant, genial, generous brotherhood amongst Irishmen, of the feasibility and beauty of which, in a little sphere, they themselves had furnished such delightful evidence," Meagher observed. "Well do I remember how cordially they used to drink my health and cheer my stammering speeches at their dinners. Well do I remember the jovial welcome and the shuffling of chairs round the fireplace, every night I came in. Early or late—the later the better—they always had a chair and a cheer for me."[59] At that time in his life, Meagher found nobility in every Irish existence. It was the British he disdained and not the Irish—not even those who supported the Crown. He would later write as he reflected on the goodness he saw in the Waterford Club:

> With all their childishness, with all their folly, with all their indolence, with all their incentives to driftless gaiety and frolic, with all their loyalty to England and her King or Queen—the darkest turpitude of all—may the social institutions flourish which bring Irishmen together, make them know each other, trust each other, love each other, and, in convivial circles, teach

them they are brothers all! This done, there is a family. From a family comes a camp. From a camp a Nation.[60]

Although he enjoyed its privileges, Meagher also became increasingly conscious of the evils of an emerging Irish class system. At Stonyhurst he had been thrown together with English Catholic students and others from all over the world, and the experience had made him sensitive to snobbery and arrogance. To his surprise, he now saw it even in Waterford, where the city fathers of either faith showed strong scorn for the tradesmen and small businessmen. The attitude disturbed Meagher when he realized that the "bitterest thing that could be said against a public man, was that his father made boots, was successful as a tailor, or tanned the best leather."[61] Yet he himself was now an educated upper-class Irishman, and he soon found that his place in the Waterford society was limited to only a few choices.

No one ever suggested that Meagher should enter his family's business or any other trade. The only acceptable option for someone of his social class and education was to become an officer in the army, to gain a position at Dublin Castle or another high public establishment, or to become a member of the bar. For a time Meagher vacillated in his career decision as he tried to see his place and future in Waterford. He was comfortable in the presence of his family, his old childhood friends, and the eternal Mount Misery across the river. He was also comfortable in the Waterford Club, but beyond that he had limited opportunity in Waterford. Restless, and twenty-one, he decided to move to Dublin in 1844 to pursue legal studies. After entering his name at one of the Queen's Inns where the barristers dined, he set out to eat the prescribed number of dinners and receive the mentoring that went along with them, to qualify him for admission to the bar. Meagher's goal, like that of many young barristers, was to attain six years' standing at the bar, after which he would become eligible for political advancement. In the meantime his lot was to languish in this elite group, waiting for a position suited to his station.

Studying law gave Meagher a rationale for moving to Dublin, where he happily found himself at the center of the Irish independence movement. The streets of Dublin were alive with the hope given to Ireland by

O'Connell and his Repeal Association. Even more important to Meagher was the work of the new literary elite he found there. Foremost among them was Charles Gavan Duffy, a Dublin journalist who in 1842 had co-founded the *Nation* as Dublin's first newspaper devoted to charting the destiny for the growing Irish movement against the British. Duffy quickly became a celebrity for his outspoken views, especially after they resulted in a charge of treason, of which he was acquitted. Meagher once had tried unsuccessfully to meet Duffy when he was visiting Waterford, but Duffy worked hard to maintain his privacy. It was only through much persistence that Meagher finally met him in Dublin.[62]

Until then Meagher kept to himself in Dublin, and he was known to be quiet and studious as he prepared himself to mingle with his fellow Irish intellectuals through a program of self-education. He reveled in the scholarship of the *Life of Petrarch,* honed his wit on *Punch's Almanac,* flirted with the atheism and anarchy of Percy Bysshe Shelley's *Essays,* pondered transcendentalism while reading Johann Gottlieb Fichte's *The Destination of Man,* delved deeply into the history and romantic philosophies of August Wilhelm von Schlegel, contemplated human ingenuity while reading William Beckford's *History of Invention,* examined with interest Johann Kohl's recent travelogue on Ireland, and became familiar with Benjamin Disraeli's advocacy of an alliance between the working class and the aristocracy as set out in the novel *Coningsby.* While it seemed of little relevance at the time, Meagher also purchased a copy of *Humboldt's Cosmos* by the naturalist Alexander von Humboldt and, after reading about the author's travels, became fascinated with Latin America.[63]

But as to Ireland and its history, Meagher's reading only convinced him further that a great gap remained. Little had been written about the history and culture of the country. In part he blamed the teachers, and he became increasingly critical of his own education at Clongowes, finding fault with the curriculum because they had failed to teach about Ireland. "That's the fault I find with Clongowes," Meagher said with cynical humor.

> They talked to us about Mount Olympus and the Vale of Tempe;
> they birched us into a flippant acquaintance with the disreputable
> gods and goddesses of the golden and heroic ages; they entangled
> us in Euclid; turned our brains with the terrestrial globe; chilled

our blood in dizzy excursions through the Milky Way; para-
lyzed our Lilliputian loins with the shaggy spoils of Hercules,
bewildered us with the Battle of the Frogs and Mice, pitched
us precipitately into England, amongst the impetuous Normans
and stupid Saxons; gave us a look, through an interminable
telescope, at what was doing in the New World; but, as far as
Ireland was concerned, they left us, like blind and crippled children, in the dark.[64]

Once he came to know Duffy and the other intellectuals who circled
around the *Nation,* Meagher gained the opportunity to help fill this
void, agreeing to help write a series of educational books called the
Library of Ireland. Meagher believed his best contribution would be to
fill in the sparse Irish history that existed, and he offered to prepare two
titles: "Williamite Wars" and "Orators of the Irish Parliament."[65]

In the meantime Meagher was becoming acquainted with the
members of Duffy's circle. Joining Duffy as co-founders of the *Nation*
were Thomas Davis and John Blake Dillon. Both Davis and Dillon had
been with the *Dublin Morning Register,* a paper that had been the voice
of the Catholic Association. Davis was the oldest of the three at twenty-
eight. Other young Irish men and women had also joined the staff of
the *Nation,* all of them eager to agitate for Irish freedom. As the *Nation*
grew, so too did the new movement that had started among its
founders and writers. It soon became known as "Young Ireland," and it
would go down in history as one of the world's recognizable revolutionary movements. But perhaps even more significant is the success of
several of its members, who ultimately numbered among the most
famous people of the period.[66]

Other important members of Young Ireland when Meagher
arrived in Dublin included William Smith O'Brien and John Mitchel.
Smith O'Brien was a prominent Protestant who had been elected a
member of Parliament. Handicapped by a lack of charisma and a reputation for arrogance, O'Brien, who was twenty years older than Meagher
and older than most members of Young Ireland, gave the association
respectability; he was still an influential and powerful man in English
politics. John Mitchel, also a Protestant and eight years older than
Meagher, had become the chief writer for the *Nation* by 1845 and

remained so until 1848, when he left to start the "extreme revolutionary" *United Irishman,* described by journalist Richard Pigott as "highly exciting and wildly incendiary."[67]

The young Meagher became involved with many others who joined Young Ireland, and many of them continued to play important roles in his life even after he left Ireland. Terence Bellew MacManus was only Meagher's age but already a prosperous young businessman in Liverpool when he crossed over to join the Repeal Association and then Young Ireland. P. J. Smyth, three years Meagher's junior, had been his school-mate at Stonyhurst and looked up to him as a leader. Thomas D'Arcy McGee, two years younger than Meagher, had previously emigrated to the United States as a boy and had already entered journalism there as a writer for the *Boston Pilot.* Returning to Ireland, he joined the staff of the *Nation.* Kevin Izod O'Doherty, about Meagher's age, was a medical student who also wrote for the *Irish Tribune,* the successor to John Mitchel's *United Irishma*n. Among the others he met was Patrick O'Donoghue, a Dublin law clerk. Michael Doheny was eighteen years Meagher's senior and had been a solicitor and law advisor for the borough of Cashel. Richard O'Gorman came from a wealthy merchant family. He was three years younger than Meagher and was an outspoken leader for Catholic emancipation.[68]

Young Ireland also included an attractive young woman, the famous "Speranza," the poetess laureate of the *Nation.* Her real name was Jane Francesca Elgee. The intellectual power of her words, as well as her refinement as a lady who sent scented notes to her friends, left a mark on Meagher. Her interest in him in turn extended beyond his mind, and she romantically described him as being "handsome, daring, reckless of consequences, wild, bright, flashing eyes, glowing colour and the most beautiful mouth, teeth and smile I ever beheld."[69] After Meagher had been exiled, she became Lady Jane Wilde when the prominent eye and ear surgeon she had married in 1851 was knighted. But it was her own verse that made her so famous as a national figure that even her flamboyant son, Oscar Wilde, found it hard to achieve a reputation in Ireland not based on his mother's acclaim.[70]

One writer described Speranza as "a tall, stately, and most beautiful lady" with "exquisitely chiselled features, dark eyes and hair, and brow— fair and lofty as that of the Athenian deity typified in ivory by Phidias."[71]

Charles Gavan Duffy described many of the personal quirks and traits of the others, as they sat in a plain apartment that served as their council chamber. Smith O'Brien was "stately, well-poised, and carefully dressed, gracious but not genial, speaking with a diffidence which implied that he regarded himself merely a peer among peers." A careless dresser and a mild and unselfish man, John Blake Dillon had "pensive brown eyes and mien of cavalier and gentleman." Richard O'Gorman was described as having a "handsome, smiling face," while Michael Doheny had "a visage like the full moon and clothes which looked slovenly and ill-made." Mitchel was "absorbed and thoughtful . . . twisting unconsciously a lock of his silken hair round his finger." McGee's face was "uncomely expressive . . . [with] large dark eyes lighted up with smiles, which were . . . too universally conciliatory." Thomas Francis Meagher, for his part, was described by Duffy as "silent and slightly foppish."[72] It was from this group that the leadership of Young Ireland emerged. Among these men and women Meagher found his political home—and he would not be silent for long.

CHAPTER TWO

Meagher of the Sword

> Abhor the sword? Stigmatise the sword? No, my lord.
>
> Thomas Francis Meagher

By 1846 Thomas Francis Meagher had been in Dublin for two years and had begun looking more critically at Daniel O'Connell and his politics. Like other Young Irelanders, Meagher came to view O'Connell as scurrilous, unprincipled, vulgar, pompous, and a bully. O'Connell's disregard for the growing agrarian problem in Ireland and mistreatment of his own tenants on his considerable landholdings also drew criticism from his compatriots. O'Connell had once stood alone as the leading figure of Irish emancipation, but during his term as lord mayor of Dublin he had taken to wearing long flowing robes and headwear that uncomfortably reminded his followers of the regalia of a king. While not the primary cause of Young Ireland's dissatisfaction with O'Connell, these personal traits as much as anything led to their view of him as unfit to lead.[1]

Aside from O'Connell's personal failings and his almost complete lack of accomplishments since his success in 1829, the root of Young Ireland's case against O'Connell in 1846 became "the Liberator's" support for patronage or place hunting, especially at the expense of repeal. At various times, O'Connell had strongly advocated repeal. Intermittently, however, he had loyally cooperated with the Whig party in a mistaken belief that they would help to secure repeal, while in the meantime the Whigs handed out patronage to quiet the Irish. Belatedly O'Connell and the Repealers came to realize that England would never agree to Irish independence, because Ireland could be used as a base for enemy invasion in the event of war.[2] But during the period of cooperation with the Whigs, "a treacherous and ruinous influence" found its way into Ireland, according to Meagher. "Government patronage shed its seeds in the hearts of the people. A fatal curse, wherever it prevails. In Ireland, the traces of it are indelibly marked in her misery and shame."[3]

In June 1846, with the Whigs newly back in power, rumor had it that O'Connell had agreed to support English liberalism. Thus, as the early twentieth century Irish politician Arthur Griffith characterized the situation, the "agitation which had been carried on for four years was to be damped down in return for a profuse distribution of patronage through Conciliation Hall."[4]

Meagher had come to Dublin two years earlier and had gained entrance into the inner circle of Young Ireland, which argued that compromise with the Whigs did not advance the ultimate goal of an independent Ireland. Such was the group's position when Meagher rose to speak at Conciliation Hall on June 15, 1846. It was the second time the twenty-two-year-old had risen to address the hall. The first speech, on February 16, 1846, had been full of platitudes, but it had been well received; however, it had not satisfied the young orator, who vowed to be better prepared the next time.[5]

Meagher's June 15 address against Whiggery provided his chance. This time he was much bolder and better informed, as he spoke on the problem of the accession of the Whigs to office. He referred to economic as well as social problems and attacked O'Connell's supporters for their acceptance of the new government. "Let me not be told that the Whigs were our benefactors, and deserve our gratitude," he said. Even though "honourable men" had been elevated to the bench by the Whigs, that was almost the only benefit to the country. Catholic barristers would make reform speeches, but they "came in for silk gowns, and other genteel perquisites," while the "sons of toil" knew no change. Meagher also attacked the Irish welfare system as it existed under British rule. "The poorhouses were built, and were soon stocked with vermined rags, and broken hearts—with orphaned childhood, fevered manhood, and desolate old age" while the "custom house was drained."[6] This bold speech from so young a man drew criticism from the older members of the Repeal Association. Meagher and his rhetoric had started to become a thorn in the side of the O'Connellites.

Undeterred by their disapproval, Meagher spoke again at Conciliation Hall on June 22, 1846, this time on the subject of youth and English Whiggery. He had given much thought to the speech and the method of delivery and presented it in a style that he was now comfortable with—a simple, self-effacing grasp of the facts at hand and recognition of the forces against him, be it his youth or his political enemies.

> If youth be at fault, it is a fault we cannot help. Each day corrects it, however, and that is a consoling reflection. If it be an intrusion on our parts to come to this Hall, to aid your efforts and to propagate your principles, I can only say it is an intrusion which your applause has sanctioned. For myself, I think it right to say, that when I came to Dublin this winter I did not expect that I should have had the honour of sustaining so conspicuous a part as I believe I have done in your councils.[7]

As Arthur Griffith later wrote of Meagher, "his was an eloquence that before was not heard. . . . Passion and poetry transfigured his words, and he evoked for the first time in many breasts a manly consciousness of national right and dignity. As handsome and chivalrous as he was eloquent, he became something of a popular idol . . . eagerly sought after in the social circles of Dublin."[8]

Meagher's speeches kept the rapt attention of his audiences, and his appearance and dress always drew notice. "Flaunting and fashionable as I sometimes am," he did not want his choice in attire to be taken as an effort to dress in English fashion. "I thoroughly hated Dublin society for its pretentious aping of English taste, ideas, and fashions, for its utter want of all true nobility," he later told Duffy. Nevertheless, the privileged Meagher believed strongly in an upper class. "I think that, in a free state, an aristocracy is a wise—an ennobling institution," he said in a speech at the Music Hall in Dublin on April 7, 1847: "I can conceive no state complete without it." Despite that view, Meagher gravitated only to upper-class intellectuals rather than to the elite in general. He wanted nothing to do with Dublin's high society, with whom he mingled only if he felt that the situation could be used for political purposes.[9]

Contradiction or not, the combination of Meagher's dapper appearance, political connections, and impressive eloquence struck O'Connell as dangerous. Already there was talk of excluding Young Ireland from Conciliation Hall, but it only inspired Meagher further. "Beyond these walls we have many incentives to love our country, and to serve her well," he said.[10] O'Connell and the association grew anxious. Meagher and the other Young Irelanders were threatening their leadership, and something had to be done. On July 11 O'Connell finally drew the line. Knowing that Meagher and Young Ireland were moving toward supporting the use of force, he asked the governing committee of the association, whose members included Meagher and John Mitchel, to affirm the association's five previous "Peace Resolutions." These resolutions called for members to use only peaceful and political means to achieve their ends. At its July 11 meeting the committee agreed with O'Connell and required that all members of the association adhere to the resolutions, with only Mitchel and Meagher abstaining. Two days later the association as a whole adopted a sixth Peace Resolution, with only Meagher dissenting this time.[11]

Meagher gave himself little time to think over the association's action and prepare a response and then went on the attack. On July 13, again in Conciliation Hall, he leveled charges directly at O'Connell. No longer politely refusing to discuss "the Liberator" directly, he launched a personal attack on O'Connell for refusing to challenge the Whig candidate at the Dungarvan election by putting forth an association nominee. If O'Connell had done so, Meagher said, it "would have taught the Whigs that the heart of Ireland was bent upon Repeal."[12]

Meagher then assailed place hunting: "I consider that Repeal is not an open question—I conceive that any Repealer taking office under the present government would be an apostate from the cause." O'Connell's supporters bridled at what they were hearing and repeatedly interrupted the speech, but Meagher carried on, bravely broaching the issue of the use of force. "I agree that no other means should be adopted in the Association but moral means and peaceful means." But at that point he hinted broadly at adopting another policy "no less honourable though it may be more perilous."[13]

The leaders of the Repeal Association by this time had become quite alarmed by Meagher's persuasiveness, and more and more were becoming dead set against the Young Irelanders and their positions as espoused in the *Nation,* which they soon banned from their halls. On July 26, 1846, matters came to a head. John Mitchel first spoke forcefully if not effectively at Conciliation Hall, asserting his extreme positions on armed revolt. Then it was Meagher's turn. Still not quite twenty-three years old, he boldly asserted his right to be a member of the association and his right to dissent on all matters, except the one for which he had joined—the Repeal of the Act of Union.

Meagher began by recognizing that an armed uprising in the Ireland of 1846 would be senseless:

> To talk, now-a-days, of repealing the Act of Union by the force of arms, would be to rhapsodize. If the attempt were made, it would be a decided failure. There might be a riot in the street—there would be no revolution in the country. . . . The registry club, the reading-room, the hustings, these are the only positions . . . we can occupy. Voters' certificates, books, reports, these are the only weapons we can employ. Therefore, my lord, I do advocate the peaceful policy of this Association. It is the only policy we can adopt.[14]

Nevertheless, Meagher refused to subscribe to the proposition that the use of arms in defense of freedom was wrong at all times and under all circumstances. In a passage that became celebrated in many anthologies and a set piece for later school recitations, he declared the principles that would earn him the distinctive title of "Meagher of the Sword." He was polite this time, speaking directly of O'Connell, giving him his due, and then declaring his own independence:

> In doing so, let me not be told that I seek to undermine the influence of the leader of this Association, and am insensible to his services. My lord, I will uphold his just influence, and I am grateful for his services. This is the first time I have spoken in these terms of that illustrious Irishman, in this Hall. I did not do so before—I felt it was unnecessary. I hate unnecessary praise:

I scorn to receive it—I scorn to bestow it. No, my lord, I am not ungrateful to the man who struck the fetters off my arms, whilst I was yet a child; and by whose influence my father—the first Catholic who did so for two hundred years—sat, for the last two years, in the civic chair of an ancient city. But, my lord, the same God who gave to that great man the power to strike down an odious ascendancy in this country, and enabled him to institute, in this land, the glorious law of religious equality—the same God gave to me a mind that is my own—a mind that has not been mortgaged to the opinions of any man or any set of men; a mind that I was to use, and not surrender.[15]

Meagher would go on to explain his dissent from the committee that had passed the Peace Resolutions:

But my lord, I dissented from the resolutions before us, for other reasons. . . . I dissented from them, for I felt that, by assenting to them, I should have pledged myself to the unqualified repudiation of physical force in all countries, at all times, and in every circumstance. This I could not do; for, my lord, I do not abhor the use of arms in the vindication of national rights. There are times when arms alone suffice, and when political ameliorations call for a drop of blood, and many thousand drops of blood.[16]

Finally, Meagher reached the *coup de maître* of his speech and delivered the words that made him famous:

Abhor the sword? Stigmatise the sword? No, my lord, for, in the passes of the Tyrol it cut to pieces the banner of the Bavarian, and through those cragged passes cut a path to fame for the peasant insurrectionist of Innsbruck. Abhor the sword? Stigmatise the sword? No, my lord, for, at its blow, and in the quivering of its crimson light a giant nation sprang up from the waters of the Atlantic, and by its redeeming magic the fettered colony became a daring, free Republic. Abhor the sword? Stigmatise the sword? No, my lord, for it swept the Dutch marauders out of the fine old towns of Belgium—swept them back to their phlegmatic

swamps, and knocked their flag and sceptre, their laws and bayonets, into the sluggish waters of the Scheldt. My lord, I learned
that it was the right of a nation to govern itself—not in this
Hall, but upon the ramparts of Antwerp. This, the first article of
a national's creed, I learned upon those ramparts, where freedom
was justly estimated, and the possession of the precious gift was
purchased by the effusion of generous blood. My lord, I honour
the Belgians, I admire the Belgians, I love the Belgians for their
enthusiasm, their courage, their success, and I, for one, will not
stigmatise, for I do not abhor, the means by which they obtained
a Citizen King, a Chamber of Deputies.[17]

The speech was not yet over, and undoubtedly Meagher had a dramatic ending planned. John O'Connell, the son of Daniel O'Connell,
interrupted him, however, afraid that young Meagher's words were
casting a spell and winning the association over as he injected passion
into his subject. As Charles Gavan Duffy recalled, one of his friends had
told him: "When Meagher began to speak he was received with coldness,
even with rudeness; but he gradually stole on the sympathies of the
audience." But when Meagher rose to the height of his theme, "The
enthusiasm of the people, suppressed for a time, broke out at last, like a
sudden storm, in bursts of ecstasy. It was perhaps the greatest speech that
historic hall ever echoed," Duffy had been told. Thus John O'Connell
could stay silent no longer: he stepped forward to stop Meagher. No one
holding Meagher's views, said O'Connell, could remain a member of the
Repeal Association. For a moment the hall stood silent, and then there
was a brief discussion among the Young Ireland group. Soon they left
Conciliation Hall en masse, never to return.[18]

The success of Meagher's "Sword Speech" was no accident. His
speeches were not extemporaneous but rather carefully prepared and
written out, a practice that sometimes left them wanting in "simplicity and
ease."[19] Meagher's dramatic oratory was the skillful melding of his education, perception, conviction, passion, poetry, and imagination, however,
and all of those things combined made the speeches brilliant. As Duffy
said, "It was like listening to the mystical sonorous music of the 'Revolt of
Islam,' recited in Shelley's shrill treble, to hear Meagher pour out passion
and pathos and humour in tones which possessed no note in perfection

The Music Hall in Dublin. After Meagher and the Young Irelanders left the Repeal Association and Conciliation Hall, they formed the Irish Confederation and held their meetings at the Music Hall. (Courtesy National Library of Ireland)

but intensity." Duffy's assessment of Meagher's contributions to Young Ireland was glowing: "He had brought to the party a force which they never possessed in perfection before—a born orator; one who could translate the philosophy of the closet into the language of popular passion, for like a great actor, he sometimes interpreted with admirable fidelity opinions which, though he shared, he did not originate."[20]

Despite the speech's acclaim among his fellow Young Irelanders, its role in the secession from the Repeal Association left Meagher demoralized. He found it disheartening that loyal and true Irish patriots could not get along and reach a compromise. For a time he reduced his speaking activity. Rumor soon sprang up that Meagher, out of despair, was going to abandon political life and live in London. Instead he returned to Waterford on a visit. There, on a road outside of town, he encountered the odd-looking old schoolmaster James Nash, the first person he had ever heard publicly suggest the possibility of armed resistance. Nash had made a deep impression on Meagher on his return from Stonyhurst. Now, four years later, he engaged Nash in conversation, only to find that the schoolteacher was a great O'Connell supporter. Although Nash agreed that there was much to drive them away, he disapproved of the withdrawal of Meagher and his Young Irelanders from the Repeal Association.

In parting, Nash shook Meagher's hand and said, with only the slightest twinkle in his eye, "My school is below there, . . . and I flog the boys every morning all round, to teach them to be Spartans." Nash recognized that Irish independence would not come easily, and Meagher never forgot him or his message. It would be a long, long road ahead for Meagher, and he would need all the Spartan stamina and perseverance he could muster.[21] The meeting on the road with Nash gave him new resolve; as he explained to his friends, he had only been thinking about spending the winter season in London. Gossip also had it that he had fallen in love. While he admitted to a "love affair," he quickly avowed that it had not chilled his ardor for the cause.[22] Meagher's moment of discouragement was only temporary, and it ultimately gave him new strength. He now realized how easy it would be to slip back into the congenial, apolitical ways of the Waterford Club, leaving the Irish cause to founder when it needed a champion more than ever. For the year was 1847, and potato blight, overpopulation, poverty, and English indifference had combined to bring mass starvation to the Irish countryside.

Notwithstanding many years of hunger and near starvation in Ireland there was really only one Great Famine: the famine of 1847. The wet summer of 1845 had helped to bring on a fungus-caused potato blight that reduced the Irish potato crop by half and cut the food supply for the Irish peasants proportionally. There was no cure for the fungus, and in 1846 the crop was all but a total failure, followed by a very poor harvest in 1847.[23]

All around Meagher, people were dying—a climax to the misery that had long haunted Ireland. The years from 1815 to 1826 had been a period of great want for the common Irish people, including a year of near-starvation in 1817. The response of the British had always been to blame the Irish for inefficient farming practices and overpopulation. The overpopulation, at least, was real: Ireland's population increased dramatically in the first part of the nineteenth century. Now, as the Irish starved, the British government at first did nothing, under the theory that the Irish had been through blights before and would know how to handle the problem. Not until 1846 did Sir Robert Peel decide that some famine relief was necessary; he imported a small amount of corn from India, which did not begin to alleviate the heavy loss of potatoes. The futility of this act became more apparent when it was found out that Ireland did not even have grist mills to grind the corn. Peel also tried to establish a public works system, which failed, and emergency hospitals, which also failed.[24] The prevailing view in England seemed to be that the Irish were simply not worth the effort. Some even argued that free trade meant the survival of the fittest: if the Irish could not survive, then they should fall by the wayside.[25] The Irish landlords either could not or would not do anything to help their starving tenants, and those who could not pay their rent were evicted.[26]

Many of the starving Irish either died or fled their homeland, with about 1 million people in each category.[27] Many, of course, went to England, where they were despised, raising resentments in the English communities in which they settled and further diminishing the willingness of the English to help them. As historian Cecil Woodham-Smith said, it was the very persons of the starving Irish as they arrived in England that sealed their doom.

> The realities of the famine in Ireland, emaciated scarecrows, once men and women, skeleton children, dirt, nakedness, fever, and the hideous diseases which hunger brings, appeared on Britain's doorstep; and the British response was one of violent irritation. How had these people been allowed to get into such a state: Why were they invading Britain, bringing fever with them, instead of staying at home? The answer was that the Irish landlords were responsible; they had not done their duty, therefore the Irish people were reduced to their present fearful condition, and now these landlords were trying to get rid of the responsibility, by shipping the poor wretches away to Britain.[28]

Irish poverty was so great that it attracted the attention of the most famous writers of the day. George Gordon, Lord Byron, told his peers that he had not seen such deplorable conditions anywhere in the Ottoman Empire; and Percy Bysshe Shelley reported that he had "no conception of the depth of human misery" until he visited Ireland. The "worse than nakedness, the rags, the dirt and the misery of the poor common Irish" appalled John Keats, as it did William Makepeace Thackeray, who was revolted by the universal filth. "An ordinary pigsty in England is really more comfortable," he declared of the dilapidated houses he had seen in Ireland during a visit.[29]

Meagher's friend Sir Charles Gavan Duffy also described the devastation that the Young Irelanders saw. "From Connaught, where distress was greatest, there came batches of inquests, with the horrible verdict 'died of starvation.' In some cases the victims were buried 'wrapped in a coarse coverlet,' a coffin being too costly a luxury. The living awaited death with a listlessness which was at once tragic and revolting. Women, with dead children in their arms, were seen begging for a coffin to bury them."[30]

In Skibbereen the famine was even worse, if that was possible. In this busy seaport, with ships carrying cattle, corn, and butter at the dock, the government rate-collector found houses deserted: the owners had been carried to their graves. Three corpses were found in one cabin, and a woman and her children had lain dead for a week in a once prosperous home. In the fields dead men were found so terribly mangled by dogs that they could not be identified. The irony of the situation was that Irish grain was still being shipped across the channel to England, where it was protected from foreign competition under the tariffs of the Corn Laws that protected British grain prices. In the midst of the famine, Ireland saw the ongoing export of Irish-grown corn and barley to England along with quantities of dairy produce. When the peasants in the southwest sought to keep the food from their lands and to retaliate for their suffering, eleven of them were hung from a gallows after only a brief trial.[31]

The landlords refused responsibility for their Irish tenants and drew back from the disaster, saying only that the Crown should provide funds to correct the situation; but no help came. As the Irish peasants slowly starved, the gains in organizing toward political independence created by the monster meetings held by Father Mathew and Daniel O'Connell began to disappear. People were simply too hungry to think much about Irish independence—even though, according to the Young Irelanders' thinking, British rule was at the root of the famine.[32]

At the beginning of 1847 Meagher could look back upon the previous year as one in which no progress had been made. He became sick of the misery around him and vowed to alleviate it, even at the risk of his freedom and his life. Together with the other members of Young Ireland who had been expelled from the Repeal Association, Meagher formed the Irish Confederation to advance the strong repeal agenda refused by the O'Connells.[33] While the famine raged in Ireland, the confederation had no political power to fight it: no government treasury to call upon, no Irish legislature to enact laws to ameliorate it, not even Young Ireland members of the British Parliament to appeal to (not that it would have helped, because the British had already turned a cold ear to the circumstances in Ireland). The only avenue they could see was to deter the Repeal Association from accepting the Whig government and to continue agitating for repeal of the Act of Union to give Ireland its own legislature and control over its own destiny.

At a large Dublin hall, the Rotunda, on the occasion of the first meeting of the Irish Confederation, Meagher addressed the membership on the subject of the despised Whig William Pitt. Early in the century Pitt had promised a better future for Ireland and a share of the wealth and prosperity of England. It was O'Connell who had translated that promise and foisted it on the Irish. And now it was Meagher and the other anti-Whig intellectuals who thought they saw clearly in the sorry history of Ireland the proof that the Whig policies had not worked and would not work despite their promises. Meagher could not ignore the horrible specter of the famine as he stood to address the meeting chair. "Sir, in what year, since the enactment of the Union, will the disciples of William Pitt find the fulfillment of that promise? . . . Tell me—is it fulfilled in 1847, when the Treasury confiscates the Island, and famine piles upon it a pyramid of coffins? A lie! exclaims the broken manufacturer. A lie! protests the swindled landlord. A lie! A lie! shrieks the skeleton from the putrid hovels of Skibbereen."[34]

Meagher's dramatic speech highlighted the necessity to end the hunger. So great was the need that soon Young Ireland attempted reconciliation with the Repeal Association in an effort to save the dying Irish. On May 4, 1847, Meagher, along with Smith O'Brien, John Mitchel, Charles Gavan Duffy, and others met with a delegation from the association, including John O'Connell. O'Connell was unable to make any concessions without the authorization of his ailing father, however, and the talks failed. Meagher and the others held out some hope for compromise until the announcement came that Daniel O'Connell had died on May 6 in Italy, where he was seeking an audience with the pope. His body was sent back to Ireland for burial—without his heart, which had been cut out to remain at the Vatican.[35]

Three months before his death O'Connell had lifted his wasted body to stand in the House of Commons, barely able to whisper: "Ireland is in your hands, in your power . . . she cannot save herself . . . a quarter of her population will perish unless you come to her relief." After his death the Repeal Association became dormant, if not dead, in the hands of his son John and ceased to be a force in Irish politics.[36] Repeal and the means to achieve it had become the sole province of the Irish Confederation led by the Young Irelanders.

Meagher's efforts for Repeal began to dominate his life, as he once again assumed the role of leading spokesman, this time for the Irish Confederation. Traveling the country to foment revolution, he attempted to gain Protestant support in Ulster in November 1847. As he soon found, the anti-Catholic feelings in the North would make it difficult. Yet he was able to make influential Protestant friends there, among them the Reverend George Pepper. It was Pepper who observed that the hall where Meagher spoke in Belfast was filled not only with militant Orangemen but also with stern O'Connell supporters, both posing threats to the young orator.

When Meagher's speech got into the secession of Young Ireland from the Repeal Association, a disturbance erupted in the hall. The O'Connell agitators attempted to take the stage, only to be restrained by the police. When Meagher announced that he was a Catholic, the Protestant Orangemen responded that this was all the more shame for him, and an antagonist claimed that the pope would rob Ireland. But Meagher was about to make an important point for the Irish Confederation, even if what he said sounded against the church. He told the crowd that he would defend Ireland against the pope and that he wanted no ascendancy. This turned the tide, and Pepper reported that deafening cheers interrupted the oration as the crowd members came to their feet and reached a crescendo as Meagher proclaimed that "the time had come for Ireland to sound the trumpet of reformation."[37]

Meagher paused his speaking tour briefly in early 1848, when he learned that a seat in the British Parliament from Waterford had fallen vacant. Fearing that a "place hunter" would be elected, Meagher sought the office for himself. Thomas Meagher, Sr., at that time was the senior member from Waterford and a confirmed "Old Irelander," not at all in accord with the liberal political views of Young Ireland. Nevertheless, the senior Meagher had a strong sense of family loyalty. He had been supporting young Thomas financially even though his son had not supported him politically when he had refused to accept an "anti–place hunting" pledge. Their political differences did not define the Meaghers' family relationship: both father and son viewed them as differences in principle, between gentlemen. No lack of affection or respect developed.[38]

Although Meagher gave an eloquent speech on February 19 decrying "place-begging," he lost the election. He did not have much time to brood, however, for on the heels of the Waterford election came word of the people's triumph in the 1848 French Revolution, the first of a series of uprisings that swept the continent in that revolutionary year. The news energized Ireland and the Irish Confederation. On March 15 at the Music Hall the confederation held a meeting to adopt a message of congratulation to the French people. Meagher read a prepared address and then moved its adoption, which he followed with an inflammatory speech of his own: "If nothing comes of this—if the constitution opens to us no path to freedom—if the Union will be maintained in spite of the will of the Irish people—if the government of Ireland insists upon being a government of dragoons and bombardiers, of detectives and light infantry—then up with the barricades and invoke the God of Battles!"[39]

British agents at the meeting heard the last phrase clearly, and within days criminal charges of sedition were sworn out against Meagher. William Smith O'Brien also spoke and was charged. The British moved on John Mitchel too, charging him with publishing "seditious" articles in the *United Irishman*. Far from professing innocence of the crime, Meagher told a crowd that his intentions were to "aggravate" the offense and that in the next few days he would speak "nothing else but sedition." The brusque Mitchel went even further. In challenging the British law he announced that he had been "indicted for 'sedition,' but I tell them I mean to commit 'HIGH TREASON'"![40]

Meagher's efforts did not cease, even though he was free on bail, awaiting his trial. The Irish Confederation selected him, along with Smith O'Brien and Edward Holywood, a Dublin silk weaver, to convey congratulations to the new Republic in France. The delegation also was there to seek support for an Irish revolution. On April 3 they were received by Alphonse de Lamartine, the head of the provisional French government, who turned down their request for help. They received an optimistic response from the United Irish Club of Paris, however. It offered to assist the confederation in the upcoming struggle, suggesting that as many as 50,000 French would join them in Ireland's fight for liberty.[41] Meagher could see that this was an unrealistic promise, and he took little comfort from the experience in Paris.

While Meagher and his deputation had failed to learn the complicated details of how to conduct a revolution, they did bring back from Paris something of great and lasting value to the Irish: a tricolor flag of orange, white, and green. In a speech on Saturday evening, April 15, 1848, Meagher said that he did not need to explain the flag's meaning, for it was obvious. "I trust that beneath its folds the hands of the Irish Protestant and the Irish Catholic may be clasped in generous and heroic brotherhood."[42] Today a flag of the same colors is the national flag of Ireland.

In the spring of 1848, as the British government watched insurrections break out in Europe, it became increasingly concerned with the threat the Young Irelanders posed if they remained in the country. In April the British Parliament passed the Treason Felony Act, under which seditious crimes would become felonies with a penalty of transportation for life. The act, which made almost all writings against the British government seditious, was particularly directed at the usual speeches of the Irish Confederation.[43] In the meantime O'Brien, Mitchel, and Meagher were still awaiting their trials under the old sedition law.

Free on bail and even more thoroughly invested in their revolutionary movement, the three men traveled to the South of Ireland at the end of April to urge the Irish Confederation clubs in O'Brien's home district of Limerick to arm themselves. Meagher and Charles Gavan Duffy went on to Carrick, where they addressed a throng of people on May 7 and then proceeded to Waterford, where they were met by a quantity of people that had not assembled since the monster meeting of June 1843. In the evening Meagher and Duffy addressed the people, urging them to procure arms at once. The following day the pair attended a meeting in Kilkenny, again stressing armament. They then returned to Dublin, where Meagher awaited his trial the following week.[44]

John Mitchel was the first person arrested under the new Treason Felony Act and incarcerated in Newgate prison. The action surprised no one—because the act had been primarily directed at him—and it silenced no one. If anything, Young Ireland and the confederation became more determined. With Thomas Francis Meagher marching at the head of his Grattan Club, sixteen of the clubs, numbering thousands of members, angrily marched in Dublin to protest actions against the "Prosecuted Patriots." At that time Meagher was starting to be singled out; at a march officers blocked the progress of the Grattan Club members until they broke through police lines to proceed with the rest of the marchers.[45]

The anxiously awaited sedition trials of Smith O'Brien and Meagher finally occurred in the middle of May. Smith O'Brien's jury could not reach a unanimous verdict after an all-day trial, and he was acquitted. The next day Meagher's trial commenced. The following morning the jury was led into court and advised the judge that they were not likely to agree, and Meagher too was acquitted. As Meagher's jurors were leaving the courtroom, one of them felt compelled to announce, "We are eleven to one, my lord, and *that one is a Roman Catholic.*"[46] A disquieted *Blackwood's Edinburgh Magazine,* an organ of the Tories and British Conservatives, commented: "These trials may be memorable in the history of the jurisprudence of Ireland, for they distinctly prove that the present system of trial is utterly unsuited for that country. . . . Meagher's recommendation was 'up with the barricades, and invoke the god of battles.' Yet in the face of this, the jury could not agree upon their verdict."[47] The Irish Confederation rejoiced at the release of the two men and once again marched in the streets, only to encounter another display of force by the police. The British government soon issued a proclamation prohibiting the clubs from marching.

Mitchel's Treason Felony Act trial came next. His supporters immediately raised charges that the jury had been selected from among those who were sure to convict him. In court, the aging Irish barrister Mr. Robert Holmes was the sole voice for Mitchel, and Sir Colman O'Loghlen, as counsel, accompanied him. Mitchel was quickly convicted and appeared for his sentencing. But before proceedings could start, Meagher and others moved forward to the bar to shake Mitchel's hand, prompting the judge to call for order. The proceeding was further disrupted when Mitchel claimed he had been found guilty by a partisan packed jury, not even selected by the sheriff under English law. After Mitchel and Barrister Holmes made their statements, applause broke out across the gallery. It came from almost every part of the court, but the chief judge focused only on Meagher and held him in contempt, demanding an apology. When Meagher refused, police surrounded him, ready to remove him to jail. The judge backed down and accepted Meagher's statement that he meant no contempt.[48] Mitchel was then sentenced to fourteen years of transportation and was soon taken in manacles to a boat and put upon the seas. Prior to the sentence Meagher had threatened that "if the worst befel [sic] us, the ship that carried him away should sail upon a sea of blood."[49]

Some of the clubs had wanted to free Mitchel even before his trial, and his sentence only added to their passion. So strong were their desires that the Irish Confederation itself banned marching to avoid conflict with the British before it was ready. It also reduced its governing council to a manageable size of twenty-one for quick decision making. The council included familiar names: Meagher, William Smith O'Brien, Charles Gavan Duffy, John Dillon, Richard O'Gorman, P. J. Smyth, John Martin, and Michael Doheny. Also included was Father John Kenyon, a radical priest who shared with Meagher the honor of receiving more votes than the others for the new body.[50] It fell on Meagher to convince the clubs that a temporary policy of restraint was necessary—an unenviable task given their lust for revenge for the arrest, conviction, and transportation of John Mitchel. "Let no foul tongue, then, spit its sarcasm upon the people," Meagher said at an early June meeting for all club members held at the Music Hall. "They were ready for the sacrifice; and had the word been given, the stars would burn this night above a thousand crimsoned graves. The guilt is ours;—let the sarcasms fall upon our heads."[51]

By June 1848 the Irish Confederation had been infiltrated by British agents. A policy of secret meetings was adopted, and the formal conspiracy of Young Ireland to overthrow the British government began in earnest. At that time the confederation set out to obtain money and arms from the United States. Agents had been sent there in the past, but they were neither good public speakers nor effective fund-raisers. The confederation now turned to Meagher, the fiery orator who had drawn thousands to the cause, for the task. At the last moment, however, his fellow revolutionaries determined that they needed Meagher's talents in Ireland. In early July, when he was only days away from boarding a boat for his American trip, they decided that he could be put to better use in organizing Munster.[52]

Meagher immediately left for the South of Ireland. On his way to Waterford he gave a speech from the window of a hotel that the police labeled seditious. On July 11 he was arrested for the second time, at his father's home in Waterford, where he had stopped after several days of inspecting the Munster clubs. As the police started back to Dublin with Meagher, throngs of Irish supporters surrounded their carriage, clamoring for his rescue. Not wanting that to be the start of the rebellion, he "mounted on the top of this vehicle, where he could be seen and heard by the vast multitude, and exhorted them to desist."[53] He was then transported to Dublin and released on bail, to appear later in the Limerick court. On July 12 Meagher gave his last speech in Dublin before moving south again.[54]

Attired in a green and gold cap and a stylish tricolor sash, Meagher stepped before an unexpectedly large crowd of fifty thousand people assembled in Slievenamon on Sunday, July 16. There he mourned the fate of his friend Mitchel, who had been taken to the West Indies: "There is a stain on the nation while he remains in Bermuda. He does not sleep—his feverish chafed spirit knows no rest.—He is listening day by day to the sound of the waves, thinking that in those sounds will come his liberty and yours."[55]

Concerned as much about the size of the Slievenamon meeting as about what was said there, Dublin Castle set about to suppress the clubs. It had also learned that the club members were gathering guns. Three days after the meeting, George Villiers, Lord Clarendon, issued an arms proclamation for all unlicensed persons in certain districts in Ireland to give up their arms and ammunition under penalty of imprisonment for a year at hard labor.[56] News of the arms proclamation reached Meagher on Thursday, July 20, while he was in Waterford visiting his father and his aunt and organizing the Waterford Confederation. Meagher now knew that the time was at hand for the revolution. He immediately arranged to travel to Dublin and then donned a tricolor sash and buckled on a sword belt, a cross belt, a cartouche box, and a sword that had belonged to a grand-uncle. As Meagher said later, he had given himself up at that time "to the gay illusion of a gallant fight, a triumphal entry, at the head of armed thousands, into Dublin, before long!" Thomas Meagher, Sr., had not the slightest faith in the success of the proposed revolution and cautioned his son against the venture. An undeterred Thomas Francis Meagher saw his home in Waterford for the last time that night.[57]

Arriving in Dublin the next day, Meagher went immediately to the offices of the *Nation* for a meeting with John Blake Dillon, Richard O'Gorman, and William Smith O'Brien. The three formulated a plan and that evening proceeded to the rooms used by the Irish Confederation, where about thirty people were assembled. Unbeknownst to Meagher and the others, the group included a spy named Dobbyn, who revealed their plans to the British and later testified against Meagher at his trial.

The following morning Meagher was greeted by the report in the *Freeman's Journal* that *habeas corpus*—the ancient and fundamental right under English law of a detainee to raise the issue of unlawful imprisonment—had once again been suspended in Ireland.[58] What the suspension meant practically is that the British would be able to detain the Young Irelanders indefinitely, without bail and regardless of the strength of evidence against them. It was the crowning blow. Even without proper training or sufficient arms, the time was ripe to capitalize on the angry mood of the peasants. In Meagher's mind the revolution had to start immediately. A plan was soon worked out to start the insurrection in Kilkenny, where they would face less force than in Dublin or other cities with large garrisons.[59] As it turned out, the plan was flawed from the start. Meagher could not have had unwavering confidence in it, especially after his visit to revolutionary France. The very idea that a partially armed and wholly undisciplined body of men with leaders unacquainted with even basic knowledge of military discipline and tactics could chase the British from Ireland was so utterly outlandish that in hindsight it is incomprehensible how anyone could have entertained it. Yet, even in defeat, the Young Ireland group knew they could awaken the world to the Irish cause; that alone would make the insurrection a success.[60]

Facing what were sure to be insurmountable odds, Meagher and his companions set out for the South to wage war. They had given no thought to arranging their own transportation and had to make public coach reservations under the name of a comrade to hide their true identities. It was an inauspicious beginning. When they arrived at their point of embarkation the coach was not yet there, and they waited in the dark and rain under a tree. There it occurred to Meagher that the path they had undertaken was not likely to lead to success, and a deep melancholy overcame him.[61]

Arriving at Ballinkeele early in the morning, Meagher met with Dillon and Smith O'Brien. They agreed that there were only three courses of action. The first was simply to let themselves be arrested and then plan an escape that would excite the peasants to action. The second was to escape now. The third was to start the insurrection. They chose the last and started for Kilkenny. It was Sunday, so the group stopped in Enniscorthy on the way so that Meagher and Dillon could attend Catholic mass while Smith O'Brien politely waited for them. The three then started to spread the word of the upcoming insurrection, urging the people to arm themselves and be ready to fight for freedom. These exhortations were later used against them at their trials. As they proceeded to Kilkenny, they could see that their supporters were lacking in both enthusiasm and numbers, even as they took pledges of support. Nor was the march forward going smoothly, as the weather frequently forced them into gloomy peasant cabins along the road.[62]

In those surroundings they became depressed by what now appeared to them to be a bad decision. "And here, at the very outset, we had evidence of the truth which a short time afterwards we learned to estimate more clearly, more painfully, and with hearts less able to bear up against it bravely," Meagher said. The long hunger had done its work, and the Irish peasantry was in no shape to rebel. As Meagher sadly realized, "cold and nakedness, . . . hunger and disease, to the last extremity, . . . had not only withered up the flesh and pierced the marrow in the bone; . . . but worse than all—oh! worse, a thousand times, than death by the bayonet, or the gibbet—had eaten their way into the soul itself."[63]

Burdened with this crushing revelation, Meagher and his comrades forged on to Kilkenny. Knowing that they needed to gain support, Smith O'Brien went out among the people and the Irish Confederation clubs while Meagher and Dillon met with a handful of the leading organizers to plan out which streets to barricade. Here they found enough enthusiasm to brighten Meagher's lagging spirits. At one o'clock the three leaders left Kilkenny. At Callan they dismounted from their horses amid a throng cheering at the top of their voices, elevating Meagher's spirits even more. Despite his dread he later recalled how the handsome young girls with "flashing black eyes" and rosy cheeks ran to throw their arms about their necks and kissed them amid the "loud applause of their own brave boys."[64]

Meagher and his group then moved on and soon found themselves confronted by the 8th Royal Irish Hussars of the British army. The troops, being mostly Irish, were friendly, giving the group hope that the Irish units of the British army would support them. With renewed enthusiasm they urged the townspeople on their route to arm themselves.[65] As the group moved down the road to Carrick, they came across "a tall, robust, gallant-looking fellow, mounted on a strong black horse." This was John O'Mahoney, who was not yet the important figure he would become in Meagher's life but at the time was serving as the head of the Confederate Clubs around Carrick. He gave Meagher hope. "Never, never, can I forget the enthusiasm of this gallant, glorious fellow," Meagher said.[66]

Finally, with their spirits lifted even further, they reached Carrick, where they witnessed a scene that Meagher described as "more like a dream . . . than an actual occurrence." There they saw a "torrent of human beings, rushing through lanes and narrow streets . . . whirling in dizzy circles, and tossing up its dark waves, with sounds of wrath, vengeance, and defiance . . . eyes red with rage and desperation . . . curses on the red flag: scornful, exulting, delirious defiances of death." Had Meagher and his group realized it, the incensed mob in Carrick was their best hope. "It was the Revolution if we had accepted it," he said later.[67]

Instead, Meagher, Smith O'Brien, and Dillon entered a house to organize their efforts, but the tumult itself thwarted them. "Within, there was this confusion and uproar of tongues," Meagher said; "without, there was the tossing and surging of the mighty throng." In the house "hundreds were blocking up the staircase . . . crowding and crushing round the table at which we sat; pressing down upon us, in their hot anxiety to see and hear us . . . drowning completely every word we uttered." Soon the enthusiasm defeated its own purpose. According to Meagher, it exhausted "our strength, . . . rendering us incapable of guiding with a firm hand the elements that swept and roared around us."[68]

As Meagher learned later, they had chosen a bad place to start a rebellion. In large part the Irish Confederation had picked Kilkenny because the clubs there had around seventeen thousand members, according to the *Freeman's Journal* and the papers that picked up its story around the country. This was in fact a grave error, and the actual number was more on the order of seventeen hundred. Worse yet, many of these were old men and young boys, leaving only about six hundred able-bodied men; only about one-third had guns, with no means to supply more than about sixty stand of arms in Kilkenny.[69] Panicked by the lack of organization and support, Meagher and Dillon left in great haste for Templederry, on the border between Tipperary and Limerick, to obtain help from Father Kenyon, a member of the Irish Confederation council and an outspoken supporter of its aims. To their profound consternation, Kenyon received them with coldness and indifference. He urged the confederation to fight, but only when they were ready; and until then he would not support a feckless insurrection.[70]

Time was now running short, and Meagher and Dillon split up, going to their areas of greatest familiarity to gather troops. Dillon had no success in Mayo, and Meagher found only a demoralized group in Waterford, whose willingness to participate in a revolution had disappeared. The cause of this, as Meagher learned later, was that Waterford's Father Tracy had refused to allow Catholics to join the rebellion. A disillusioned Meagher traveled back alone to join the other leaders, who were expecting him to arrive with troops.[71]

The 1848 rebellion did not have a final ending because it never really began. A group of rebels, led by Smith O'Brien, succeeded in setting up a barricade at Ballingary and made plans to ambush the police as they approached. Aware of the danger and believing that they faced up to three thousand insurgents, the police ran to the top of a hill and into a large stone house belonging to Widow McCormick. Smith O'Brien's group attempted to smoke them out by starting a hay fire around the house, which caused the police to dispatch Widow McCormick herself to meet with Smith O'Brien and advise him that they would accept terms. As he walked up to a window of the house to tell the police that he wanted their arms and not their lives, he was surprised when his ragged troops started to pelt the house with rocks. The police responded with fire, killing one man and wounding another. A return volley by the Irishmen expended all of their ammunition, and they regrouped a short distance away.[72]

Smith O'Brien made a final effort to rally the people, but it was thwarted by a priest who shouted out against the madness of the uprising and advised the men to return to their homes. Terence Bellew MacManus could see that the cause was hopeless and implored Smith O'Brien to fall back. But he would not do so until it became apparent that the people would no longer participate in an armed rebellion. Smith O'Brien could easily have been shot by the police; although he had chosen death as the only honorable way to end the affair, he was denied his wish and finally forced to retreat. He was soon captured, on August 5, at Thurles.[73]

Right before the revolt began, some of Thomas Francis Meagher's staunch friends from the Waterford Club begged him to give up his revolutionary activities and travel abroad with them to Italy, Greece, and Egypt. So ingratiating and sincere were they that he briefly considered going with them to enjoy the warmth of their friendship in safety from the pursuing British. In the end he politely declined their offer.[74] Now, a few weeks later, Meagher's circumstances had definitely changed: he found himself climbing out of an old hayloft after several nights of sleeping among the wretched peasants, who, like him, had no other place to go. On this particular day a clergyman approached Meagher with a plan to escape to America.

Still filled with the spirit of a revolutionary leader, Meagher declined, because he believed that "[w]hen the Government comes to wreak its vengeance on our failure, the people shall still see we are at their head." The clergyman presented a second proposal: Meagher would surrender on the condition that he be allowed to leave the country. Meagher pondered the proposition for a time and then agreed to it, but only on the condition that all members of the revolutionary movement be allowed to do the same. A response from the British government soon came in the form of a letter from the lord lieutenant, Mr. Redington, who agreed, provided the revolutionaries pleaded guilty to high treason. Although Meagher immediately rejected the offer, British newspapers soon carried a false story of his offer to surrender if his life was spared. Recognizing that he could not force the press to retract the story, the libeled Meagher decided to come out of hiding to face charges and preserve his reputation. On August 12 he made his whereabouts near Rathgannon known and was quickly arrested.[75]

The British, plainly troubled that the rebellion had gone as far as it did, saw the arrest of Meagher, O'Donoghue, Smith O'Brien, and MacManus as an opportunity to extract revenge and mute any criticism that the government was too lenient on the insurgents.[76] Thus, rather than charging Meagher and his fellows under the Treason Felony Act, the Crown decided to charge them with high treason. It was one of the most serious crimes of the day, with a Draconian penalty. Unlike the new Treason Felony Act, which had served to convict and transport John Mitchel, high treason specified that the convicted be tortured by being drawn on a hurdle to a place of hanging and there hung, followed by dismemberment of the body. The punishment had been stopped in England in 1814, but it had not been abolished in Ireland. Even though there was no recent precedent for its imposition, Meagher and many Irish Catholics knew that the punishment had been used as recently as the sixteenth century against 105 Catholic martyrs in London charged with the crime of "spiritual treason" for failing to recognize the true religion of the country.[77]

On Monday, October 16, 1848, throngs of Meagher's supporters crowded the streets of Clonmel, all hoping for a glimpse of the young patriot who was coming to trial. When he finally appeared in the dock, he was quiet, dignified, and composed. His usual flamboyant dress had been replaced with a plain black frock coat and a light-colored waistcoat; on his finger was a large gold ring set with a miniature carving of his hero, John Mitchel.[78]

As he sat in court Meagher observed that, in a Catholic country, the panel from which the jury was to be picked had only eighteen Catholics out of a total of three hundred. Even though he had not expected anything different, he felt compelled to point out the disparity, so he arose to address the court: "Personally, I care not whether I am to be tried by Protestants or by Roman Catholics. Though I am myself a Roman Catholic. I feel that my cause, my honor, my liberty, my life, are as safe in the hands of a jury composed exclusively of Protestants, as they would be with a jury composed exclusively of Roman Catholics." There was loud applause in the courtroom, which was silenced by the judges.

Then a jury was selected that included only a single Catholic, a known British loyalist.[79]

Meagher was the last of the four revolutionaries—now being called the "State Prisoners"—to be tried; Smith O'Brien, MacManus, and O'Donoghue had already been found guilty. The case against Meagher was somewhat weaker than the cases against the other three, because he had not participated in the same events, had not appeared in arms at Mullinahone, and had not erected barricades at Killenhaule as he had been charged. Nevertheless, Meagher's pride as a revolutionary would not allow him to raise these points.

Notwithstanding his client's reluctance, his counsel, Isaac Butt, did try to convince the jury that Meagher should not be convicted. The argument did not go over well; when John Mitchel heard of it, he criticized Butt. "I have seen a part of Butt's speech in defence of Meagher—bad." On October 21, the jury predictably returned a guilty verdict, but knowing the harsh punishment high treason demanded and the weakness of the case against Meagher, they made a "unanimous recommendation of mercy from the prisoners youth, and other circumstances."[80]

When it came time to sentence the four, Chief Justice Blackburne, a grim old man, sentenced Smith O'Brien, on October 9, in an imposing manner. Mr. Justice Moore passed sentence on MacManus and O'Donoghue in an unimpressive fashion. All three were sentenced to death. It was then Meagher's turn. A dignified man and an impressive speaker, Mr. Justice Doherty seemed somewhat insincere as he expressed his grave sorrow before reading the sentence: "[Y]ou . . . Thomas Francis Meagher, be taken hence to the place from whence you came, and be thence drawn on a hurdle to the place of execution, and that . . . you be there hanged by the neck until you be dead, and that afterward the head . . . shall be severed from [the] body, and the body . . . divided into four quarters, to be disposed of as Her Majesty shall think fit."[81]

These ancient words settled like darkness over Meagher and the hushed courtroom, but he did not ask for leniency or assign error to the proceeding that convicted him. Instead, in a quiet voice and conversational tones, he defied the judges:

My Lords, you may deem this language unbecoming in me, and perhaps it may seal my fate. But I am here to speak the truth

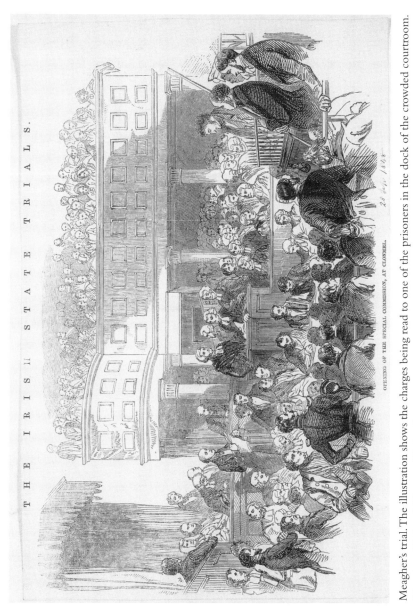

THE IRISH STATE TRIALS.

OPENING OF THE SPECIAL COMMISSION, AT CLONMEL.

Meagher's trial. The illustration shows the charges being read to one of the prisoners in the dock of the crowded courtroom.
(Courtesy National Library of Ireland)

whatever it may cost. I am here to regret nothing I have ever done—to retract nothing I have ever said. . . . Judged by the law of England, I know this crime entails the penalty of death; but the history of Ireland explains this crime, and justifies it. Judged by that history I am no criminal—you [addressing MacManus] and you [addressing O'Donoghue] are no criminals: I deserve no punishment—we deserve no punishment. Judged by that history, the treason of which I stand convicted loses all its guilt, is sanctified as a duty, will be ennobled as a sacrifice. . . . Pronounce, then, my lords, the sentence which the law directs; I am prepared to hear it. I trust I shall be prepared to meet its execution. I hope to be able, with a pure heart and perfect composure to appear before a higher tribunal—a tribunal where a Judge of infinite goodness, as well as justice will preside, and where, my lords, many—many, of the judgments of this world wille [sic] be reversed.[82]

The Reverend George W. Pepper, the Protestant minister from Ulster who had befriended Meagher in Belfast, described his statement as "grand and noble." Pepper witnessed the proceedings from the back of the courtroom. Later, when he reflected back on the events of 1848, he remembered that the Irish Tory newspapers had proclaimed that the Irish revolt had been crushed. Pepper denounced the Tories as fools, who "might as well attempt to crush the Andes or the Rocky mountains."[83] John Mitchel, after hearing of the proceedings, predicted that the sentences would be commuted and noted in his journal: "All the four—O'Brien, Meagher, M'Manus, O'Donoghue—sentenced to death. But the enlightened Spirit of the Age—the devil take his enlightened cant!—is going to spare their lives, and *only transport them for life*. I have seen . . . [a]lso the few words spoken by poor Meagher after conviction; brave and noble words."[84]

Meagher's defiance of the court did not please the judiciary, and the lawyers' attempts to have the convictions of the State Prisoners overturned on a writ of error were to no avail.[85] O'Brien and MacManus then took their cases to the English House of Lords, but Meagher on principle refused to join them. He would not seek justice in England, and for that he earned the praise of Mitchel: "Right, brave Meagher!"[86]

Soon a rumor emerged in Ireland that Meagher's escape had been arranged and that his father had brigantines cruising off the coast to pick him up.[87] Meagher would not have attempted escape, however, for he knew that he could not be restored to society in Ireland. Thus he prepared to meet his death. His personal belongings were meaningless to him, save those that signified the cause that was to cost him his life. Among them was his "'82 cap" from his membership in the '82 Club, which had been started in commemoration of Grattan's 1782 declaration of legislative independence. On November 9 he wrote from Clonmel Gaol to his friend "Johnny," offering him his "'82 cap." "It is the only thing I have worth giving you," Meagher said. "It will remind you . . . of the cause for which I suffer imprisonment, and have been condemned to death."[88]

But death had to wait, as public opinion surfaced against the dreadful punishment. The British officials were not only faced with clamor for a pardon or reduction in Meagher's sentence but also had a serious problem of credibility because of an event that had arisen a few years earlier. In 1832 General Sir Charles Napier, an Irishman, had been directed by a letter approved by Lord John Russell, now prime minister of England, to lead a group of insurrectionists in Birmingham as they prepared for a march on London. While the letter had been subpoenaed for the trials of the State Prisoners, the judges refused to admit it into evidence. It was brought to light by the press, however, and it showed a surprised public that Lord Russell himself had actively planned to commit the same type of acts that the State Prisoners had committed. Under the circumstances Russell could not let the death sentences be carried out. It became apparent to the government that the best way to avoid a real revolution was for the British Crown to show mercy. Finally, an act of royal clemency came, transmuting the State Prisoners' sentences to transportation to one of the British penal colonies for life.[89]

Meagher never avoided responsibility for the failure of the rebellion:

> The defeat of 1848 was not the defeat of a whole people. It was nothing more than the rout of a few peasants, hastily collected, badly armed, half-starved, and miserably clad. . . . I feel, however, it would not be candid of me to conceal the opinion I have frequently stated in private, that we who went to Tipperary did not put the question properly to the country—did not give the

1849 etching of Thomas Francis Meagher with a revolutionary inscription. The inscription reads: "From the blood which stained the scaffolds of 1798, the 'felons' of 1848 have sprung." The date appears to be April 27, 1849, from Kilmainham prison. (Courtesy National Library of Ireland)

country a fair opportunity—did not adopt anything like the best means for evoking the heroism of the people, and bringing it into action.[90]

But Meagher also thought that another factor was key to the defeat of the Irish people. In his view, which became public, the Catholic priests were also at fault:

I do not, of course, applaud them for the part they acted. With the belief that is rooted in my mind I could not do so. For I firmly believe that, had the Catholic priests of Ireland preached the revolution from their altars—had they gone out, like the Sicilian priests, or the Archbishop of Milan, and borne the Cross in front of the insurgent ranks—had this been the case, I firmly believe there would have been a young Nation, crowned with glory, standing proudly up by the side of England at this hour.[91]

This rebuke of the priests did not sit lightly with the clergy and many Irish Catholics, and it drew criticism of Meagher from the Irish community for the rest of his life.

In the years following, Meagher reflected many times on his personal reasons for becoming involved in the rebellion. In 1855 he felt compelled to explain his defiance of the British to Elizabeth Townsend, the New York Yankee socialite who became his second wife. Meagher admitted to her that he might have lacked judgment, yet he neither overstated his involvement in the effort nor sought to disown it. Ultimately he stood by his belief that the cause was just: "In the last attempt of the Irish [?] in Ireland, it was my fate to be involved. . . . Through much . . . flattery and exaggerated colouring, the fact and the truth of my short course in public life are clear enough, and that there is nothing in it all—not a word, an act, a sentiment, from first to last—you would fear to own, or blush to own, I feel personally satisfied."[92]

In the summer of 1849 Meagher, now in Kilmainham prison in Dublin, made preparations for his exile: settling bills and writing to friends. One of the bills was from Henry FitzGibbon, a tailor in Dublin, who had delivered a black frock coat and tweed trousers on December 13, 1848, and a "super rifle green cloth cloak," a satin vest, and a black

Thomas Francis Meagher and William Smith O'Brien. The two are pictured in 1848 or 1849, when they were imprisoned in Kilmainham Gaol in Dublin after being sentenced to death for treason. Meagher is left center, and Smith O'Brien is seated. (Author's collection)

rib cap and trousers on January 8, 1849, all during the time when Meagher was in prison.[93]

Two weeks before his departure Meagher took out his volume of *Shelley's Poems* and inscribed it with an original verse of his own titled "My Poor Old Country." It ended with a postscript: "The history of Ireland explains my crime—explains and justifies it."[94] He gave the volume to "Miss Cooper," whose identity is otherwise unknown. Meagher had many female admirers, and one of them had supposedly followed him to prison when he was arrested. When the death sentence was announced, the story goes, she died of a broken heart.[95] Unknown even to his closest friends, Meagher had also become secretly engaged to "Miss O'Ryan," whose parents violently opposed the match once they learned of it.[96]

Having passed his last days saying good-bye, Meagher sailed out of Dublin harbor on July 9, 1849. He and the other three State Prisoners were bound to Tasmania aboard the British warship the *Swift*. Before they left, the group published parting addresses calling for an end to the dissension among Irish of all creeds and unity for the common good of Ireland. Only a few days later, Protestant Orangemen on their annual march through Catholic neighborhoods would kill four people and burn several houses and churches. Irish Catholics immediately raised the cry that this was a far greater tragedy than that perpetrated by the Young Irelanders; but to no one's surprise, the Protestant Orangemen went unpunished, except that the Orange leaders were deprived of their commissions as justices of the peace.[97]

Hearing that the *Swift* had sailed out on the Atlantic bound for Tasmania, John Mitchel sadly noted in his journal:

> I know not three other men so expressly formed as O'Brien, Martin, and Meagher, for a life of tranquil enjoyment, and the discharge of all peaceful duties in proud obedience to the laws of the land. But they could not stand by and see diabolical injustice wrought without end, under this foul pretence of law;—they would not be parties to the slaughter of their countrymen by millions that this foul pretence of law might flourish for ages to come—"and of its fruit their babes might eat and die."—therefore they sail this day in a convict-ship with the concentrated quintessence of all the offal of mankind.[98]

CHAPTER THREE

Exile

The story can be easily told. . . . You know I was a "rebel"—and you
know I am an "exile."

Thomas Francis Meagher to Elizabeth Townsend

"The *Swift* lies at anchor a little outside the light-house on Kingstown
pier. A ten-gun brig, very trim, bright and rakish." This was how Thomas
Francis Meagher described the ship that was to take him to Tasmania. On
July 9, 1849, he was put on board along with William Smith O'Brien,
Terence Bellew MacManus, and Patrick O'Donoghue, and read the rules:
surprisingly, they were to be treated as "supernumeraries" rather than
common prisoners. After eating a dinner of the ship's regular food, which
included "two pounds of hard beef steak—plate of biscuits—jug of tank
water," they were put in passenger cabins, where the prisoners slept, with
locked doors for the night. The following morning they were off the
coast of Waterford. Meagher's heart was heavy with grief at what he
knew would be the last sight of the estuary of the River Suir, a place
familiar to him since his youth. "I pass by, and my own people know
nothing of it," he bewailed in his diary. "Erin mavourneen farewell."[1]

Meagher's homesickness must have been intense. He remained
firmly committed to the cause, of course, for somewhere in the middle
of the ocean he symbolically affirmed his attachment to Ireland by
changing his name to O'Meagher. Many Irish adopted the use of the

patrimonial "O," and presumably Meagher believed that "O'Meagher" would clearly identify him as an Irishman to the rest of the world. While the name change did not stick, it remains suggestive of his emotional state as the *Swift* took him farther and farther from home.[2]

After more than three months' uneventful sailing, except for a day's sojourn in the bay at the Cape of Good Hope, Meagher, Smith O'Brien, O'Donoghue, and MacManus finally arrived in Hobart Town. About that same time John Martin and Kevin O'Doherty arrived on the *Elphinstone*. Only Martin, who had received a lesser sentence of seven years' transportation, could look forward to returning to Ireland in his lifetime. The isolated island in a remote southern corner of the world—250 miles across the Bass Strait south of Australia—was beautiful, with a rocky coastline, rolling hills, remarkable mountains, and the fauna and flora suited to its temperate climate. As the *Swift* pulled into the harbor at Hobart Town, the prisoners' spirits rose as the long voyage ended: they began to see the natural beauty of their country of exile and to hear Irish voices.[3]

Indeed, there were many Irish in Tasmania and many prisoners. The British had begun sending convicts to Tasmania, then called Van Diemen's Land, in 1803. Their guards and their guards' families accompanied them. Some of them decided to settle on the island. Soon sheep raising was introduced, and free settlers arrived to colonize. But a large portion of the population consisted of freed transported prisoners. Transportation had developed in England as a separate and distinct punishment from imprisonment, and legal principles did not permit two punishments for the same crime. Thus the convicts were usually held in probation stations instead of prisons for up to several years before they were allowed to become pass holders and take employment and receive wages as part of the general population of the island. When Meagher and the other State Prisoners arrived, Tasmania had a population of over 65,000, of which almost 30,000 were transported criminals.

As this society grew, transportation and the landing of more prisoners in its midst became objectionable, even to the British. By the time Meagher arrived, there was a move afoot to abandon transportation and rename Van Diemen's Land as Tasmania. Transportation ended in May 1853, and on January 1, 1854, the name "Tasmania" was adopted to separate the new society and its future from the dismal past of Van Diemen's Land. Of course, many of the freed convicts and the settlers were Irish, and the island's substantial Irish community ranged from prominent professionals to thieving bushwhackers. The Young Irelanders found they would not lack supporters in this far-away land.[4]

When Meagher arrived in Tasmania, officials recorded his physical description in the log of the *Swift:* five feet nine inches tall, clean shaven, with a fair complexion, round head, brown hair, long visage, medium forehead, nose, mouth, and chin, and light blue eyes. No weight was given. His trade was listed as "law student."[5] After being booked in the prison records in Hobart, Meagher received his ticket of leave. He was lucky, although he did not feel that way. Even before the State Prisoners left Ireland, Earl Grey, Britain's secretary of state in charge of colonial affairs, had written to Sir William Denison, the lieutenant governor in charge of the British penal colony, to tell him that Meagher and the Young Irelanders were of superior rank in society and should be treated as gentlemen. There was no question of hard labor; instead, the loss of fortune and social position would in itself be suitable punishment. Nor were the prisoners to be placed in the usual probation station, where prisoners worked for the government until they earned the right to become "pass holders."[6]

The State Prisoners were allowed to skip these steps. Provided that they behaved themselves properly during their voyage, they were granted immediate freedom if they promised not to escape. This freedom was to be under a "ticket of leave," a written instrument through which transported prisoners were honor bound by their parole not to escape unless they notified the government first that they were revoking their promise, to give the police a fair opportunity to arrest them. Generally prisoners did not gain tickets of leave—which entailed the right to buy property, marry, and control many aspects of their own lives—until after proving themselves as pass holders.[7]

All of the Young Irelanders accepted their tickets of leave except Smith O'Brien, who refused on principle to give his promise. He was sent to Maria Island off the coast for imprisonment among "the most desperate convicts." The others were allowed to live at large, but each within a limited district, with no two of them nearer than thirty or forty miles from each other. John Mitchel found this scheme calculatedly demoralizing: "It is not easy to understand the object of so carefully separating the prisoners, and planting each by himself in the midst of a felonious population, unless it be, by depriving them of one another's society, to force them into association with such miscreants as they are likely to meet, that so they may become at last the felons their enemies call them," he said. "Or, possibly, it is done with a view to more easily reducing them singly to submission."[8]

Meagher was assigned to Campbell Town, seventy-five miles north of Hobart in the center of Tasmania's budding wool-growing district. He was the first of the State Prisoners permitted to leave the *Swift* when he was put on a night coach at half past three in the morning for a twelve-hour trip to his new home. Campbell Town was the third largest city in Tasmania, but it had only one main street, which had buildings on only one side, and about three side streets.[9] The people Meagher found there were the type that he would decry as "regenerated swindlers!! chastised and chastened forgers!! circumcised murderers!! renovated burglars!!"[10] John Mitchel agreed with Meagher's assessment of the average resident's character: "of the whole population of V.D. Land, more than *three-fourths* are convicts, or emancipated convicts, or the children of convicts, begotten in felony, and brought up in the feeling that their hand must be against every man, as every man's hand is against them."[11]

Meagher stayed in Campbell Town only a few days before he found it necessary to escape the "village notabilities" who hounded newcomers. He soon moved to a hotel in the even smaller village of Ross, five miles south. In November 1849 he wrote a friend that he was moving to a "pretty little cottage," where he hoped "to spend some quiet pleasant days, 'all alone, by myself,' with my pipe and my books."[12] There on the shores of beautiful Lake Sorell his only neighbors were two or three distant shepherds. The lake itself was seven miles wide and about eight and a half miles long. In its middle was an island of some sixty acres, which Meagher rented, along with his house site on the shore, from one of the wealthiest sheep ranchers in Tasmania. Once a week Meagher took provisions to the island for his "farm-servant," Tom Egan, an Irish lad from County Kilkenny who had himself been transported to Tasmania for a minor crime.

At first it seemed as if Meagher had decided to build a new life for himself. He kept himself busy cultivating the land for his own use and acquired farming stock consisting of four bullocks and a "wicked old" pony who would think nothing of "doing his 60 miles between

Meagher's cottage on Lake Sorell. Meagher was isolated high in the mountains of Tasmania on a beautiful but lonely lake. After his marriage, Meagher and his wife, Catherine, lived here until he escaped. From an original done by Meagher's fellow exile John Mitchel. (Courtesy Archives Office of Tasmania)

breakfast and dinner." The remainder of his domestic animals included "a few sheep, also—two Kangaroo dogs—two watch dogs, and two saddle horses" that Meager described as being cheaply bought. In that wild and remote country, he believed it was absolutely necessary to have "a couple of good horses," because all journeys in the interior of the country were made on horseback. There was only one regular road between Launceston and Hobart for buggies, with all others being mere track ways.[13]

Lake Sorell and the Tasmanian countryside were beautiful, the weather was pleasing, and the freedom was adequate, considering that for most Young Irelanders it was an alternative to the death penalty. For some people it would have been an idyllic setting; for the urbane Meagher it was a prison. He soon became bored, frustrated, and unhappy, as were the other Young Irelanders; their spirits were buoyed only by infrequent meetings with each other and the promise of escape. The threat of arrest haunted them all, because local penal officers had the ability to jail them instantly for parole infractions.[14] Most of all, they missed civilization and the company of their own kind. Ultimately not one of them was willing to accept his fate and simply settle down to a new life far away from Ireland. "But I peopled the lonesome scene with friends who were far away, and made it teem with memories and visions of the dear land of my birth," Meagher said later.[15]

Although thousands of native Irish in Tasmania had been sent to the penal colony over the years, most of them did not have the refinement of the intellectual, privileged, and sophisticated Young Irelanders. They were rough-and-ready Irish peasants and laborers of a class that had been denied education and privileges for centuries. The Young Irelanders had been settled, Meagher wrote, "amongst a people whose vulgarities and vices are ever staring us in the face, and whose dull and dogged insensibility to every-thing that is generous and truthful . . . renders them a people most besotted, depraved, and loathsome."[16]

Meagher and the others all thought of escape. It seemed to Meagher that only John Martin, who had the possibility of freedom in seven years, had accepted his existence, living quietly and obscurely, not "uttering a single word against anything or anybody." But Meagher's sentence was for life, and he could only wonder when he would be allowed to leave the island. "And if it comes in ten, fourteen, or twenty years—is it not destined to come as a *special favour*—as a *special act of grace*—or somehow else that will make me loathe it, more or less? For, I have been sent *here for life,* and any shortening of that sentence must be an act of mercy!"[17] As much as he desired his freedom, Meagher abhorred the thought of receiving a shortened sentence from the Crown.

John Mitchel finally arrived in Hobart on April 7, 1850, aboard the *Neptune.* He had been the first of Young Ireland to be transported, but he had been sent to Bermuda on a convict ship. Suffering from asthma there, he applied to be transferred to a new penal colony in Cape Town; but when he arrived there, the citizens demonstrated against the landing of Irish prisoners so strongly that his boat was sent to Tasmania. Mitchel accepted his ticket of leave. Because he had been ill, he was given permission to reside with his brother-in-law, the quiet John Martin, in Bothwell.[18]

Within a few days Mitchel and Martin set out to meet Meagher at his cabin on Lake Sorell. Riding up into the mountains on a steep and uncertain path, through rain and snow, they were finally stopped by their own fatigue several miles short of Meagher's small cottage. Word was sent to him to meet them in the hut of one of his neighbors. There Mitchel and Martin stayed by the fire until Meagher, accompanied by Kevin O'Doherty, came through the door. Mitchel later wrote, "I know not from what impulse, whether from buoyancy of heart, or *bizarre*—perversity of feeling—we all *laughed* till the woods rang around; laughed loud and long, and uproariously, till two teal rose, startled from the reeds on the lake-shore, and flew screaming to seek a quieter neighbourhood." Yet the gaiety of the four Young Irelanders soon ceased as they began to consider the plight of Smith O'Brien, still in prison and being subjected to strict confinement and insolent treatment by his British jailers.[19]

Almost as dismaying was the state of the revolutionary movement, particularly among those who had emigrated or escaped to America. Even in far-away Tasmania the men heard of the factions that had developed among the Irish in Boston and New York "on the momentous question, who was the greatest man and most glorious hero, of that most inglorious Irish business of '48; and each imagines he exalts his own favourite 'martyr' by disparaging and pulling down the rest—as if the enemy's government had not pulled us all down, and ridden roughshod over us," Mitchel wrote. "It seems I had my faction, and Meagher a still stronger one. If our respective partisans could but have seen—as we discussed this question of our own comparative importance—how bitterly and how mournfully we two smiled at one another across the gumtree fire in that log-hut amongst the forests of the antipodes, perhaps it might have cooled their partisan zeal."[20]

Despite the sorry circumstances, the exiles found great comfort in their mutual continued passion for revolution and their now even greater hatred of the British. Having concluded that his friends were "*unsubdued*," Mitchel later wrote in his *Jail Journal:* "The game, I think, is not over yet."[21] For Meagher the next stage of "the game" concerned William Smith O'Brien. Feeling he could not sit idly by as Smith O'Brien's health declined in prison, Meagher could not restrain himself from challenging the British. Early in 1850 he wrote a letter to Governor Denison requesting relaxation of the severe discipline that Smith O'Brien was subjected to on Maria's Island, but the request went unheeded. Driven to action, Meagher began plotting Smith O'Brien's escape.

The escape was to be accomplished with funds and assistance from the New York Irish Directory, which held the money that had been raised for the 1848 rebellion but had arrived in Ireland too late. Dr. J. C. McCarthy, a local physician from Hobart and a supporter of Smith O'Brien, also agreed to help with the project. The plan involved hiring a sailing ship and crew to rescue Smith O'Brien from the island. When the money from New York did not arrive, Dr. McCarthy committed to finance the project himself, upon assurances of repayment from Meagher, who had shown him a letter from Irish supporters in America expressing an intention to cover the expenses. This was sufficient for Meagher, who boldly went out and purchased a half interest in the cutter *Victoria,* renting the other half for a year. Most of the over five hundred pounds for the purchase came from his father. According to the plan, the boat was to take Smith O'Brien to Tahiti or some other island under the French flag; from there he could easily get to the United States. But when the plan was finally executed, it failed miserably because of "the rascally conduct of the Captain who made away with the ship."[22]

Smith O'Brien, who had not even been informed of the escape plan until just before it was to occur, was ordered into solitary confinement. He was becoming broken in body and spirit and felt an obligation to repay Dr. McCarthy, so he recanted his previous position and accepted a ticket of leave.[23] Although Smith O'Brien came from a wealthy family and had considerable funds at one time, he had left all his money in trust for the care of his wife and children and had no funds to contribute toward his escape. When he left prison, he thought the debt was only two hundred pounds and would take him a year of work as an underpaid schoolteacher to repay it. Of course, the debt was much higher, and Meagher took responsibility for it. Confronted with a financial crisis, for he had no money either, Meagher forwarded the bill to his father for payment. After waiting for an explanation, the senior Meagher finally sent payment, along with a cryptic note: "The adventure in which you risked so much had been excessively improvident and fruitless."[24]

Meagher's depression at the failure to accomplish Smith O'Brien's escape was compounded by a personal crisis. Meagher had been secretly engaged to a Miss Ryan when he left Ireland; however, his fiancée's parents had discovered the arrangement and would have nothing to do with their daughter marrying an exile. Thus he received a letter the Saturday before Christmas of 1850 in which the young lady begged him "to burn or send back all her letters which latter request I have complied with." Depressed by the event, he found the "gloom and solitude" of his existence deepening around him.[25]

In this state Meagher took to wandering the roads of his district in Tasmania. "I was idly living on from day to day," he confessed in a letter to his friend Kevin O'Doherty; he was lonely and hoping to make new friends.[26] Always well met and eager to engage total strangers in conversation, he came across the entourage of Dr. Hall and his family, who were making their way toward the town of Ross, where the doctor had just been appointed physician. The group included the six Hall children and their caretaker, a beautiful young girl named Catherine Bennett, the daughter of Bryan Bennett, who had come to Tasmania as a convict.[27] Meagher was attracted to her immediately; he fell in with the group, walking with them for several miles and all the time chatting with Catherine. The young woman was enthralled that this famous man was paying attention to her, for Terence MacManus had become a frequent visitor to her family home in New Norfolk and had often talked about Meagher.

Meagher's sad heart found new hope in the presence of the young woman; as he later described it, "a solitary star shone down upon me, making bright and beautiful the desolate waters of the mournful wild lake on the shore of which I lived in that wilderness."[28] After many visits to the Hall home for the sole purpose of seeing Catherine, Meagher proposed, and the couple became engaged. As a convict, Meagher had to receive permission to marry, which was granted on January 21, 1851. They planned to marry a month later.[29]

The announcement did not sit well with the Young Ireland exiles. Smith O'Brien had once chided Meagher about avoiding "cupid and his darts," only to receive a firm denial. "You are quite wrong," Meagher had said. "I shall never condescend to honour Van Diemen's Land as to make it the scene of my nuptials." Thus Meagher's engagement took Smith O'Brien and the others by surprise. As John Mitchel wrote to O'Doherty about Meagher's decision to wed: "About Meagher, you are dumb. Perhaps I ought to be so, too. I was astonished beyond measure when he told me (about a fortnight ago) that the thing was settled, irrevocable, booked, and he had not ever hinted to me the thing before." Having expecting Meagher at least to have found a mate with some sophistication, Mitchel continued: "But I was even more astonished the next time I went up and saw the lady." Trying to view the situation in the best light, Mitchel ended: "Yet still, if she have some sense and spirit and can assume that gentle ascendancy over him which is so salutary to many men, the thing may do well."[30]

In a letter to his friend O'Doherty, Meagher explained his state of mind: the letter from his fiancée in Ireland breaking their engagement had devastated him, and his isolation—many miles from his closest comrade—had a deadening effect on him. "It is no wonder," he later wrote, "that my heart should have turned to one, in whose love I felt assured that peace, and health, and gladness would be returned to it."[31] It was not a propitious way to begin a marriage.

Meagher realized immediately that his marriage to Catherine would not win the approval of his fellow exiles: "I know full well, that in the world's estimation . . . I shall not elevate myself by the connection on which I have passionately and proudly set my heart." He also knew that his life in Tasmania with Catherine would not bring him the trappings of his upper-class life in Ireland, but he rationalized that it was not important: "Let the world pursue its own course and seek enjoyment, wealth, and grandeur through the glare of gold, and old family plate, and the emblazonery [sic] of crests and shields—beneath a milder and a purer light—that which a gentle, noble nature sheds—I desire to tread my path through life."[32]

In fact, Meagher was ultimately unwilling to settle for a life of obscurity, whatever comfort he found in his romance. Adding to his unrest was the revocation of the tickets of leave of O'Donoghue, O'Doherty, and MacManus, who were imprisoned during the Christmas season of 1850 for illegally meeting with each other. The event incensed Meagher: "They were clothed in the vile yellow dress of the chain-gangs—compelled to ... work, in company with the vilest ruffians that were ever bred upon the earth—and to every indignity which such an abominable fellowship could inflict, they were forced patiently and silently to submit." Meagher had been able to escape from a like sentence, "thanks to the speed of a gallant little grey horse, mounted on which I dashed through the police, and got back to my own boundary before they had time to arrest me."[33]

MacManus was released on a writ of *habeas corpus* early in 1851; his ticket of leave had been revoked, so he was no longer honor bound not to escape. Plans began for his getaway. MacManus's subsequent run for freedom offered hope to all of the Young Irelanders that their time in Tasmania might be shortened by their own escapes. Coming at the time when Meagher was fulfilling his commitment to marry young Catherine Bennett and settle down with her in the forests of Tasmania, the news unsettled him. The irony of the event would be even more biting: MacManus, before leaving the island, risked his freedom to attend Meagher's wedding, where the guests were told to keep his identity a secret. With MacManus and some of their other comrades present at Ross, Bishop Willson married the unlikely couple at Dr. Hall's residence in a Roman Catholic ceremony on February 22, 1851.[34]

After the wedding, Thomas Francis Meagher and Catherine Bennett Meagher moved into his mountain property at Lake Sorell. Soon friends started to visit, among the first of whom was John Mitchel. With him was John Martin, who immediately wrote to Smith O'Brien: "Mitchel and I went up by invitation to see the happy couple at Lake Sorell the second Sunday of their honeymoon. The bride looked well and so did the groom." But Martin's praise for Catherine ended there. "She seems a very quiet, gentle, inoffensive girl," he said. "It is a pity (so far as I learned) she neither sings, or plays, nor draws, nor paints, nor has any decided turn for literature, or any great enjoyment or interest in it, or any feeling of patriotism, or any enthusiasm of character, or any marked talent, or accomplishment or decided character or (as I incline to think) much tendency or capacity to receive impressions from the decided character of a husband." As if by way of justification for the marriage, Martin added: "no doubt he regards her as very beautiful. I trust in heaven the poor fellow will be happy with her—and she with him."[35]

Several weeks later, after hearing that Catherine was ill, Martin visited again. He learned that "Meagher had walked down to Ross for supplies for his sick wife and walked up again, leading the horse and cart conveying them." He also found out that there was "rather a serious quarrel between him (Mrs Meagher on his side) and the Halls. Dr and Mrs Hall made injurious representations about his conduct towards his wife. Though his wife is on his side, I am vexed beyond expression at the vile entanglements he gets himself into—he has hardly any common sense in some respects."[36]

While his friends marveled at his choice, Meagher put the best face he could on his marriage. Eight months after his wedding he wrote to a friend in Ireland: "whilst I am writing these few words (in the thick of the Wild Australian Bush close by the shore of a lonely but lovely Lake) my wife is sitting, at the other end of the little table, the very picture of a fine Irish girl!—working away with her needle, in the brightest good humour."[37]

Despite such assertions of contentment, underneath Meagher continued to chaff at his new life. Around the same time, he wrote to another Irish friend, Dick Sargeant: "the climate is exceedingly fine, and effects, in a very short time, a most delightful improvement even in the worst cases of physical prostration." But he also told Sargeant that the longer he was away from Waterford and his old friends there, the more constantly he prayed to be among them once more. "Of that, however, I entertain hardly any hope. My 'pleasures' are there of 'Memory'—they do not live in the future but in the past. That I am doomed for life to this hateful land, I painfully and deeply believe. Hence I shut my eyes to the morrow, and never bestow a thought except upon what has already taken place." In this letter he made no mention of his new wife.[38]

By the fall of 1851 Meagher had purchased a boat that was built at Hobart Town and hauled up to Lake Sorell over mountains by six bullocks, a distance of eighty-five miles through swamps and forests.[39]

From the mast of the boat, which he had named *Speranza,* he flew the Irish tricolor. Perhaps his young wife did not know the origin of the name, but his Young Ireland friends surely would have recognized the tribute to the exotic Jane Elgee, by now Lady Jane Wilde, who at one time had viewed Meagher somewhat romantically.

Around this time, too, Meagher began planning his escape. He later rationalized it as motivated by a desire to provide a better life for his new bride:

> I had not been four months married, when I saw that she had to share the privations and indignities to which her husband himself was subject. A prisoner myself, I had led another from the altar to share with me an odious captivity. . . . Without her, I might have hardened my heart, and to have stoutly borne the lot assigned me. But that she should have to drink from the bitter cup that was given me to drink; that her days should come and pass away in solitude, and that to the brighter scenes and nobler cares of life she should be held there, in that dreary hermitage, a stranger;—this I could not bear. Hence I came to the determination of breaking loose from the trammels which bound me to that hateful soil, and, flying to another land, beckon her across the ocean to a home, the foundations of which in the midst of a free people, would be laid in joy.[40]

This explanation seems more than a little self-serving. Most likely his planned escape had more to do with his unhappiness than with Catherine, whose entire family was in Tasmania.

The problem that Meagher and the other exiles had in escaping from Tasmania was twofold. First were the logistical problems of escaping from the constables and finding both a boat to take them off the mainland and a ship to take them to a safe port. The second problem was more complex, for they needed somehow to flee without violating the promises not to escape that they had made to obtain their tickets of leave. With the eyes of the world on them as leaders of the Irish cause, their honor could not be sacrificed for mere freedom. The matter was always subject to interpretation, however; according to P. J. Smyth, who investigated the matter, "a condition of the parole was that the Govt. could revoke it at any moment without cause assigned. In like manner the prisoner was free to resign it."[41]

Meagher relied on this view and started to lay the groundwork for his escape. In April 1851, when he was required to renew his parole, he did so in a document handed to a police magistrate in open court, using carefully chosen words: "I hereby pledge my word of honor not to leave the colony so long as I hold a ticket of leave." In January 1852 final arrangements were made. Catherine, who was by then pregnant, went to wait with her people until she received word that Meagher was safe. At that point she would sail for Waterford, where Meagher's father would receive her.[42]

With these plans in place, Meagher addressed a letter to the magistrate of his district, on January 3, 1852:

> Sir:—Circumstances of a recent occurrence urge upon me the necessity of resigning my ticket of leave, and consequently withdrawing my *parole*.
>
> I write this letter, therefore, respectfully to apprise you, that after 12 o'clock to-morrow noon, I shall no longer consider myself bound by the obligation which that *parole* imposes.
>
> In the meantime, however, should you conceive it your duty to take me into custody, I shall, as a matter of course, regard myself as wholly absolved from the restraint which my word of honor to your Government at present inflicts.
>
> To the Police Magistrate of the District of Campbelltown.[43]

The police magistrate received Meagher's letter at eleven o'clock the same morning he sent it, and Meagher remained in his cottage at Lake Sorell until seven o'clock in the evening. At that time four friends—who, interestingly, were new acquaintances rather than Young Irelanders—came as planned to tell Meagher that the police were on their way to arrest him. Once he received word, he left his cottage and waited in the bush a short distance away until his servant brought the news that the police had arrived and were sitting in his kitchen. Mounting their horses, Meagher and his friends rode down to the cottage. Meagher alone proceeded to a position close to the stable, which was "within pistol shot of the kitchen door." There he told the servant to go tell the police he was waiting for them.[44]

After two or three minutes the police appeared. According to Meagher, "I rose in my stirrups, and called out that I was the prisoner they came to arrest, and I defied them to do so. This challenge was echoed by my friends with three loud and hearty cheers, in the midst of which I struck spurs to my horse, and dashed into the wood, in the direction of the coast."[45]

Meagher's neighbor, a man named Kean, confirmed the basic facts of this story. Kean reported, when questioned, that he had observed Meagher call out to the police, who would not answer because they were intimidated by the presence of "three or four persons" who accompanied Meagher. This was the attempt to take him into custody that Meagher had envisioned when he crafted the language of his parole renewal and resignation, and he believed himself absolved from his promise not to escape.[46]

Having outdistanced the slowly pursuing constables, Meagher rode toward the coast. Reaching the mouth of the Tamar River, he located two fishermen who had been waiting for him and was rowed out into the Bass Strait. There they unfurled a small sail and proceeded through high seas that threatened to swamp the little craft. Finally reaching the barren and uninhabited Waterhouse Island, the fishermen waited with him for two days; but having exhausted their provisions, they left on the third day, not to return again. Meagher was now alone and faced starvation until a band of escaped convicts came to the island and provided a degree of hospitality and food for him. After ten days the boat *Elizabeth Thompson* arrived at last, much later than had been arranged. It was bound for London by way of Brazil.[47]

The ship that Meagher escaped on was captained by a man named Betts; even though it was of British registry, the captain did not want to pass up the offer of nearly six hundred pounds sterling to take aboard an escaped prisoner. As part of the bargain, the captain agreed to conceal Meagher's identity from the rest of the crew to prevent him from being captured again. Long days passed on the seas, and finally the ship rounded the southern tip of South America. It stopped long enough for Meagher to observe that the Indian tribes there lived in huts in the middle of misery and filth, a scene that he would be reminded of later when he arrived in Montana toward the end of his life and observed the Bannack

Indians. Meagher finally reached Pernambuco, Brazil, in time for St. Patrick's Day. Even with an Irishman as his host, he had to keep his identity a secret for fear that word of his whereabouts would reach the British. He then transferred to the brig *Acorn* and set sail for New York.[48]

Catherine, meanwhile, remained with her family in Stonefield, where she kept Meagher's departure a secret as long as she could. Not hearing from him, she became anxious about his safety. "The last letter I received from my dear husband was written the day he left Lake Sorell," she told a friend. "I got two letters from certain friends and just a few pencilled words from my husband, the moment before he stepped into the boat which was waiting for him." She took consolation that one of her friends had seen him in the boat "sailing off beautifully." Optimistically she said that "our days of separation, I earnestly hope, will not be long." Catherine had other things on her mind as she waited for word from her husband. In early 1852 she gave birth to Henry Emmet Fitzgerald O'Meagher, only to watch him die four months later on June 8, 1852. Shortly after Meagher arrived in New York, Catherine buried Henry in a small churchyard at the parish of Father Dunne in Richmond. Eight months later she would depart for Ireland and then on to the United States.[49]

For his part, Meagher had made good his escape but still had to survive the furor that followed. Although he had revoked his ticket of leave in a manner he thought appropriate, the British immediately complained of his breach. Lady Denison announced in Tasmania that she believed the Irish had no concept of honor and should all be treated as ordinary felons. The *Hobart Town Advisor,* a newspaper that supported the British, also announced that Meagher had escaped without honor, a sentiment that was soon seconded in Australia by the *Sydney Morning Herald*.[50]

The debate surrounding Meagher's escape continued long after he reached America, with even some of his fellow exiles lambasting his methods. Although Meagher had informed Charles Gavan Duffy late in 1851 that he was planning to withdraw his parole, none of his fellow Irish exiles were party to the details of his escape plan; and some were now critical of its execution.[51] According to the Young Irelanders who believed that Meagher had not followed the dictates of a strict code of honor, he should have delivered his letter personally to the constables. The principal charges came from the unpredictable John Mitchel and his brother-in-law, John Martin. In mid-January 1852, after they heard of the escape, Martin wrote to O'Doherty, declaring that both he and Mitchel had concluded that Meagher was not "free in honour to go."[52] But there was no uniform agreement among those still in Tasmania, and O'Doherty and Smith O'Brien believed that Meagher had comported himself admirably. O'Donoghue, in his defense of Meagher, committed what to the State Prisoners was an unpardonable sin. He exposed them all by attacking the British government and its governor of Tasmania, Lord Denison, for allowing criticism of Meagher; O'Donoghue's ticket of leave was withdrawn as a result, and he was ordered to be taken to a probation station and become part of a chain gang.[53]

The concern over the proper manner of revoking paroles was not entirely noble on the part of the Irish exiles, for they feared that heightened restraints might be put on them to prevent their own escapes. It seemed particularly unconscionable to Mitchel, a family man, that Meagher had left his pregnant wife. Had Mitchel felt more respect for young Catherine, he undoubtedly would have had more to say.

The disagreement over Meagher's escape finally escalated until Martin proposed that Meagher should turn himself over to the British authorities; Mitchel and Martin wrote Meagher, asking him to return to Tasmania. This position seemed absurd to Smith O'Brien, who wrote to Martin that Meagher had taken a judicious course and had acted with great discretion, although he would allow that he wished the circumstances had been different. But Smith O'Brien stopped short of condemning Meagher, all the while believing that the matter could be explained to the satisfaction of all except Meagher's most avowed detractors.[54]

In New York Meagher immediately tried to set matters straight and preserve his reputation. In a letter to the *New York Daily Times* on June 5, 1852, he explained the matter. According to P. J. Smyth, Meagher's good friend from Stonyhurst who wrote about the event many years later, "the only anxiety of his personal friends was that he should be clear as regarded the parole, they agreed that if he were not he should immediately return and give himself up to the Authorities." Meagher had agreed to return to Tasmania if his friends were not satisfied and presented the matter to John B. Dillon, Richard O'Gorman, William Mitchel, T. Devin Reilly, and Smyth, who had agreed to accompany him if necessary. The group "unanimously agreed that he had satisfied the parole obligations."

According to Smyth, however, "to put the matter beyond dispute" it was referred to "an independent tribunal of American gentlemen," which included Horace Greeley, the Honorable John McKeon, and Felix Ingoldsby. The status of these men shows Meagher's prominence and the seriousness with which the public took the matter: Greeley was the editor of the *New York Tribune*. McKeon was a former congressman and a U.S. district attorney, and Ingoldsby was a prominent merchant. Smyth recalled: "They went minutely into the whole case, and decided—that having regard to the nature of the parole, the circumstances under which it was imposed, &c. the prisoner was not bound to place himself in the position in which he was before accepting it; that he was bound to give the authorities a fair and reasonable opportunity to capture him dead or alive and that that he had done."[55]

In general, the New York Irish agreed, even going so far as to embrace a popular ballad celebrating Meagher's heroic escape. Ten stanzas long, the ballad recounted Meagher's transport, his imprisonment, and the controversial flight:

> He called for a ticket of leave, that was fair,
> In order you know for to take the fresh air,
> When his time it was up, believe what I state,
> For to keep up his honor he returned back straight.
>
> . . . .
>
> With a good case of pistols, all in his right hand,
> Like a Hector so bold young Meagher did stand,
> Is it me that you want, young Meagher did cry,
> Here now try your best, for your skill I defy.
>
> Young Meagher that moment, he bid him good-bye.
> To his horse he gave spurs, and he opened their eye,
> From Van Diemans [*sic*] Land, he gave them leg bail,
> And he sailed to New York on the back of a whale.[56]

The paradox of the whole ticket of leave question became apparent when John Mitchel himself escaped on June 12, 1853. As early as January

1853 word had reached Mitchel of Meagher's successes in America. With his own escape pending, Mitchel had started to moderate his previously strong views that Meagher had escaped without honor. "He is now in America; and has been generously hailed and welcomed there," Mitchel said. "I have seen some of his speeches and lectures; and one may easily guess that he will keep most of the favour he has won." On January 1, 1853, Mitchel entered in his journal the comment: "A year ago, our comrade Meagher formally withdrew his parole; and then, with the assistance of friends, made his escape."[57]

Patrick O'Donoghue was the next to leave: in December 1852 he simply boarded a boat, leaving Launceston without giving notice to anyone. As the time neared for Mitchel's own escape, one of his proposed strategies was to bribe the constables. His break for freedom was finally made only moments after handing the police magistrate in Bothwell a copy of a note withdrawing his parole that he had "just despatched to the governor." Relying on the confused gentleman's few moments of indecision, Mitchel burst outside, where he mounted a horse and gained his freedom with the help of P. J. Smyth, who had traveled from Dublin to Tasmania to assist him.[58]

The correctness of Mitchel's escape was not impressed upon Duffy, still in Ireland, who accused him of also behaving dishonorably. Finally, in May 1854, William Smith O'Brien, John Martin, and Kevin Izod O'Doherty were pardoned, which none of them had requested.[59] The pardon not only freed them from Tasmania but allowed them to go back to their beloved Ireland. Thus Meagher's impatience had defeated him. Ireland, of course, was the place where the young revolutionary most longed to be.

CHAPTER FOUR

A New Life

A rebel under a Monarchy, I am a Conservative under a democratic Republic.

Thomas Francis Meagher to Smith O'Brien

Meagher disembarked from the *Acorn* into the heart of the Irish diaspora, where he found himself welcomed as a hero. He had watched Irish peasants mournfully boarding ships bound to the United States as a child in Waterford and as a young revolutionary in Dublin. Now they and their descendants were becoming a powerful political force in the United States, particularly in New York, where Irish immigrants made up 20 percent of the city population in 1850. Many of the New York Irish lived in grinding poverty in the city's worst slums, forced to make their way in the face of anti-Irish discrimination, anti-Catholicism, and growing ethnic intolerance. Opposition strengthened their commitment to each other, to the church, and—even as they worked to build new lives in America—to the cause of Irish freedom. At the same time, questions of tactics, philosophy, personality, and petty jealousy divided America's Irish community. In New York Meagher would experience both the warm welcome due a noted patriot and hero and close scrutiny and criticism from rivals.

By the 1850s the sheer number of Irish immigrants had placed their concerns on the agenda of United States politicians; among those concerns was the fate of the heroes of 1848. In early 1852 United States senator James Shields, himself Irish-born, proposed a Senate resolution of sympathy for Meagher, Smith O'Brien, and the other imprisoned Irishmen in Tasmania. Senator William H. Seward of New York represented the sentiments of his Irish constituents by speaking in its favor. The Irish press in America also had kept the prisoners' fate in the public eye, and the editors of the *Boston Pilot* gleefully informed their readers of Meagher's escape when news of it reached the United States.[1] In London the *Times* had also alerted its readers. "It appears that a gentleman in Dublin has received a letter from his brother-in-law, an assistant-surgeon in the British navy . . . which states that Meagher has escaped, and that the Government officials had searched his house in vain. He had fled beyond capture and pursuit."[2]

Meagher arrived in New York a short time later, eager to take his place once again among the voices for Irish freedom. He immediately sought out fellow Irish revolutionary John Blake Dillon, who had escaped to New York right after the failed 1848 insurrection. Dillon took Meagher to Brooklyn—with its high concentration of Irish immigrants. A huge crowd soon assembled and asked him to speak, although Meagher, perhaps with false modesty, pointed out that he did not deserve the attention because he had not fought any battles in Ireland.[3] That argument did not deter his fellow Irish or the United States at large. Almost immediately, invitations for Meagher to speak started pouring in from all over the country.

It soon became obvious to his new country that Meagher had not come to the United States devoid of revolutionary zeal. To the contrary, those long months in Tasmania had given him even more time to contemplate his imprisonment at the hands of the British and the continued fate of his country and his compatriots. Very soon after his arrival, the *United States Democratic Review* published a lengthy article by Meagher in which he leveled an attack on the British and on O'Connellism and called for armed revolution. "We do not blame the England of the aristocracy for its cruelty—we do not complain of cruelty," he proclaimed.

> Cruelty is a thing of which conquered nations, pretending to decency, never complain. With men it is the nurse of vengeance and redemption, and that which made O'Connell's career a curse,

and a blight upon the Irish name, was his eternal whine for mercy and equality, and his eternal begging cry of being a loyal slave, and therefore, deserving of better treatment.... No aristocracy in history, no class of human beings possessed of hereditary property over the lives and land of an unarmed nation, ever gave up that property, those priv[i]leges, that class distinction and pre-eminence, without the hardest fought, and bloodiest contest they were capable of making.[4]

Soon Meagher's life became a series of speeches, receptions, testimonials, and social engagements. When the fall lecture season started, he was featured as a principal orator, along with the likes of Daniel Webster, Horatio Seymour, and William Makepeace Thackeray.[5] Invitations poured in from as far away as Ohio, Indiana, Illinois, Boston, Philadelphia, and the South. His fellow Irish formed Meagher Clubs, and militia companies renamed themselves the Meagher Guards. People danced to the music of the "T. F. Meagher Polka"; New York City offered a civic reception, which Meagher sensibly declined; and Fordham gave him an honorary degree.[6] The *New York Herald* predicted that Meagher would have a successful career in the United States. "The Irish patriot," it reported, "wants no material aid—means no humbug—but intends to settle down, a plain republican, in this land of freedom and equality."[7]

The welcome he received bowled Meagher over; after enduring the desolation of Tasmania, he enjoyed being back in the limelight. Meagher's commitment to Ireland remained strong, but the adulation he found in the United States proved tremendously seductive. Until Ireland finally broke free of British rule, he vowed to stay in the United States and took out his first citizenship papers within three months of his arrival. A side benefit to becoming an American citizen was that, as an Irishman, Meagher was a British subject: he relished disavowing his loyalty to the queen.[8]

At the beginning of 1853, when Meagher had been in the United States for over six months, he found that his reputation had spread, giving him ready access to the politically powerful. Before the inauguration in 1853 president-elect Franklin Pierce summoned Meagher to visit him in Concord, New Hampshire. Invited to the inauguration, Meagher also spent part of a day with Pierce at Washington's fashionable

Willard Hotel. There Senator James Shields, at that time probably the best-known Irishman in America, introduced him to Washington society.[9] Meagher also had put together his major speeches in Ireland and believed that they would make a great book; however, "When I was thinking of bringing out my speeches, three or four of the leading publishers, to whom I applied, declined having anything to do with the business on the ground that . . . they should have to . . . depend upon the Irish population—but this support, they said, was very unsafe." As it turned out, "Not much more than 2,000 copies have been disposed of, and . . . of the purchasers two thirds have been Americans." The title of the book was *Speeches on the Legislative Independence of Ireland.* Meagher had actually taken his manuscript to several established publishers, who all saw it as only of interest to Irish readers. A new publisher, Redfield of Nassau Street, finally agreed to publish the book. But Meagher later confided in a friend that he had made no money from the venture, which he had undertaken looking for a profit.[10]

As Meagher was being feted in the United States, his wife left Tasmania on February 5, 1853, aboard the *Wellington,* bound for Ireland. After a hard ocean voyage that lasted over four months, she arrived in Waterford on June 27, 1853. To her surprise, an immense throng of well-wishers greeted her as she stepped from the ship at the quay. Only a few weeks earlier the *Waterford Mail* had rekindled thoughts of her husband by reprinting a lecture that he had given in New York on the insurrection of 1848. Now Meagher's townspeople had an opportunity to pay tribute to the revolutionary leader by proxy through his wife.[11]

Meagher's father, Thomas Meagher, Sr., and the mayor of Waterford officially welcomed the flustered Catherine. The mayor then addressed her with a prepared speech: "Your husband is of no ordinary character. The son of one of our most esteemed citizens, he grew up amongst us with manly and gracious trait of character." Ever a politician, the mayor focused more on Meagher's personality than on his cause. Meagher, he said, had plunged "into a course of action on which we, of all shades of politics offer no opinion, save this one: we believe that the purest of motives and the most honourable of intentions were the principles which guided him."[12]

That was not the end of her public reception. On July 4, 1853, the town assembly room filled with Waterford citizens to offer an official welcome to the attractive young woman. The mayor presided, and an official resolution of welcome was passed by those in attendance, followed by more speeches, expressions of respect for Meagher, and hearty good wishes for the united prosperity of the Meaghers upon their expected reunion in America.[13]

The young Mrs. Meagher, plainly of more common origins than her husband, soon became an object of inquisitiveness. The *Waterford Chronicle* obligingly informed its readers:

> She is a very beautiful girl of we should say about twenty-two years. Her face is of that splendid Spanish model that has found so many admirers among Poets and Painters; but there is about it a native sweetness and simplicity of expression that springs more from the heart than from the country . . . her large brilliant eyes give clear indication of a mint above the ordinary stamp. Her person is tall and commanding; rounded and elegantly formed.

Finally, the *Chronicle* could not resist a pun: "in fact, she is really a most splendid woman . . . [with] whom we are certain any man (*at least any Irishman*) would cheerfully consent to be transported."[14]

On Saturday, July 9, 1853, Catherine Meagher left Waterford for what she believed would be forever. Safe in the company of her father-in-law, she was on her way to America to be reunited with her husband. The pair first traveled to Dublin, on their way to Liverpool, from which they would depart.[15] Staying at the Imperial Hotel, they were soon inundated with throngs of men and women wishing to pay their respect. For a time Catherine Meagher privately received as many of the visitors as she could, favoring Meagher's personal friends. As the day wore on, the overwhelming number of people who called on her made her realize the true enormity of her husband's fame in Ireland. She could hold up no longer and toward the end of the day had to excuse herself from appearing at another large reception like the one she had received in Waterford. Because she could not attend, a deputation organized for the purpose drafted a formal welcome, which was read to her. Unsure of how to respond, she shyly prevailed upon her father-in-law to draft a written reply, in which he offered her grateful acknowledgment. The *Dublin Nation* politely said that they were "aware of the considerations which governed Mrs. Meagher in thus declining the public honors so universally tendered to her. And cordially we recognise their propriety."[16]

The sailing of the *Arctic* temporarily spared Catherine from more embarrassing public appearances. The trip was probably a pleasant one; the *Arctic* was a 285-foot-long ship with two hundred first-class cabins, and Catherine and Thomas had been joined by Meagher's brother Henry. Henry Meagher held a high position in the Vatican as chamberlain to the Quirinal—a position described as somewhat like the aide-de-camp to a king—as well as holding a commission in Prince Albrodini's regiment of the Papal Guards. The trip to America was short, and the three arrived in New York harbor on Saturday, July 25, 1853.[17]

New York's Archbishop John J. Hughes was among the first to visit the group after they had checked into the Metropolitan Hotel, where Thomas Francis Meagher lived when he was in town. Hughes invited Thomas Meagher, Sr., to ride with him in his carriage to visit a mutual friend at Fort Washington, setting off an exhausting series of invitations to Irish events.[18] Soon the *Irish American* suggested that a "public entertainment" be given for Thomas Meagher, Sr., "because Ireland has no honester, more faithful, or more independent representative in the British House of Commons." Meagher's father did not prove to be anxious to attend gatherings in the hot East Coast summer. Described by Mitchel as a "small and meager" man "of an aspect and manner somewhat dry and cold," Meagher, Sr., was much more retiring than his spirited son.[19] To an invitation to attend his son's own birthday celebration in Boston, he replied: "I regret, however, that my infirm health, not improved by the fatigue of my recent voyage across the Atlantic, and a warmer climate here than I have been accustomed to, oblige me to observe strictly a rule that I have found it prudent to adopt, of avoiding the excitement of public entertainments."[20]

During the first part of Catherine Meagher's stay in the United States she did some traveling with her husband, visiting Niagara Falls, the Catskills, and Lake George.[21] Meagher, however, soon felt compelled to continue his lecturing and attendance at Irish functions without his wife or his father. As Catherine's long-awaited reunion with her husband turned into just a visit, it became apparent to all that the match was ill fated. Meagher no longer saw in Catherine what he had found in the forests of Tasmania at the depths of his depression. In the United States he was surrounded by influential Irish leaders and invited to gatherings attended by U.S. dignitaries, and Catherine simply could not measure up to their expectations. "It is said they do not suit," Lucy Smith O'Brien wrote to her husband, William. "His fault, I am told. I pray it is not true. What will the poor girl do?"[22]

It also became apparent that Catherine Meagher should best be kept out of sight. As the *Irish American* noted: "As regards Mrs. Meagher, we yield to none in respect for that lady; but we think the mode of complimenting her should be in unison with her retiring disposition, and rendered as graceful and appropriate as possible."[23] By October Catherine, in the company of Meagher's father, had left to return to Ireland. She was pregnant, just as she had been the last time she had parted from her husband.[24] Six months later she died in Ireland, far from her husband and even farther from her own family. She had fallen victim to complications attending the birth of a son, Thomas Bennett Meagher.

Meagher grieved at the news of Catherine's death. Despite his failure to provide for her or to invite her to share in his life in the United States for his private reasons, he had thought she was well placed in Waterford under the care of his respected father. He also worried about his infant son, who remained in his father's custody. Although Meagher intended to send for the young Thomas Bennett when he could provide him with a stable home, that day never came. Meagher died without ever seeing his son.[25]

Although the exact date of his birth is not known, Bennett was baptized in Waterford on March 30, 1854. Years later, on May 26, 1872, when Thomas Bennett Meagher accepted an appointment to the United States Military Academy, he certified "on honour" that he was eighteen years and one month of age. To add confusion to the record, the academy records show that Bennett was eighteen years and eight months old when he entered on September 1, 1872; and nineteen years and zero months when he left in January 1873. Perhaps born prematurely, there is little doubt that Thomas Francis Meagher was his father and always acknowledged Bennie as his son.

If Catherine was in any way responsible for the failure of their marriage, it was Meagher who faced public criticism for abandoning his wife. Soon criticism for some of his other actions—including his mode of escape from Tasmania—also gathered strength. Reports of both his fame and the attacks against him reached John Mitchel in Tasmania. Now planning his own escape, Mitchel was in a kinder mood than when he had led the charge questioning the honor of Meagher's escape: "a close friend of Meagher . . . gives us a pleasant account of all the actings and sayings of that ex-prisoner, formerly of the Dog's-head, Lake Sorel [sic], but now of the Metropolitan Hotel, Broadway; how the *gobemouches* worried him; how the . . . priests scowled upon him; how the ladies smiled upon him; all which one can very well imagine."[28]

Mitchel's allusion to scowling priests referred to an issue that would haunt Meagher even more intensely after Mitchel finally made good his own escape to New York: the ongoing tension between the Young Irelanders and the Catholic Church. It had started immediately after the failure of the insurrection of 1848. "There was bitter wrath among the Clubs at the opposition priests had offered to the movement," said Charles Gavin Duffy later. Meagher too had said that the effort would have been a success had the priests actively supported it.[29] That view did not sit well with defenders of the Catholic hierarchy; nor did the view of many Young Irelanders that a free Ireland should embrace the separation of church and state.

Criticism of these views—and accusations of anticlericalism—began to haunt Meagher when his family assembled in New York. The first shots were fired when Meagher was in Boston to celebrate his birthday at the invitation of the Meagher Club of United Irishmen and the Meagher Rifles. Many out-of-state well-wishers attended the grand affair held at Faneuil Hall, but there were also those in Boston who believed that Meagher was not a true Catholic. The *Irish American* reported: "There was no effort left untried, in Boston, to *kill* the Banquet."[30]

The attacks on Meagher heated up in September, when an editorial appeared in the *Shepherd of the Valley,* a strict Catholic organ. Specifically, the *Shepherd* castigated Meagher for his view of the correctness of separation of church and state, which he believed was provided in the United States Constitution. The *Shepherd* went further, however, accusing the Meagher group, with Mr. P. Lynch, editor of the *Irish American,* as their spokesman, of "openly announc[ing] that that clique has definitely rejected the religion of Jesus Christ as a humbug, as an old woman's story, unworthy [of] the serious attention of practical men."[31]

That charge was hogwash, of course. Meagher remained a devoted Catholic his entire life, although he never repudiated his belief that

the priests had done Ireland a disservice by not supporting the revolution. Nor did he repudiate his commitment to an Irish Republic,
free from state religion. In a lecture on February 28, 1854, in the
Musical Hall of San Francisco he asserted that Irish republicanism was
not incompatible with the Catholic religion, but his East Coast rivals
remained unconvinced.[32]

The arrival of fellow exile John Mitchel in New York did not help
Meagher's position within the American Irish Catholic community.
The always-loyal Meagher had fully forgiven Mitchel for accusing him
of escaping Tasmania without honor and was among the first to board
the steamer *Prometheus* when it brought the Protestant Mitchel to
New York harbor in November 1853.[33] By December the two had
agreed to found a new weekly Irish American newspaper, the *Citizen,*
modeled after the *Nation of Dublin,* which Mitchel had once edited.[34]
Meagher left the fledgling paper in Mitchel's hands to travel to California, where he had already scheduled a lecture tour. In Meagher's
absence the erratic Mitchel quickly set about alienating much of the
New York establishment.

Showing little concern for the Catholicism of his friend and associate
Meagher, the outspoken Mitchel almost immediately got himself into
trouble with Archbishop Hughes. Having just arrived in America, he
took it upon himself to dictate political opinion to the Irish who had
been there for years. His worst offense was his attack on the Catholic
Church, claiming that it was part of the "Nativism" that existed in the
United States, usually attributed to Yankee Protestants. He was already
well on his way to alienating many in the North when he declared
that he would be more comfortable with a plantation in Alabama,
"well stocked with healthy negroes." With that parting shot he abandoned the *Citizen* and left for the South.[35]

Mitchel's outrageous pronouncements marginalized him from the
Irish American scene; but Meagher was able to rise above his association with Mitchel and, for the most part, the scurrilous attacks of rival
newspapermen and politicians. He did so by politely but irrevocably
distancing himself from the blunt, ego-driven divisiveness of his old
revolutionary comrade. It was just as important, however, that Meagher
retained a good relationship with Archbishop Hughes, among the most
powerful Irish Catholic figures in America. Perhaps Meagher's brother's
post with the Vatican helped him here, or perhaps it was his own honest

commitment to Catholicism, but Hughes was willing to accept Meagher's assurances that he remained always true and faithful to his church as well as to his country.[36]

Still, it was not an easy time for Meagher. It must have been painful to see Young Ireland—the movement to which he had committed his youth—destroyed by internecine squabbling. The first comrade lost to Meagher was D'Arcy McGee, the first Young Irelander to arrive in America. Escaping Ireland immediately after the insurrection by crossing the Atlantic disguised as a priest, McGee quickly started a newspaper, the *New York Nation,* which alienated Archbishop Hughes when it assailed the priests for their lack of involvement in the movement. Hughes banned McGee's paper from his diocese, and in a short time the *New York Nation* failed.[37] By the time Meagher arrived in New York, McGee was in the process of falling out with Young Ireland and was among those who questioned Meagher's commitment to the church.[38]

In early January 1854 the often depressed Patrick O'Donoghue died, reportedly from diarrhea but more likely from alcoholism. A vital part of Young Ireland, O'Donoghue had been with Meagher in Tasmania and New York. The papers reported: "Through nervous irritability and a mind shattered by suffering, producing jealousy and distrust of all who came within his reach, O'Donoghue had become estranged from those who, under other circumstances, would have been his fast and ardent supporters." Separated from his family for some time, O'Donoghue had been awaiting the arrival of his wife and daughter and his brother, who had sailed from Dublin. When they arrived, the seas in the bay were so rough that the vessel could not be boarded, and O'Donoghue died before his family could disembark. Many friends attended his dismal funeral, but conspicuously absent were Meagher, who was still in California, and Mitchel, for whom no excuse was offered. An insensitive Mitchel, directing a eulogy toward the widow in the *Citizen,* said that O'Donoghue had devotion to the Irish cause but "was not great or gifted."[39]

Mitchel managed to antagonize other Young Irelanders as well. Charles Gavan Duffy, still editing the *Nation* in Ireland, serialized some excerpts from Mitchel's recently published *Jail Journal,* only to have Mitchel assail him for his part in the trials of the Young Irelanders in 1848. According to Mitchel, Duffy had lacked integrity when he refused to acknowledge that he had written articles that were allegedly seditious and had also attempted to defend himself by producing "evidence of character" at his own trial. An upset Duffy responded heatedly, claiming that Mitchel himself had not escaped Tasmania with honor, causing shame to his American supporters. In the *Nation* on April 29, 1854, Duffy called on Meagher to distance himself from Mitchel to avoid charges that he, like Mitchel, was anticlerical. Even though it was Mitchel being attacked this time, Meagher had become so sick of the constant harangue about his own escape that he advised Duffy that he would no longer communicate with him until his derogation of Mitchel had been withdrawn.[40]

As Young Ireland disintegrated before his eyes, Meagher continued to face personal attacks. He finally took it out on James McMaster, editor of the *Freeman's Journal,* who accused Meagher of moral failing in breaking his parole in Tasmania. In his attack McMaster denounced both Mitchel and Meagher as a "vain, blustering set of braggarts that did so much to spoil the work of O'Connell, and to make Ireland a laughing-stock to the world." To McMaster, the two were "the very worst specimens of an excrescence. . . . Spouters without industry to work for their livings, without modesty or prudence to keep themselves out of scrapes with the police, without courage to strike a blow when nabbed in the very midst of their brag, without brain to understand, or else fortitude to abide by the conditions they accepted in the convict colony, and without shame to make them hang their heads in silence, instead of vaporing and blowing."[41]

Upon reading this invective, Meagher went to McMaster's office on July 18 to request a retraction. McMaster refused, and Meagher returned home to ponder the matter for several hours. Finally, his resentment boiled over and he took to the street again, walking near McMaster's residence on Sixth Street near First Avenue. Upon encountering him, Meagher attacked. McMaster received repeated blows from a riding whip before he pulled out a revolver and fired. The ball grazed Meagher's forehead and eyebrow, and he received powder burns. While McMaster was attempting another shot, Meagher wrenched the revolver from his grasp and also took his loaded cane. Wrestling McMaster to the ground, and leaving him there "bleeding and panting," Meagher went in search of the police. When the officers arrived, Meagher requested that both he and McMaster be taken into custody. The two were taken before Justice Wood, where they were bound over and freed on $500 bail each. McMaster's injuries were reported to be serious. Despite Meagher's aggressive behavior, the press was not intimidated. Meagher was still bedeviled by the nagging rumors and innuendos that continued to surround his escape.[42]

A bright light shone amid this turmoil. Eighteen months after Catherine Meagher's death in Ireland, Thomas Francis Meagher met Elizabeth Townsend at a social gathering in New York. She was the daughter of Peter Townsend, a successful New York businessman and a member of the established American family that had once owned the Sterling Iron Works, the firm that had cast a chain to block the Hudson River during the American Revolution. Upon their second meeting he revealed his love to her and received the response that she could deeply love him. Only four days after his initial introduction, Meagher proposed; to his joy, Elizabeth accepted at once. "I know not whether you observed it or not, but the moment I was introduced to you, I was overcome with this consciousness—with this belief," Meagher later wrote to her. "And until I met you again—until, indeed, I revealed to you the secret with which my heart was throbbing, almost breaking, this consciousness—this belief was to me a torture. I could not—dare not—hope for such a wife. I felt, however, it would be a relief for me, even though my love was not returned, to let you know I loved, and deeply loved you."[43]

Even though Elizabeth had accepted his proposal, Meagher felt that he had to enter the marriage with a clean breast: "The story can be easily told. . . . You know I was a 'rebel'—and you know I am an 'exile.' You know I was married and you know there has been left to me a little fellow, who knows not what a mother would have been. Of other events and aspects of my life, you may not be aware. But, familiar with those I have mentioned, you know the worst, and you know the best."[44]

Elizabeth's father, Peter Townsend, did not receive the news of the engagement gladly, and the New York City gossips had a field day. In an article published on November 3, 1855, under the heading "A Fifth-Avenue Romance," the *New-York Daily Times* described the "rather romantic antecedents" of the forthcoming marriage.

About a year since, a distinguished Hibernian formed the acquaintance of a celebrated belle, Miss E   T   d, daughter of a wealthy Fifth-avenue merchant. Four days after the first introduction, the swain proposed and was accepted—by the lady only. The parents, alas! were obdurate. The father declared that his reasons for disapproving of the match were of a serious nature, and based on some unpleasant antecedents in the life of the candidate for his daughter's hand. Stolen interview resulted, and, finding eventually that the young lady was determined to stick to her lover, the cruel father made his will, and disinherited his daughter. It is understood that the parties are to be married in a few days.[45]

The reporter's account of Peter's response was a dramatic fiction, but it was not completely divorced from reality. When Townsend died in 1885, in his eighty-fourth year, it turned out that two years before he had made a will that unevenly divided his considerable estate among his children, giving the widowed Elizabeth Meagher substantially less than an equal portion.[46]

On November 14, 1855, at the residence of his friend and supporter Archbishop John J. Hughes on Madison Avenue, Elizabeth Townsend married Thomas Francis Meagher. Formerly a Protestant, she became a devout Catholic. Meagher had been taken immediately with Elizabeth, and the attraction endured. Almost a year after marrying her, Meagher described his wife to Smith O'Brien, who was still in exile in the British penal colony. "She is so beautiful, so intelligent, so cultivated, so generous, so gentle and unaffected." His first wife, Catherine, had never received such admiration from him; nor had she come from a prominent and rich New York family.[47]

Peter Townsend had many reasons to oppose the marriage of his well-bred daughter to the capricious Meagher, who was a Catholic and had no regular means of support other than his lecturing. But in Meagher's favor were his English education, his eloquence, his culture, and his fame. In the end Townsend relented; because Meagher had no regular employment, the newly married couple moved in with him in one of the new fashionable brownstones at 129 Fifth Avenue, between Nineteenth and Twentieth Streets.

Meagher's marriage to Elizabeth clearly marked a new phase in his life, but he was loath to leave Ireland completely behind. "I long— earnestly and fondly throb—to see Ireland, and especially poor Waterford, for a little while once more," Meagher wrote. "Everyday, I grow fonder and fonder of the old scenes and the old faces which lit them up and beautify them."[48] He also fondly remembered Speranza. A newly married man, he couched this nostalgia in a piece he wrote about Tasmania and the time he spent sailing on his boat *Speranza* on Lake Sorell. At the end of 1856, Meagher published a piece remembering Christmas Eve at Lake Sorell. He wistfully quoted the words of a "friend" about his sailboat and then wrote: "This *Speranza* was the *Lady [of the] Lake,*" in obvious reference to Lady Jane Wilde, the poetess laureate of the *Nation* who had been enamored of him a decade ago in Dublin.[49]

Nevertheless, Meagher continued to look to the future and to contemplate seriously how he would make a living for himself and Elizabeth in the United States. He finally considered three alternatives. The first, of course, was to continue on the lecture circuit. "Were I single, perhaps, I'd hold on to lecturing," he explained in a letter to his friend Smith O'Brien. He also had been trained in the law but realized that he had not yet "enough of law to realize speedily a profitable practice." His third idea was to publish a newspaper. In the end he would split his time among the three endeavors, but initially he accepted the enormous challenge of entering the brutal world of New York publishing as he founded the *Irish News* in the spring of 1856.[50]

The full-sized weekly paper listed Thomas Francis Meagher as editor and sole proprietor.[51] Although publishing never provided him with what he deemed an adequate income, he initially had high hopes for his new weekly, announcing an ambitious editorial policy. He intended to cover the events in any country in the world with a substantial Irish population where he could find a correspondent. Meagher encouraged his Young Ireland friends to contribute articles, and he asked Smith O'Brien "to send me for publication a few of your reminiscences abroad. Those of India, Italy, and Greece, would be delightful."[52] He confidently announced that his readers could expect to see "regular monthly correspondence" from California; Pernambuco and Rio de Janeiro, Brazil; Buenos Aires and Montevideo, Argentina; Lima, Peru; Valparaiso, Chile; Tasmania; and Sydney and Melbourne, Australia. Meagher pointed out that South America, and particularly Buenos Aires and Valparaiso, had generations of Irish, with around six thousand in Buenos Aires alone. He had made contacts there en route during his escape from Tasmania and hoped to enlist the proper correspondents.[53]

The Irish News.

THOMAS FRANCIS MEAGHER, } EDITOR AND PROPRIETOR.

{ THREE DOLLARS PER ANNUM. Single Copies, 6 Cents. Publication Office, 29 Ann St., cor. of Nassau.

VOL. I.   NEW-YORK, SATURDAY, APRIL 19, 1856.   NO. 2.

Publications.

THE IRISH NEWS,

EDITED BY THE PROPRIETOR.

THOMAS FRANCIS MEAGHER,

DEDICATED TO THE SERVICE OF THE

IRISH PEOPLE,

AT HOME AND ABROAD.

Will be published every Saturday, on and after the 19th of April, at 29 Ann street, corner of Nassau, New-York.

Publications.

Annals of the Four Masters,

7 VOLUMES QUARTO, IN IRISH, WITH AN ENGLISH TRANSLA-
TION BY O'DONOVAN. $45.

Publications.

COMPLETION OF THE SIXTH YEAR.

HARPER'S NEW MONTHLY MAGAZINE,

FOR MAY.

A TRIP TO THE SILVER MINES OF CENTRAL AMERICA.

COMMODORE PERRY'S EXPEDITION TO JAPAN.

The *Irish News*. Meagher started his own newspaper in 1856, and its masthead listed him as editor and proprietor. The *Irish News* was a full newspaper published weekly. (Author's collection)

The *Irish News* also carried regular reports from Dublin, where P. J. Smyth was the correspondent; from Meagher's hometown of Waterford; from the Irish Militia units in New York; and from locations across the United States. Prominently mentioned was the schedule of the 69th New York Militia, which Meagher later headed in the Civil War.[54] A militia unit in South Carolina had been named the "Meagher Guard," and its history was proudly featured in the May 3, 1856, edition.[55] Soon Meagher reported that his news departments—Irish, American, and Foreign—were not mere reprints as in most weeklies but rather a "condensed epitome" of the history of the day and that the *Irish News* had twice as many pages as the average weekly and four times as many as most weeklies.[56]

At first Meagher kept politics out of the *Irish News,* sticking to his original vision of making "the paper a pleasant 'home journal' for our people out here." His plan was that the paper would also include "a few features of more personal interest, to render it welcome to the more literary portions of the American public." This was not the typical revolutionary "Meagher of the Sword" speaking, and at least for a few short months he appeared to be a recently enlightened peacemaker. Meagher said as much when he told Smith O'Brien: "I may, however, indicate in a sentence my political tendencies—A rebel under a Monarchy, I am a Conservative under a democratic Republic."[57]

In fact, Meagher was not emotionally equipped to stand on the sidelines and merely observe political controversies. Born to a life of political strife, he could not remain silent for long on the issues of the day, and the *Irish News* drifted rather quickly toward political debate. Soon Meagher was using the "pleasant home journal" to attack anti-Irish journalists in New York and anti-Irish politicians in Britain. He jumped headlong into the most divisive issue of the day: the abolition of slavery. Coming from Ireland, where some argued that the lives of the starving peasants under British rule were worse than those of the slaves in the South, Meagher's view was that abolition was impractical. Slavery, he admitted, "has its dark side; and it would be well, perhaps, if we could get rid of it." Nevertheless, he believed, there was no way to eliminate it "in our time," so efforts should be confined to "alleviating the evils that accompany it."[58]

Even those ills, Meagher felt, were exaggerated by abolitionists. "The general impression of the South, in the minds of Northern people," he wrote in the *News,* "is a sort of mingling up of bowie-knives, revolvers, slave-drivers with broad-brimmed hats and long whips, shrieking negroes, blood and murder, and all that." Meagher had been to the South, however; he had come to "mix with the people" and "could discern none of those social corruptions that are said among us to disfigure Southern society."[59]

Meagher's friend Archbishop John Hughes expressed the view that the church had never interfered with established slavery except by "religious and moral suasion" and that slavery existed by a "Divine permission of God's providence."[60] Meagher weighed in on the 1856 presidential campaign, throwing his support actively behind Democrat James Buchanan, in the belief that he would benefit the Irish in America. Although Buchanan was generally favored to win the Irish vote anyway, Meagher campaigned hard for the Democratic contender. He ran articles to prove that Catholicism was consistent with slavery (Buchanan favored its continuation in the South) and otherwise supported Buchanan's candidacy.

Among other tactics Meagher used the letters of Bishop John England of Charleston, South Carolina, to bolster Buchanan's position against abolition. Starting on October 18, 1856, Meagher began running a series of editorials directed to Irish Catholic voters that were based on letters condoning slavery that Bishop England had written years earlier.[61] After reading England's letters, Meagher claimed, "not a solitary Irish Catholic vote . . . will be found for Fremont, in the ballot-box. . . . The Irish vote—the Irish Catholic vote which the Fremont orators and writers, pamphleteers and bill-stickers, have labored to evoke in favor of Sectionalism and Sedition—will be a unit—swift, sure, and telling—for Buchanan, the Sovereignty and Unity of the States."[62] Meagher's support for the Democrats and his anti-abolition position did not go unnoticed in New York. The *New-York Daily Tribune* attacked his position: suggesting that "perhaps the *[Irish] News* had adopted the regular Democratic slave breeding doctrine, that it is no more harm for an aristocrat to kill an Irish waiter than it is to kill a [black man]."[63]

When Buchanan handily won the White House in November 1856, Meagher publicly lauded the results while privately hoping for a reward for his support. As he wrote to his friend Smith O'Brien, "My disinclination to 'place-hunting' no longer exists. That is, I have no objection to taking a place under the American government—nor any in looking for one for any friend of mine or yours. The same feelings which induced me to regard such gifts with contempt and enmity in Ireland, operate in the contrary direction here. I would rejoice . . . in serving the American Republic."[64]

True to his word, Meagher actively sought a position in the new government, claiming, perhaps speciously, that the *Irish News* was "[t]he *first* journal in America . . . devoted to the interests of Irish citizens, which espoused the cause, foretold and openly hailed the nomination of Mr. Buchanan."[65] Writing President Buchanan that he was "in rather sad want of a position, with some emolument attached to it," Meagher expressed particular interest in a consulship in Latin America. "As long as I am compelled to remain here," he told the president, "my time and brain is the property of the public, rather than my own." When Meagher did not hear back from Buchanan, he fired off a second letter, saying that he would prefer a post in Nicaragua. Again he received no answer, so he made a formal application to Secretary Lewis Cass for a post in Venezuela, as a first choice, with Ecuador or Argentina being satisfactory.[66]

In his request Meagher downplayed his revolutionary past, which he thought could undermine his chance at a diplomatic post; but he played up his fame, writing the president once again to remind him that there was a movement on in Ireland "in which the most capable and powerful men of all parties actively participate. . . . The object is to restore me to the land of my birth." He also emphasized their common ethnicity: he was of the same race as Buchanan's father, he explained (though in fact Buchanan was Scotch-Irish), which should count for something. The appointment never came, and a dejected Meagher felt betrayed. He had worked hard for Buchanan's election and expected at least the courtesy of a reply.[67]

Although on its face Meagher's interest in a Latin American diplomatic post appeared merely self-serving—a result of his recent marriage and his need for "a position, with some emolument attached"—in fact he had long been interested in Central America, and particularly Nicaragua. The 1849 California gold strikes had emphasized the need for travel somewhere across the isthmus of Central America. The United States had obtained a treaty in 1849 with the Nicaraguans for an exclusive transit route and soon granted Commodore Cornelius Vanderbilt's Accessory Transit Company rights to build a canal across the isthmus within the next twelve years. Violence erupted in 1850, however, when the British tried to block Vanderbilt's plans. As a result of negotiations, Britain controlled the Caribbean port of San Juan del Norte, while the United States owned the vessels, hotels, restaurants, and land transportation along the entire transit route.[68]

The issue of control in Nicaragua did not rest there. As the 1850s proceeded, Meagher and his Irish friends could see that the British were still contending for control in the area. The Nicaraguans were unhappy. In 1855 a faction of them offered the American filibuster William Walker funds and generous land grants if he would bring a force of U.S. mercenaries to their aid. The Tennessee-born adventurer, who had already failed in an attempt to take control of Sonora in Mexico, was glad to have another opportunity and leaped at the chance. With fifty-eight U.S. followers, joined quickly by reinforcements, he landed in Nicaragua on May 4, 1855, and seized Granada. The stunned government surrendered, and the United States quickly recognized a new puppet liberal government, with Patricio Rivas as president and Walker in command of the Nicaraguan army.[69]

Not long afterward Walker seized the presidency for himself. Among his first official acts were the declaration of English as the official language and the legalization of slavery. He called for the United States to annex Nicaragua as a slave state and received some support from Southern sympathizers. Walker soon found himself under attack, however—the deposed President Rivas had appealed to Guatemala, Honduras, El Salvador, and Costa Rica. In October 1856 Walker was driven into the countryside.[70]

Meagher was tremendously taken with Walker, whose bravery and daring had captured his fancy, and saw in him the best chance for defeating British interests in Central America. Meagher explained the situation in a May 10, 1856, *Irish News* editorial:

> The question seems to us to have simply come to this—who will have the supreme right of way between the Atlantic and Pacific? . . . Will the United States give way, leaving England to put up a toll-gate . . . and plant her Red Cross there . . . in token of her ownership of the road? Will America consent to pay the toll, struck by the Parliament whose Stamp-Act she cut

to pieces and flung in the foolish face of old King George, and without a murmur, and with perfect good grace and ease of heart, consent to pass from one part of her domain to another, through a double file of sneering Red coats?[71]

Walker soon lost any control he had over Nicaragua. Under a truce arranged by Commander Charles H. Davis of the United States Navy, Walker returned to the United States, where he was taken into custody for violating the Neutrality Act. Walker retained Malcolm Campbell, Meagher's legal partner, as his counsel, but the case never came to trial; charges were dropped when representative Alexander Stephens pointed out that "the only legitimate sovereign of that country was William Walker."[72] After repeated attempts to resume control of the country, Walker was captured by a British warship in 1860 as he tried to enter Honduras, and he was turned over to the Hondurans. On September 12, 1860, he was executed by a firing squad.[73] Only three weeks earlier, on August 21, Meagher (with his profession listed as "Agent") had arrived in New York harbor aboard the *Ariel,* which had departed from Aspinwall, Panama.[74]

Meagher's travels to Central America had started two and a half years before William Walker's death. In March 1858, almost a year after Walker had been deposed in Nicaragua, Meagher turned the *Irish News* over to his associate editor, James Roche. "I visit Central America— Costa Rica especially—for the purpose of ascertaining the true condition of things there, and becoming familiar with a noble region, for which there inevitably approaches an eventful future," he told Roche.[75] The "eventful future" Meagher spoke of could have included the possibility of Irish immigration, a revolution styled after the filibustering William Walker, or both.[76] Meagher repeatedly denied all such rumors and insisted that he was merely going "to collect material for lectures and writings upon the country." His traveling companion, however, was his Stonyhurst schoolmate Don Ramon Páez, the eldest son of South American revolutionary General José Antonio Páez, "an accomplished linguist, a botanist, a geologist, and a splendid draughtsman," who would take "the scientific and artistic portion of the work" they were to do. Meagher would take the rest.[77] He clearly had more in mind than just a literary foray.

Meagher had still not had contact with his young son in Ireland, prevented by his exile from going there. But Elizabeth could go to Ireland and took this opportunity to visit there, returning to New York on June 23 aboard the *Persia,* which had sailed out of Liverpool.[78]

Meagher obviously intended to assess Central America as a place for Irish immigration, with the idea of ameliorating the condition of his compatriots in New York. The impoverished condition of the New York Irish was widely recognized. Archbishop John Hughes called New York's Irish slum-dwellers "the poorest and most wretched population that can be found in the world—the scattered debris of the Irish nation."[79] In an early *Irish News* column Meagher commented on their situation:

> The crowding of emigrants into such cities as New-York and their being compelled to remain there huddled together and pent up, is a mischief concerning which volumes might be written. . . . The tenement which the emigrant, in the vast majority of cases, is forced to resort to . . . is by a thousand degrees less wholesome and affords less shelter than the rudest hut which could be thrown up on the prairie or within the forest. . . . Of the temptations which lead to drinking, debauchery, and riotousness in great cities, among the struggling and hard-pressed especially, it is needless for us to speak.[80]

Soon Meagher joined many other Irish professionals in looking for ways to improve Irish life in America. He thought part of the solution lay in leaving the city. In the *Irish News* he touted the work of the Irish Aid Society of New York, which helped "deserving Irishmen who have large families, and require aid to reach a home in the West."[81] Immigration to Costa Rica was another option, he believed; with funds provided by Judge Charles P. Daly, an American of Irish descent, and his wife, Maria Lydig Daly, he went to investigate in 1858.[82]

For several years the government of Costa Rica had offered land grants as an inducement for European immigrants. Shortly after Meagher arrived, the Costa Rican government passed a new colonization law encouraging immigration.[83] Nevertheless, Meagher wrote his patron Maria Daly in New York, reporting that the unstable government made immigration inadvisable.[84] Regardless, he remained enamored with Costa Rica. He wrote three articles for *Harper's Monthly Magazine,* lauding the country's landscape and economic prospects and returned there on several occasions.

On one trip, having already made plans to go independently, he gratuitously volunteered to carry dispatches from the government to the American consul there. He created somewhat of a furor by billing the government for the trip. In January 1860 he and Elizabeth went again, staying an entire year, for part of the time as the guest of Costa Rican president José María Montealegre. On that occasion Meagher's unofficial diplomatic experience had garnered him a position as a representative for businessman Ambrose W. Thompson, who wanted land and other concessions to build a railroad across the isthmus. Although Meagher successfully negotiated with the Costa Rican government, the U.S. Senate refused to approve the agreement, and the million-dollar deal fell through.[85] On January 25, 1861, Thomas and Elizabeth Meagher returned to New York aboard the *Ariel,* which had departed from Aspinwall, Panama.[86]

Even as he had explored Central America and worked to establish the *Irish News* in the competitive world of New York publishing, the energetic Meagher also looked into building a law practice. Though his legal experience was limited, his fame was an asset. Soon after the initial editions of the *Irish News* started to hit the streets of New York in 1856, an announcement appeared in the paper that Meagher had opened a law practice with Malcolm Campbell under the name "Meagher and Campbell." It was largely Campbell's practice, with Meagher lending his well-known name and putting in limited time. "Mr. Meagher may be consulted daily, on law business *only,* at No. 82 Broadway, from three till five o'clock P.M.," the ad read.[87] But as things developed Meagher sometimes became active in representing clients—and he fared well. As a lawyer in early 1857, for example, Meagher had an opportunity to join William Walker's cause—defending Walker's director general of emigration to Nicaragua, Joseph W. Fabens.

Fabens had been arrested in New York on January 20 along with A. C. Lawrence and several associates for violating the Neutrality Act of 1818.[88] In pretrial arguments Meagher proved himself an able advocate and more than a match for the prosecuting district attorney, John

McKeon. Meagher and McKeon were both Irish, and the contest quickly became personal. In one instance Meagher derided his opponent: "Should I stray from the main circumstances of the case, the District Attorney, with the sympathy which exists between mutual offenders, will forgive me." In his final argument, he leaped on McKeon's ignorance of Irish history. McKeon, Meagher reported, had asked him "if it would gratify me to see General Walker landing in Ireland? He had my answer on the spot . . . He has forgotten there was such an Irishman as Theobold Wolfe Tone, [who invited] a French squadron . . . of 'strangers'—'foreigners' to the very root of their tongues" to Ireland to drive out the English. "What brought them there? The invitation of the Democratic revolutionists of Ireland. What brought William Walker into Relajo bay? The invitation of the Democratic revolutionists of Nicaragua."[89]

Although the commissioner who heard the pretrial arguments decided to send the case to the grand jury, the case never seems to have surfaced again after Meagher's argument. During the proceeding he had smartly raised the possibility that President Franklin Pierce himself was implicated in land dealings in the area; Fabens, who had at one time been a United States counsel in Nicaragua, had threatened to reveal information about well-known persons' involvement in a land scheme there.[90] While there was no final decision, the results of the case indicate that Meagher represented his client well.

Meagher also participated as a lawyer—albeit in a most unusual way—in the celebrity trial of his day: the defense of congressman Daniel Sickles for the murder of Philip Barton Key, the U.S. attorney for Washington, D.C. Meagher was saddened when he heard of the event, because he had known Key, the grandson of Francis Scott Key (author of the "Star-Spangled Banner"), since 1852. Meagher also knew Sickles and had seen him often, as they both patronized the lobby restaurant of the Astor House in New York across from City Hall. On one occasion as a lawyer Meagher had been able to refer a potentially lucrative case to Sickles.[91] But in 1859 Sickles discovered that his twenty-three-year-old wife, Teresa Bagioli Sickles, and Key had been having an affair. As described by Teresa in a written confession of her infidelity, "I have been in a house in Fifteenth street, with Mr. Key. . . . There was a bed in the second story. I did what is usual for a wicked woman to do."[92]

The infidelity and the murder created a sensation, and well-known lawyers throughout the country rushed to defend Sickles. He had engaged prominent New York attorneys James T. Brady and John Graham and an equally prominent and politically connected Washington attorney, Edwin Stanton. Before the trial Sickles also engaged Thomas Francis Meagher, as much for his name and oratory as for his legal skills, which were limited as a trial lawyer. Sickles and his other lawyers knew that Meagher had tremendous standing with the Irish community, and the surnames of the twelve jurors—Arnold, Davis, Neale, Hopkins, Bond, Kelly, Harper, Knight, Wilson, McDermott, Moore, and Wight—indicated that the Irish were represented on the jury. All of the members of the Sickles defense team stood to gain from the publicity of the famous trial, and Meagher, like the other defense lawyers, served "without fee or reward."[93] Meagher's principal responsibility at the trial was to sit at the defense counsels' table; as *Harper's Magazine* said, he was only to be content "with suggestions to his seniors." Many thought this was fitting, including George Templeton Strong, a New Yorker who kept a diary throughout the trial and described Meagher as an "expatriated wind-bag."[94]

Even though Meagher did not take an active part in the trial, he could understand the devastation that Sickles suffered. He also knew, as a master orator, how to magnify sentiment so that it touched his listeners' hearts. Thus Meagher waited for a moment at the trial when the courtroom would be filled with the most passion. It occurred on the trial's eighth day when Sickles, overcome with emotion, broke into sobs in the courtroom. Soon many in the courtroom were also in tears, and Sickles was led out to compose himself. Meagher knew the pivotal moment in the trial had occurred and started to write furiously. He saw it as imperative that the scene of the manly Sickles crying openly in court should be brought to the jury's attention again.[95]

On the nineteenth day of the trial, as James T. Brady was making his final statement to the jury, he pulled Meagher's account of Sickles's breakdown from the papers lying on the counsel table and introduced its well-known author to the jury. "My friend and brother, Meagher, . . . who gave a dignity to the criminal dock in his native land, . . . instituted a legal inquiry, and made a suggestion which . . . I shall quote as quite germane to the matter in discussion." Brady then read verbatim from Meagher's manuscript:

You beheld the scene of the 12th of April. . . . Recall this scene. Think of this—think of the tears you shed yourselves as this stricken victim was borne by—think, think of this—and then may we well say to the jury, if your love of home will suffer it—if your genuine sense of justice will consent to it—if your pride of manhood will stoop to it—if your instinctive perception of right and wrong will sanction it, stamp "murder" upon the bursting forehead that has been transpierced with the thorns of an affliction which transcends all other visitations, and for the scandal, the dishonor, the profanation, and, in the end, the devastation which provoked this terrible outburst, this tempest of grief, this agony of despair.[96]

On April 26 the jury returned a verdict, acquitting Sickles on the grounds of temporary insanity, which was one of the earliest uses of that plea in the United States. The event created great jubilation for his trial team. Stanton actually did a jig in the courtroom, and Meagher exclaimed again and again that the victory was "glorious." It was glorious indeed for Sickles, who escaped penalty and went on to become a major general in the Union Army during the Civil War. After Sickles was wounded at Gettysburg and had his leg amputated, Meagher, who himself had become a general but was not in the army at that time, would travel from New York along with James Brady to sit at the bedside of Sickles.[97]

Despite his successes in America, Meagher still missed Ireland but doubted he would ever see a successful revolution or be allowed to return. "Ireland, I believe," he wrote his comrade Smith O'Brien in 1857, "has thoroughly settled down into a loyal province, and has the strongest repugnance to be disturbed."[98] Not long afterward, however, Ireland seemed as if it was once again beginning to wake up when James Stephens founded a new revolutionary group, the Irish Republican Brotherhood. In 1858 Stephens brought his fiery message of continued struggle to New York. Meagher's love of Ireland had not lessened, but he had more at stake than he did as a young man. While he still longed for a free Ireland, he knew that another failed effort would not further the Irish cause. Ultimately Meagher joined the movement, but not as a leader and not until it was well established and looked like it might have some possibility of success.

Stephens came to the United States in 1858 in part to solicit Meagher's support and met with Meagher within days of his arrival. Accompanying Stephens to this meeting was John O'Mahony. Both O'Mahony and Stephens had played a small role in the 1848 uprising, and both had fled to France after the insurrection failed. On the streets of Paris, amid the revolutionary attitude that prevailed there, the two became well versed in the art of revolution. They claimed to have fought on the Republican side when Louis Napoleon staged a coup d'état in 1851.[99]

O'Mahony had been in New York since 1853 and had written as a Gaelic scholar for Meagher's *Irish News,* but his primary mission in the United States was to build a revolutionary organization in the heart of the exile community. In 1855, along with Michael Doheny, another expatriate Young Irelander, O'Mahony started the Emmet Monument Association. Its goal was to erect a monument honoring Robert Emmet, who had given an immortal speech from the dock after the Irish rebellion of 1803. The group's bland name barely concealed its real purpose, for many of the Irish knew that before he died Emmet had dramatically proclaimed, "Let no man write my epitaph. . . . When my country takes her place among the nations of the earth, *then,* and *not till then,* let my epitaph be written."[100]

In the meantime there was no effective organization in Ireland to foment revolution until 1856, when Stephens returned as an organizer. Stephens was disappointed by what he found: "The ardour of Young Ireland had evaporated as if it had never existed." Even William Smith O'Brien, who had just returned to Ireland from exile after a pardon from the British, told the rough-toned Stephens: "You see, Mr. Stephens, the respectable people of the towns especially are quite indifferent to . . . nationality."[101] But Stephens had started to think big, and he and O'Mahony soon hatched a plot that would require considerable money being sent from the United States along with at least five hundred men, "preferably armed with Lee Enfield rifles." The main recruitment would be in Ireland, where at least ten thousand men were to be enrolled with no less than fifteen hundred having firearms. Finally, a messenger from the United States showed up in Ireland with a mere eighty pounds and an explanation that there was no real revolutionary organization in New York, only a group of sympathizers. Stephens then knew he had to start building a revolution in Ireland from the ground up; only a few days later, on St. Patrick's Day, he founded the Irish Republican Brotherhood in Dublin.[102]

While in France, Stephens and O'Mahony had followed the successes of the Italian revolutionary Giuseppe Mazzini, who had modified the ancient Sicilian Carbonari organization when he formed Young Italy. Following Mazzini's tested organizational scheme, Stephens organized the Irish Republican Brotherhood into "circles" with himself as the "head centre." Under Stephens were the "centres" of the circles, to which a limited number of captains reported. In turn, a limited number of sergeants reported to the captains, and each sergeant controlled a limited number of privates. Secrecy was paramount: each man was sworn in only by his immediate superior and theoretically knew only his superior and the other members on his level.[103]

With his organization barely in place, Stephens set sail for New York in the belief that Irish Americans would be a source of both funds and troops. He also needed an American leader for his organization and intended to recruit one while he was there. By the time he reached New York, he had thought it over and had two candidates in mind. One was the erratic and cynical John Mitchel, who had been brilliant in his denunciation of the British but was not a great speaker or a great leader. Stephens jotted down his real opinion of Mitchel in his diary: "Anybody who has met him and knows his position here might well ask him *how* he is less a slave *now,* than he was in Ireland. His answer would be indignantly caustic and every one of his *followers* would cheer him to the echo."[104]

The more desirable candidate, because of his great oratory and his large following, was Meagher, although in Stephen's caustic opinion he rated only slightly better: "As to the 'man of the Sword' he has performed such patriotic feats within the last lustrum as most assuredly make the angels weep. Still I must do Meagher the justice to say that I believe his heart infinitely more with everything generous, and even noble, than Mitchel's is, and but for his proverbial *weakness,* he would, as in his best moments, do good service to Ireland."[105] The weakness to which Stephens referred was Meagher's ever increasing tendency toward overindulgence in alcohol.

Stephens had another, equally important purpose in pursuing Meagher and Mitchel: to obtain money. A large sum, said to be many thousands of dollars, had been collected in New York in 1848 to support the Young Ireland–led rebellion. While a portion of the funds had been used for the legal defense of the State Prisoners and a portion used later to aid in the various escapes from Tasmania, a substantial amount remained under the control of a Directory that prominently included Meagher and Mitchel as members.[106]

After a rough sea voyage in steerage, a bedraggled and nearly penniless Stephens stepped off the boat in New York harbor. He first met with Michael Doheny, one of the older members of Young Ireland. Doheny deplored Stephen's attempts to draw Meagher and Mitchel more tightly into the fold; he accused Stephens of "running after them" and over-estimating their importance in Irish American affairs. Stephens ignored the criticism, observing that "Doheny is jealous of every man who would dispute the position he fancies he holds or may hold, as chief of the Irish people." When Stephens visited his old friend from Paris, John O'Mahony, he heard a more positive assessment of both Meagher and Mitchel. O'Mahony advised Stephens that he had to win them both over in order to secure funding from the Directory.[107]

For his part, Meagher had already heard from O'Mahony about Stephens's growing influence in Ireland and was looking forward to talking with him. Their meeting, however, held in Meagher's study at his father-in-law's residence on Fifth Avenue, did not begin well. Meagher immediately committed a *faux pas* when he did not recognize Stephens. The bedraggled, poorly dressed stranger who accompanied O'Mahony was not recognizable as the man Meagher had met briefly ten years earlier. Stephens did not like what he saw either and was appalled by the grandeur of the house. In his diary he decried it as a "servile imitation of European dwellings" of the upper class, tasteless in design and decoration, which even Dublin could improve upon. Stephens also had choice words about Meagher: "The intellectual and moral portion of the head is small, and his measured way of speaking would scarcely reconcile one to the genius of Shakespeare."[108]

Despite the inauspicious beginning, Meagher was characteristically cordial and, according to Stephens, "seemed greatly struck; pronounced me the Tone of our generation; expressed not only sympathy but a desire to forward my views far as he could." Meagher's fawning comment, of course, compared Stephens to Theobold Wolfe Tone, the leader of an armed rebellion against the English in 1798 and an Irish martyr. Meagher also agreed to present Stephens to the Directory, yet he had seen enough of Stephens to know that he was not the type of person he wished to follow into revolution. That aversion was not lost on Stephens, who said that Meagher's offer, "though pleasant, had one drawback; he said nothing about *going heartily to work with us.*"[109]

John Mitchel, in his typical style, had sent Stephens a somewhat obtuse and insulting telegram asking him to come to the South to talk about "business." As Stephens had no money at all, his comrade Doheny financed the trip. Meagher, on his way to the capital with former Young Irelander D'Arcy McGee, invited Stephens to join them as far as Washington.[110] The trip was uncomfortable for Stephens. McGee, who had moved permanently to Canada and was just visiting the United States, no longer sympathized with the revolutionary movement. Almost as disturbing to Stephens was Meagher's heavy consumption of food and drink. An offended Stephens noted in his diary that Meagher drank excessively on the trip and bragged that he had paid only three dollars for his bottle of brandy. Stephens concluded that Meagher was a "*gourmand* and nothing more."[111]

When the ill-matched group arrived in Washington, Stephens found that his fare to Knoxville, Tennessee, would take sixty-three of the sixty-five dollars he had been provided. McGee finally found twenty dollars in his pocket and gave it to him, but Stephens had already missed the train that day. Meagher and McGee took Stephens to a reception, where Meagher introduced him to President Buchanan. Stephens could have lauded Meagher for giving him the opportunity to meet the American president, but instead his only comment was that Buchanan had the expression of a "philandering tom-cat." Stephens was finally ready to depart, and the always-gentlemanly Meagher expressed his gratitude to him for coming to America: "Stephens, you have done me a great deal of good. Before meeting you, I felt as *if half my soul were wandering I know not where; and you have given it back to me!*" The cynical Stephens could not stand his dramatics and later wondered in his diary whether Meagher's soul might not turn up on the shores of the Dead Sea![112]

Whatever misgivings Meagher had about Stephens as a leader, he initially offered his backing and gave Stephens a document saying that he supported his quest to obtain money from the Directory. Meagher also gave him a letter to present to Mitchel: "This will be handed to you by our gallant friend, Stephens—one of the truest of the true—and, I verily believe, the Wolfe Tone of our generation. And now, wishing every mother's son of us, a happy new year." After meeting with Stephens in Knoxville, Mitchel agreed to write five letters to other members of the Directory to free up the money that Stephens sought. Mitchel never disclosed to Stephens the content of the letters, however, and they did not produce the result that Stephens wanted.[113]

Meagher soon had second thoughts about supporting Stephens, probably brought on by news from his substantial connections in Ireland that the revolutionary efforts of the egocentric Stephens had not enrolled the number of insurgents in Ireland that he had claimed. On January 26, 1859, in the offices of the *Irish News,* Meagher handed Stephens a letter that he had written: "I have come to the conclusion, after some days of conscientious reflection, that, if it be not criminal, it is unworthy of me, in any way, however trivial or indirectly, to urge or authorize a revolutionary movement, in the hazards of which, from a conviction of their utter uselessness, I feel at present no disposition whatever to participate." Meagher's letter then requested Stephens to "erase my name from the paper you did me the honour to submit to me for my signature a few weeks ago."[114]

Stephens recorded no response to Meagher's letter in his diary. Nor would the letter have come as a complete surprise to Stephens and his comrades, Doheny and O'Mahony, who always had some doubt among themselves that Meagher and Mitchel would give the support to the revolutionary movement that they so badly desired. Stephens gave up on obtaining money from the Directory and considered Meagher and Mitchel men of the past. That assessment might not have been completely fair—what was true was that Stephens regarded Meagher and Mitchel as aristocrats, while they regarded him as a "leveler."[115]

Having been rebuffed by Meagher, Mitchel, and the Directory, Stephens and John O'Mahony set out to organize by themselves the American branch of the Irish Republican Brotherhood. Stephens officially named O'Mahony as "supreme organizer and Director of the Irish Revolutionary Brotherhood in America." Communications from Ireland were to go directly to O'Mahony as "chief centre," and anyone violating the order would be considered a traitor. According to O'Mahony's own account, the original organization was formed from a small remnant of the Emmet Monument Association.[116]

Sometime before April 1859 O'Mahony renamed the American Branch of the Irish Republican Brotherhood the Fenian Brotherhood, a name based on his research in translating Geoffrey Keating's *History of Ireland*. The name stood for "Feonin Erin" or Irish Militia, an ancient group that had been organized before Christianity came to Ireland.[117] In time it became common to refer to both the Irish and the American organizations as the Fenian Brotherhood and to their members as Fenians.

Even without Meagher's and Mitchel's active support, the organization grew in strength and eventually earned Meagher's respect under John O'Mahony's leadership. Meagher was inducted into the Fenian Brotherhood by O'Mahony but did not take the "Pledge of Initiation" until the fall of 1864.[118] Before then Meagher would play a small role in helping stage one of the events that provided the Fenian Brotherhood its best recruiting opportunity: the funeral of Young Irelander Terence Bellew MacManus, who died in 1861.

After being the first to escape Tasmania, MacManus had found his way to San Francisco. His name became legend there, even though he lived out his life in relative obscurity. Although MacManus was buried the day after his death, it soon dawned on the California Fenians that his passing provided a golden opportunity to create a revolutionary martyr. His body was removed from the ground, and a mass funeral was held in San Francisco, where over twenty thousand mourners lined the streets. MacManus's remains were then transported to New York, where Meagher asked Archbishop Hughes to conduct a requiem mass. With thousands lining the streets, the event turned out to be an inspiration for the American Irish to join the Fenian Brotherhood.[119]

MacManus's body was then returned to his beloved Ireland for Catholic services and burial. Although there was no evidence that he had ever been a Fenian, Archbishop Paul Cullen of Dublin refused to permit services for him at the Catholic Cathedral because of the church's policy, which prohibited secret societies and also forbade any Catholic priest from saying a funeral mass for their members. Finally, a funeral was arranged at the Mechanics Institute in Dublin, where tens of thousands paid tribute to MacManus and lined the path to the cemetery. Father

Lavelle, in defiance of Cullen, recited a Catholic burial ceremony over the grave.[120] The whole MacManus affair enlivened the Irish throughout the world, among them Thomas Francis Meagher, who lectured in Boston, Roxbury, and Philadelphia in March 1861 on "The Life and Times of Terence Bellew MacManus," repeating the address in New York, at Irving Hall, on April 3.[121]

The funeral of MacManus and the rejuvenation of Irish nationalism came on the eve of the Civil War, a confluence that profoundly influenced Meagher's future. The Fenians viewed the Civil War as an opportunity to train and make an Irish expeditionary force out of their militia units. Thus it was that Thomas Meagher, formerly a Southern sympathizer, joined the 69th New York Militia shortly after the South fired on Fort Sumter. His service as commander of the Irish Brigade would become the stuff of legend.

CHAPTER FIVE

For the Union and for Ireland

YOUNG IRISHMEN TO ARMS!

TO ARMS YOUNG IRISHMEN!

IRISH ZOUAVES

One hundred young Irishmen—healthy, intelligent and active—wanted
at once to form a Company under command of

THOMAS FRANCIS MEAGHER

Advertisement in *New-York Daily Tribune*

The spring of 1861 found Thomas Francis Meagher pondering his
position on the pending war against the Southern states. Before the
Confederate Army fired on Fort Sumter, Meagher openly favored the
South.[1] His lecture tours had taken him deep into the region. He was
impressed by the people he met there, calling them "sober, intelligent,
high-minded, patriotic, and kind-hearted." Upper-class himself, he had
much in common with the Southern aristocrats, perhaps even more
than with the working-class Irish who dominated New York. Even at the
height of his involvement with Young Ireland, Meagher had embraced
the idea of a continued aristocracy, and the attraction endured.[2] In his
typical boldly definite manner, he left no doubt about his belief that the
evils of the North, as he saw them, were not present in the South. "There
are no cadaverous, sapless, man-forsaken females, turning politics into a

burlesque, philosophy into farce, and religion into reproach. There are no long-haired fanatics preaching a millennium of free love. There are no Hiss Committees, no convent-burners, no addlepated ranters, no Know-Nothings." As for slavery, he simply set it aside.[3]

Meagher had even argued for Southern rights one day with his father-in-law, a staunch Unionist. The debate became heated when Peter Townsend characterized the Southern secessionists as rebels. "You cannot call eight millions of white freemen '*rebels*,' sir," countered Meagher; "you may call them '*revolutionists*' if you will." Later that day, at Delmonico's, an outspoken Union protagonist stopped mid-harangue when he recognized Meagher, acknowledging that he might have spoken too heatedly in Meagher's presence. "I tell you candidly and plainly that, in this controversy, my sympathies are entirely with the South," Meagher responded; but he was not as sure as he sounded. Within months, he would find himself heading off to defend the Union.[4]

Behind Meagher's change of heart was—as always—a complex blend of self-interest and love of Ireland. He had supported James Buchanan in his successful run for the presidency, only to be ignored by Buchanan when he had asked for a position in the government. He no longer felt compelled to support the Southern Democrats, particularly since the Catholic Church in the North had joined the cause of maintaining the Union.[5] More important, however, was the Union's growing Fenian support. Trained, battle-hardened Irish regiments would make a formidable expeditionary force to free Ireland, according to Fenians, and many Irish leaders saw that alone as reason enough to fight for the Union.

Michael Corcoran, a colonel in the "Irish Rifles," the militia company that became the 69th New York Regiment, was among those who advanced that proposition. Four years Meagher's junior, Corcoran came to the United States in 1849. In Ireland he had worked for the Crown as a revenue policeman, arresting outlaw distillers during the day while fighting against the English landlords with the rebel Ribbonmen at night. His double life soon came under suspicion, and he left Ireland for New York. There he joined the Irish Rifles in 1851. In the next few years Corcoran's hard work and devotion to Irish freedom earned him a series of promotions in the Irish Rifles. At the same time he was also advancing as a local precinct politician within the hierarchy of Tammany Hall, resulting in his election as a school inspector and then an appointment to a well-paying job in the post office. On a less public front, he had become the military commander of the Fenian Brotherhood in 1859 and was the Brotherhood's acting "head centre" in April 1861.[6]

Corcoran and other Fenians spoke frequently among themselves about the opportunity that the Civil War presented. Though fearful that the American war might result in needless deaths and deplete the Fenian ranks, Corcoran also saw the Civil War as a training ground. Before he left New York with the mobilized 69th, Corcoran addressed a circular letter to all Fenian centers: "I am leaving in great spirits and hope. My last wish and most ardent desire is that the organization should be preserved in its strength and efficiency, and that every man will do his whole duty. We will not be the worse for a little practice, which we engage in with the more heart because we feel it will be serviceable in other fields."[7]

Meagher soon came to share this belief. He still favored the South, but he almost switched his allegiance on St. Patrick's Day after he observed the strength and vigor of the 1st Regiment of the Phoenix Brigade under a green flag that had been presented to them by a group of New York Irish ladies. The glorious vision of an all-Irish regiment—a common organizing tactic in the nineteenth-century militia—certainly played to Meagher's martial spirit. In fact, his friend Michael Cavanagh believed that the sight of the proud Irish regiment renewed Meagher's faith in the possibility of a free Ireland and that it was at this moment that Meagher decided to back the Fenian movement fully.[8]

Then the Confederacy fired on Fort Sumter on April 12, 1861, and that act pushed Meagher completely into the Union camp. He was not alone. On April 20 the *Irish American* published its backing for the North. "Irish-Americans, we call on you . . . to be true to the land of your adoption in this crisis."[9] Two days later Meagher met Robert Nugent, a leading Fenian and a lieutenant colonel of the 69th New York State Militia. Nugent's regiment was to depart for action the next day, and Meagher told him how upset the attack on Fort Sumter had made him: "*Damn them! that didn't let that 'flag' alone.*"

"As you feel that way, Mr. Meagher," said Nugent, "perhaps you might take a notion of coming with us?"

"I do not know but I might," Meagher said.

"You'll think over this, Mr. Meagher!" Nugent exclaimed.

A pondering Meagher promised: "I will think of it."

When Nugent left, Meagher's longtime friend Michael Cavanagh, who had observed the exchange and was well aware of Meagher's Southern sentiments before Sumter, approached him. "Did you mean that, Mr. Meagher?" he asked.

"Yes! I did mean it," Meagher answered.[10]

The 69th was fully enrolled when Meagher finally decided to join the Union cause, but Corcoran made an exception for his distinguished countryman. Corcoran also gave Meagher permission to raise a company in New York to serve under him, with the understanding that the company would be incorporated into the 69th in Washington, D.C., after the War Department approved the increased strength.[11] Meagher quickly issued his newspaper advertisement for recruits in New York.[12]

Within a week Meagher's rolls were complete. And so it was that Thomas Francis Meagher, no longer a young man at age thirty-eight, entered the war as a captain in the 69th New York State Militia and as the head of his company of Irish Zouaves. The term "Zouave," originally used to describe French Algerian units who wore brilliant uniforms and conducted quick, spirited drills, had come to describe any stylishly uniformed and intense fighting units. The fashion-conscious Meagher liked the idea of flashy uniforms and personally designed parade uniforms for his Zouaves that included pantaloons, which were not worn on the field. Even the fighting uniforms had gold stripes on their trousers and red trim on their jackets—a poor choice, according to Civil War journalist David Power Conyngham. The bright colors made them "a conspicuous mark for the enemy," Conyngham claimed, and the Zouaves "suffered desperately" in their first real taste of battle at Bull Run.[13]

Meagher's own gaudy parade uniform drew the negative, anti-Irish attention of journalist Henry Villard, who reported on the camps of the state militia units for the *New York Herald*. A German immigrant, Villard was partial to the exclusively German regiments out of New York and also liked the "Garibaldi Guards," which included Italians, Frenchmen, and Hungarians. But he absolutely disdained the Irish regiments, which he described as consisting of a "very low order of elements," and was downright insulting in his description of Meagher:

Speaking of these men, another apparition of those days rises before me. Thomas Francis Meager, the Irish exile, well known

Colonel Robert Nugent and Brigadier General Thomas Francis Meagher. (Collection of Jack McCormack)

for his political martyrdom and his great natural eloquence and literary talent, . . . had devised a most extraordinary uniform for himself, of the Zouave pattern, literally covered with gold lace. It was a sight to see him strut along Pennsylvania Avenue in it, with the airs of a conquering hero.[14]

Villard later claimed that he observed Meagher mounted on a horse, wearing a plain uniform and holding a cocked revolver in his right hand, which was rested on his hip. "The leer from his eyes and a certain unsteadiness in the saddle indicated plainly that he had braced himself up internally for the fight."[15]

Meagher only had a brief time to get his men ready, drilling them either in one of the large rooms at Hibernian Hall or at a billiard saloon at Tenth and Broadway. Captain Michael Phelan, who operated the saloon, was a veteran and organizer of the 9th—New York's first Irish regiment—and a good drill instructor. But Meagher was in a hurry to join Corcoran and the rest of the 69th, which had shipped out to Washington on April 23, and the troops had little time to prepare. On May 22 Meagher's Irish Zouaves left for Washington to join the 69th, then occupying the buildings and grounds of Georgetown College as a temporary cantonment.[16] Admittedly the outlook for his undertrained Irish soldiers was not good, and Meagher was compelled to state publicly that it was "a moral certainty that many of our countrymen who enlist in this struggle for the maintenance of the Union will fall in the contest." Even so, the risk was worth it to Meagher, for he too looked forward to freeing Ireland: "if only one in ten of us come back when this war is over, the military experience gained by that one will be of more service in a fight for Ireland's freedom than would that of the entire ten as they are now."[17] Meagher surely meant this statement as exaggeration—although it turned out to be near the truth—because like many of his contemporaries he would have expected a short, relatively easy victory.[18] It was not to be.

Meagher was promoted to acting major not long after he arrived with his regally outfitted Zouaves in Washington. He also was assigned to handle some of Colonel Corcoran's correspondence and write letters, such as the letter to Judge Charles P. Daly, thanking him for his support of the 69th, which was signed by Corcoran but was clearly

Meagher with Zouaves of the 69th. This photograph shows Captain Thomas Meagher of the New York 69th Militia in Virginia, seated with members of Company K. (Collection of Michael J. McAfee)

Thomas Francis Meagher. He is pictured here in a self-designed uniform, probably intended for battle. (Courtesy U.S. Army Military History Institute)

Officers of the 69th. This photograph, taken at Fort Corcoran, Virginia, shows the officers of Colonel Corcoran's 69th. Corcoran is the tall man standing in front of the cannon, and Meagher is on Corcoran's left, with his arms folded on the cannon. (Courtesy Library of Congress)

in Meagher's scrawling jagged hand with phrasing typical of the great orator.[19] Meagher's company, along with the rest of the 69th, was placed under the command of Colonel William Tecumseh Sherman, who became known for his famous "March to the Sea" that helped to end the Civil War.[20] In 1861, however, Sherman had just returned to the army after working as a banker in San Francisco, as the head of a military school in Louisiana, and as the president of a transit railway in St. Louis. Despite his civilian ventures, Sherman was a committed military man who had ranked sixth in his West Point graduating class of 1840, and he was a stickler for military discipline—something Meagher knew little about.

Sherman had reservations about the informally trained militia units that were part of his command. But he—and the North in general—had no option but to rely on the volunteer militia units, better known for parading than for fighting. In addition to the 69th, Sherman's brigade included four other volunteer regiments: the 13th New York, the 29th New York, the 79th New York, and the 2nd Wisconsin. Given the circumstances, Sherman considered his troops to be "good, strong, volunteer regiments, pretty well commanded," and he believed he had "one of the best brigades in the whole army." Four of the regiments, including the 69th, accompanied Sherman to the Battle of Bull Run on July 21.[21]

On Sunday morning, July 21, well before dawn, the 69th received orders to move forward from their camp at Centreville. In command was the tall, gaunt Colonel Michael Corcoran, ably assisted by Lieutenant Colonel James Haggerty. They and their men were eager to join the fight, but they were not happy with their treatment by Sherman. While advancing, they noticed that "regiments of other divisions" had been supplied "baggage and provision wagons," while the 69th was "peremptorily denied any facilities of the sort," according to Captain James Kelly, who made the official report as acting colonel of the regiment. Moreover, according to Kelly, the "regiment numbered one thousand muskets and was attended by one ambulance only, the other having broken down."[22] Borne on the single ambulance was the wounded Captain John Breslin, who had been shot by the accidental discharge of a loaded musket before the battle. He had been ordered to stay with his regiment by Colonel Sherman instead of being returned to Washington for medical

Civil War mass being celebrated for the Irish New York 69th. Thomas Francis Meagher, then a captain, is shown wearing a white hat with a black band, standing in the middle of the group to the left. Standing in front of this group, closest to the priest, is Colonel Michael Corcoran, the commander of the 69th. (Courtesy Library of Congress)

attention, and his suffering became worse as the vehicle jounced along.[23] The overall disrespect with which the army and Sherman were treating the Irish did not go unnoticed, and both Kelly and Meagher would have something to say about it after the battle.

The 69th's advance was followed by a steady march to within a mile and a half of the enemy's battery; the lack of sleep and lack of logistical support took their toll. The 69th arrived at the field of action "greatly fatigued and harassed, and but for their high sense of duty and military spirit would not have been adequate to the terrible duties of the day," according to Kelly.[24] But the men of the 69th were there to fight, and fight they did to the best of their abilities.

After waiting for what seemed an eternity, they received their orders from Sherman, who deployed the 69th into a line of battle in the woods to await the enemy's attack. Finally ordered to advance, the regiment marched forward through trees and obstacles to reach the ravine of Bull Run. Breaking their line, they crossed the stream single file and then climbed the bank of the ravine to a meadow. There, reforming into two lines, they marched forward until they were close to the enemy. The regiment halted, awaiting the order to charge. Seeing a group of Confederate Louisiana Zouaves start to retreat, Acting Lieutenant Colonel Haggerty and some of his men gave pursuit. The Louisiana troops, ironically also made up of Irish immigrants, fired. Their aim was true, and they wounded several of the Union troops, including Haggerty, who was killed, "shot through the right side by a rifle ball." After the battle there were rumors that Haggerty's body was mutilated by the Confederates after the "four sergeants" in charge of the body had to leave it when they were attacked by the Confederate Black Horse Cavalry. Meagher denied that "any mutilation of the kind took place in any instance," but one thing was clear: the war had started for Meagher and the 69th.[25]

As the rest of the regiment continued to wait, they were assailed with a continuous fire of muskets and artillery. The regiment fell into a line directly in front of the entrenched batteries of the Confederates. When they received the order to charge, the 69th proceeded forward with other Union regiments, only to be repulsed. They reformed, charged again, and were repulsed again. They tried to reform again but could not.[26] As one participant reported,

Then another valley, then another, and we charged up the heights to their battery with all the impetuosity of our race; but we were like "sheep sent to the slaughter." The cannon belched forth their shells in our midst, killing our men in groups, and scattering them in all directions. But even they halted, tried to close up, and fired again; and then, just as we seemed to carry our point, we found ourselves fired into on the right flank and rear by the Rebel cavalry, who emerged from the woods and struck down and picked off all the men near them.[27]

Then an overall panic started the retreat of the Union Army, and the 69th was carried with it.

Meagher had been mounted during the battle; when his horse went down, "I was knocked head over heels and fell senseless on the field." He could have been captured but was saved when "a private of the United States Cavalry galloping by, grasped me by the back of the neck, jerked me across his saddle, and carried me a few hundred yards beyond the range of the batteries." Meagher walked with the "Fire Zouaves" of the 8th and 71st New York militia until he climbed aboard an artillery wagon. As the wagon crossed Bull Run, one of the horses drawing it was shot. "Here I was pitched into the water," Meagher said. After "struggling through the river," he soon rejoined the retreating 69th.[28]

Meagher, whose entire military training had been in the three months prior to the battle, received both praise and criticism as a military officer. In her diary Maria Lydig Daly, then one of his supporters, wrote that word had reached her that "Meagher behaved very gallantly when the ensign who bore the green flag was killed. He seized it . . . calling to his men, 'Remember Frontenez' [sic]." She was referring to the famous battle cry "Remember Fontenoy," used many times in the Civil War by the Irish. It had its beginnings over a century before when an Irish Brigade had fought in the battle of Fontenoy under the king of France and had routed the English Coldstream Guards on May 11, 1745. Some reported that Meagher had said to "think of Ireland and Fontenoy." It did not matter. Said either way, it became the stuff of legend.[29]

Maria Daly continued in her diary: "Meagher . . . showed the greatest coolness and courage. He remained with Colonel Corcoran and was the last to leave the field. He was indefatigable in his attention to the wounded and dying. When parties of the enemy came up in search of prisoners, he lay down upon the ground and feigned death until they passed, and then continued his charitable work. Behold, indeed, an Apostle of Christ, a follower of his self-denying Master!"[30] If Maria Daly had read her own diary several months later, she would have choked on those words, because by then she had taken a different view of Meagher. Her change of heart was fueled by jealousy of his growing popularity, rivalry with the dynamic Elizabeth Meagher, and unflattering accounts about Meagher's behavior on the battlefield.

William Howard Russell, a British journalist who reported from the front at Bull Run and who was known for his pro-Confederate views, wrote the worst of those accounts. Russell reported for the *London Times*, the leading British newspaper of the day. Even before the *Times* could make it back across the Atlantic, however, the *New-York Daily Tribune* carried a story, presumably based on Russell's report, that Meagher had run away from the battle at Bull Run. Even more damning, Meagher was quoted as saying that the "Southern Confederacy ought to be recognized to-morrow [sic]; they have beaten us handsomely, and are entitled to it."[31] The *Tribune* denied the story, stating that Meagher "bore himself with distinguished gallantry"; but other newspapers were less charitable, and Russell's charges against Meagher spread around the world. Judge Charles Daly received a letter from Father Bernhard O'Reilly in Europe, saying that in Ireland he had heard "every body around me condemning the cause of the Federal Government. . . . Russell's letters were read with avidity, & made even Irishmen question the gallantry of the 69th & its officers." But Meagher was still a hero to those who knew him. In Dublin, O'Reilly was questioned by Meagher's old "friends of Clongowes, and many & many a voice did I hear among the Jesuits and among others say, 'God be praised!' or 'God bless him!'" he said.[32]

As an Englishman, Russell was likely ill-disposed to Meagher, and the overall bias of his reporting in favor of the South also casts doubt upon the veracity of his account. So does a lack of any supporting evidence. According to at least one other newspaper reporter, Meagher performed admirably in the Battle of Bull Run. "It was a brave sight—that rush of the 69th into death-struggle. . . . Coats and knapsacks were thrown to either side, that nothing might impede their work, but we knew that no guns would slip from the brave hands of those fellows, even if dying agonies were needed to close them with a firmer grip. As the line swept along, Thomas Meagher [their commander] galloped towards the head, shouting, 'Come on, boys! You've got your chance at last!'"[33]

Sherman would say in his official report of July 25 that the 69th, being third in the line of battle, topped a hill and there faced the roar of cannon, musketry, and rifles from a far superior enemy force. After holding their ground for some time, they finally fell back in disorder. With the help of Corcoran, Colonel Sherman organized his brigade, many of whom were fleeing, into an irregular square formation. They began their retreat back through Bull Run Creek on the same path they had used to arrive. Finally, Sherman's troops became dispersed and returned randomly to Fort Corcoran, where they continued to camp.

Though Sherman respected the 69th's performance in the battle itself, he criticized their behavior in the aftermath. By July 25 Sherman had his troops back under control—all, that is, except the 69th, which received harsh criticism from its commanding colonel. According to Sherman, the 69th had become "extremely tired of war, and wanted to go home [and] were so mutinous, at one time, that I had the battery to unlimber, threatening, if they dared to leave camp without orders, I would open fire on them."[34] The imputation that the men of the 69th were somehow not up to the task—that after their first taste of battle they were ready to go home—was unfair. The 69th enthusiastically rejoined the fray in the fall of 1861. Even Sherman acknowledged that the 69th performed acceptably at the Battle of Bull Run itself. The issue was not being "tired of war," as Sherman characterized it. Rather, the troops were angry over what they perceived as Sherman's anti-Irish bias and over the colonel's apparent lack of respect, which they felt was due them as volunteers. Sherman's unwillingness or inability to issue the 69th baggage and supply wagons and an additional ambulance rankled the volunteers, who had come to defend the Union of their own free will.

More significantly, however, the conflict arose from a disagreement about when the militiamen's term of duty ended. The regiment had volunteered in early April for only ninety days; but due to transportation difficulties the recruits were not mustered into the Union Army until almost a month later when they reached Washington, even though they had served as guards for a railroad en route. Some of the men claimed that they were entitled to their discharges ninety days from enrollment and were near the end of their commitment in early July. According to the muster rolls, however, they were to be discharged ninety days from the date they were mustered in. Having had the matter explained to him by Colonel Corcoran, Sherman submitted the question to the War Department, which held that the muster roll determined the length of service and that the regiment was to be held in service until approximately August 1.[35]

Although Sherman saw the War Department's decree as the final word, Meagher did not. Either he had not heard about the War Department's ruling or he had decided to ignore it. Thus he approached Sherman at reveille within a few days after Bull Run and graciously said to him, "Colonel, I am going to New York to-day. What can I do for you?" Sherman took offense. "How can you go to New York?" he asked. "I do not remember to have signed a leave for you." Meagher answered that he did not want leave, because his engagement was over after three months and he had already served more than that time.[36]

The matter escalated into an argument; according to Sherman's recollections, Meagher said that "if the government did not intend to pay him, he could afford to lose the money; that he was a lawyer, and . . . was then going home." Sherman noticed that "a good many of the soldiers had paused about us to listen, and knew that, if this officer could defy me, they also would." So he said to Meagher, "Captain, this question of your term of service has been submitted to the rightful authority. . . . You are a soldier, and must submit to orders till you are properly discharged." Sherman "had on an overcoat, and may have had my hand about the breast" when he told Meagher, "If you attempt to leave without orders, it will be mutiny, and I will shoot you like a dog!" At that point Meagher did as he was commanded and returned to his quarters to consider a plan of action.[37]

In the afternoon President Abraham Lincoln himself visited the demoralized Union troops and unwittingly became involved in the controversy. After touring the camp, he gave an inspiring address that included allusions to the imprisoned Colonel Corcoran. He concluded his remarks with an offer of redress for individual soldiers in the case of legitimate grievances; surprisingly, Meagher took him up on this offer. Sherman told the story: "In the crowd I saw the officer with whom I

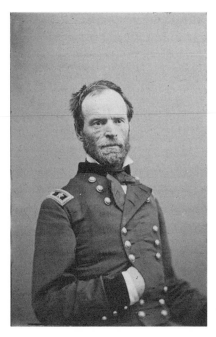

Major General William Tecumseh Sherman.
(Courtesy Library of Congress)

had had the passage at reveille that morning. His face was pale, and lips compressed." According to Sherman, Meagher said, "Mr. President, I have a cause of grievance. This morning I went to speak to Colonel Sherman, and he threatened to shoot me." A puzzled Lincoln, who did not know anything about the matter, finally said to Meagher in what Sherman described as "a loud stage-whisper, easily heard for some yards around: 'Well, if I were you, and he threatened to shoot, I would not trust him, for I believe he would do it.'" Sherman said that the men "laughed at him" and Meagher left the encounter humiliated.[38] If Sherman's account is to be trusted, it was an unusually tongue-tied moment for the great orator Meagher.

Perhaps the incident could have been avoided if Meagher and Sherman had understood each other better. To Sherman, the professional soldier, the issue was simply not allowing troops to be dismissed while battles were being waged. To Meagher, the issue was respect for the Irish. He realized, however, that he was no match for Sherman within the confines of the military and wisely chose not to take the matter any higher. He still felt it his duty to stand up for the Irish and perhaps to defend his own honor. Once he and his fellow members of the 69th had been discharged, Meagher returned to New York to take up his real weapon, the pen. A civilian once more, he lashed at Sherman, calling him a "rude and envenomed martinet" in an article for the *Irish American* that exposed what he perceived as Sherman's anti-Irish bias.[39] Though Meagher believed he had the last word, he would have to deal with Sherman again, and Sherman's enmity would come back to haunt him.

In the short term, however, Meagher's brush with Sherman did nothing to discourage his enthusiasm for the Civil War. Irish feeling was still running high, and Meagher felt certain he could recruit a brigade of five thousand men to fight for the Union. In September 1861 he wrote directly to secretary of war Simon Cameron: "Authorize positively to organize an Irish brigade of 5,000 men. I can do so forthwith and have it ready in thirty days to march." A delighted Cameron accepted at once; but because it was a matter of raising state militia, he advised Meagher to seek authorization from New York's governor Edwin Morgan, who also promptly accepted the proposal.[40]

Meagher set about recruiting Irishmen from anywhere he could find them and almost immediately was in trouble. Pennsylvania's governor A. G. Curtin wrote to Cameron that New York recruiters were not authorized to solicit troops in his state, naming "Colonel Meagher" as one of the violators.[41] More trouble came from Southern sympathizer S. C. Hayes, a longtime resident of Philadelphia, who neutralized a fine recruiting speech that Meagher gave there by raising Meagher's rumored mistreatment of his Irish Tasmanian wife, Catherine, and his subsequent marriage to Elizabeth Townsend, a Protestant Yankee. These arguments, he claimed later, limited Meagher's recruiting success in Pennsylvania to only a "corporal's guard."[42]

Another potential obstacle loomed. As Archbishop Hughes said before the year was out: "There is being insinuated . . . that the purpose of this war is the abolition of slavery in the south." But Hughes was of the opinion that if the Catholics were asked to fight only for abolition, "then, indeed, they will turn away in disgust from the discharge of what would otherwise be a patriotic duty."[43] Hughes was prescient. Irish enthusiasm for the war had already waned dramatically by September 1862, when

Return of the 69th. In this lithograph published in 1861 the Irish 69th Regiment is shown returning home from the first Battle of Bull Run and being escorted by the New York 7th Regiment. Meagher is pictured on the left, astride a horse and doffing his cap. (Courtesy Picture Collection, The Branch Libraries, The New York Public Library, Astor, Lenox and Tilden Foundations)

Lincoln finally issued the Emancipation Proclamation, which further chilled Irish willingness to fight on the side of the North.

In September 1861, however, Meagher's vigorous enlistment campaign quickly bore fruit. The Irish recruits came flocking in, and the brigade's ranks filled quickly. Given that the Confederates had captured the 69th's original leader, Michael Corcoran, the question then arose: who should be named brigade commander? Logic dictated Meagher, but he soon learned that he was not everyone's first choice. Many of New York's Irish upper class, including some of his former friends like Charles and Maria Daly, strongly supported the idea of the brigade but now had reservations about him as its leader.

Maria Daly, who had effusively praised Meagher's performance in the Battle of Bull Run, now became one of his main detractors. Her particular criticism centered around Meagher's tactics to convince all the original members of the 69th Regiment to join the Irish Brigade: "I think it was very inexcusable in Meagher to brand those who chose to stay behind as being impostors, to say that as the best of the Regiment would be with him, there could be no regiment with the number '69' on their caps parading Broadway in their absence."[44]

It is likely that Maria Daly spoke for her husband, Judge Charles Daly, as well. A man of inestimable wisdom, charm, intelligence, and influence, Judge Daly had spent his entire life in New York, rising to prominence as a justice of the Court of Common Pleas and lecturer on the law at Columbia. As president of the Friendly Sons of St. Patrick, he also advanced the interests of the Irish.[45] The Dalys had known Meagher for a long time, and at first they had shown great respect for him. It was Maria Lydig Daly who had arranged the funds for his first trip to Costa Rica, for which she had received Meagher's sincere appreciation.[46]

Now, however, Maria Daly wrote in her diary that Meagher—the man she had a few months earlier called "an Apostle of Christ"—was "very despotic and very ambitious" and "double-faced," with "a very domineering, arrogant disposition." She also accused him of being drunk during the Battle of Bull Run. The abrupt change in her assessment of Meagher occurred at about the time when she sensed that Elizabeth Meagher had a political agenda to promote her husband as the best-known Irishman in the nation—a move that Maria Daly feared would usurp her own husband's prominence. "I do not quite like

Mrs. Meagher's manner and think that she rather desires to keep all the glory and renown to herself and her husband," she wrote. A convert herself, Maria Daly even questioned Elizabeth's sincerity about her adopted Catholicism: "she had a pretty little formula which she had written out about her not having had the blessings (which she deeply regretted) of having been born in the Ancient Faith."[47] In the middle of November, when the various regiments of the Irish Brigade were ready to go to war, the two women competed for attention by the presentation of regimental flags. Elizabeth Meagher presented the colors to the 88th, which then became known as "Mrs. Meagher's Own." Maria Daly and her committee had a special green flag with an Irish harp made by Tiffany and Company for the 69th.[48]

Once Meagher had lost the support of the Dalys, and with it the approval of many of the established Irish in New York, General James M. Shields became the leading candidate for brigadier of the Irish Brigade. A judge, soldier, and U.S. senator, Shields was well known long before Meagher reached New York. In fact Shields had spoken favorably of a bill introduced in the Senate to grant asylum to Meagher and his fellow exiles in Tasmania. Ironically, Shields was also Meagher's own first choice for command. In a memorandum written around July 1861, President Lincoln himself wrote: "Thomas Francis Meagher, as well as Senator Latham & Gen. Denver, desire the appointment of Shields. Bishop Hughes thinks Corcoran should be appointed; and my own judgment concurs in both cases."[49] Shields would have been an ideal commander, experienced as he was in war; but he had been a major general in the Mexican War and sought a higher command, commensurate with his rank.[50]

Meagher's advocacy of Shields lends credence to reports that he did not initially aspire to lead the brigade himself. Meagher's friend W. F. Lyons, who served under him as a captain, affirmed that view. "All along he wished, and, so far as he was concerned, intended that General Shields should take command," Lyons said.[51] When Lincoln appointed Shields and Corcoran (who was still a prisoner of war) to other commands, however, the position of leader of the Irish Brigade remained open. At that point Meagher's ambitions may have begun to change. Meagher, then a captain, was offered a position as aide-de-camp, with the rank of colonel, on the staff of Major General John C. Frémont but politely turned it down.

Meagher was offered colonelcy of the 69th, most of whose members had reenlisted at his urging. He refused that post as well.[52]

By the end of 1861 a surreptitious campaign had begun to have Meagher named the permanent commander of the Irish Brigade. Probably with his knowledge, but surely without his editing, an awkward, anonymously authored, and unsigned document titled "Reasons Why Colonel Thomas Francis Meagher Should Be Appointed Brigadier General of the Irish Brigade" was delivered to President Lincoln. Written in a hand different from Meagher's usual jagged, right-slanted, nearly illegible penmanship, the pamphlet gave ten reasons why he deserved the appointment.[53]

First, the document pointed out that Meagher had served with the 69th Regiment and that he had convinced a large number of Irishmen with sympathies for the South to join the Union, despite the fact that "the emissaries of Rebellion carefully circulated and cultivated the idea that this regiment was illtreated [sic] because it was an Irish one." It went on to say that Meagher had delivered an address at "Jones Wood," where he pointed out that the Lincoln government "was the best and most liberal towards adopted citizens this Nation ever had." Lincoln was also told that "two hundred thousand Irishmen and the sons of Irishmen are enlisted under the Nation's flag . . . owing to the influence which Colonel Meagher [has] over his countrymen."[54]

But what probably most impressed Lincoln about Meagher was the document's promise of recruiting Irish soldiers for the Union, even outside the country. It stated clearly that Meagher had influence, particularly in Ireland, "where millions of Irishmen look to him as their prophet and their guide," and he had "already drawn many Irish . . . from their own country to this for the sole purpose of joining *his brigade,* and fighting under *his lead* for the Union Cause." If a war with England should arise, "no man could, by his influence with the Irish race, so effectually strike a blow at the power of that country by attacking her in Ireland, in the Canadas, in Australia, nay in England itself as Colonel Meagher."[55]

The prospect of obtaining troops directly from Ireland was one that President Lincoln would not take lightly, as the North was attempting to mount a large force against the Confederates. Often suspected as a strong possibility, foreign recruitment of Irish soldiers even had the support of Archbishop John Hughes. In November 1861 Archbishop Hughes was dispatched by his friend Secretary of State Seward to Europe on what was thinly disguised as a peace mission to the French government and the Vatican. When Hughes arrived, the *London Times* immediately saw that the real purpose was to promote the cause of the North and reported that Hughes had "worked the Irish element in the States for a considerable period, and ha[d] used it in favor of Mr. Seward."[56]

Completing his diplomatic assignment in Paris and in Rome, Hughes went on to Ireland, where he made speeches in July 1862 that were laden with animosity toward England. Soon he was literally preaching the Fenian position: that the Civil War was a fine training ground for future rebellions. "The Irish have, in many instances[,] . . . entered into this war partly to make themselves apprentices, students as it were, finishing their education in this, the first opportunity afforded them of becoming thoroughly acquainted with the implements of war," said Hughes. "If you undertake a revolution and have not so measured your strength you commit a great crime," he told an assembled group of young men from Nenagh.[57] Lincoln probably had no doubt that appointing Meagher a general could only help that effort. Thus, on December 20, 1861, Lincoln advised Cameron: "Let Thomas Francis Meagher, be appointed a Brigadier General of volunteers."[58]

Meagher quickly followed up his appointment by writing directly to Lincoln with a list of persons he wanted appointed to his staff, all of whom Lincoln also approved.[59] After that Meagher felt comfortable communicating directly with the president and frequently found that it achieved his desired results. Yet it was not always effective. In early 1862, having achieved the leadership of the Irish Brigade, Meagher sought an even broader Irish ethnic command and proposed that several Irish regiments from various states be consolidated and placed under him. This time the request was refused by the army, however, which notified Meagher that "the sentiment of Union that has brought them into rank shoulder to shoulder with the natives of this and other countries is inconsistent with the idea of army organization on the basis of distinct nationalities, and to foster such organization among those who are fighting under the same flag is unwise and inexpedient."[60]

Despite the army leaders' ambivalence toward ethnic units, they understood that ethnic loyalty overshadowed many other connections and that recruitment by the Irish general for an all-Irish Brigade would help to

Brigadier General Thomas Francis Meagher. He is shown here in formal dress in a rare side view. (Author's collection)

bring the troops they needed. They also understood the need to promote ethnic leaders like Meagher, whose appointment was meant to be a compliment to the Irish. Despite its political nature, Meagher's appointment was a signal achievement. For the Irish in America, it gave them a military leader that they could point to as one of their own. It also bred new hope for the cause of Irish freedom. For Meagher personally, it meant being elevated to an elite group of Union generals—numbering no more than seven hundred before the end of the war—that commanded more than two and a half million men. In addition, it set the stage for a bright political future. Little did Meagher know that the prestige of his new rank only foreshadowed disaster, both for himself and for the Irish, who would be decimated in the Civil War.

CHAPTER SIX

The Slaughter Pen

Come, my countrymen, fling yourselves with a generous passion into the armed lines.

Thomas Francis Meagher

The Virginia woods rang out with the sounds of gaiety and laughter, punctuated by the beat of horses' hooves and the frequent raising of voices in Irish song. As the day wore on, the sounds became louder and more boisterous. After a tedious winter Brigadier General Thomas Francis Meagher and his staff had prepared the day's festivities to honor St. Patrick's Day. The men had been encamped near Alexandria, Virginia, since early fall of 1861 and were desperate for a break from the monotony of camp life. Many generals in the Army of the Potomac, including Major General Joseph Hooker, attended the event. The Irishmen, donning colorful clothing, delighted their distinguished visitors with foot races, hurdle races, wheelbarrow races, sack races, weight casting, running after a soaped pig, and a dance contest including Irish jigs, reels, and hornpipes. Part of the day's highlight were the refreshments: "copious draughts of rich wine" and "potations of spiced whiskey punch, ladled from an enormous bowl, holding not much less than thirty gallons." Civilians from New York and Washington, including the officers' wives, attended the proceedings, and the *Irish American* reported that "the gay ladies . . . added much [to the event], by their vivacity, and their picturesque costume, by their brilliancy and witchery."[1]

Father William Corby, a Jesuit priest from Notre Dame University who served as brigade chaplain, had whiled away the long winter with Meagher and the Irishmen, conducting masses and hearing confessions. He had plenty of time to keep a detailed diary, and he reported on the St. Patrick's Day celebration at length. According to Corby, the event grew from Meagher's "natural fondness for sports, and with a desire to keep life and energy in his command." But before the contests began, "all attended Mass and listened to the sermon; he [Meagher], in person, acting as master of ceremonies, directing the band when to play during the divine service."[2]

The act earned Corby's everlasting respect for Meagher. He was aware of Meagher's weaknesses, reporting in his diary that sometimes Meagher drank too much. "It is to be regretted that, at times, especially when no fighting was going on, and time grew heavy on his hands, his convivial spirit would lead him too far," Corby wrote; but he added: "by no means must it be concluded from this that he was a drunkard. It was not for love of liquor, but for the love of sport and joviality that he thus gave way, and these occasions were few and far between." Even when Meagher was under the influence Corby found him "never sinking to anything low or mean, beyond indulging too freely in unguarded moments." More important than his occasional excesses, in Corby's estimation, was Meagher's proud Catholicism. "Wherever he went he made himself known as a 'Catholic and an Irishman,'" Corby reported. Meagher "loved his faith, and assisted in making religion take a front rank."[3] To Corby, that made up for a myriad of smaller sins. Not all agreed with his assessment.

The St. Patrick's Day festivities enlivened what had been an almost unbearably dull winter. From early fall 1861 until spring 1862 the Irish Brigade had been quartered on the Virginia side of the Potomac, a short distance from Alexandria, in the grip of a mire of porous and soaked reddish clay that bogged down even powerful horses and that the troops found it nearly impossible to walk through. The absurd name for this slimy enclave was "Camp California," but there certainly was no similarity between that sun-drenched state and the Virginia

Father William Corby. Seated at the right, Corby was the Irish Catholic chaplain of the Irish Brigade. Despite seeing some faults in Meagher, Corby was always his supporter. (Courtesy Library of Congress)

mud, which, after winter rains, was some of the worst boot-grabbing muck in the country. In this bleak environment the soldiers had been given endless picket duty, drilling, policing, and other camp assignments, all exceedingly monotonous and carried out under the threatening dark winter skies.[4]

Meagher found himself depressed as he shared in the boredom of the brigade and camp life. Despite experiencing the deaths of comrades at the first Battle of Bull Run, he still had romantic notions about war. He envisioned his troops upholding Irish honor as they had at the historical battle of Fontenoy in France in 1745. There Irishmen had attained victory by using smoothbore weapons, which were deadly at close range. Although Meagher could have secured for his men the newer .58-caliber rifles that were more accurate at long range, he chose the older .69-caliber smoothbores because he envisioned a daring and fierce charge by his soldiers firing "buck and ball," followed by a bloody bayonet charge.[5]

Emotionally ready to dash into battle, Meagher became disillusioned by the monotony of camp life. He found the busy-work confusing and insignificant. On March 4, 1862, shortly after he had received his commission, he wrote from the headquarters of the Irish Brigade at Camp California to his brother-in-law Samuel Latham Mitchell Barlow, complaining about orderlies riding into camp every few minutes with orders and circulars and "every other form of urgent epistolary missive," each of which he had to acknowledge as brigadier.[6]

Experience in actual battle, where the Irish troops were used as cannon fodder, would bring further disillusionment. Meagher knew some of the men would lose their lives, but he would be shocked by how many. Father Corby realistically referred to the brigade as "a body of about 4,000 Catholic men marching—most of them—to death." Corby was not alone in his prediction. In New York, Maria Daly, after attending a mass for five thousand departing Catholic soldiers, said, "I could scarcely *restrain* my tears, for I felt it was like a mass for the dead."[7]

Undeterred by the impending doom, the 69th New York, the 88th New York, and the 63rd New York—all Irish regiments—confidently marched into the Civil War under the command of their inexperienced general. They would be joined later in the Civil War bloodbath by the largely Irish 116th Pennsylvania and the non-Irish 29th Massachusetts, which was soon replaced by the Irish 28th Massachusetts.[8]

Meagher's first real taste of battle would come in June 1862, when his brigade was involved in a series of engagements as the North tried to take Richmond, Virginia, in the Union Army's advance up the Virginia peninsula. The Irish Brigade would participate in the battles of Fair Oaks, Gaines's Mill, Savage Station, White Oak Swamp, and Malvern Hill, all within a few miles of each other and all of great importance to the success of the campaign. Major General George B. McClellan had brought the Army of the Potomac up the Virginia peninsula to within six miles of Richmond in May 1862, and the Irish Brigade joined the battle to take the swampy peninsula on June 1.[9]

On the preceding day Meagher and his troops had held another celebration. The men had become restless; to relieve the boredom of regimental life they collected a purse and organized a steeplechase around a hastily constructed course. Meagher embraced the event and offered as a prize the skin of a jaguar that he had shot on a trip to Central America. Cheers and shouts of laughter came from a nearby field, where the men were engaged in a game of Gaelic football. Commanding officers came from other brigades, and General Israel B. Richardson and General William H. French joined the festivities as judges. In the final race of the morning, drummer boys competed aboard mules for a purse of thirty dollars. As the morning wore on, the men erected a makeshift theater and hastily studied parts for a play and lettered and posted crude handbills advertising a great evening of entertainment. But it was not to be. That evening marked the beginning of the Battle of Fair Oaks and the brigade's first real look at the specter of bloodshed, mutilation, and death in the Civil War.[10]

Around midday on May 31 the Irishmen heard "considerable firing in front," which continued to increase in rapidity and loudness. At about one o'clock Meagher became concerned and ordered his command to place themselves under arms immediately, anticipating that an order to advance to the scene of action might soon reach them. Within minutes Captain Norvell, the assistant adjutant-general of the division, arrived at Meagher's tent and delivered an order from General Richardson, commander of the division, to get his brigade instantly under arms and to take only two days' cooked rations in their haversacks, leaving behind their overcoats, knapsacks, and blankets. Glad that the waiting was over, Meagher advanced eagerly—all the more so when he met some retreating Union soldiers, "who informed us that the Federal arms had met with a severe reverse, and that as some New York troops were implicated it was specially incumbent on us to redeem the honor of our State and the fortunes of the day."[11]

Duty-bound to uphold the reputation of the home state of the New York 63rd, 69th, and 88th, the Irish hurried to reach the scene of battle, only to find that the route was through a swamp. The infantry barely proceeded with great difficulty through the stagnant water, rotting trees, and brush, past croaking frogs and slithering snakes. While the foot soldiers were able to advance, the horses of the cavalry and artillery, pulling cannon and watertight chests of ammunition, sank up to their bellies in the mud, and no amount of whipping and yelling could free them. In this desperate situation members of one of the Irish Brigade's regiments, the 63rd New York, were ordered to fall back to defend the batteries that were stuck in the mud instead of advancing into battle. Later, after the Union troops were defeated, Meagher complained that "the participation of the Sixty-third New York Volunteers in the dangers of the day would have added to whatever credit the rest of the brigade has had the fortune to acquire."[12]

Struggling into the night, the exhausted soldiers finally reached the site of that day's battle. "It was between 9 and 10 p.m. when the head of our Brigade entered on the scene of that day's terrible conflict," Meagher reported. He must have been dismayed when they were able to see through the gloom, "and we were apprised of the fact and it was impressed upon us startlingly by the appearance of numbers of surgeons and chaplains with lanterns in hand searching over the ground to the right and left of our advance in column for the dead and wounded, who they said were scattered in every direction around."[13]

While the search went on, Meagher's bedraggled troops secured their arms, reclined on the open field, and soon fell asleep. As gray dawn awoke them, they found to their horror that they had been sleeping with the dead. Father Corby was dismayed: "Many a poor soldier lay cold in death just where he fell in the battle of the previous evening, and we saw the ghastly appearance of their bodies, which had been, as it were, our bed-fellows, and a shudder passed through our hearts. . . . Taking a hasty look over the locality, I saw on every side dead men, dead horses, broken muskets, caissons smashed to pieces, and general destruction of life and property."[14]

A sleepless Meagher was already mounted at 4 A.M. amidst the grisly remains, ready to take action, when he realized the Confederate forces were bivouacked in the woods surprisingly nearby. Meagher hastily roused his drowsy men. The troops barely had time for some hardtack and water before they were confronted with brisk firing from the enemy immediately in front of them. Taking care to avoid the bodies of the dead and dying, they assembled for battle after General Edwin Sumner, the corps commander, had addressed them with a few words of encouragement.

As the firing in the woods increased in intensity, Meagher received his orders: the 69th New York started downhill toward a railroad. The reports of muskets and the whirring sound of bullets passing by told them that they were under attack from Confederate troops positioned behind the trees and in a few nearby houses. Their moment had arrived, and Meagher and the brigade were now fully in the battle. It was a challenge the Irishmen had both feared and wanted. Meagher was ready to lead his troops into battle and direct them during the fight. He would soon find out to his dismay, however, that he was not always in charge of his own men. In the heat of battle, division staff officers or other brigadiers with more military experience would convey many orders to the regiments of the Irish Brigade.

While the battle raged, division command ordered the 88th New York to proceed by a flank movement to occupy the railroad to the left of the 69th and go forward under Meagher's command. The troops dutifully started their struggle through tangled underbrush, fallen, rotting trees, and heavy patches of mire and swamp. But then they encountered even more difficulty—this time caused by human error. A division staff officer countermanded Meagher's order to advance but did not see to it that the order was communicated to the two lead companies of the 88th. They did not hear the new order and continued to the railroad, where they were exposed to the unobstructed fire of the enemy from the woods. Support arrived after the conflicting order was finally recalled, but to no avail. The Union Army, including the Irishmen, could not maintain its position and withdrew, leaving its dead and critically wounded on the field.

The countermand that caused the unnecessary exposure of his troops infuriated Meagher. The 88th, he reported, "had to display itself in an opening before they reached their position on the railroad which was exposed to the unobstructed fire of the enemy from the woods." The angry Meagher was also certain that the negligent countermand had ruined the chances of the whole army on that day: had his two companies "not sustained the fire of the enemy, I believe the issue of the day adversely to the Army of the Potomac would have been materially influenced."[15]

Despite the confusion and the rout, Meagher performed admirably in his first taste of real battle as brigadier. David Power Conyngham, a journalist who later described himself as an "honorary member" of Meagher's staff, reported that Meagher was "indefatigable, riding from line to line, cheering on the men. The general was all the time under fire."[16] Meagher's reputation would soon become subject to the inconsistencies in Civil War reporting. While Conyngham lauded Meagher's battle performance, a taciturn General Richardson, the commander of the division, only begrudgingly allowed that "I was ably assisted by all three of my brigadiers." Richardson's report suggested that the 69th and 88th had been ordered forward only to relieve other troops, with no mention of securing the railroad.[17] At Fair Oaks, however, the dash and vocal charge of the brigade and its green flag had already given Meagher's Irish a reputation for fighting. "The rebels cannot stand their charge of Bayonets, when accompanied with their wild Native Shout. It is said the Green flag is a terror to them," said young Thomas Darby.[18]

The Union Army had suffered great casualties at Fair Oaks, and the officers of the Irish Brigade had to engage themselves in the unpleasant search for their wounded upon the body-strewn battlefield—and the burying of the dead.[19] The destruction caused by the Irish Brigade's first real battle sunk in slowly. Meagher had witnessed what Conyngham described as "the horrors of that sad scene;—the blood and carnage of the fight; the wild shouts of victory and vengeance; the ghastliness of the dead, piled in all shapes and forms; the groans of the wounded, who call on you in mercy to shoot them, and put them out of pain." The situation, if possible, was worse at the makeshift hospitals. "It looks like a perfect butcher's shambles," Conyngham said, "with maimed and bloody men lying on all sides; some with their arms off; some with their legs off; some awaiting their turn; while the doctors, with upturned cuffs and bloody hands, are flourishing their fearful knives and saws around, and piles of raw, bloody-looking limbs are strewn around them: while some who have died on the dissecting-table, add to the ghastly picture."[20]

Despite the heavy loss, Meagher's initial response, before the horror set in, was positive. In his June 4, 1862, report he wrote: "I am happy to inform you that in killed and wounded the brigade has only lost 2 officers (Lieutenants King and O'Connor, Eighty-eighth New York Volunteers, of whom the former died yesterday morning and the latter lies severely though not mortally wounded) and something less than 50 men."[21] Still, Meagher felt that his brigade was undermanned; his letter

David Power Conyngham. Conyngham, a journalist with the *New York Herald,* is shown seated to the right of the man standing with a group during the Civil War. This picture was taken at Bealton, Virginia, at the tent and wagon of the *Herald.* (Courtesy Library of Congress)

to the aide-de-camp of the governor of New York on June 21 said that "what we must want is 600 recruits—these to be equally divided amongst the three original Regiments of the Brigade."[22] Meagher had every reason to believe he could successfully recruit in New York, because his efforts at Fair Oaks were being described as heroic. The lithographers at Currier and Ives immediately went to work publishing a scene showing him on horseback, with a sword over his head, leading his brigade into battle.[23]

Members of the brigade had a few weeks to recover from the rout at Fair Oaks. In mid-June their ranks received reinforcements, when the army assigned the 29th Massachusetts to the Irish Brigade to bring it up to a full complement of four regiments. The 29th was composed not of Irishmen but of New England Yankees, which caused problems. There was much grumbling by the men of the 29th. "Strange to tell we

Meagher at the Battle of Fair Oaks. This is an original lithograph published in New York by Currier and Ives at 152 Nassau Street, entitled "GENL. MEAGHER AT THE BATTLE OF FAIR OAKS VA. June 1st, 1862." The caption reads: "The bayonet charge of the Irish Brigade at this battle, was the most stubborn, sanguinary and bloody of modern times. Again and again they advanced with the cold steel, and were as vigorously met by the enemy. In one place on the field of carnage, three men were found on each side that had fallen by mutual thrusts. But at last the battle terminated in favor of the Union arms, the Rebels gave way in flight, and the victorious 'Army of the Potomac' continued their advance on Richmond." (Courtesy Library of Congress)

have been attached temporarily to Meagher's Irish Brigade," said George W. Barr, noting "the indignation of the men," who could "not expect much satisfaction from such villainous associates."[24] With this attitude, integrating the Yankees into the Irish Brigade did not go smoothly. Meagher extended a welcome by presenting them a "magnificently embroidered Green flag" with their regimental number, only to have the 29th's colonel, J. H. Barnes, refuse to bear it on the field because his unit was not Irish. Meagher retrieved the flag. After removing the "2," he presented it to the 9th Massachusetts, an Irish regiment from another brigade. A short time later the 29th was transferred out of the Irish Brigade to be replaced by the all-Irish 28th Massachusetts.[25] If giving Meagher a non-Irish regiment was an experiment, it did not work. The remainder of his career as a battle commander would be as a leader of Irishmen. The men of the 29th could not have been more grateful to get out of the Irish Brigade. On January 4, after the disastrous battle of Fredericksburg, Thomas Darby, a sergeant, wrote that "our Regt. has always been fortunate and did not participate in the last battle, but had we not been transferred from Meagher's . . . we would have to have taken an active part in the last battle and probably would have suffered as the other Regts have."[26]

Even though it had been driven back at Fair Oaks, the Union Army remained on the peninsula until invigorated Confederate forces under their new general, Robert E. Lee, attacked them in what would be known as the Seven Days battles, starting on June 25. Meagher's troops had now had a respite since early June, and he received orders late in the afternoon of June 27 to report to Brigadier General William H. French. French had orders to aid General Fitz John Porter, who was a few miles further up the peninsula on the north side of the Chicka-hominy in the vicinity of Gaines's Mill and the Watt house. Porter was being forced backward by the enemy.[27]

In what was known as the Battle of Gaines's Mill, French led his brigade and Meagher's brigade on a quick march to the Chickahominy, where they crossed the swollen stream on one of the few bridges in the area. Meagher reported that as they crossed they were met by "an immense cloud of dust, through which teams and horsemen hastily broke . . . followed by crowds of fugitive stragglers on foot, whose cry was that 'they had been cut to pieces.'" To turn the retreat back, French ordered the deployment of a company of the 69th to drive back the runaways. According to Meagher, this "had the effect of almost instantly checking a rout which if not arrested at that moment would have been attended with the most fearful consequences."[28]

The involvement at Gaines's Mill had started well for Meagher's men, and it would get better. Major General McClellan reported that as the battle moved on into late afternoon General Porter's forces, though increased to some thirty-five thousand, "were probably contending against about 70,000 of the enemy." With such odds against him, Porter reported his position as critical. "The enemy attacked again in great force at 6 P.M., but failed to break our lines, though our loss was very heavy," McClellan said. Again "about 7 P.M. they threw fresh troops against General Porter with still greater fury, and finally gained the woods held by our left." At that point McClellan called on mounted troops to drive the enemy back, but to no avail; and he reported: "This reverse, aided by the confusion that followed an unsuccessful charge by five companies of the Fifth Cavalry, and followed as it was by more determined assaults on the remainder of our lines, now outflanked, caused a general retreat from our position to the hill in rear, overlooking the bridge."[29]

It had now become the goal of the Union Army to retreat in an orderly manner from its positions at Gaines's Mill, and fresh troops were needed to stop any advance of the Confederates that would hinder the recrossing over the Chickahominy bridges. At this point the Irish Brigade became fully engaged in the fray, with passion and fury. "French's and Meagher's Brigades now appeared, driving before them the stragglers who were thronging toward the bridge," McClellan said. "These brigades advanced boldly to the front, and by their example, as well as by the steadiness of their bearing, reanimated our own troops and warned the enemy that re-enforcements had arrived." As the evening turned to dusk, the Confederates, "hearing the shouts of the fresh troops, failed to follow up their advantage." This gave the Union forces time to regroup, and McClellan proudly reported that the men had rallied "behind the brigades of Generals French and Meagher, and they again advanced up the hill ready to repulse another attack."[30] In addition to McClellan's glowing report, the Irish Brigade also received tribute from the Confederate side. Confederate Major General Daniel H. Hill heard loud cheers coming from the Union ranks only two hundred yards away from his line. "The cheering, as we afterward learned, was caused by the appearance of the Irish Brigade to cover the retreat," Hill said.[31]

The advance of the Irish Brigade, under fire of the enemy, did not stop until General Porter commanded them to do so in person. At that time Porter directed Meagher to relieve the regulars under Brigadier General George Sykes on the front line.[32]

At midnight Major General Porter returned from McClellan's headquarters and directed French "in the name of the general-in-chief, to hold [his] line on the front until all the rest of [the] force had crossed the river." There members of the Irish Brigade remained throughout the night. French noted that they were "far to the front" and "lay in close proximity to the enemy—so near that numbers of their men and officers were taken crossing our lines of pickets to communicate with

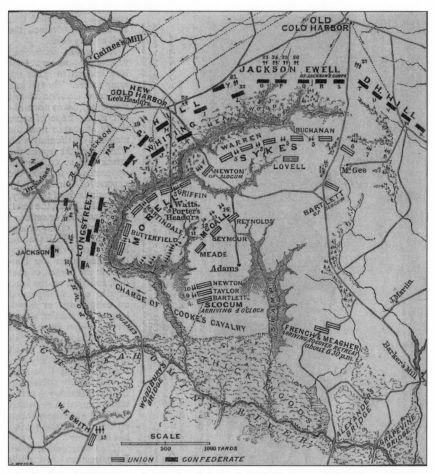

Meagher's Irish Brigade at the Battle of Gaines's Mill. This map shows the position of French's and Meagher's troops (in the lower right) as they arrived at the battlefield at about 6:30 P.M. to cover the Union retreat. The original battlefield map was made by Jacob Wells. (Courtesy Library of Congress)

regiments which had bivouacked on our right and left, separated by the darkness of night."[33] In the middle of the night General French ordered his forces and Meagher's troops to recross the Chickahominy, which was accomplished before sunrise the next morning on a bridge that was being demolished. The 88th, which was ordered to keep in the rear of the column to defend the passage of the wounded and stragglers, and Meagher and his staff finally crossed in the rear of the brigade. They headed "with celerity" for Fair Oaks Station, where French's men had heard "very heavy firing."[34]

The Battle of Gaines's Mill was over for the Army of the Potomac and for Meagher, and it turned out to be the highlight of his military career. In the late summer of 1863, when James Turner was writing a history of the Irish Brigade, Meagher told him to put "great stress on this rapid march of our's [sic] to Gaines's Hill, and our effectively covering the broken and routed forces of Porter, for I consider it the most successful and masterly achievement of the Brigade for the two year's [sic] of its existence—all the more so that we didn't fire a shot."[35]

The Irish Brigade, still under French's command, rested at the Fair Oaks encampment until ten o'clock on the night of June 28. Then Meagher and the Irishmen—without the 69th, which was on picket duty—marched through the dark a few miles to Savage Station and then on to Meadow Station. There they held a position until ordered to report to General Richardson, which they did about four o'clock the following afternoon, on June 29. But that was not soon enough. Earlier in the day Major General Samuel Heintzelman had informed McClellan that "Gen. Richardson has ordered Genl. Meagher to join the Division and has sent to arrest him for not obeying the order."[36] Meagher did report later that he was in fact "temporarily placed under arrest until 8 o'clock the following day."[37] While not stated, the likely cause of the arrest was confusion. It seems to have been quickly straightened out and treated by Meagher, and apparently everyone else, as a matter of little consequence, although it must have dumfounded him at the time.[38] Meagher was back in command the next day, June 30, after Colonel Robert Nugent had taken command of the brigade at the battle of Savage Station in the late afternoon of the June 29 and the march through White Oak Swamp that evening.[39]

What Heintzelman and Richardson might not have known was that Meagher's brigade, or at least the 69th Regiment, was involved in the battle of Savage Station that afternoon, under General Sumner. Heintzelman himself was to have been in the battle, but Sumner was in "utter amazement, that General Heintzelman had left the field and retreated with his whole corps (about 15,000 men) before the action commenced." According to Sumner, "at 12 o'clock m. [noon] . . . I saw the necessity at once of concentrating the troops . . . at Savage Station."

This was necessitated when the Confederates crossed the Chicka-hominy in pursuit and "the enemy came in upon me at 4 o'clock P.M. in large force." Sumner lauded Meagher's troops: "The assault was met by Burns' brigade . . . and finally by the Sixty-ninth New York (Irish) Regiment." At last "we drove the enemy from the field, and thus closed the battle of Savage Station." According to Richardson, "on Saturday, June 28, I was ordered to get my division ready for a move . . . to Savage station, and late in the afternoon I was ordered to detach the brigade of General Meagher to that station, to report to Major General McClellan for duty, which was done."[40]

As the Army of the Potomac made further plans to retreat to the James River, General Richardson received orders "[l]ate at night," on June 29. With his brigades, including Meagher's, he was to serve "as a rear guard with my division in covering the movement of the army across the White Oak Swamp" and then break up the bridge crossing White Oak Creek so the Confederates could not follow.[41] By the time Captain Rufus King, Jr., commanding Batteries A and C of the 4th U.S. Artillery, came to the bridge, preparations were being made to demolish it; he barely had time to get across. Finally, Meagher's brigade came across the bridge under command of Colonel Nugent, and the bridge was destroyed. By this time day was breaking on June 30, and the Union army prepared to hold off the pursuing Confederates. The Irish Brigade, having slogged all night through the swamp, deployed on a hill to the south of the bridge and there, along with King's battery, awaited the Rebels. The batteries "commenced firing between 1 and 2 o'clock p.m., firing very rapidly and drawing the entire fire of the enemy's batteries upon us," King said. To his surprise, he received some unexpected help. Meagher was back in charge of his brigade, and he "stood by one of the pieces, and, exposed to the hottest of the fire, assisted the men in running the gun forward," King reported. As the artillerists started to run out of ammunition, King's anxiety was relieved when Meagher "kindly volunteered to ride to General Richardson and have ammuni-tion sent to me as soon as possible."[42]

On July 1, shortly after 6 P.M., Sumner ordered Meagher to advance the 63rd, 69th, 88th, and 29th Massachusetts into battle. While they awaited orders, these regiments had been under incessant bombardment from the Confederates. Despite that, they had successfully occupied the banks of a ravine to the right of Sumner's corps and in so doing helped protect the right flank of the army.[43] The Irish Brigade also had had a small but intense battle on July 1 against the celebrated Confederate "Louisiana Tigers," a battalion from New Orleans referred to as "the desperados of the Southern service," according to Michael Cavanagh. In what was later called a "regimental duel," the Irishmen encountered the Tigers at close quarters. They had no time to affix their bayonets and so instead used their muskets as clubs against the knives and pistols of the Southerners. No winner of the melee was declared.[44]

The 69th and the 88th performed particularly well during the engagement, succeeding in outflanking the enemy until the Confederates were forced to draw back from the range of fire. In the meantime the 63rd and the 29th preserved the second line of attack under fire until Meagher ordered them to support an artillery battery. As Meagher was observing the movement of his troops, an aide of General McClellan rode up and requested that one of his Irish regiments be detailed to accompany a battery of artillery that was moving up in relief, the previous battery having exhausted its ammunition. With only the 63rd at his disposal at that time, Meagher ordered its acting commander, Lieutenant Colonel Henry Fowler, to accompany the battery. To Meagher's great consternation Fowler refused the order, claiming that he did not have to take orders from Meagher because he was under special orders from another general.[45]

Father Corby, who witnessed the event, said that Meagher went "wild with rage" and commanded Fowler to surrender his sword to Captain John "Jack" Gosson, placing Captain Joseph O'Neil in command. As Meagher recalled, "having no doubt whatever that the officer representing himself as an aide of the general-in-chief [McClellan] had the authority which he professed to have, I . . . directed Captain O'Neil, the next senior officer of the regiment, to assume the command, and to have the disputed order instantly complied with." But the troops of the 63rd themselves seemed unwilling to comply with the order, even though they stood somewhat reluctantly by the artillery battery until it was withdrawn. Apparently General Fitz John Porter, as general in command of that part of the field, had in fact given Fowler orders to remain there to support another battery of artillery when it came forward. It fell upon another priest, Father James Dillon, to calm the men and convince them to obey O'Neil's orders.[46]

As night fell and darkness obliterated the lines of fire, Colonel Nugent of the 69th requested that his regiment be relieved "until such time as his overheated arms would be sufficiently cooled to render them efficient." Upon personally getting news of the situation to General Edwin Sumner, Meagher received permission to withdraw all the regiments of his brigade. Shortly after 9 P.M. on July 1 they left the field, ending the involvement of Meagher's Irish in the major peninsula battles.[47]

The peninsula battles had drastically reduced the Irish Brigade. The 69th New York alone had lost 222 men, killed, wounded, or missing after the battle. The 63rd and 88th New York combined lost 238 men.[48] On July 16, 1862, Major General McClellan ordered Meagher to New York to recruit. He urged Meagher to "use his utmost exertions to hasten the filling up of his regiments and to rejoin his command at the earliest possible moment," sending on squads of men as they were signed up.[49]

Even though Meagher had been called to New York to recruit, the Irish Brigade stayed on the peninsula in the vicinity of Harrison's Landing, sometimes encountering the enemy but not engaging in any meaningful combat. Around the middle of August the Army of the Potomac began its withdrawal from the peninsula. It had been within six miles of Richmond yet had not taken the Confederate capital.[50] Meagher's disenchanted troops shared the frustration of the rest of the Union Army as they marched through the decimated countryside. When the Irish Brigade passed back over some of the hard-won ground of the peninsula, they saw the devastation that the war had caused the South. With able-bodied men off to fight, only women and children were left to attend the crops. The little food that remained was taken by the "stragglers and bummers" of the Confederate Army when they took the retreating Union Army's place.[51]

From Harrison's Landing, Meagher marched to Newport News, where they were boarded onto boats and sent to a camp at Aquia Creek in Virginia on the Potomac. But McClellan could not make up his mind on how to use his brigade. "Meagher's brigade is still at Aquia," he wrote to Halleck. "If he moves in support of Franklin, it leaves us without any reliable troops in and near Washington. Yet Franklin is too weak alone."[52]

Camping only two days there, the brigade became involved in a series of meaningless movements that sent them first to Alexandria to their old campground at Camp California then immediately to Arlington Heights and next to the forward lines to support General John Pope to cover the Union's retreat from a second disastrous encounter at Bull Run. The brigade was soon on its way back to Aquia Creek and then turned around again to go by transport to Alexandria. Finally, a few days later, the brigade marched with Sumner's troops toward Rockville, Maryland, where they stopped for a while. Meagher was back from recruiting for some of this period, and during all of this movement the Irish Brigade and Meagher were not always prompt to respond to orders. When the call came on August 27 to make one of the movements, Meagher had trouble mobilizing his command, noticeably keeping two troop trains waiting until they were finally boarded and headed toward their destination hours late.[53]

Meagher had not done as well on his recruiting trip as he had been expected to, though he had tried his best. On July 25 Meagher spoke in the armory of the 7th Regiment, over Tomkins Market, pressuring his fellow Irishmen to join the Union Army. "I here this night call upon my countrymen . . . to throw themselves forward, and pledging themselves in life and death to it, to stand to the last by that noble little brigade," he called to ringing cheers and prolonged applause as he addressed the mass meeting of Irishmen. "Come, my countrymen, fling yourselves with a generous passion into the armed lines," he urged. "Come, my countrymen, one more effort, magnanimous and chivalrous, for the Republic. . . . Come my countrymen . . . as you exult in the gallantry of James Shields—and as you point with the highest pride to the staunch loyalty . . . of Michael Corcoran . . . you should emulate their example, as you are inspired by it." These words excited the crowd to a fever pitch and evoked tremendous cheering—but brought in many fewer recruits than Meagher had anticipated.[54]

When Samuel Barlow sent Meagher's recruiting speech to General McClellan, McClellan responded: "Much obliged to you for the copy of Meagher's speech—give him my regards & tell him that I am very anxious for his success—we want many more 'wild Irishmen.'"[55] But Meagher's fellow countrymen did not come into the Union Army as they had previously. Although he could point out the rise of James

Major General George Brinton McClellan. (Courtesy
Library of Congress)

Shields in America to the potential recruits, it had a hollow ring, because
the Senate had just turned down Shields's promotion to major general.
Meagher felt this was a slight to the Irish, and he picked up his pen to
complain to President Lincoln. "Recruits come in slow, though thousands upon thousands cheer me as I entreat and exhort them to rally
round and stand to the last by the Glorious Flag of the Union," Meagher
wrote. "The Irish-born citizens . . . are fiercely indignant at the action of
the Senate in regard to their gallant countryman, and keenly feel it as an
injustice to him, and an insult to them."[56] But Lincoln could do nothing.

Even more significantly, Meagher found that the mood of the Irish
in New York had shifted dramatically from the previous year. His
recruiting effort fell far short of the thousand men he expected.[57] In the
end, only three hundred new recruits left for the South aboard the *Key
West* after receiving an additional bounty of $10 each from the Produce
Exchange for a total of about $140 upon joining the brigade. With
them, in "tasteful gray uniform faced with green," was a new brigade
band to "cheer the tedium of camp life with some of the fine old music
of Fatherland, to which every true Celt is so passionately attached."[58]

Meagher returned to his brigade in August and awaited the next
battle with his few new soldiers. It would turn out to be the Battle of
Antietam, the bloodiest of the Civil War, and Meagher was in poor

condition to face it. The horrors of the peninsula campaign and the loss of many Irish troops had finally sunk in, chilling his ardor. Any thought that Meagher had of returning to New York as a victorious leader after a short war had quickly disappeared after the failure of the North to take Richmond. He knew also that more fatalities among his native Irishmen would be certain. These undeniable truths would test the mettle of any man, and Thomas Francis Meagher, the classically educated Irishman who wrote poetry and only wanted equality for his country-men, was deeply disturbed. In the face of these fatalities, he began to drink more and more frequently, no doubt supported in his "unfortunate habit" by the prevalent heavy drinking among both enlisted men and officers during the Civil War.

On September 4, 1862, General Robert E. Lee made the first incur-sion of his Army of Northern Virginia onto Union soil as he crossed the Potomac River at Harper's Ferry and proceeded North toward Pennsylvania. By September 5 Lieutenant General Henry Halleck had General McClellan in pursuit of Lee; Meagher's brigade, under command of General Sumner, commander of the second corps, marched through Maryland, entering Frederick on September 12.[59]

Two days later, on September 14, while the Irish Brigade was encamped about a mile outside of Frederick, Meagher received orders to proceed immediately to the support of General Hooker, who was at the time hotly engaged with the enemy to the west of Frederick in the passes of South Mountain. The brigade made "a rapid and exhausting march over the rocky hills and through the tangled woods from their encampment." But then, "owing to the favorable reports from the head-quarters of General Hooker, the brigade had an hour or so to take rest and refreshment."[60]

By the time Meagher's refreshed troops reached the South Moun-tain battlefields, the Confederates had been put to retreat. According to Meagher, "the Irish Brigade had the honor of leading the pursuit of the rebels from South Mountain through Boonsborough and Keedysville." This took the brigade to Antietam Creek, where the Confederates were positioned on the other side, "drawn up in line of battle on the heights near Sharpsburg and overlooking the Antietam." Quickly the "brigade was halted and deployed in line of battle to the right and left of the Sharpsburg turnpike, the Eighty-eighth and Sixty-third Regiments New

York Volunteers being on the left of the road and the Sixty-ninth New York Volunteers and the Twenty-ninth Massachusetts Volunteers being on the right."[61] Lieutenant Colonel James J. Smith of the 69th reported that on September 16 and 17, before being called to battle, his regiment with the brigade "was posted as a support to the Twenty Pound Gun Battery, that was in position on the knoll on the right of the Sharpsburg Road, on the East side of Antietam Creek."[62]

Even though they were "protected by the hill on the slope of which they lay," the Irish Brigade's regiments were shelled by artillery and "lost several good men even in this comparatively safe position." The brigade had to remain there until the morning of September 17, "when, the men having breakfasted, a sudden order came for the brigade to fall in under arms, and take up the line of march." The moment was now at hand for the Irish Brigade under Meagher's leadership to proceed across Antietam Creek to the battlefield to confront the Confederate enemy.[63]

Following the lead of Major General Israel B. Richardson, their division commander, Meagher and the Irish Brigade proceeded north less than a mile and crossed the creek at Pry Ford.[64] Leander M. Vaughan was with Company E of the 29th Massachusetts and described the initial movement of Meagher's troops on September 18 toward the ultimate battle. "There was no bridge, our pontoons were a long way in the rear, so we had to wade with the water about to our waist, lifting the cartridge boxes to keep the am[m]unition dry, going up out of the water directly into battle," Vaughan said.[65] From there the division proceeded about one mile in a southwesterly direction toward the Roulette Farm, which was only a short distance from a hill, over which the sounds of battle came.

Meagher said he and his troops were "following the lead of Major-General Richardson, who conducted the brigade to the field of battle, under cover of the rising ground and depression which intervened between us and the enemy." Arriving at a cornfield, Richardson ordered the soldiers to drop "everything but the cartouch-boxes," a command that Meagher said was "instantly obeyed . . . with a heartiness and enthusiasm which it was rare to expect from men who had been wearied and worn by the unremitting labors of a nine months' campaign." Deploying his brigade into a line, Meagher proceeded across the field, only to have his troops confronted by a fence. His men became targets of the Confederate fire as they topped it. "I had the misfortune to lose the services

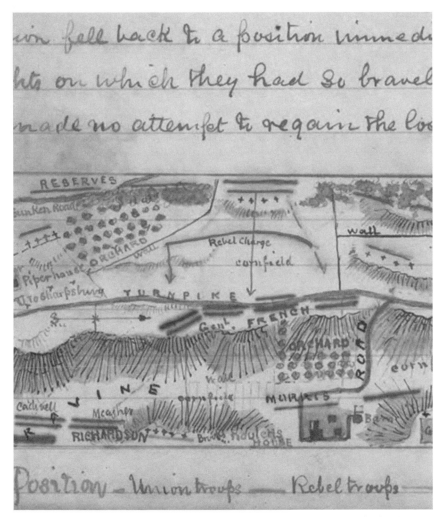

Sketch showing Meagher's forces at Antietam. This sketch on the bottom of a handwritten report shows the position of Meagher's Brigade in the lower left near the Roulette house close to the sunken road, which is marked as a turnpike on the sketch. (Courtesy Library of Congress)

of many good officers and brave men," he said. Despite these early losses, the brigade continued forward to face the enemy "within 300 paces of our line" with a "clover field of about two acres interposed."[66]

"[T]he enemy was drawn up," Meagher reported, "and . . . from their double front they had delivered and sustained a fire before which Sedgwick's forces on the right and French's on the left were reported at the time momentarily to have given way." But Meagher was convinced that "owing to some reason which as yet has not been explained, the Irish Brigade had to occupy and hold a gap in the line of the Union army, which the enemy perceiving had flung a formidable column to break through, and so take the two divisions last named on their flank and rear." His regiments took the charge head-on, and the movement of the enemy through the Union battle lines was checked "by the impetuous advance of the Irish Brigade, which in a great measure filling up the gap through which the rebel column was descending to the rear of the Federal lines, drew up in line of battle within 50 paces of the enemy." Meagher was able to add proudly: "Never were men in higher spirits. Never did men with such alacrity and generosity of heart press forward and encounter the perils of the battle-field."[67]

Private Henry H. Robbins from Plymouth, Massachusetts, who was a soldier in the non-Irish 29th Massachusetts, was nevertheless proud of his Irish comrades as they approached the enemy. "We marched to within about five hundred yards of the enemy and halted," as he reported it. "The rebels saw the green flag of our Irish Brigade, and knew that Brigade was coming in, and immediately formed a whole division in our front." Meagher's description of the enthusiasm of the Irish was echoed by Private Robbins: "As soon as we were ready we started at 'charge bayonets' and halted within about 100 yards of their lines and poured into them. The effect was awful. Our poor fellows fell like grass all along the lines; but the fall of the enemy was yet more awful. Their killed and wounded lay in piles one [sic] top of another. . . . We went round after the battle and piled up the dead rebels. They looked like a lot of haystacks."[68] In the meantime, as the battle had raged on, Private John Dillon, the color guard of the 63rd New York, was hit by the enemy but stayed on the field, aware of the honor and responsibility of maintaining both the Stars and Stripes and the "Green colors" in front of the regiment during battle. "When we were relieved I was not able to walk out, wea[k]ness from the loss of blood," Dillon said.[69]

Meagher had been ordered to fire only two volleys and then follow it up with a bayonet charge. Instead he permitted his brigade to fire five or six times before he "personally ordered them to charge upon the rebel columns." Meagher said he was "relying on the impetuosity and recklessness of Irish soldiers in a charge" and that he "felt confident that

before such a charge the rebel column would give way and be dispersed."
But the tactic did not work. He had to admit that the Confederate fire
"literally cut lanes through our approaching line." When the brigade was
"within 30 paces of the enemy," Lieutenant Colonel James Kelly was
shot in the face; and Captain Felix Duffy fell dead in front of his troops.
The Irishmen could go no farther, but they maintained their ground
until relieved by another brigade.[70]

Toward the end of the brigade's battle, Meagher was suddenly thrown
from his horse and carried from the battlefield. "My horse having been
shot under me as the engagement was about ending, and from the shock
which I myself sustained, I was obliged to be carried off the field," he
explained. But the incident set off a storm of controversy: allegations of
drunkenness were again leveled at Meagher, despite his involvement in
the success of the Irish Brigade at Antietam. Nowhere is this more
evident than in the report of Colonel David H. Strother, a member of
General McClellan's staff, who observed the charge of the Irish Brigade
and noted: "On the center General . . . Richardson and . . . Meagher
moved in handsomely and joined battle. The fire became tremendous.
Our troops advanced, wavered, broke, and fled, then rallied and advanced
again, leaving the earth strewed with blue jackets." Strother observed
that after the Rebels had advanced and were turned back by Sumner's
troops, the "Irish brigade made a gallant rush on the center and forced
the enemy back behind" its artillery battery.[71] The following day Strother
noted in his diary: "Meagher was not killed as reported, but drunk, and
fell from his horse."[72] General McClellan confirmed that Meagher's
horse had been shot and so did General Hancock, but neither said he
was drunk.[73] Meagher's conduct was lauded by Major General Edwin
Sumner, his corps commander, who credited Meagher for his zeal and
devotion along with a number of other general and staff officers.[74]

Meagher's heroic bravery in leading the charge at Antietam was widely
reported in the New York newspapers. Whitelaw Reid of the *Cincinnati
Gazette,* however, who was in Washington and not at Antietam at the time,
spread a damaging story. He reported:

> The General in question . . . was not in the charge at all!—did
> not lead or follow it! He was too drunk to keep the saddle, fell
> from his horse . . . several times, was once assisted to remount

by Gen. Kimball of Indiana, almost immediately fell off again, was too stupidly drunk to answer the simplest question Gen. Kimball put to him about the disposition of his brigade, and was finally taken up on a stretcher, covered with a cloth, and carried off the field—the bearers circulating the story as they went that Gen. Meagher was dangerously wounded.[75]

There is no apparent record of General Nathan Kimball himself ever accusing Meagher of being drunk at Antietam. Frederick Hitchcock, however, an adjutant to the Pennsylvania 132nd Volunteers, who had just been mustered into the army on August 22, 1862, claimed: "Just as we were moving back, the Irish brigade came up, under the command of General Thomas Francis Meagher." According to Hitchcock, "Meagher rode a beautiful white horse, but made a show of himself by tumbling off just as he reached our line. The boys said he was drunk, and he certainly looked and acted like a drunken man." He said that Meagher "regained his feet and floundered about, swearing like a crazy man." But Hitchcock made no mention of Kimball having interrogated Meagher and put him back on his horse, and his source of information seems to have been "the boys."[76]

Whether true or not, the tales of Meagher being drunk at Antietam never did die down. Many months after the event, after Meagher had resigned from the army, T. C. Grey, a *New York Tribune* correspondent, wrote to Sydney Howard Gay, managing editor, regarding planned surveillance of the battle areas in Virginia from a balloon. He gratuitously stated that Meagher had been drunk at Chancellorsville and that "[a]t Antietam I myself saw him carried from the field in a beastly state of inebriation. I state this thinking that possibly you have never heard facts in relation to Meagher."[77] Perhaps the biggest flaw in the credibility of the reports of Grey, Hitchcock, Strother, and Reid is that not one of them reported that Meagher had actually been seen drinking. And not one of them allowed that Meagher might have suffered a blow to the head when he fell and that his behavior might have been due to a concussion, which could have been mistaken for drunkenness.[78] But there is also no doubt that Meagher drank to excess on many occasions.

On November 9 a young private named William McCarter of the Irish Brigades' recently joined Pennsylvania 116th was serving as Meagher's secretary and noted in his memoirs how he saved Meagher from being badly burned one night when he almost stumbled into a fire. Meagher was "very drunk," according to McCarter. Despite that, Meagher would always be a hero to McCarter and "was one of the very few military leaders who never required or would ask any of his command to go where he would not go himself."[79] There would always be a dichotomy between the views of Meagher's detractors, who were quick to report him drunk in battle, and the views of his supporters, who were equally quick to proclaim his steadiness and bravery in battle. As the target of the charge of drunkenness, Meagher joined an elite group of prominent generals that included Ulysses S. Grant and Joseph Hooker. In fact the same Frederick Hitchcock accused Hooker, again relying on statements that he claimed were made by a third person.[80] Rightly or wrongly, these reports set off a storm of controversy about Meagher. No one reported seeing him drinking, but some who were disposed to a critical view of Meagher and the Irish quickly adopted the allegations as fact and spread them.

The Reverend John H. W. Stuckenberg was the Methodist chaplain of the newly formed Pennsylvania 145th, which was temporarily assigned to the Irish Brigade just after Antietam. Stuckenberg had not even met Meagher at the time, but he had already formed a prejudiced opinion. "[T]he general—Meagher . . . is very profane and I am told frequently gets beastly drunk," Stuckenberg said. "At one of the battles they say (At Antietam I believe) he was so drunk that he fell from his horse." Stuckenberg at that time detested the Irish. "The very fact of being placed in an Irish brigade was very displeasing to us . . . . [T]he Irishmen in this brigade are rough, a week ago yesterday many were drunk." All of this was written before Stuckenberg got to know Meagher; when he did, he had a different view. Some months later, when he was encamped near Falmouth, Virginia, Stuckenberg wrote about Meagher: "There is something dashing, spirited, proud and dignified in Gen. Meagher. He dresses finely and rides well and the very finest horses. He is calculated to excite admiration, rather than love; and the men will obey him because they fear him, rather than because they love him." Meagher was no longer the vile drunk that Stuckenberg had described a few months ago, and experience had shown him another side of the general. "To me he was always kind," the minister concluded.[81]

The drinking controversy aside, in the Battle of Antietam, the Irish Brigade had seen its most intense action—and the results were disastrous. Of the slightly under 1,000 men of the three Irish regiments from New York that were part of the brigade that went into battle that day, 512 were lost. The day before the battle the brigade had received a number of recruits, eager to fight. At the end of the battle 75 of them lay dead or wounded on the field. What had once been a proud brigade had been quickly whittled down to the strength of a regiment in one day and less than two months later would be reduced to a battalion.[82]

The diminished brigade was not again called to action at Antietam, but Meagher himself was given a strange duty the day after the main battle, on September 18. After Confederate sharpshooters had fired upon the Union troops since early morning, a Confederate flag of truce appeared on the battlefield in the afternoon. It was immediately reported to Brigadier General Winfield S. Hancock of the U.S. Army, then commanding the 1st Division of the 2nd Army Corps. Upon learning that Confederate General Roger A. Pryor appeared to be part of the party carrying the flag, Hancock summoned Meagher to meet with Pryor and learn of his wishes. It turned out that they were not calling for a truce. The whole matter had been arranged by the pickets of the two armies on an informal basis for the purpose of removing the wounded, some of whom had been lying on the ground for thirty hours. According to Pryor's wife, Sara Agnes Pryor, her husband was at the time approached by a "Federal officer," who said: "General, I have just detected one of my men in robbing the body of one of your soldiers. I have taken his booty from him, and now consign it to you."[83] Soon after Meagher and Pryor met, however, another flag of truce appeared from the Confederate side, and Meagher was again called upon to meet the bearer. This time it turned out to be a Confederate lieutenant colonel coming to collect the wounded and bury the dead, until he was also notified that there was no truce. Hostilities commenced again in a few minutes.[84] Finally, a real truce was called. It produced the strange scene captured by artist Alfred T. Waud for *Harper's Weekly*, showing Confederate and Union soldiers mingled together near the Dunker church as they went about the grim work of removing their dead and wounded.[85]

Despite its huge losses, the Army of the Potomac was victorious at Antietam but did not risk renewing the attack with its diminished

"The Truce at Antietam," by Alfred T. Waud. (Courtesy Library of Congress)

forces. Confederate General Robert E. Lee and his army fell back across the Potomac and entrenched there. In late October Meagher's brigade crossed the Potomac and encamped at Bolivar Heights in Virginia—a scenic spot a little above the junction of the Shenandoah and the Potomac and Harper's Ferry. Soon the men were able to put the loss of their comrades aside at least momentarily and amuse themselves from day to day with races and evening parties. Because the camp was within fifty to sixty miles of Washington, Elizabeth Meagher was able to visit. After she met Father Corby there, he remarked that she was a "lady of marked character and possessed of more than an ordinary degree of refinement and excellent social virtues."[86]

On November 2 the brigade broke camp at Bolivar Heights and marched southeast toward the gaps of the Blue Ridge Mountains. Upon reaching Warrenton, Virginia, Meagher found out that General McClellan had been relieved of his command of the Army of the Potomac and replaced by General Ambrose Burnside. Many in the Irish Brigade mourned the event, and on November 9 Meagher issued an order for the Irish Brigade to "assemble under arms, with overcoats and without knapsacks, precisely at 6 o'clock A.M., so that your command may be fully prepared to receive and greet . . . General McClellan, who has been, for so many months, the earnest, indefatigable, upright, generous, the highly gifted, . . . the patriotic chief of the Army."[87] A new commander meant a change of plans and left the Irish Brigade entirely unsure of their ultimate destination. It also left Meagher without the benefit of the relationship between McClellan and Meagher's brother-in-law, Samuel Barlow. Meagher had never asked McClellan for personal favors, however, and McClellan had never shown favoritism to Meagher or his brigade, instead sending them into the teeth of battle on each opportunity. Under Burnside nothing really changed for Meagher and the Irish Brigade. They ended up in Falmouth on the north bank of the Rappahannock opposite Fredericksburg. There they "settled down in earnest; built log huts, roofed them with tents, and built chimneys of sticks and mud—for here was plenty of mud," according to Father Corby.[88]

In the meantime the Confederates were massing on the hills behind Fredericksburg, actively building fortifications for their infantry and putting their heavy artillery in position. In early December the Union Army constructed a pontoon bridge across the river, and it became apparent to all the soldiers that they would soon be asked to face the "grape and canister, and the tens of thousands of muskets, well protected behind the carefully constructed breastworks."[89] Uranus Stacy of the 27th Maine infantry observed that "Meagher rode among the ranks, and was cheered tremendously. He is a fine looking man."[90] On Thursday, December 11, at precisely 7:00 A.M., the Irish Brigade left camp and proceeded toward the Rappahannock to a "well-sheltered valley." Once there, "the fire of our batteries and those of the enemy, incessant and terrible as it was, taught every man of the brigade to prepare himself equably and sternly for a desperate conflict." Resting overnight, Meagher and the brigade proceeded onward the next day to a position close to Fredericksburg. The men halted, "ankle-deep in mud, and with little or nothing to contribute to their comfort." They knew they were going to cross into Fredericksburg the next day, and Meagher reported that his "officers and men laid down and slept that night in the mud and frost, and, without a murmur, with heroic hearts composed themselves as best as they could for the eventualities of the coming day."[91] They awoke to the "roll of the drum at five A.M." Orders had been given to cross over the Rappahannock on the upper pontoon bridge to join the Union troops that "had crossed the previous evening and night, numbering

probably 20 or 25 thousand men." At "half past ten A.M." the brigade
took its place in the mass of Union troops. Marching four abreast at the
"[d]ouble quick," the Irish Brigade—constantly under fire from Confederate batteries only roughly a mile away—descended the "open face
of the hill down which" they had to go to reach the upper pontoon
bridge leading to Fredericksburg.[92] The crossing was perilous, but the
brigade finally reached the streets of Fredericksburg. Sometimes under
fire, the Irish Brigade bedded down in the area just south of the Middle
Bridge near the wharf on Water Street for the night, but few slept,
knowing that they were "not over probably . . . 1000 yards from the
enemy's front" and that they would be going into battle the next day.[93]

The next morning, Saturday, December 13, was the awful day of the
Battle of Fredericksburg. Meagher's troops were aroused before sun-up
by Confederate shells bursting in the middle of the Rappahannock
on whose banks they lay. Shortly after breakfast McCarter noted that
"volley after volley of musketry broke upon our ears, as if proceeding
from the Confederate works on Marye's Heights behind the town."
They knew that this was "[t]he very place, as we were soon given to
understand, which was to be assaulted by Hancock's entire division," of
which the Irish Brigade was a part. The men could not see the battle,
because it was blocked by the buildings of Fredericksburg and a low
uprising of the land. From the roar and din of continuous musket and
artillery fire, however, they knew that "French's division was now engaged
in real earnest," as the musket fire increased to "one long unceasing roll
and roar of death and destruction" and the "smell of burning powder
almost suffocated us."

When the firing finally ceased for a time, McCarter thought for a few
minutes that it was possible that "our boys" had "taken the coveted
heights." But this was not to be. "A few minutes more told the tale of the
terrible defeat and retreat of the gallant French with scarce half of his
men." The other half were "dead, wounded and dying on the battle
ground immediately in front of Marye's Heights." A little later, reality set
in as Hancock, "[i]n a voice like thunder, . . . gave the order to the [Irish
Brigade], 'Fall in.'" Next came Meagher with the same order. "The troops
were soon in line with loaded muskets, anxiously awaiting further orders."
Meagher appeared again on horseback with two orderlies, "bearing in

their arms large bunches of green boxwood." Sprigs of the boxwood were stuck in the caps of the men, to identify them to their comrades and to the enemy as Irish, and the brigade was now ready for battle.[94]

As Meagher addressed his troops and encouraged them to go bravely into battle, three men of the 63rd were hit and killed and—as "mere masses of blood and rags—were borne along the line."[95] McCarter observed General Meagher "again in the distance at the head of the column, waving his glittering sword overhead." Finally the order to advance was given, and the brigade "headed up the street to the other end of the town, our route to the point to be assaulted on Marye's Heights."[96]

"The Brigade, . . . by regiments about 10 yards apart, marched steadily onward amid this terrible rain of fire and death, till arriving at the other end of the town," McCarter wrote. The route selected had been north up Water Street to George Street and thence West until George joined Hanover Street, continuing on to the battlefield. While marching, it was observed that "[c]annon balls and shells were now flying faster than ever, and dropping thick in every part of Fredericksburg, crashing through roofs, windows and walls." Finally, upon nearing the stone wall that sheltered the Confederate infantry, "that most terrible military command, 'Fix Bayonets[,]'" was given. Although this was done with "the yells and cheers of the men," the bayonets would never be used, because none of the troops got that close to the enemy.[97]

The men encountered obstacles along the way to the battlefield, including board fences and "a canal, probably 4 or 5 yards wide" that had to be crossed. But perhaps the most demoralizing obstacles along the way were the dead and wounded of French's defeated division, which littered the battlefield. "The ground on top of the embankment was literally covered with dead Union soldiers of French's Division, shot down while attempting to cross it," McCarter reported.[98] Those of French's command who could had withdrawn; now the time had come for Meagher and his Irish Brigade to take their place. Father Corby said that "the place into which Meagher's brigade was sent was simply a slaughter–pen."[99]

As the Irish Brigade was advancing out of Fredericksburg, Meagher dismounted from his horse, leaving it with an orderly, and proceeded on foot with his troops. He would have preferred to stay mounted, because he had a very painful sore on his knee that made it difficult to

The Stone Wall. This 1886 etching accurately depicts Confederate infantry sheltered behind the famous stone wall below Marye's Heights at Fredericksburg on December 13, 1862. (Courtesy Library of Congress)

advance on foot, as all of the battle officers had been ordered to do by General Hancock. Meagher struggled forward and with the aid of two wounded soldiers crossed the mill race. Advancing over the dead and dying bodies of French's troops, the brigade took about half an hour to assemble into a line facing the enemy, with Meagher arranging the order of his regiments and relaying orders to Colonel Nugent of the 69th to throw out two companies as skirmishers. As the regiments were forming into a line of battle, they drew down still more fire upon themselves. Finally, on Meagher's order, the line advanced at the double-quick against the artillery batteries of the enemy until they came in range of the rifle pits behind the stone wall.[100]

According to Colonel Patrick Kelly, commanding the 88th New York, the Irish "formed [a] line of battle . . . between the hours of 10 and 11 A.M., as near as I can judge." Marching "by the right flank," they crossed "the mill-race on a single bridge, where we filed to the right and reformed [a] line of battle under a terrific enfilading artillery fire from the enemy."[101]

Captain Patrick J. Condon, commander of the 63rd New York Infantry, reported that at the outset of the advance he "passed by General Meagher here, waving his sword and closing us in."[102] The Irish hero-ically kept up the advance until a board fence temporarily stopped them. As they crawled over the fence, they became sitting ducks for the fire that burst in their faces out of the Confederate rifle pits. With most of the troops stopped, Colonel Robert Nugent, Meagher's best battle officer, kept on until he was badly wounded. Major William Horgan lumbered forward toward the stone wall by himself until he was killed.[103] The 116th Pennsylvania was assigned to the left flank of the Irish Brigade. Its commander, Colonel Dennis Heenan, was wounded during the battle. Command was taken by Lieutenant Colonel St. Clair Mulholland, who was also wounded. The 28th Massachusetts was in the middle of the Irish Brigade's line; Peter Welsh, its color sergeant, writing to his wife on December 25, told how "our troops had to lay down to escap[e] the raking fire of the batteries and we had but a poor chance at the enemy who was sheltered in his rifel [sic] pits and entrenchments." Welsh, who had "seen some hot work at south mountain and Ant[i]etam," said that "they were not to be compared to this," where "every man that was near me in the right of the company was either killed or wounded."[104] In the meantime Kelly and his 88th, now on the other side of the mill race, "advanced in line of battle under a most galling and destructive infantry fire." They were soon confronted by another obstacle: they "crossed two fences, and proceeded as far as the third fence." There his men "maintained their position until their ammunition was exhausted, and more than one-half of the regiment killed and wounded." Faced with undeniable devastation, Kelly and Colonel Richard Byrnes of the 28th Massachusetts met and agreed in desperation "to go over the field and collect the remnants of our regiments, which we did, meeting in the valley near the mill-race."[105]

McCarter described how the Irish Brigade "reached the top of the hill, and the level ground, within 200 yards of the first line of Rebel Rifle Pits, and a long stone wall running close across their front, . . . where a blinding fire of musketry met them in the face, and which for but a few seconds, staggered the line." Parts of the brigade advanced until they had "gained, to within about 50 paces of this wall," but they were repulsed when a Confederate brigade, "said to have been then 2,400 strong, suddenly sprung up from behind it . . . , and pouring volley after volley in our faces, at once stopped our further progress." Meagher, "who at this time, was on the extreme left of his Command, seeing the very critical position of his men, the terrible slaughter that was being made among them, with no prospect of success, ordered the 5 regiments of his Brigade . . . to be closely massed together in double line of battle." Meagher gave the command: "Load, and Fire at Will," and his brigade made another brave attempt against the enemy. According to McCarter, "A few moments after, [Meagher] was very severely wounded himself, in the thigh, by a cannon ball, and carried off of the field." That was the last time McCarter ever saw him, being wounded himself shortly after.[106]

Whether Meagher's wound was due to being hit by the enemy or was the same injury he already had as he entered battle, he had to quit before the battle was over. General Hancock acknowledged that Meagher had "led his brigade to the field under a heavy fire; but, owing to a serious lameness, making it difficult for him to either ride or walk, he was unable to bear that prominently active part which is usual with him." As his command moved toward the enemy, Meagher himself was forced to hobble back through the crowded field of dead and wounded toward

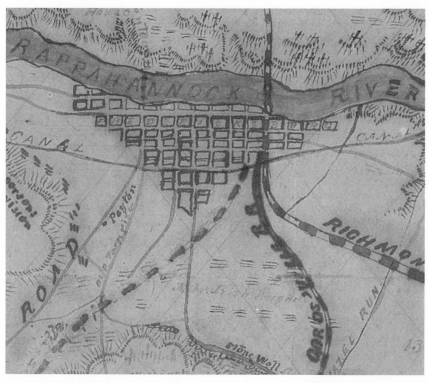

Meagher's Irish Brigade at Fredericksburg before the stone wall at Marye's Heights. This hand-drawn contemporaneous map shows in light markings the position of "Meagher's Irish Brigade" close to the stone wall at the Battle of Fredericksburg on December 13, 1862. The map bears the inscription "To James G. McCabe, Jr, from his friend James W. B." and the initials "JWB" as well as the handwritten date "1863." (Courtesy Library of Congress)

Fredericksburg to get his horse. Reaching the streets of Fredericksburg, he found his mount and started to rejoin the brigade.[107]

The 63rd and the 69th were also decimated and forced to retreat. As Meagher, now mounted on his horse, proceeded up a Fredericksburg street to return to the battle, he "almost at once was confronted" with their remnants. Meagher halted the men and remained with them in a spot where he could view the ongoing battle. At that time he had been commanded to fall back to the street from which the brigade had started "in order that their cartridge boxes might be refilled," according to Hancock's report. From that spot Meagher viewed the battle and became fearful that the Confederates might break through the Union line and come toward Fredericksburg. He also became convinced that the brigade's hospitals "were dangerously, if not fatally, exposed."[108] Meagher sent two officers to General Hancock with a request that he be allowed to retreat across the river with what was left of his brigade. After taking a quick count, he had concluded that the Irish Brigade had been essentially destroyed, with less than three hundred members still useful, and even some of them were maimed. His concern now was the survival of his remaining troops. He did not have enough troops to be available for further battle, but he had to have enough able-bodied men to assist the badly disabled. "I was solely actuated by an affectionate and intense concern for the wounded officers and soldiers of my command," Meagher later explained when his decision came under criticism.[109]

Finally, as shells and rifle balls threatened the hospitals of the 63rd, the 69th, and the 88th, one of Meagher's officers returned from General Hancock and gave Meagher the mistaken impression that he had been authorized to remove his brigade from the city, which he did. "I did so under the impression that Brigadier-General Hancock had given me such authorization, . . . which impression, a few hours later, I discovered was erroneous. I should not, however, have brought over my command to the opposite side of the river, nor have dreamed of asking permission to do so, but for the horrible accidents to which the wounded of the brigade were exposed." A few days later Hancock had an opportunity to read Meagher's report of his actions and concluded that Meagher had "candidly and fully explained" the event.[110] At the time when he found out that Meagher had crossed the river, however, Hancock was not happy, and he said that those were circumstances "I very much regretted at the time." Hancock ordered Meagher to return to battle. But when Meagher complied the next morning, in place of his brigade were only about 280 men able enough to return across the Rappahannock to Fredericksburg. "This little band," Meagher said, "unswerved and unde-terred, still full of heart, inspired by a bright sense of duty, sorrowful for their comrades, but prouder and still more emboldened that such men had fallen bravely as they did, awaited the word that was once again to precipitate them against the batteries and defenses of the enemy."[111]

The Battle of Fredericksburg was over for the Irish Brigade. It was time for Meagher to make a cold assessment of the damage to his Irish countrymen and the benefits to his American country. To be sure, the

Irish had gained respect, even from at least one Englishman; as a *London Times* correspondent with the Confederate Army observed, "never . . . was more undoubted courage displayed by the sons of Erin than during those six frantic dashes which they directed against the almost impregnable position of their foe."[112] Despite the controversy that surrounded his withdrawal from the battle, Meagher's own reputation in high places was enhanced by the telegram that Anson Stager sent to Edwin Stanton on the day of the battle, saying that "Gen Meagher of the Irish Brigade had his horse shot from under him but he is in front of his men cheering them on."[113]

The losses to the brigade were incomprehensible, leaving Meagher not only devastated but angry. He vowed not to let his remaining troops sink into depression. When a new flag for the Irish Brigade arrived the day after the battle, it gave him an opportunity for a commemoration (it could not be called a celebration under the circumstances). On Monday, December 15, only two days after the brigade's suicidal charge on Marye's Heights, biographer and friend Michael Cavanagh reported that Meagher had assembled his men at a small theater in Fredericksburg for what became known as the "Death Feast." There, amid the noise of a continuing Confederate bombardment, Cavanagh describes an elaborate banquet, complete with viands cooked in neighboring houses and served by a crew of military waiters. According to Cavanagh, "those guests who looked below the surface, soon discovered a deeper and nobler cause" for the banquet. "For what time could be more opportune for giving public expression to the feelings of bitter indignation against the political partizanship [sic] which drenched the neighboring fields with the blood of the nation's best and bravest defenders?"[114] Though Meagher's full speech on the occasion was never published, according to Cavanagh it "gave expression to the out-spoken sentiments, not only of his own command, but of the army and the people of the loyal States." Cavanagh cited the words of an unnamed officer of the Irish Brigade who at the time of Fredericksburg was an invalid in New York: "May God visit as He will, with a just judgment, the man or men who caused so much good, true, loyal blood to be shed in vain; so many brave children of the people to be led up to slaughter, to destruction, to the coldest blooded murder."[115]

Given the decimation of the town of Fredericksburg and the number of dead and wounded on the streets, the scene that Cavanagh paints of a fine banquet is so surreal that one wonders whether it could actually have occurred, at least in Fredericksburg. Father Corby and David Power Conyngham do not mention it in their reminiscences. Lieutenant Colonel St. Clair Mulholland of the 116th Pennsylvania, however, said that it did occur, on December 14 rather than December 15, with an early adjournment being ordained by a shell "passing through the ceiling of the room" and knocking "the plaster down among the viands."[116] It is clear that Meagher had been involved in what the army command would likely consider a protest, and it would become his undoing in the Union Army.

After receiving a medical leave, Meagher prepared to return to New York to recuperate. "I am quite safe with the exception of a bruised knee," he wrote his wife, Elizabeth, on December 17. But he could not leave yet: "I am remaining for the present with what is left of my noble Brigade," but he would return home "as soon as my wounded are cared for."[117] In the meantime Elizabeth and her family anxiously awaited word of Meagher; and Samuel Barlow wrote to him: "If you have again escaped unharmed we shall conclude you bear a charmed life as from all accounts your Brigade has been fearfully cut up in the performance of its usual duty on the battle field." Barlow added that he saw General McClellan in New York on a daily basis: "he often speaks of your Brave Brigade & of yourself."[118]

On Christmas Day a somber Meagher reached New York in company with the embalmed remains of Major William Horgan, whose bullet-torn body had been recovered from the battlefield at the spot of farthest advance. The Irish claimed that his position within twenty-five paces of the stone wall was the farthest advance of the entire Union Army. The major's casket was taken to the headquarters of the Irish Brigade at 596 Broadway and remained there for two days until it was moved to the City Hall for another day before burial. Having taken care of all the arrangements required of him, Meagher limped home to celebrate Christmas with his wife. He was still an invalid and remained in New York for a few weeks under a surgeon's care.[119]

CHAPTER SEVEN

A General without a Command

> I did not absolve myself of my obligations . . . from which death alone
> can free us.
>
> Thomas Francis Meagher, June 16, 1863

On February 12, 1863, Thomas Francis Meagher walked out of the executive mansion in Washington, satisfied that he had obtained promotions for some of his brigade commanders. He had just had a personal meeting with President Abraham Lincoln to appeal for promotions for Colonels Robert Nugent and Patrick Kelly. Lincoln had listened carefully and then wrote to Henry Halleck, the commander in chief of the army: "Gen. Meagher, now with me, says the Irish Brigade has had no promotion," noting that both Nugent and Kelly held regular army grades as captains.[1]

Before going to Washington, Meagher had been on medical leave in New York, recuperating from his knee injury. "I find that he is suffering from a 'Furunculous Abscess' of the left knee, which quite disables him for active duty in the field . . . to prevent loss of life or permanent disability," Dr. Francis Reynolds, the chief medical officer of Hancock's Division at Fredericksburg, reported on December 15, when he recommended a twenty-day medical leave for Meagher. On January 11 Dr. William Edgar noted that Meagher was "suffering from a wound over the left knee joint." On February 3 Edgar reported that he was "still suffering from the results of a wound over the left knee joint" and that he was unfit for duty for an additional ten days.[2] Meagher's absence from the army was so long that his file in the War Department noted that he was "absent without leave." Meagher enclosed Edgar's last certificate in a letter he wrote from 129 Fifth Avenue to the "Adjutant General, U.S.A.," advising that on February 11 he would report to Major General John E. Wool "in person at the War Department" and that he had previously notified Wool in person of "my presence and stay in this city." He added that Wool had "signified his approval of my remaining here until I was sufficiently recovered to enable me to resume my duties in the field."[3]

Now recovered enough to rejoin his troops, and after what he thought was a successful meeting with Lincoln, Meagher headed for Falmouth. But his spirits sank upon his arrival when he had to make a grim assessment of the strength and condition of his Irishmen and found the brigade to be in deplorable shape. The men had fought heroically on the front lines, and their decimation was a measure of their bravery. Out of the 2,250 members of the original 69th, 88th, and 63rd Regiments who had left New York in late 1861, Meagher had only a little over 600 men left. Adding in the remaining members of the 116th Pennsylvania and 28th Massachusetts, the total brigade now had only 139 officers and 1,058 enlisted men.

The demoralizing numbers prompted Meagher on February 19, 1863, to write directly to secretary of war Edwin Stanton, advising him that "the Brigade has ceased to be a Brigade, and hardly exhibits the numerical strength which qualifies it for a higher designation than that of a Colonel's command. . . . I do most respectfully and earnestly beg that the three original regiments of the Brigade . . . be temporarily relieved from duty in the field; and, being so relieved, have the opportunity of restoring, in some serviceable measure, their exhausted ranks." Meagher pointed out to Stanton that such a privilege had been granted previously: "decimated regiments from Maine, Massachusetts and Connecticut have been ordered home." He asked "no more for what is left of . . . [the] brave officers and men than that which has been conceded to other commands, exhibiting equal labors, equal sacrifices, and equal decimation." He acknowledged that asking for a temporary leave in the middle of the war could put the reputation of the Irish and his own

General T. F. Meagher U.S.A. This is the title given to this photograph in the files of the Library of Congress, where it forms part of the Civil War glass negative collection. (Courtesy Library of Congress)

reputation at risk; however, he explained, "Doing your duty to your men . . . oftentimes demands a resolution higher far in a moral estimation than that which the orders delivered on the eve of battle exact."[4]

Meagher had every reason to believe he would receive a prompt response from Stanton. The two men were not close friends, but they knew each other well from the time when they had served together as co-counsel at the murder trial of Daniel Sickles in 1856, where they had mounted a successful defense. Stanton ignored the request, however.[5] Meagher did not foresee, but Stanton may have appreciated all too well, that the Irish, and for that matter the nation, had become increasingly disenchanted with the war, and the risk of desertion while on leave was high. Stanton may have also taken offense at Meagher's statements given at the "Death Feast" in Fredericksburg, which to him smacked of defiance.

Not hearing from Stanton, Meagher decided to pursue political avenues that he thought were available to him as a leading Irishman and to force the army's hand. On February 26 he made a formal request to the army. According to Meagher, his request to withdraw "the three old regiments of my Brigade" had already been approved "by the General Commanding the Army of the Potomac, after it had been previously approved by the intermediate Generals," with the condition that "a Regiment outside the Army of the Potomac, and at least equaling the numerical force" of the regiments to be withdrawn would be "sent to replace the latter." He now requested a leave of absence to visit Washington "so as to facilitate the fulfillment of the condition." As Meagher explained, "Congress adjourns in less than a week, and the undersigned respectfully submits that his proceeding to Washington, on the matter in question, will enable him to secure the co-operation of influential and active friends, who, immediately after the 4th of March will have left for their different States, and, therefore, begs that, if the accompanying request be not considered unreasonable, it may be granted with as little delay as possible."[6] Meagher had submitted the request that he had made to Stanton to General Hancock, who passed it on to General Hooker, now commander of the Army of the Potomac. It was Hooker who had set the condition when he issued an order: "The Commanding General cannot entertain the proposition for the temporary withdrawal of the Irish Brigade from the Army, without positive assurances, that it will be immediately replaced by an equal body of troops." Meagher did not get the leave he asked for, and Hooker could not have appreciated the threat to take the matter to Congress.[7]

Although Meagher inwardly fumed at what he perceived as another show of disrespect for the Irish, he could do nothing. It was time to celebrate St. Patrick's Day again, and he threw himself into preparing for the March 17 event. In the four days before the festival, a race course was marked out, invitations to all the officers of the Army of the Potomac were issued, and a quartermaster was sent to Washington to bring back quantities of food and liquor, with Meagher himself being in charge of mixing a strong punch. According to Father Corby, the versatile Meagher also "directed the military bands when and how to play during the Mass" that was held that day.[8] The whole affair went off as planned, amid much gaiety despite the situation's underlying misery. Unveiled at the proceeding was a new "Song of the Irish Brigade," which "was sung by Captain Blake, in his best style." It spoke of the decimation of the brigade in the Civil War, but a verse directed at Meagher spoke more of freedom for Ireland:

> But sure, our chieftain, of his race,
> Was ever foremost 'mid the brave,
> . . . .
> We swear it now, and evermore—
> To free green Erin, land of slaves,
> And banish tyrants from her shore.[9]

The St. Patrick's Day celebration was only a brief respite from the woes that beset Meagher and the Irish Brigade, and he longed to return to New York either to recruit new volunteers or to further the advancement of his plea that the brigade should be withdrawn from the conflict. Meagher submitted another medical certificate from Dr. Reynolds, and the army granted him another medical leave to seek treatment in the hot baths of the North, and soon he was back in New York.[10]

Unsuccessful at either recruiting volunteers or gaining leave for his men, Meagher returned from New York to take charge of his command on April 27. The Army of the Potomac was preparing another advance toward Richmond, which would start by crossing the Rappahannock in the vicinities of Fredericksburg and Chancellorsville. The Irish Brigade was already being positioned to cross the river in the area north of Chancellorsville. Meagher's first official act would be to write a report to General Hancock explaining why he had not taken command a day earlier when he arrived on the Rappahannock.[11] Colonel Kelly of the 88th New York had been acting as commander of the Irish Brigade, and Meagher had to relieve him of the command personally. Even though the 63rd New York was at Banks' Ford, located about two miles upstream from Fredericksburg, Meagher "learned that Colonel Kelly had, an hour previous, proceeded to the United States Ford." Meagher "set out at once . . . , taking the corduroy road leading up from Banks' Ford to the Warrenton pike" on the north side of the river, because he was "ignorant of the River road," which was on the south side.[12] Meagher found the 69th and the 116th posted at "United States Ford, at which I arrived some time about 5 P.M." But Kelly "had left something more than an hour before, to return to Banks' Ford." Meagher explained that he had stayed overnight there, because to go back to Banks' Ford he would have to take "the only route (that of the Warrenton pike) with which I was acquainted," which would have been slow. The next morning "orders arrived for the regiments of the brigade stationed at the United States Ford to proceed" back to Banks' Ford, where Meagher finally caught up with Kelly and relieved him.[13]

After two days of troop movement, on April 28 and 29, Meagher's brigade as part of Hancock's division marched across a pontoon bridge at United States Ford that had just been completed at 3:30 P.M. by troops under General Darius Couch.[14] Once again Meagher was ready to lead his brigade into battle, but confusion started right away. As Hancock reported, "At 8 P.M. the entire division had crossed the pontoon bridges at that point. It immediately proceeded through the Wilderness, and encamped within half a mile of Chancellorsville at 10 P.M." But Meagher's brigade did not advance with the division. The 88th New York had been split off and put with the combined 5th New Hampshire and the 81st Pennsylvania under the command of Colonel E. E. Cross of the 5th. These regiments "were left to serve as a rear guard to the ammunition train of the corps until it had crossed the United States Ford." Entirely ignoring Meagher, General Hancock put the other four regiments of the brigade "under command of Col. R. Byrnes, Twenty-eighth Massachusetts

Volunteers"; they "were posted on a road leading from the main road toward Banks' Ford."[15]

On May 1, at 1:30 P.M., the call to battle sounded for Hancock's division to come to the relief of the command of General George Sykes. Hancock moved his troops forward in the direction of Fredericksburg, along the "Plank Road" and "the old Turnpike leading to Fredericksburg" near the Chancellor house. The 88th New York, which arrived from its rear guard duty, was placed in reserve, still under Colonel Cross. While there had been some firing during the day, according to Hancock, "[t]he combat was not renewed, except by the fire of artillery down the turnpike, from the position we had abandoned, and we bivouacked for the night. A rifle-pit was dug along our entire line and an abatis felled in front." At about 1:30 P.M. the next day, May 2, Sykes's command was withdrawn and Hancock's division, with the 88th New York, was ordered to withdraw after it.[16]

In the meantime Meagher had again taken command of the 63rd and 69th New York, the 116th Pennsylvania, and the 28th Massachusetts. On May 1 Meagher and the brigade spent a long day waiting, "with every ear listening anxiously for news that was so difficult to obtain," said Major St. Clair Mulholland of the 116th. The next morning, with the Union army falling back to take up a defensive position, Meagher's brigade moved to the right of the line closest to the Rappahannock. According to Mulholland, "rumors of a column of the enemy moving . . . to strike the right were heard and all felt anxious and nervous." At that time "General Meagher came down the right of the brigade, . . . addressed the men and begged them to make a good fight." Soon after Meagher's appearance, the men heard "a tremendous storm of musketry." The occasion was the Confederate attack—26,000 strong under Stonewall Jackson—on Major General Oliver Howard's 11th Corps. Howard's troops soon gave way in a panicked retreat. Rather than facing the enemy, Meagher's brigade now had to stop the retreat of their own comrades in arms. They were "every one of them panic-stricken, frantic, almost insane, their only desire to get to the rear," Mulholland said. As night settled, "the fugitives were quickly gathered into squads, forced to the rear, and the front of the line was cleared for action." Finally order was restored, and "a day full of anxiety had been passed."[17]

The next day, Sunday, May 3, the troops of the Irish Brigade had been listening to the "continuous roar of artillery and volleys of musketry" since early morning when orders came shortly after ten o'clock for the brigade to move south toward the Chancellor house. St. Clair Mulholland understood that they were to "join the balance of the division which was at that time beating back" the Confederates. As the brigade took the road from the United States Ford and moved south toward the battle, Mulholland observed that "[s]treams of wounded men flowed to the rear. Men with torn faces, split heads, smashed arms, wounded men assisting their more badly hurt comrades, stretchers bearing to the rear men whose limbs were crushed and mangled, and others who had no limbs at all." The entire scene was bedlam, according to Mulholland. "Shells screamed through the trees and, as the Regiment approached the front, the whir of the canister and shrapnel was heard and musket balls whistled past."[18]

Hancock later reported that the Irish "did not return from detached service until the morning of May 3, and did not report to me until the action was nearly decided—about 10.30 p.m." Yet he did acknowledge that Meagher's troops had been of service. "Brigadier-General Meagher's command had been posted in the woods on the right of Leppien's battery, supporting it." Hancock was "not able to speak of the service of General Meagher's [command] while they were engaged with the enemy" because "they were detached, and under the immediate orders of General Hooker."[19]

To add to the confusion, Major General Darius Couch, the commander of the 2nd Army Corps, had also issued orders affecting Meagher's troops. Captain Rufus D. Pettit, the commander of Battery B of the 1st New York Light Artillery, reported that on the morning of May 2 the first section of his battery "was detached by Colonel Morgan and sent in charge of First Lieutenant Sheldon to Scott's Mills, to report to the commander of the Irish Brigade."[20]

According to Mulholland of the 116th Pennsylvania, Meagher's troops had in fact advanced on May 3 close to the Chancellor house. "The Irish Brigade was engaged in supporting the Fifth Maine Battery, commanded by Captain Leppien." This is what Hancock had also observed. But the battery did not do well, and "all the officers and [men] belonging to it had either been killed, wounded, or had abandoned their pieces, . . . and all the

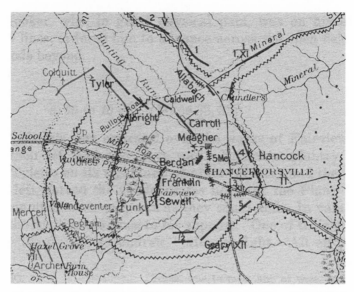

Chancellorsville battle map. This map shows the position of Meagher's troops at 9:45 A.M. on May 3, 1863, when they helped to remove the battery of the 5th Maine Artillery from the field as part of Hancock's retreat. (Author's collection)

guns were silenced except one." As the Union infantry started to retreat from the Chancellor house, the possibility that George Leppien's valuable artillery would be left on the field was becoming real. Major Scott, of General Hancock's staff, soon approached Mulholland and ordered him "to bring out a sufficient number of men to haul the abandoned guns off the field." According to Mulholland, "My regiment at this time occupied the left of the brigade line, and was nearest the battery. I at once . . . led my men toward the abandoned battery, and . . . removed three of the guns off the field, and to the rear." He acknowledged that men of the 63rd and 69th assisted in removing the guns.[21]

Meagher's version of the events that day at Chancellorsville was somewhat different than Hancock's or Mulholland's. After the battle Meagher directed Lieutenant Edward Whiteford, aide-de-camp of the 88th New York, to write a report on the activities of the Irish Brigade. According to Whiteford, "personal orders were received from General Couch to advance the brigade (then supporting the Fifth Maine Battery) through the woods in their front, but were immediately countermanded

by him, and skirmishers ordered to be thrown out." At that time Whiteford himself "received orders . . . from General Meagher to throw out 50
men of the Twenty-eighth Massachusetts." Whiteford then observed that
the "fire which the enemy concentrated on the above battery compelled the men to desert the guns, the horses at the time being either all
killed or wounded." After Whiteford had reported "the fact to General
Meagher," he "was ordered by him to tell Major Mulholland, of the One
hundred and sixteenth Regiment Pennsylvania Volunteers, to save the
guns with his men, at any risk." Whiteford observed that Mulholland's
men took the guns "out of stiff yellow clay, where the guns were stuck,
and under a galling fire of the enemy, by which some 4 or 5 of his men
were either killed or wounded." Whiteford's report made no mention of
Scott supposedly ordering Mulholland to bring off the batteries.[22]

The whole matter of who had ordered whom to bring the abandoned guns off the battlefield created some controversy. "Who brought
off the guns of the Fifth Mine Battery?" queried J. H. Lebroke in the
opening line of his May 27 letter "To the Editor of the Press." According
to Lebroke, "After the battery had ceased firing, one of the gunners
went to General Hancock for a detail to haul off the guns. He sent a
detail from the Irish Brigade under the command of Lieutenant-Colonel
Mulholland and Lieutenant Wilson, of Hancock's staff." On May 10
letters were written separately from both Hancock's headquarters and
Meagher's headquarters to Mulholland, expressing gratitude for his
efforts in bringing off the guns.[23] Despite Hancock's apparent reluctance to acknowledge Meagher's involvement on the battlefield at
Chancellorsville, both Meagher and his brigade were definitely engaged
there. According to Colonel A. Van Horne Ellis of the 124th New York
Infantry, he was "ordered to support Meagher's Irish Brigade, which, it
was said, was about charging with the bayonet." His regiment "lay
down behind it in line of battle, with a battery on our left, and were
here shelled by the enemy in the liveliest manner." About 4 P.M.
Meagher's brigade retired from the field, according to Ellis.[24] As to
Meagher's own participation, Frank Henry of the *New York Times* wrote
to Abraham Lincoln on May 3, saying that a correspondent from a
Philadelphia paper who had been on the field of battle told him that
"Gen. Meagher is *again* wounded."[25] Henry's report was incorrect and
may have been based on rumor or malice. According to Mulholland,

Meagher appeared on the night of May 3 "in full uniform" and "walked up and down the brigade line."[26]

In the meantime Peter Welsh, the color sergeant of the 28th Massachusetts, was with his regiment when "we fell back sunday [*sic*] after the battery was brought in about half a mile and built a breast work all along our line[;] in a few hours there was miles of breast work built." They remained there until they retreated across the Rappahannock.[27]

Meagher and the Irish Brigade would await the Confederates from a new position until May 6, when they were ordered before sunup to retreat across the pontoon bridge at the United States Ford. For participation in the battle Major General Hooker cited his brigade commanders, John C. Caldwell, Samuel K. Zook, and Meagher, as having performed their duties "faithfully and well."[28] The words rang hollow to Meagher, however, who lost another ninety-two men in the battle and who felt more than ever that his brigade deserved time away from the battlefield to recover.[29]

Unable to accept the slaughter of the Irish any longer, offended by the lack of response to his request for relief for the Irish Brigade, dissatisfied with the way the command of the regiments of his brigade had been taken from him, and unwilling to continue as a brigadier general unless the army built up his command again, Meagher tendered his resignation from the army on May 8, 1863, in frustration and anger. "The memorial was in vain. It never was even acknowledged," he wrote, referring to his request to Stanton for relief of the Irish Brigade. But Meagher was not so offended that he totally burned his bridges with the army, and he left the door open for his reassignment. "In tendering my resignation, however, as the Brigadier-General in command of this poor vestige and relic of the Irish Brigade, I beg sincerely to assure you that my services, in any capacity that can prove useful, are freely at the summons and disposition of the Government of the United States." But he had enough of the killing in the Civil War. "I feel it to be my first duty to do nothing that will wantonly imperil the lives of others."[30]

By May 20 the resignation had been accepted, without Meagher's reassignment. One reporter said that "habitual drunkenness accounts for the prompt acceptance of Brig. Gen. Meagher's resignation."[31] Meagher soon found himself giving his parting address to his command. "Suffice it to say that, the Irish Brigade no longer existing, I felt that it would be perpetuating a great deception were I to retain the authority and rank of brigadier-general nominally commanding the same. I therefore conscientiously, though most reluctantly, resigned my command. That resignation has been accepted, and as your general I now bid you an affectionate farewell."[32]

The army's quick decision to accept Meagher's resignation outraged the Irish community. The *Irish American* expressed their views: "the War Department have not only inflicted on him and his brave Brigade an unmerited and outrageous injustice, but have done the National cause an irreparable injury by their neglect and ill-treatment of a body of representative citizens, whose valor on every battle-field elicited the generous encomiums of the foes against whom they fought."[33] The wholehearted support expressed by the *Irish American* was not universally felt. Some Irish apparently blamed Meagher for leading his troops to their death. Father Corby said, "I have heard many blame Meagher," but Corby was quick to point out that the criticisms were not valid. "Gen. Meagher and his brigade simply obeyed the orders of superior officers, and went in at the time and place assigned them. Had Gen. Meagher disobeyed such legitimate orders, he would have been liable to be cashiered, and thus have disgraced himself and his race for all future time."[34]

Significantly, many of his officers agreed with the *Irish American's* view that Meagher's resignation was a great loss. Before he left, fifty-nine commissioned officers commended his leadership in a letter dated May 20 from Falmouth, Virginia:

> We regard you, General, as the originator of the Irish Brigade in the service of the United States, we know that to your influence and energy, the success which it earned during its organization is mainly due; we have seen you since it first took the field—some eighteen months since—sharing its perils and hardships on the battle-field and in the bivouac; always at your post, always inspiring your command with that courage and devotedness which has made the Brigade historical, and by word and example cheering us on, when fatigue and dangers beset our path; and we would be ungrateful, indeed, did we forget that whatever glory we have obtained in many a hard fought

field, and whatever honor we may been privileged to shed on the sacred land of our nativity, that to you, General, is due to a great extent, our success and our triumphs.

Not to be outdone, twenty-nine noncommissioned officers of the brigade offered their own tribute:

> Beloved General—Seldom, if ever, has a more mournful duty devolved on a soldier than now devolves on a few of that devoted band of Irishmen that rallied at your call around the Green Flag of our native land, and who are here now to evince their sincere and heartfelt sorrow at the loss of an indomitable leader, a brave companion, and a stern patriot, as well as to extend their congratulations at your returning in all your manly pride and spotless integrity, to the domestic scenes of your own fireside. . . .
>
> The first to lead us to victory, we fondly hoped it would be your proudest honor, as it was your highest ambition, to lead us back again to our homes, but through the inscrutable wisdom of an all-wise War Department it will be reserved for you instead to welcome back what has been, or will be left, of what was once known, and proudly so, as Meagher's Irish Brigade.[35]

Thus Meagher left the Union Army and once more headed home to New York. He arrived home soon after the Battle of Chancellorsville, his leg still sore and his spirits dashed by the heavy casualties to his once proud Irish Brigade. While the testimonials of his officers and men had been sincere, others blamed him for leading his fellow countrymen to death. He needed some time to reflect quietly on the events of the last two years. Instead of returning immediately to the dusty streets of New York and the bustle of politics, he headed to Manhattanville to spend some time at the home of his friend Dan Devlin.

With Meagher in seclusion, rumors began to circulate. One had him planning to leave for France to visit "his venerable father and other members of his family, from who he had been separated for many years." Another had him planning to enter politics. In fact, Meagher wanted only a quiet life for a few days. When incorrect information was issued about a political meeting he was to attend, the *Irish American* immediately declared that it was authorized to "state emphatically" that "when General Meagher does speak on the war, or any other of the great questions of the day, he will speak at his own chosen time and place."[36]

Meagher did not stay in seclusion for long. The next two years would be a period of confusion, during which he would undermine his bold stance against the military's treatment of the Irish and would alienate his fellow Irish Americans with his embrace of Republicanism. These years would also mark the period when much of his drinking was no longer convivial. Meagher would sink further into a pattern of overindulgence that would tarnish his reputation.

When he first returned home, however, Meagher still had the support of the Irish. His resignation had sparked an uproar among the Irish community over the failure of the army to rebuild the Irish Brigade or, lacking that, to reassign the brigade's regiments. This state of affairs enraged the editors of the *Irish American,* who protested: "To keep them where they are now, in their reduced condition, is not merely a cruelty—it is a crime."[37] Their indignation fueled Meagher's own. Nevertheless, he felt strongly that the Irish Brigade's remaining units should stay together. The goal of all his efforts had been an *Irish* fighting force, and he began to wonder if his resignation would spell the end of his old command and the dispersal of the Irish into nonethnic units. Thus, despite his continued anger at his brigade's mistreatment at the hands of Stanton and Hooker, Meagher painfully began to reconsider his resignation. When General Lee's Confederate troops invaded Pennsylvania in June and threatened the large cities of the North, Meagher thought he saw an opportunity to revive the Irish Brigade.

On July 13, 1863, Meagher wrote to secretary of war Edwin Stanton. "I have now to request permission to withdraw my letter of resignation, and beg to renew the offer of my services to the government which accompanied the letter."[38] Once before Meagher had written directly to Lincoln and received authorization to raise troops. This time, too, he sent a dispatch directly to President Lincoln, asking for authorization to raise three thousand troops. Lincoln's speedy reply advised: "Your dispatch received. Shall be very glad for you to raise 3,000 Irish troops."[39] While Meagher got the answer he wanted, he inappropriately avoided Stanton; the secretary of war, who had ignored Meagher's request for leave for his men the year before, again did not respond. While Stanton did not react immediately to the slight, he would have several opportunities in the coming years to help Meagher—and he would always refuse.

In the meantime the army had finally acted on the old regiments of the Irish Brigade, consolidating them and mustering out some of the old officers. To Meagher, the proud Irishman, this diminishment of the brigade was still another rebuke. What he wanted now was to rebuild a complete Irish Brigade. To the *Irish American* the reassignment was a grave injustice, and its pages openly championed Meagher and complained about his treatment by the army.

Prominent New Yorkers agreed with the *Irish American* that Meagher had been poorly treated and were determined to rectify the situation as best they could. "For the neglect which he received" from the War Office in Washington, reported the *Irish American,* "he shall here . . . receive a just recognition for the services which he rendered in the defence of the Union and for the unsurpassed gallantry which he, and the noble little command which he here raised, showed on every battle field from Fair Oaks to Chancellorsville." Praise for Meagher continued to flow at a banquet held in his honor at the Astor House on June 16, 1863, where New York's mayor George Opdyke presented Meagher with a resolution passed by New York's Common Council honoring his service. Then Alderman Farley presented him with the Kearney Cross for valor as a gift from the citizens of Philadelphia.[40]

Speaking to the gathered dignitaries, Meagher took the opportunity to reaffirm his support for Lincoln and the Civil War: "Let the army . . . proceed, beat back the enemy, crush the insurrection, restore the Constitution and reinstate the Union." He also took the opportunity to explain away his resignation. The Irish Brigade, through casualties, "had ceased to exist," and he had resigned in protest and from a sense of honor: "as I had no command, it was but decent of me to relinquish the emoluments of a sinecure." But Meagher made clear that his loyalty still rested with the Irish of his command, vowing: "I did not absolve myself of my obligations . . . from which death alone can free us." He then dramatically declined the proffered resolution of the city, deferring his acceptance until the end of the war.[41]

Meagher's support for Lincoln separated him from the majority of his compatriots, most of whom supported Lincoln's Democratic rival, General George McClellan, in the 1864 presidential campaign. The New

Thomas Francis Meagher with the Kearney Cross. Meagher is shown here in civilian clothes, wearing what is believed to be the Kearney Cross awarded to him. (Courtesy Montana Historical Society, Helena)

York Irish had their reasons to dislike Lincoln and the war that was his legacy. The large casualty numbers had quelled Irish enthusiasm for the war. Added to that was Lincoln's famous Emancipation Proclamation freeing the slaves in Rebel territory, which went into effect on January 1, 1863. The act further alienated many of the New York Irish, who, barely eking out a living in the crowded city, saw free African Americans as a direct threat to their livelihood. Their suspicion only increased when a number of former slaves were used to replace striking Irish longshoremen. To make matters worse, Lincoln signed into law the first Conscription Act on March 3, 1863, to draft men into the Union Army. The law was not designed to be even handed, and the workingmen of the North found much in it that dissatisfied them. Black men were exempt from the draft, which theoretically applied to all white men between the ages of twenty and forty-five. In addition, the act allowed the rich to hire substitutes or simply purchase an exemption for three hundred dollars.[42]

Most of the Irish in New York supported a quick end to the war through a negotiated peace, but Meagher stayed solidly behind Lincoln. He shared this position with Archbishop John Hughes, who in June 1863 told his congregations that peace "appears at this moment to be ridiculous[,] . . . [because] it requires two sides to make peace," while "one side can make war." In August 1863 Hughes again addressed the need for the continued use of force. "If I had a voice in the councils of the Nation, I would say, let volunteers continue, and the draft be made," he said. "If three hundred thousand men be not sufficient let three hundred thousand more be called upon, so that the army, in its fullness of strength, shall always be on hand for any emergency. This is not cruelty; this is mercy; this is humanity—anything that will put an end to this draggling of human blood across the whole surface of the country."[43] Meagher shared this desire to end the war with a decisive military victory rather than through negotiations. He must also have recognized that the 1848 rebellion might have had a different outcome if the Irish priests had shared Hughes's martial spirit. At any rate Meagher no doubt took comfort in the pronouncements of Hughes, which armed him with the moral authority to lead his Irish countrymen to the slaughter—if the Irish would just join him.

Their willingness to do so was questionable, although Meagher did temporarily catch the popular imagination. A day after his martial address at the Astor House in June, men gathered at a meeting of the T. F. Meagher Literary Union. There they loudly applauded one of the speakers "when he dwelt with fervor on the hopes of Ireland through the restoration of the Union" and his expectation of seeing "a gallant array of armed men marching under Gen. Meagher to reestablish the glories of Eire."[44] Nevertheless, Meagher's personal popularity would not translate into acceptance of his cause. Determined once more to organize a brigade, he called a meeting of all the returned officers of the Irish Brigade for Saturday, July 11, at "General Meagher's chambers, at 41 Ann-street." His timing could not have been worse. On that same day the names of the first draftees were drawn by lottery in New York City. The next day they were published in the Sunday papers.[45]

On Monday an angry, mostly Irish mob stormed the streets, attacking the staff of the draft office with clubs and setting their building on fire. It was the beginning of four days of increasingly violent riots. Fire crews were called to put out the fire; but instead the New York firemen, who had just lost their draft exemption under the new law, joined in the destruction. As the mob grew out of control, one of the rioters knocked New York's chief of police unconscious; others attacked the offices of abolitionist Horace Greeley.[46] Pillaging and robbing their way down Third and Fifth Avenues, the mob broke into an armory to obtain arms and attacked an orphanage where black children lived, mutilating and then lynching a black disabled coachman. A sixteen-year-old Irish boy hacked off the coachman's fingers and toes before dragging the corpse through the street by the genitals, finally setting the body on fire. A mob of longshoremen attacked a black sailor, striking him with stones, stabbing him with knives, and then savagely beating him to death. Other black men were killed and thrown into rivers, and a number were hung from trees or lamp-posts. Frightened African Americans across the city left their dwellings in search of safe places to hide.[47]

The War Department had known that the draft would not go easily in New York and had sought to counter the coming resentment by sending an Irishman to organize and oversee its operation. They had chosen Colonel Robert Nugent for the job, promoting him to vice provost before sending him into the impossible situation. Nugent had served under Meagher as the leader of the 69th until he was injured at Fredericksburg. The *Irish American* praised the choice, stating that the selection was a "wise and deservedly popular one." But Nugent's promotion did nothing to quell the unrest. Although he issued an order under his own name canceling the draft, it did not stop the rioting; and Nugent's house was gutted by the mob. Eventually he ordered the mob fired upon, killing quite a number, but even then the rioting continued. In an effort to stop the riots, an ailing Archbishop Hughes issued a statement to the Irish: "If they are Catholics, I ask, for God's sake—for the sake of their holy religion . . . to dissolve their bad association with reckless men, who have little regard either for divine or human laws." In the end it took six thousand troops from West Point and the Gettysburg battlefield to restore order.[48]

In the middle of the riots Tammany Hall Democrats drafted an ordinance to appropriate a large sum of money to pay the exemption fee for every New York City man conscripted by the draft. Tammany Hall's act affirmed Nugent's view that the riots were in part politically motivated; according to Nugent, "the Democratic politicians are at the bottom of this riot, and . . . the rioters themselves include not only the thieves and gamblers that infest this metropolis, but nearly every one of the vast Democratic majority."[49] Despite this view, responsible Irish all over New York were appalled by the violence. The *Irish American,* for example, was quick to criticize the attacks on blameless people: "The assaults on unfortunate negroes and the burning of their houses and their Orphan Asylum cannot be condemned in language too severe. These poor people were innocent of any complicity in bringing about our present troubles." Nevertheless, the *American* continued to stand with the Democrats and against the draft, complaining: "from the tone of the Republican journals it is evident . . . that they are determined to force the Administration to push the obnoxious draft at every risk of renewed bloodshed and disorder."[50]

Meagher apparently remained silent during the draft riots; but he spoke out later in a letter to the Reverend George W. Pepper, a Methodist minister from Ireland. Pepper was an old acquaintance; he had watched Meagher's trial for treason in Clonmel. Now he had resurfaced as a Republican political activist in Ohio and had invited Meagher to deliver an address to the Unionists there in an attempt to defeat Clement L. Vallandigham, a gubernatorial candidate. Vallandigham was the leader of the peace Democrats, sometimes called "Copperheads," whose outspoken beliefs about the war had gotten him charged, convicted, and exiled for treason.[51] Arrangements were made for Meagher to go; but as the time neared he had to write Pepper and cancel, explaining that "very urgent business calls me to Washington." Instead Meagher sent a letter in which he explained his views on the recent events in New York. He was at his dramatic best when he blamed the peace Democrats for the "riots of New York, . . . where Copperheads abound, and the venom, as well as the slime, the fangs, as well as the slippery skin, of the reptiles, warn the community of danger."[52] Meagher's letter was soon published in New York in Horace Greeley's abolitionist *Tribune.* Two days later Meagher drew the rebuke of the *Irish American,* perhaps marking the first time that he had been publicly criticized on those pages. The editors fumed that "the opinions of the mass of our countrymen on this particular question are opposed to those to which General Meagher gives expression." They then castigated the Republican party, "whose hands are red with the blood of naturalized citizens, shed in violent attempts to deprive our people of the franchises guaranteed to them."[53]

Thus Thomas Francis Meagher, a leader of Young Ireland, a revolutionary in the 1848 uprising, the leader of the Irish Brigade, and one of the most significant Irishmen in America, was now officially at odds with one of the leading Irish American newspapers. For Meagher, the draft riots had personal consequences beyond his break with the *Irish American.* The riots crushed his recruiting effort, because now no volunteers were to be had in New York. But there were other sources of Irish troops, and word started to spread that recruiters were enticing Irishmen to come to America as laborers, with the intention of quickly enlisting them into the army with the promise of better wages. Some of the charges of "federal enlistments" were even published as early as April 1863 in the pages of the *Irish American,* which cited as its source an accusatory letter written from the town of Skibbereen to the *Cork Examiner.* The *American* reported that the letter was a lie "to blind the world" to the evils of English rule and later sought to prove that the young Irishmen who were arriving were just part of the normal emigration, commenting that "it has not at all been shown that the proportion of young men to females and old men among the emigrants is greater this year than it was in years past."[54] Still, suspicion lingered.

The Confederacy took the Union's recruitment in Ireland seriously, and it came to the attention of Judah P. Benjamin, secretary of state of the Confederate States of America. He queried James M. Mason, the Confederate agent in London, about the matter. Mason wrote back that indeed someone was giving a small bounty to Irishmen to emigrate to the United States. Benjamin thought the matter significant enough that he sent a counteragent. First Lieutenant James L. Capston was instructed to go to Ireland and use "all legitimate means to enlighten the population as to the true nature and the character of the contest now waged on this continent, with the view of defeating the attempts made by the agents of the United States to obtain in Ireland recruits for their armies." Benjamin specifically instructed Capston to "relate to them the story of Meagher's brigade, its formation and its fate."[55]

The matter continued to bother the Confederacy. On September 4, 1863, Benjamin wrote to the Reverend Father John Bannon of Richmond, directing the priest to go to Rome and attempt to obtain sanctions from the pope to stop the Irish recruitment. No significant meeting between Bannon and the pope was recorded, but A. Dudley Mann, another Confederate emissary, did gain a papal audience in November 1863. Mann informed the pope about the recruiting and made an oblique reference to Meagher when he noted that "in consequence thereof an instance had incurred in which an almost entire brigade had been left dead or wounded upon the ground."[56]

It is not known if Meagher supported direct recruitment from Ireland. In any event, it did not provide him with the quantity of troops he needed. Even the continued enticement of the brigade forming the core of a trained Fenian expeditionary force could not attract enough men to form a new Irish Brigade. The idea of forming an army of "trained and tried" soldiers to strike at England had continued to engage the New York Fenians, however, and may have been the subject of discussion at a private meeting that Meagher held with all officers of the old Irish Brigade on the evening of September 28. It certainly was openly discussed among the troops. As a member of the old brigade reported, "oftentimes, during the lull of battle, have I heard one Irish soldier exclaim to another:—'Arrah, Paddy, what harm if this was for the poor ould dart!' . . . we are already tasting the sweets of our revenge."[57] Nevertheless, not even the incentive of training men to fight England could override the scorn that the New York Irish now had for the war.

Although recruitment had not gone well, Meagher wanted more than ever to be back in the Union Army. His support for Lincoln had strained his relationship with the Irish patrons upon whom he depended for his social position, work as an attorney, and popularity on the lecture circuit. It had also strained his relationship with his father-in-law, who was an active McClellan supporter. To make matters worse, Samuel Barlow, Meagher's brother-in-law through Barlow's marriage to Elizabeth's sister Alicia, was a friend and staunch supporter of McClellan and ended up being his unofficial campaign manager.[58] Unable to live comfortably with Elizabeth at the luxurious home of her father, Peter Townsend, Meagher believed that reenlisting in the army was his best option. It would get him away from a scratchy domestic situation and could help him secure a political appointment once the war was over.

Because Meagher could not raise the troops he promised, however, he had to give up hope of rejoining the army as a commander of his own brigade. He needed a new appointment and looked to anyone who could help him. One of the people he sought out was Captain James R. O'Beirne of the 57th New York, whom he had met under bad circumstances on the previous St. Patrick's Day. Then still in the army, Meagher had sought to raise the dwindling spirits of the Irish by directing festivities honoring the occasion. Wanting to keep the entertainment of the day going late into the evening, he became angry when two or three officers, including O'Beirne, failed to extend the celebration. Meagher had been drinking; he lost his temper and lashed out against them. Once he realized what he had done, he immediately wrote his amends: "I would not, for the world!, that any friend, whom I esteemed, . . . should have any unpleasant recollections . . . ; and hence am eager and impatient to remove any impressions with which some inadvertent and graceless act on my part may have clouded to your eye the introspective vision of St. Patrick's Day."[59]

After this rocky start, Meagher and O'Beirne became fast friends. In Meagher's estimation, O'Beirne was a young man on the rise whose friendship he wanted to cultivate. So he started corresponding with O'Beirne, who was recuperating at a New York hospital from a wound he had received in the field. Meagher's attentions flattered the young man, who responded with respect and affection. In the fall of 1863

General Thomas Francis Meagher in formal uniform. Meagher inscribed the back of this photograph "To Alice Barlow, With the affect. Regards of Thomas Francis Meagher, Brigadier General Commanding the Irish Brigade, Army of the Potomac, New York, Jan. 24th/63." (This item is reproduced by permission of *The Huntington Library, San Marino, California*)

O'Beirne asked Meagher to be present at the christening of his new-born child and to sponsor the infant as a godfather. Although Meagher was out in the country in Orange County, New York, and did not receive the letter in time to attend the christening, he wrote back with enthusiasm, letting O'Beirne know just how much his friendship meant: "The approval and friendship of intelligent minds and sound chivalrous hearts I dearly prize."[60] Once Meagher's recruiting efforts had failed, he would turn to O'Beirne as a sounding board for his effort to rejoin the army. Meagher wrote: "I would wish very much to have the command of a Veteran Division, and remain in active service until the War was brought to a triumphant issue for the Union . . . or Heaven pleased that I should die 'with harness on my back.'"[61]

During the summer of 1863, while spending time at Peter Townsend's rural property in Southfields, Orange County, New York, Meagher was asked to contribute to a history of the Irish Brigade being written by James Turner, who had been a member of the 88th New York. Meagher had been in touch with McClellan, who was himself out of the army. Meagher informed Turner: "General McClellan told me that, in his report of the battle of Antietam, he has mentioned the conduct of the Brigade on that occasion with special distinction, and in such a manner as, he is confident, will gratify us all. The report may be published before your book goes to press—or before, at all events, the proofs are completed—if so we must have this testimony to our credit set forth in full."[62]

While waiting for word that he was back in the army, Meagher continued to campaign for Lincoln. It was a lonely task. Not many Irishmen came forward that fall to support Lincoln. One of the few who did was Colonel Patrick R. Guiney of the 9th Massachusetts Volunteers, perhaps the only member of his regiment to call himself a Republican. Meagher had corresponded with Guiney about their mutual beliefs. On October 7, 1863, in a fit of frustration, he wrote a letter to Guiney that would later be his own undoing. "As for the great bulk of the Irishmen in this country, I frankly confess to an utter disregard, if not a thorough contempt of what they think or say of me," Meagher stated. "To their own discredit and degradation, they have suffered themselves to be bamboozled into being obstinate herds in the political field."[63]

Meagher's letter to Guiney left no doubt about his fundamental disagreement with the majority of Irish Americans. As bad as it sounded, however, his real grievance was not with the Irish, whom he condemned for their blind allegiance, but with the leaders of the Democratic Party. "To have been a Democrat in the days of Andrew Jackson was to have been . . . the devoted friend of the country, whether it was right or wrong," he wrote Guiney. "Now-a-days to be a Democrat, is to be the partisan of a selfish and conscienceless faction, which . . . would cripple the national power." Meagher intended his letter to be confidential, and Guiney thought he had put it in good hands when he mailed it to his wife, Jennie, with instructions that it should be kept "safely for me." But that did not happen, and a year later the letter was made public.[64]

The long days of summer had given Meagher time to reflect on the struggle in America and his part in it. There was growing pressure on him to join his native Irish in New York and call for an end to the war; but that he could not do, for it would not save the Union. At the same time the successful prosecution of the war would end the institution of slavery in the South—something he had never come out against. Finally, he wrote two letters for publication (one on September 5 and another on September 26) to the *Irishman* in Dublin, where his old friend P. J. Smyth was editor. The letters were picked up by the Loyal Publication Society of New York, a group that published pamphlets and broadsides supporting the Union and opposing Copperheads or Southern sympathizers. They published the letters under the title *Letters on Our National Struggle*. The interested public would soon know that Meagher was now totally in favor of abolition—and not only that: he had clearly given the matter some thought and reconciled the experience of the Irish. It was not just jobs that Irishmen in New York had lost to emancipated slaves that concerned Meagher, but the greater good of the Republic.[65]

Meagher's first letter dealt only with the "sentiments . . . of the Irish public—so far as speeches and newspapers can be taken to interpret them truthfully," which he regarded as a "partisanship of the Irish public with the aristocrats of Carolina and Virginia." Despite the apparent Irish sympathy for the South, Meagher honored the Irish soldier. "I turn with pride and exultation to those of our race who stood true to the Government of the United States, and in the vindication of its honor and prerogatives pledged the fire of their hearts and the vigor of their arms." As no one but Meagher could put it: "In the honored graves in which many of them sleep to-day they are not on trial for their loyalty and heroism."[66]

The second letter elaborated on the slavery issue, on which Meagher in his newspaper days a few years before had rationalized to come down on the side of the South. "I cannot forget my friend, Mr. Smith O'Brien, asking me, more than once during his visit to this country, how it was that I could bring myself to be an apologist of the slavery existing in the South. . . . I told him I was not in favor of slavery, but was devoted to the Union; and that, as the Union involved the slavery he condemned, I had to accept the latter to befriend and serve the former." Meagher declared: "At first, and for some time, this war was prosecuted with the single purpose of reinstating National authority." But "as the war went on, new developments occurred; and amongst these, the emancipation of the slaves in the Revolted states became a military necessity. . . . Thus the inexorable logic of war compels the justice which fidelity to the Constitution solemnly withheld," which "was not only in conflict with their humanity and conscience, but falsified the spirit, and neutralized the glory of [the] Republic."[67]

It was now unmistakably clear that Meagher was against slavery, and he sought to raise the reputation of the Irish to the loftier plateau of his new thinking.

> Thank God! that disgrace has been averted from our race . . . ,
> in upholding with their strong arms the honor and authority of
> the Government, to which, on ceasing to be exiles and becoming
> citizens, they swore allegiance, proved themselves worthier of a
> better and brighter destiny than that which has, for a winter of
> centuries, shrouded the land of their birth in a dense mist of
> misery and humiliation—the most woeful and death-like that
> ever darkened the hopes and memories of a nation.[68]

As the fall days shortened in 1863, Meagher still had not been given orders and longed to be associated once again with the officers and men from his old brigade. He knew that their period of enlistment would be up soon, and many of them would be coming home. This time the army had learned its lesson, however, and the soldiers were furloughed for the winter to recruit and to encourage their own reenlistment—an action that Meagher had requested the year before, which had been denied by General Hooker.

On October 5, 1863, Meagher wrote to Secretary of State Seward:

> If my services to the National Government, in connection with the Irish Brigade, in the Army of the Potomac, have been of sufficient importance to constitute for me a claim to the consideration and good offices of the Government, I think the time has come for me to request a favor from it. . . . I have felt mortified and unhappy that I was not . . . in the field, face to face with the enemy, in support of our glorious Nation.

His proposal this time was that he "reorganize the officers and privates of the returned New York Volunteer Regiments into a 'Veteran Corps' and that, with the view of . . . speedily organizing this Corps, I should be reinstated in my commission as Brigadier-General. . . . I am almost certain, that being duly empowered, and sufficient inducements being guaranteed to the returned volunteers of this city and neighborhood, I could, between this and New Year's Day organize a Corps of Veteran Soldiers (from 5 to 7,000 strong)."[69]

On November 26, 1863, Meagher had a special audience with President Lincoln for the purpose of introducing Charles G. Halpine to him. Lincoln had been feeling unwell and had been confined to a sick room. Meagher's appointment was the only one he had for the day; nor did he receive anyone the next day. Halpine, a native-born Irishman, had been a member of the 69th at the first Battle of Bull Run and then served in the army in other capacities. But his fame came when he wrote under the pseudonym Private Miles O'Reilly, who freely expressed his opinions about the war as a seemingly ignorant Irish enlisted man.[70]

Meagher's resignation was finally canceled just before Christmas, and he attended a gala affair held at Irving Hall honoring the brigade's non-commissioned officers.[71] There he gave the address for the evening. At least with the members of the fragmented units of the old Irish Brigade, Meagher was in good standing; significantly, his wife, Elizabeth, sat in one of the stage boxes along with the wives of some of the other officers.[72] Nonetheless, there was no possibility that Meagher would be reassigned to join the Irish.

It was not until late spring of 1864 that Meagher was finally sent to Washington to return to duty in the Union Army. It had taken a long time, and his appointment was likely due to Lincoln's belief that he could help the campaign among the Irish enlisted men. There was no command waiting for Meagher; nor did he have any definite post to report to. It was an ironic position for the general, who had resigned from the army earlier because he did not have troops to command and did not want a sinecure. This time he accepted it gratefully and did his best to support the Lincoln administration.[73]

In Washington the army told Meagher that he was to report to City Point, Virginia, but his orders were still unclear. He knew only that he was to go to City Point, where the army commanders had gathered, and contact General Grant for further orders. In the meantime, on the boat transporting him, he met Colonel Theodore B. Gates of the 20th New York State Militia, who was also headed to City Point, where he served as commander of the City Point Post. Like Meagher, Gates had been the commander of Irish troops, although his men were mostly from Ulster. As battle commanders, both men had seen their commands suffer tremendous losses: Meagher at Antietam and Fredericksburg, Gates at Gettysburg. The two men hit it off handsomely, and Gates invited Meagher to visit his camp.

The men disembarked in City Point on Monday, August 8, 1864, and Meagher showed up at Gates's camp on Friday, a day later than invited. Gates observed that Meagher "got very drunk some how [*sic*]." He stayed that way through Saturday. On Sunday Meagher spent the day "between this and Gen. Grant[']s . . . Gen. Meagher is drunk." On Monday Meagher left camp to visit the 5th Corps for the day; when he returned at ten that evening, Gates noticed with surprise that "Meagher . . . for a wonder was tolerably sober." The sobriety was short lived, however, and when Meagher awoke the next morning he "drank about a quart of whiskey & went to bed again & has been there all day drunk," according to Gates's diary. The next day Gates reported that "Meagher still keeps himself in bed & drunk." Finally, on Thursday, August 18, Gates had seen enough of Meagher and sent him a note advising that quarters would no longer be provided for him. Abashed and depressed, Meagher left later in the day in a gentle rain.[74]

Still without a command, Meagher had time to visit General Hancock in September at his encampment. As it was nearing the third anniversary of the Irish Brigade, he proposed a celebration; wishing to commence it in a religious manner, Meagher asked Father Corby to conduct services. Invitations were issued to Hancock and his generals, many of whom attended. A crude altar was constructed in the woods, seating was provided, and Father Corby recited a mass. Then Meagher took over as master of ceremonies. The program included music as well as glorious speeches by a number of generals, the best of which, according to Corby, was Meagher's. But at the end of the day the gathering broke up, bringing Meagher another sad parting from his beloved Irish Brigade.[75]

In the following four weeks Meagher returned to New York to await news of his future in the army. Despite his bout with alcohol, he had apparently impressed Grant sufficiently to obtain an assignment or at least an order to duty. On September 11 Grant sent a telegram to Halleck, letting him know that Meagher could be reached at his residence in New York and requesting Halleck to order Meagher to proceed to Nashville. It was Meagher's misfortune, however, to be ordered to report by telegraph to his nemesis, General William Tecumseh Sherman. After his last encounter with Sherman, after the first Battle of Bull Run, Meagher had publicly called him an "envenomed martinet," and Sherman had not forgotten it.[76]

Then Meagher's luck got even worse. When he arrived in Nashville, he was faced with the devastating news that the letter he had written to his friend Colonel Patrick Guiney the previous fall had been published in the newspapers. His private words to Guiney that he had "discarded with the haughtiest insensibility and disdain the 'Irish Opinion'" ran in the *New York Times* under the headline: "The 'Irish Vote'—Views of Gen. Meagher." As the *Times* treated its readers to a shocking viewpoint from the great patriot, the editors of the *Irish American* excoriated Meagher, citing what they called an "unwarranted and un-called for attack" on his fellow Irish. They claimed that Meagher himself was under control of a faction that was simply using him. With that the *Irish American* formally bid "*adieu*" to Meagher, decreeing that "between him and the people who loved and trusted him once he has opened a gulf which he never can bridge over."[77] The letter's publication clearly undermined Meagher's usefulness to Lincoln, who had counted on him to woo the Irish. Nevertheless, Meagher busied himself in Nashville giving political speeches for Lincoln's reelection. Soon the Lincoln campaign found another way to use Meagher's letter: the full text of the letter was put in a "Campaign Document" as part of an "appeal to intelligent Irishmen upon the duty they owe to the country."[78] Either way the letter was used, it could only appear to the Irish that Meagher had yielded to pressure and authorized its publication and that in so doing he had intentionally affronted the Irish—his luck had run out with them.

The article created a furor not only in America but also in Ireland. A. M. Sullivan, a lawyer who was a member of Parliament, wrote to editor Patrick Meehan of the *Irish American:* "I tell you that the picture of the Irish in America drawn by Meagher is a cut to our hearts here, and a glory to our West British defamers."[79]

The political campaign wore on Meagher. For relief from its divisiveness, he decided to give a lecture on the general subject of "Poets," giving a brief sketch of poetry and citing as illustrations excerpts from Geoffrey Chaucer, Edmund Spenser, William Shakespeare, Lord Byron, Thomas Gray, and Thomas Campbell. But it was in the verse of Robert Burns and Thomas Moore that Meagher gloried that evening, until he also felt compelled to mention the exotic Irish poetess Speranza, who had remained in his heart from his Young Ireland days. Perhaps only a single person in the audience would have known of Meagher's deep attraction to Speranza: the ubiquitous Reverend George W. Pepper, who had come to the lecture all the way from Georgia, where he was now serving as a chaplain in General Sherman's command. Pepper, who had heard Meagher speak in Ulster and at his death sentence in Clonmel, reported after the lecture that Meagher had entirely lost his English accent.[80]

It was a great show of loyalty on Pepper's part to travel to Nashville to hear Meagher speak. To do so, he had faced not only the risk of travel during the war but also the possibility of rebuke from Sherman. In fact, upon being informed of Pepper's trip to hear Meagher, Sherman chuckled: "Ah yes, Mozart Hall." This was likely a reference to the proslavery and pro-Southern New York political organization Mozart

Hall, which had been formed to challenge Tammany Hall. It was an unfair connection, which revealed how deep Sherman's distrust of Meagher ran.[81]

While Sherman was certainly aware of Meagher, by the fall of 1864 he still had not given him any orders. It was one of the busiest times of the war, and Meagher could not stand idle any longer. Not wanting to address Sherman directly, he prevailed upon General J. D. Webster to send a telegram for him. Webster informed Sherman that "Brigadier-General Meagher desires me to inquire if there are any orders for him, and to say that he is unwilling to remain unemployed at a time when the service of every soldier seems needed."[82]

Sherman tersely responded to Webster that he would not force Meagher on a commander who did not want him. Nevertheless, he knew of Meagher's relationship with President Lincoln and knew that he could not refuse to try to help him in some way. Like Meagher, he used Webster as a go-between, instructing him to tell Meagher that "if he will get any department commander to make application for him I will order him to report. . . . Unless he can do this I have no orders for him." Then Sherman relented somewhat, suggesting that Meagher "might see General Thomas or General Schofield."[83]

The following day Sherman assigned Meagher to General George H. Thomas when he ordered Thomas to organize the furloughed troops into battalions. On November 15 Thomas assigned Meagher to report to General James B. Steedman of the Department of the Cumberland and to take charge of the convalescents of the 15th and 17th Army Corps. Thomas implied that Meagher had been forced on him when he communicated with a grumbling Steedman, who wondered why his organization was being tampered with. "Your organization of convalescents, &c., is correct, and as I intended," Thomas told Steedman, "but General Meagher having reported to me for duty, I must find a command for him."[84]

Despite his balking acceptance of Meagher, Steedman soon found that they had much in common. Steedman was six years Meagher's senior and also had been a lawyer and a publisher before the war. He proved to be a steadying hand for Meagher. On November 25 he turned over the command of the 15th and 17th Army Corps in the District of Etowah to Meagher, renaming it the "Provisional Division of the Army of the Tennessee," a unique designation in the Union Army. While it was not a battle command, it was a division; and as commander

Meagher could expect that he might at some time be named a major general. His first assignment was to "occupy . . . the garrisons and block-houses on the Chattanooga and Knoxville railroad . . . , and to have full charge of the defenses of those lines."[85]

With a new army career ahead of him and a possible promotion, a relieved and energized Meagher wasted no time in organizing his division. He commanded well in the last months of 1864, and Steedman expressed his appreciation in a January 12, 1865, letter:

> Your administration of the affairs of the district of the Etowah, . . . as well as your splendid success in protecting the railroad and telegraph to Knoxville and Dalton, the steamboat transportation on the Tennessee river, the public property exposed to capture by the enemy's cavalry, and the harmony and good order maintained by you throughout the district . . . have given me much satisfaction, and secured for you the confidence and esteem of the Major-General commanding the department—as well as the officers of the entire command.

Steedman's letter soon found its way to the *Irish American,* as Meagher started to repair his reputation among the Irish.[86]

In due course a decision was made to transport Meagher's provisional division to the East, but he was not initially ordered to go with it as commander. He became anxious and in time prevailed upon Steedman to inquire about the army's plans for him. On January 10, 1865, Steedman wrote to Brigadier General William Whipple, chief of staff of the Army of the Potomac, asking if Meagher was to accompany his command to Savannah and expressing his desire to do so. It was finally decided that Meagher would remain in command. He prepared to transport his troops by train to Nashville and then by boat down the Cumberland River to the Ohio River, up the Ohio to Pittsburgh, and finally overland by whatever means were available to an East Coast port where the troops would board boats for the South to join General Sherman. A major relocation of a least six thousand troops carried with it substantial responsibility. Had it gone well, it would have been a feather in Meagher's cap. Despite a promising sendoff from Tennessee, however, Meagher's movement to the East became a well-documented disaster.[87]

The first mishap occurred after the division had barely gotten underway, when a renegade conductor ordered one of the troop trains to steam through Tullahoma Station without stopping as he was supposed to. Meagher overtook the train at Murfreesborough and was able to reassemble his command at Nashville two days later.[88] Other adversities awaited him. As the provisional division reached Cincinnati, Murat Halstead, the editor of the *Cincinnati Commercial,* wrote the War Department, saying that Meagher's drunken officers were shamefully mistreating their troops and had deserted them.[89] The War Department asked Colonel Lewis B. Parsons, chief of rail and river transportation, to investigate the matter. Parsons reported: "I have not seen a Cincinnati paper for some days, but a gentleman casually informed me that there had been some complaint in reference to neglect on the part of the commissary department." The complaint applied, he believed, to "the small force under General Meagher proceeding east by Pittsburg [*sic*]." In a separate telegram to C. A. Dana, assistant secretary of war, Parsons confirmed that the complaint was not general but applied specifically to Meagher's troops, "some 2,000 or 3,000 arriving . . . from Nashville." Meagher responded promptly to the allegations, claiming that no misconduct had occurred. He blamed whatever problems there were on the inefficiency of the railway officials, noting that he was not short over one hundred men, which he said was excusable considering that he had moved over six thousand men more than two thousand miles.[90] The exchange should have put Meagher on notice that the War Department was closely watching his progress, but he did nothing to close up the order of his straggling command as they struggled up the Ohio River in unaccommodating winter conditions.

Instead Meagher continued on ahead of his troops to Pittsburgh, where he made plans to set out alone for New York. When Major General Halleck, chief of staff of the Union Army, inquired about Meagher's position on January 23, Colonel O. Cross, deputy quartermaster general in Pittsburgh, advised Halleck that he did not know where Meagher was. Cross said that Meagher's troops had not yet arrived in Pittsburgh and that he was unable to say where they were. Later that same day, however, Halleck received word directly from Meagher, who was in fact in Pittsburgh, asking for assistance. Meagher "has 7,000 men and wants transports ready in New York," Halleck reported to Lieutenant General Ulysses S.

Grant. But Halleck had his reservations about the matter: "If Meagher's command stops in New York it is feared that very many will desert, and there are no quarters for them on Governor's Island." As Halleck and Grant pondered the matter into the evening, they became increasingly worried about Meagher's troops going to New York and finally ordered him to proceed to Washington.[91]

Meagher did not receive the late evening order because by that time he was in New York. Unaware of the orders that had been sent to Pittsburgh for him, Meagher telegraphed Halleck on January 24 that he had come to New York "to make arrangements for proceeding with all practicable speed to Savannah." He also reported confidently that his division of close to sixty-five hundred men was still coming up the Ohio River but would not reach Pittsburgh for a few days. Instead of asking for further orders, Meagher took it upon himself to arrange his own movement; he informed Halleck that he was going to Baltimore to await the arrival of his troops, because he had ordered them to go there after they reached Pittsburgh.[92] Making the confusion over Meagher's destination even worse, on January 24 Grant changed his mind about Meagher going to Washington and told Halleck to order Meagher directly to Fort Fisher in North Carolina.[93] It was left to subordinate officers to straighten out the mess.

Colonel Cross in Pittsburgh had a dilemma, because Meagher was in New York headed to Baltimore and Halleck had ordered his provisional division to Washington. Cross took it upon himself to issue orders for Meagher's troops to go to Washington after they arrived in Pittsburgh. In Washington they would embark on ships from the port of Alexandria for the South. It had now become apparent to Halleck that Meagher was not in a position to marshal his troops or to command them. Orders—some contradictory—continued to fly among the military commanders until Meagher and his troops were finally ordered to Annapolis. Halleck advised Grant that "General Meagher's division is ordered to embark at Annapolis. It will be slow work, as the transports must be coaled and provisioned by lighters. The weather is rapidly moderating, and an effort will be made to-morrow to make a channel for the transports at Alexandria."[94]

Meagher's troops started to arrive at Annapolis around February 1, and Major Robert N. Scott at Annapolis was able to inform Halleck that about a thousand of them were already on board transports waiting to embark to the South.[95] In the meantime Meagher had made his way to Baltimore together with some of his troops that he had directed there. Late in the evening of February 4 Scott had to inform Halleck that Meagher was not coming to Annapolis until the following afternoon and that he was holding up the transportation of his troops who had arrived.

Meagher had taken quarters at Barnums Hotel in Baltimore. At 5:30 in the afternoon Scott forwarded Meagher a telegraph from Halleck that authorized Scott to give orders "in my name" that "[e]ach transport must start as soon as it is loaded, Meaghers Provisional Division will go to Beaufort N.C. reporting to General Palmer at Newbern."[96]

At four o'clock on February 5 an angry Halleck telegraphed Scott: "No one will wait for General Meagher's arrival, and if such orders have been given they will be countermanded." It was not until the evening of February 5, however, that Halleck was able to report to Grant that "over 2,000 of Meagher's division are off." That was the only good thing Halleck had to say; he also reported that Meagher's troops "are in utter confusion, and he seems to be ignorant of what troops he has, or where they are." In total frustration, Halleck looked for someone to blame for Meagher's involvement with the provisional division. "It is strange that General Thomas should have intrusted [sic] men to such an officer."[97] On February 5, 1865, Scott issued an order from Halleck to the "Commanding Officer, U.S. Troops onboard Steamer New York," directing him to report to Brigadier General Palmer upon arriving in Beaufort, North Carolina. "You are directed to communicate this order to the Commanders of any portion of Genl Meaghers Provisional Division whom you may find at Beaufort or with whom you may communicate en route, and to direct them to be governed by its provisions."[98] Scott forwarded Meagher a copy of his order the same day and commented: "The commanding officers of troops on board Steamers Cahawba and Alhambra sailed under your orders for them to await your arrival at Beaufort N.C."[99]

By half past ten on the morning of February 6 Scott was able to report to Halleck: "All of Meagher's battalions have arrived, except one that was frozen up at mouth of Kanawha River." A half hour later he reported: "There is great uncertainty as to arrival of battalion alluded to this morning as being behind. General Meagher could give me no information last night." By this time Grant had heard enough of Meagher's dereliction and decided to take action to get rid of him. On February 6 an angry Grant shot back a telegram to Halleck: "If Meagher has lost his men it will be well to send some officer from Washington to look after them and relieve Meagher. If he has lost his men it will afford a favorable pretext for doing what the service would have lost nothing by having done long ago—dismissing him."[100]

Grant's decision to rid the army of Meagher did not immediately end Meagher's military service. Both Grant and secretary of war Edwin Stanton were aware of his relationship with President Lincoln; recognizing that dismissing Meagher would require Lincoln's approval, they awaited his word. In the meantime evidence against Meagher mounted. On February 9 Major Robert N. Scott wrote Halleck directly, "accusing . . . Meagher of drunkenness at Annapolis while moving his troops." When Scott had gone on board the ship *Ariel* a few days before to deliver orders to Meagher, directing his troops to New Berne, North Carolina, he noted on a copy that he had kept: "Copy furnished to Capt Flagg . . . his commander (Genl Meagher) being too drunk to understand anything."[101] The army started a file on Meagher's alleged intoxication, beginning with Scott's report. The notation on the file wrapper states: "Maj. Scott reports that in obedience to instructions he delivered certain orders to Genl Meagher on evening of 5th inst., on board Str. Ariel at Annapolis, Md. and that for reason of intoxication, . . . the said Genl M. did not, or could not, understand the purport of said orders. In verification of which Capt. Flagg, A.Q.M observed to Maj. Scott, 'it is a pity to see the Genl so' meaning Genl. Meagher."[102]

Two days later, on February 11, Grant placed on Scott's letter the following endorsement: "I would respectfull[y] recommend that Brig. Gen. T. F. Meagher, for the condition of his command in coming from Tenn. to Annapolis, and for his condition on receipt of orders for their further movement be mustered out of the service." Grant could not have made this decision easily or lightly, because he himself had been forced to resign from the U.S. Army in 1854 under charges of excessive and debilitating drinking. In a wartime army, where there was much drinking, removing an officer for inebriation was extremely difficult unless specific dereliction of duty could be related to it. Scott's report had supplied that needed element.[103] Grant continued to push for Meagher's dismissal, telegraphing Halleck on February 20: "Has Gen. Meagher been dismissed? If he has not, I think it will be well to relieve him from duty."[104] At two o'clock that same day Halleck telegraphed Grant: "The President has not acted on Meagher. The Secty of War thinks you had better order Schofield to relieve & send him home." Grant took action immediately, ordering General Schofield to relieve Meagher without delay with orders to "proceed to his place of residence."[105] In turn, Schofield issued the order relieving Meagher.[106] The matter was finished as far as Grant was concerned. Although Meagher was not out of the army, he was out of Grant's command and no longer in a position to get in his way.

Additional evidence against Meagher came from General Palmer, who reported that those troops who had arrived in New Berne were in disarray. Palmer wrote to Meagher's nemesis, Sherman, noting that

> the Provisional Division of the Army of Tennessee, under the command of General T. F. Meagher, has just arrived. This consists of about 5,000 men, composed of squads or detachments from nearly every regiment of your army, and no complete organization of any kind. There are with this some fifty officers only, and after taking out the commanding officers of the brigades with the staff officers there is scarcely one officer to each 200 men, and the whole command is but a mob of men in uniform. . . . I neglected to state that no wagons or transportation of any kind arrived with General Meagher's command.

On March 9 Major General G. W. Schofield, who was with the Army of Ohio at New Berne, reported to General Grant that "the fragments brought here by Meagher, are little better than militia."[107]

On March 10 Meagher reported by letter to the adjutant general that he was back in New York; three days later, however, he requested permission to visit for St. Patrick's Day and was granted a three-day visit to the Army of the Potomac.[108] The purpose, of course, was to visit the remnant of the Irish Brigade that was now in the South. On March 18, 1865, Meagher was present at its camp near Petersburg, Virginia, to celebrate St. Patrick's Day. As usual, horse races, foot races, and sack races were the order of the day, and the men honored Meagher by asking him to present a handsome whip to the winner of the hurdle race.[109]

Although disgraced in the eyes of his superiors, Meagher still retained the respect of the men he had commanded in battle. He also retained the respect of his opponents. Shortly after the Confederate surrender, the Reverend George Pepper, Meagher's friend from Ireland, talked with Confederate general Robert E. Lee about the Irish soldiers in the Union and Confederate armies. Lee lauded his own Irish officer, Major General Patrick Cleburne: "On a field of battle he shone like a meteor on a clouded sky!" Yet Lee singled out Meagher as the most significant leader of Irish troops in the Union Army. In Lee's opinion, Meagher did not have the military genius of Cleburne, but he still rivaled him in bravery and in the affection of his soldiers. Pepper quoted Lee as saying of Meagher: "The gallant stand which his bold brigade made on the heights of Fredericksburg is well known. Never were men so brave. They ennobled their race by their splendid gallantry on that occasion. . . . Their brilliant though hopeless assaults upon our lines excited the hearty applause of my officers and soldiers, and General Hill exclaimed, 'There are those d____ green flags again!'"[110] Lee's bright assessment of Meagher in battle contrasted sharply with Meagher's miserable failure at transporting his provisional division at the end of the war, and the two situations defined the upper and lower bounds of his military performance. Despite the dismal end of his military career, Meagher had shown commendable bravery in battle and had been a great motivator of his fellow Irishmen in the heat of a fight. But given the less glamorous administrative job of moving his provisional division across country for long distances, he simply could not perform his duties and sank deeply into the drinking that was his undoing in the end.

Meagher was still in the army, although with no hope at all of any future reprieve, when Lincoln's assassination on April 14, 1865, compounded his difficulties. Lincoln had consistently responded to Meagher's requests and supported his Irish troops. He had endorsed Meagher's reappointment in 1863 and had prevented his outright dismissal in 1865. In turn, Meagher had thrown his wholehearted support behind Lincoln, even to the point of antagonizing his wife's family and his own Irish constituency. Over the years he had established the privilege of being able to communicate directly with the president. Unlike President

James Buchanan, Lincoln usually responded promptly to his requests. Now it appeared that Meagher's last hope to recover his reputation had died with the president. He was still resourceful, decisive, and confident when sober, however, and he was quick to take action. The day after Lincoln's assassination, he appeared at the White House for a hastily arranged meeting with Andrew Johnson, the new president, and laid out his aspirations. These included a promotion, continued assignment to duty in the Union Army, and—in case the Union command decided to press charges—dismissal of any court-martial or other proceedings against him.[111] Although Meagher left a formal written request with Colonel Brownstone, an aide in the White House, they might have totally forgotten to act on Meagher's visit except for a stroke of good luck. During a chance encounter with a cousin of his friend Captain James O'Beirne, he learned that O'Beirne had been promoted to major and was serving the new president as a special aide. Meagher wasted no time in penning a letter to him from New York:

My dear Major,

. . . I shall entreat your kind offices in my favor. The President is very cordially disposed towards me—He will, I believe, favorably consider any reasonable request which I may make him, or which may be submitted him, on my behalf, by my friends—At an interview I had with him, by appointment, the morning after the assassination of Mr. Lincoln, I spoke to him about myself, just as frankly and fully as I have spoken to you, the Sunday evening previous to the assassination. On his suggestion, I shaped my wishes in a written memorandum, which under an envelope marked "confidential," I requested Colonel Browning to place in his hands. This memorandum contained three propositions.

Ist—That all proceedings hostile to me, by Court Martial or otherwise, be stopped.

IInd—That in consideration of my services in and out of the field etc. a brevet promotion be accorded me.

IIIrd—That on such promotion being made, I should be assigned to duty.

Now, however, that the army is about to be reduced it may be well for me to modify the last two propositions, or rather substitute others more opportune and attainable—Could you ascertain if there is any Territorial Governorship vacant? Next to a Military Command, this is precisely what would suit me best—Indeed, for every reason, it might prove greatly more advantageous than the latter—It would enable me, after a little, to enter Congress; and once there, I have no fear but that I should make myself Master of the Situation—to my own credit, to the gratification of my friends, to the confusion and mortification of my enemies, and to the honour of our race. You have here, in these few timid words, my wishes, my ambition, my anticipations; and I confide them to you, Jim, assured you will do all in your power to assist me in giving them effect—I beg you to write to me on the Subject, and shall be delighted to receive any suggestions in relation to it, you think it wise to make— with friendliest regards to Mrs. O'Beirne and affectionate good wishes for the Great Responsibility,

> Believe me always
> Most faithfully
> Your friend,
> T. F. Meagher
> Brig. Gen'l[112]

Despite Meagher's face-to-face meeting with President Johnson and his contact through O'Beirne, nothing resulted from his requests, although there is no evidence (other than Meagher's letter to O'Beirne) that he was ever under any threat of court-martial. On May 1 the War Department, as part of a general mustering out of volunteers, finally called for Meagher's resignation. He delivered it on May 12, leaving his future prospects less promising than ever.[113]

But that was not the last of Meagher's attempts to obtain the rank of major general. On June 20, 1865, he wrote to O'Beirne again, saying that "it would be most advantageous for me to have my Brevet, as Major General." Meagher also noted that he had read in the paper "this morning . . . that the Governorship of Idaho Territory is vacant. Entreat the President to let me have it, and all will be forthwith right and glorious with me. Urge this at once." Accompanying the letter were two one-page documents. One explained why the envelope was from the Astor House in New York. "I happen to enclose this letter at the Astor House—But, of course, I'm at my father-in-law's. 32 East 23rd Street." The note said: "Let me have Idaho." The other was also in Meagher's unmistakable handwriting: "It is ordered by the President, that the communication from the War Department, accepting the resignation of Brigadier General Meagher be forthwith cancelled, and that his commission as Brevet Major General be forthwith made out." R. D. Massey, secretary for military affairs, scribbled on the back of Meagher's envelope, forwarding it to the "Secretary Of War for his special perusal and considerations." No further action was taken by the War Department. An unsigned copy of Meagher's "order," in a neater hand, was also placed in the file, but Meagher received no response to his request to be breveted as a major general.[114]

Although the unsigned order to promote him became a permanent part of his army file, Thomas Francis Meagher was never promoted to brevet major general.[115] This fact was sometimes ignored by the media.[116] In 1867, eight days after Meagher's death in Montana, John C. Foley of New York asked the adjutant general to provide him and "some of the exc officers of this Brigade in this City" with the precise "rank of the late Brig. Gen'l Thomas Francis Meagher." Apparently there was still doubt, even among the Irish who had served with him, as to whether Meagher had received a brevet promotion to major general.[117]

CHAPTER EIGHT

The Way West

I leave this evening for the far west, for one of the richest of our new territories.

Thomas Francis Meagher, July 17, 1865

Thomas Francis Meagher saw his life change dramatically in the last half of 1865. In June he was unemployed in New York and seeking a new course. By December he had just finished a treaty negotiation with the Blackfeet Indian tribe on the plains of the Missouri River. During the intervening six months he moved to Montana Territory, having been appointed territorial secretary en route. Despite the great contrast between New York and Montana, Meagher's decision to move west had an undeniable logic. His letter condemning the Irish Democratic political machine—and, by extension, its Irish followers—had made him *persona non grata* in New York's Irish circles. With nothing more he could do for the Irish or his own career in the East, he began to look farther afield.

Before the war Meagher had embraced the belief that migration from the cities could improve the situation of Irish immigrants. In his newspaper, the *Irish News,* he had touted the services of the Irish Aid Society of New York, an organization that helped resettle Irish families in the West.[1] He also had traveled to Costa Rica to explore the possibility of establishing an Irish republic in the young country through mass migration. While Costa Rica was politically too unstable to provide a suitable new home, he was more impressed with the western United States.

Meagher had visited California during the winter of 1854 and found there the type of landscape and society he thought might suit the Irish. He scheduled three lectures on Irish topics at the Musical Hall in San Francisco.[2] After that he had visited the mining camps in the California mountains, where he spent most of his time among the miners in Grass Valley, rough-and–ready Nevada City, and at the Forks of the Yuba River. He had stayed in whatever accommodations were available, including a hotel that had no doors or windows and no one to collect his bill when he left. Despite the hardships, he found that the country offered a rich diversity, pleasant companionship, and endless possibility.[3]

Meagher fondly recalled walking through five feet of snow to pay his respects to the famous dancer Lola Montez, who despite her name was an eminent Irishwoman, the Countess of Landsfeldt. He claimed to have found her with her arm in a cast, recovering from a slap given by her pet grizzly bear. In another California gold town he had incongruously delivered a lofty lecture on the "Fine Arts of Athens" while he sat in the corner of a Methodist church next to a stove upon which he had placed candles so he could read his manuscript. In a typically expansive letter, Meagher touched upon what he saw as the nature of California: "the floor of which is of precious stones, the gates of which are golden, and the roof whereof is azure . . . which animate and beautify society, and in the growth and spread of which republicanism finds its true expression." Now, over ten years later, it occurred to Meagher that the true republicanism he sought for his fellow Irish might be had in the West. But instead of California, Meagher set his sights on the new goldfields of the Rocky Mountains.[4]

An invitation-only lecture at the Traveler's Club, on the corner of West Fourteenth Street and Fifth Avenue, piqued Meagher's interest in Montana Territory. On the summer evening of June 23, 1865, he listened as a rugged westerner named Captain James Liberty Fisk talked about the three pioneer wagon trains he had led from St. Paul to the Idaho and Montana gold mines. Meagher grew increasingly excited as he listened to Fisk's energetic description of the rich goldfields and the beauty of the country. When he heard Fisk say that a fourth train would leave from Minnesota later that summer, he grew impatient to learn more. After Fisk's talk, Meagher pressed him into conversation. Soon the two agreed that Meagher would go on the next expedition and use his connections to obtain a military escort for the settlers through Indian-controlled territory.[5]

Meagher wanted a letter of recommendation from the Catholic bishops in New York and approached them with trepidation, because even staunch Irish defender Archbishop John Hughes, who had died over a year before, believed the Irish were ill equipped to live on the western frontier. Meagher did not have the standing with the other priests in the New York archdiocese that he had enjoyed with Hughes, so he was especially pleased to obtain letters of introduction from them to the missionary priests in the West and to the Catholic bishops in St. Paul.

Having secured the requisite introductions, Meagher enthusiastically began to arrange his departure from New York. He knew he would be safe in Montana under the religious guidance of Father Pierre Jean De Smet, a Catholic missionary to the Indians who had come to the upper Missouri region in 1840 and who had already become famous. Meagher wrote his father and his son in Ireland, with great assurance: "The territory I go to includes that vast Indian territory which has been the scene of the great Father De Smet's labours and successes."

> I carry letters of introduction (written in the warmest and most complimentary terms) from the good Father Provincial here and the Rector of St Francis Xavier's College to father de Smet, and the Bishop of the Territory, who is also a Father of the Society of Jesus—The good Father Rector, in his letter to the Rev. Father Provincial of the Province of Missouri, says—"Through all the battles which the General has led his soldiers, he has ever proved himself to be a true Christian with a truly Irish faith."

The recommendation from the rector so pleased Meagher that he told his father: "I value such a commendation more than any other I have received for my conduct in the war."[6]

Meagher's letter to his father also included a separate note for Thomas Bennett Meagher, who was now eleven years old. Meagher had never seen his "dear little Bennie." "I leave this evening for the far west, for one of the richest of our new territories," he told his son. Always holding out the prospect that soon he might have the means to see both his son and his father, he added: "I entertain the liveliest hopes that this enterprise will prove a profitable one to me, and that it will enable me to pay you a visit in France next Summer."[7]

By late July Meagher found himself in Minnesota actively working with Fisk on the expedition. Carrying through on his promise to Fisk, Meagher, together with Minnesota governor Stephen Miller and General Henry Hastings Sibley, telegraphed President Andrew Johnson on July 25, asking for troops to accompany the expedition.[8] The request was not even acknowledged. The telegraph served a secondary purpose, however, by once again reminding the White House that Meagher had requested an appointment.

In Minnesota Meagher obtained audiences with Bishop Thomas Grace and Archbishop John Ireland of the St. Paul diocese. He found both priests sympathetic to his plan to populate Montana with Irish settlers. As it turned out, John Ireland had already been involved in a movement to relocate Irish Catholics to the West. In 1864 he had been made president of a group of local Irish patriots named the Minnesota Irish Immigration Society, whose mission was to promote Irish settlement in Minnesota and surrounding states.[9]

Meagher, Grace, and Ireland all agreed that one major obstacle stood in the way of successful Catholic settlement: the immigrants, they believed, needed access to priests in their new home. Meagher had a plan, which Ireland duly recorded:

> It was [Meagher's] wish, he repeatedly stated, to colonize Montana with Catholics, drawing settlers principally from Irishmen in Ireland and Irishmen in America. He would at once take steps to secure priests and would write to All Hallows College in Dublin to engage there ten students, for whose tuition he would make himself responsible. He would, furthermore, he added, take steps to have a bishop in Montana.[10]

While in St. Paul, Meagher also spoke at a benefit for the Irish Immigration Society, which welcomed him as an Irish patriot and war hero. The event offered an occasion to reassert himself as a leader in Irish American politics. Instead of using the opportunity to lay out a vision for a better Irish future, however, Meagher's bitterness led him to rant against the New York Irish political leadership and the blindness of their followers, calling on the Irish "to emancipate themselves from the control of the politicians who have held them in an ignoble captivity for many years, and to whose vulgar dictation they have surrendered the intelligence and high spirit which should be as precious to them as their citizenship." Meagher also came out in favor of African American suffrage, saying that "the black heroes of the Union army have not only entitled themselves to liberty but to citizenship."[11] He soon found out that even in St. Paul he was not out of reach of the *Irish American,* which attacked his position on racial matters. In an article entitled "Gen. Meagher on Negro Suffrage," the *American* sarcastically wrote that Meagher had "beautiful diction and fervid eloquence" but continued to alienate the Irish people with the "new-fangled notions of the circle of friends in which he now finds himself."[12]

In the article disparaging Meagher, the *Irish American* also inadvertently paid him the compliment of announcing that he had been breveted major general—which was untrue. Not wishing to press his luck with President Johnson, who, he believed, was considering his other requests, Meagher had withdrawn his request for the rank.[13] The compliment aside, the point had been made: even though Meagher was no longer in New York, he was not out of the East Coast Irish community's reach. The *Irish American* had also made it clear that he would no longer be accepted as a leader unless he hewed to Democratic positions.

To Meagher, their position mattered little. He had given up on the possibility that New York could offer a positive future for the Irish or for himself. Life there was barely an improvement "from their distressed and downcast condition in the old country," he wrote in a public letter. "An Irish laborer, with his wife and children hived into a badly plastered den in the back part of a tenement house in New York, for instance, is very little better off than he was at home." The West, on the contrary, offered hope: "somewhere in these glorious new States—with his own hearth-stone under his unshackled foot . . . the Irish emigrant does, indeed, radically and essentially improve his condition."[14] Thus Meagher ignored the *Irish American*'s attack to focus on the business at hand in St. Paul. He continued to promote the Fisk expedition, and on August 2 he gave a lecture on the Idaho Territory. Andrew Fisk, James's young nephew, attended the lecture and noted on August 13, 1865, in his diary that the "St. Paul paper says Gen. Meagher has received his commission and expects to have an escort."[15] Although that prediction did not become a reality, Meagher's fortunes began to look up when he received an official appointment as secretary of Montana Territory.

In 1865 Montana Territory was a little more than a year old. The position of territorial secretary had never been filled, but not for want of trying. First President Abraham Lincoln offered the job to the Reverend Henry P. Torsey, LL.D., president and professor of medical and moral philosophy and natural science at Wesleyan Seminary and Female College in Maine. Torsey, who had no wish to leave his academic position for the wilds of the West, declined. Next President Johnson offered the job to Brigadier General John Coburn, a former state representative from Indiana, but Coburn too turned it down. Finally Thomas Francis Meagher's name surfaced in the White House when they received his telegram requesting troops to accompany Fisk. Knowing that Meagher was headed to Montana anyway and that he had once wanted a territorial position, Johnson offered him the job.[16]

Although the appointment came as a complete surprise, Meagher accepted immediately. Territorial secretary was not the high-level government position he had initially sought, but he was tired of the uncertainty in his life and was willing to accept any job that offered a salary and the possibility of a political advancement. Certainly secretary was better than no appointment at all, and Bishop Ireland made the most of it when he read the letter of appointment to the August 2 meeting of the Immigration Society, proudly announcing that "Gen. Meagher had accepted the appointment with a view of being a help to his countrymen who should emigrate to that Territory." Meagher then responded with a lengthy address. "That the inevitable necessity of the Irish race has been for some time past, is at present, and will continue for some time longer, to overflow in the emigration to the new world, must be admitted," he said. A free Ireland could have prevented this state, making "the emigrant ship . . . a stranger." Instead "the depletion of Ireland by the emigrant . . . [has become] an almost fatal calamity. But it is a calamity which for the time being cannot be averted," Meagher continued; therefore, it has become "our sacred duty . . . to direct that emigration into salutary channels, and transform it from a curse . . . into a benediction."[17]

On August 16 Meagher wrote Fisk that instead of accompanying the wagon train he planned to begin his trip to Montana immediately. By August 23 he had reached Atchison, Kansas, on the Missouri River. He left the next day on the Overland Stage, reaching Denver by August 29 and staying there until September 6. Meagher then traveled to Salt Lake City, where he arrived on September 16, staying a few days before leaving on September 19 for the final leg of his journey to Bannack, Montana's territorial capital. While in Salt Lake City, Meagher wrote secretary of state William H. Seward about delay and uncertainty in his travels due to concerns about Indian troubles.[18] It was his first encounter with the growing conflict between the Great Plains tribes and the onrush of settlers—a conflict that would dominate much of his career in Montana.

When Meagher finally arrived in Bannack, the territorial capital was a mere three years old. In those years the region's non-Indian population had ballooned to over twenty thousand after large gold strikes convinced miners, merchants, and freighters that there were fortunes to be made. The territorial governor in 1865 was Sidney Edgerton; but when he had first arrived in Bannack in 1863, the community had still been part of Idaho Territory. Lincoln had appointed him to serve as Idaho Territory's chief justice, but Edgerton never performed the judicial duties he had been sent to carry out. Even though there was a crying need for judges and courts, Edgerton believed that he could not serve as a judge until he took the required oath. He had been assigned by Idaho's governor to the eastern side of the Rocky Mountains, where there was no one who could administer the oath, and snow had blocked his initial attempt to reach the Idaho capital of Boise across the Rockies.[19]

Edgerton never did travel to Boise City to have the oath administered but remained in Bannack, where he watched as vigilante justice reigned, absent courts and judges. He was not idle, however. Receiving support from the citizens of the gold-rush towns of Virginia City and Bannack to break away from Idaho, Edgerton set out for Washington, D.C., in January 1864 to lobby for the establishment of a separate territory to be divided from Idaho at the summit of the Bitterroot Range.

Sidney Edgerton. (Courtesy Montana Historical Society, Helena)

He left his wife, Mary Wright Edgerton, who was expecting a child, along with their young daughter and a niece in the crude mining camp.[20]

Edgerton's efforts in Washington were successful, and on May 26, 1864, President Lincoln signed the "Organic Act" creating Montana Territory.[21] Soon afterward he appointed Edgerton as territorial governor. It was a bad match. The former Ohio congressman was a hard-line abolitionist with an iron will, a "radical of radicals," according to his nephew Wilbur Fisk Sanders.[22] The new territory was filled with Confederate sympathizers and Union Democrats. Thus it was not surprising that the *Montana Post* reported that in the first Montana legislature Edgerton "met with a good deal of opposition, and some of it tolerably violent."[23]

The next appointed officials after Edgerton to come to the territory were the territorial federal judges, who arrived in 1864. Hezekiah L. Hosmer, a Shakespeare scholar and former secretary of the House Committee on the Territories, was appointed chief justice. The two associate justices were Lorenzo P. Williston, a Pennsylvanian who had already served as a judge in Dakota Territory, and Lyman E. Munson, a Yale graduate and practicing New Haven attorney. They were all men of considerable legal ability and all staunch Republicans who judicially and politically supported Governor Edgerton.[24]

The territorial secretary arrived at last, when the dusty and travel weary Meagher stepped down from a stagecoach in Bannack City on September 23, 1865. What he found there matched no portrayal in his mind's eye of anything he had ever contemplated as a capital. Amid the sagebrush of a high mountain basin were scattered a few hundred small log buildings along the gold-laden Grasshopper Creek. One of these rough cabins, where the Edgertons lived, served as the governor's mansion. The creek itself had been named for the insects that abounded in the dry, hot summers. Meagher was not initially impressed, saying later that "every collection of log huts is called a city in this ambitious country."[25]

Even with little advance notice of Meagher's arrival, a lively group of well-wishers greeted him. The dead may also have greeted him: even with the presence of the three territorial judges, vigilante justice still reigned in Montana Territory. One of its most avid practitioners, in fact, was Edgerton's nephew, Wilbur Fisk Sanders, who had accompanied his uncle west. Starting in December 1863, Sanders served as the prosecutor of George Ives. When twenty-three of the twenty-four miners assembled for the trial found Ives guilty of murder, Sanders immediately made a motion that Ives "be hung by the neck until he was dead." The meeting approved the motion; and though Ives pleaded with Sanders, asking for time to write his mother and sisters in the states and to make a will, Sanders denied his request. Within a "few minutes," the body of Ives was left hanging in the street. Shortly afterward, Sanders and seven others agreed to form a vigilance committee.[26]

Twenty-four men took the vigilante oath of silence and fidelity. They then set about their gruesome work of apprehending and hanging members of a gang of road agents, who had been robbing and murdering travelers with seeming impunity. Soon Bannack's sheriff, Henry Plummer,

Wilbur Fisk Sanders. (Courtesy Montana Historical Society, Helena)

was implicated in the road agents' work and was also hanged.[27] More bodies were left swinging from trees and gallows in the Montana Territory; when Meagher arrived in the territory, there had been more than two dozen executions.[28]

The vigilantes typically displayed the suspended, lifeless bodies following public hangings. When Meagher arrived, the area was in the middle of a spate of such events. If he did not see the bodies, he certainly read about them. On the day after his arrival the territory's only established newspaper, the *Montana Post,* reported on the hanging of Tommy Cooke, a pickpocket. In its September 30 edition the *Post* ran an extensive story about Meagher in addition to stories about the hangings of John Morgan and John Jackson and the separate hanging of a robber named Jack Howard. The *Post* edition of October 7 reported that a man with the label "Robber" was found hanging in Confederate Gulch; two more men were found "dangling" at the Prickly Pear toll gate; and a fourth man named Con Kirby was also found "dangling in the air."[29] As Thomas J. Dimsdale, the editor of the *Montana Post* and himself a member of the secret vigilante organization, commented in 1865, "swift and terrible retribution is the only preventive of crime, while society is organizing in the far West."[30]

A few days after his arrival Meagher had a brief meeting with Governor Sidney Edgerton. Soon afterward Edgerton, who had already sold his interest in a gold claim in Nevada City on September 12, announced with very little preparation or warning that he was leaving the territory with his family for Ohio.[31] He had not obtained permission to leave his post in Montana, but it seems to have been the style of the day. All three of the territorial judges—Hosmer, Williston, and Munson—had gone east during their tenures, prompting John Owen to note: "our Terr. officers Seem to have a fondness for Hibernating at the East." In addition, several of the succession of Idaho Territory's governors had simply left their posts when it suited their interests.[32]

Four months later, while Edgerton was still on the East Coast, he was called upon to justify his absence. He responded with a letter to secretary of state William Seward claiming hardship. Among his excuses was that Meagher, the territorial secretary, had not arrived until September 1865, giving him no time to request leave before the winter months prevented travel.[33] Seward did not accept the argument, and further exchanges of correspondence only worsened the matter. One of Edgerton's complaints was that he had funded many of the territorial expenses out of his own pocket, and he pointed a finger of blame at Meagher, saying that he had arrived without funds or a bond and did not intend to post one. Edgerton's final argument, perhaps his lamest but also the truest, was that he had left to obtain education for his daughter. Secretary of the interior James Harlan finally impressed on Seward that Edgerton needed to be in the territory to govern effectively. When Harlan recommended Edgerton's removal, Seward agreed. Their correspondence was placed in a private file.[34]

Meanwhile, fully expecting that Edgerton would return, Meagher set out to do the best he could in Montana as acting governor. His charisma led to early broad-based acceptance in the territory. Meagher even had initial favorable relations with Edgerton's nephew, Wilbur Sanders, who had stayed in Montana in part to look after his uncle's political interests. Together with three others, Meagher and Sanders set out to visit the Oro Cache lode and others in the area. As reported in the *Post*, "The genial souls of that auriferous region expressed their happiness at the sight of the General, and Mr. Brown drank to 'The health of the friends of the Secretary in Ireland, and also to the health of his own friends in America,' which was immediately replied to by that gentleman with, 'The health of the friends of both of them, the world over.'"[35]

Thomas Dimsdale, editor of the *Montana Post*, also initially welcomed Meagher. Born in the north of England to a family of iron masters, the diminutive Dimsdale had come to the territory to try his luck in the goldfields two years before Meagher arrived in Montana. With an education obtained at Rugby and Oxford, his literary talent far exceeded his mining abilities. Dimsdale became Montana Territory's foremost recorder, and much of early Montana territorial history is seen through his eyes.[36]

Initially Meagher appreciated Dimsdale's considerable literary talent and intellect, and Dimsdale respected Meagher's oratory and idealism, as one who stood for justice and had fought to save the Union. On September 23 Dimsdale introduced Meagher in the *Montana Post* by reprinting an article from the *Salt Lake City Daily Telegraph* that proclaimed Meagher "a thorough Irish gentleman, of manly instincts, a great traveler, and an eminent scholar."[37] Dimsdale followed that with an even warmer welcome the next week:

Thomas Josiah Dimsdale. (Courtesy Montana Historical Society, Helena)

General Meagher has arrived among us, and we doubt not that the public reception of this evening will be an earnest of the high appreciation in which he is held as a soldier, as a citizen, and as a man. Our new secretary is no partisan. His banner is the stars and stripes, under which he has fought for the country, and this he regards as the flag of a nation, and not of a party. . . . Not as a politician, but as an American citizen, General Meagher enters this Territory, inspired with the firm determination to do justice to all men.[38]

In addition, on October 21 the *Post* published a biographical sketch of Meagher that resounded with heroism, honor, and dignity, if not accuracy. The sketch cited Meagher's "honest and chivalrous revocation of his parole" in Tasmania, glossing over the controversy that had long clouded his reputation. It also presented a revisionist history of Meagher's Civil War experience, exaggerating his role in the defeat of Confederate general John Bell Hood in Tennessee and, even more remarkably, citing him for successfully delivering 7,000 western troops to General Sherman—the failed mission that had caused him to be relieved of his command.[39]

The article's most conspicuous error was its promotion of Meagher to "Major General, having been placed on a list of brevets at the end of the war by President Johnson himself."[40] At least on that score the *Post* soon quietly corrected itself, later referring to him as a brigadier general, his true rank. Dimsdale later gagged on his own words when Meagher allied himself with the territory's Democratic majority, and Meagher soon felt the sting of the retaliatory pen wielded by the small, frail Englishman.

Meagher also received a hero's welcome from his fellow Irish, including members of the Fenian Brotherhood. Shortly after he arrived in Bannack, Meagher met the territory's steadfast Fenian "head centre," Andrew O'Connell. On September 30 the Fenian Brotherhood chapters of Virginia City and Nevada City organized a torchlight procession for Meagher that proceeded from Nevada City to Virginia City. Thirty-two torches were marked with the letters "FB," standing for Fenian Brotherhood, while five larger torches boasted the design "'98 and '48" (the years of the last two Irish rebellions) and slogans such as "Robert Emmett [*sic*] Circle F.B., Nevada City, M.T." One slogan in particular captured the group's militancy: "A soldier's Life is the Life for me."[41]

The march ended in a reception at the Planter's House Hotel, where Meagher had taken up residence. The *Post* reported that Meagher told the assembled Fenians that he "belonged to no party—never could be yoked, broken, coaxed, or otherwise tamed to any party" and would vote for the measures and for the men "as he believed and was convinced would best promote the material interests, the democratic development, the republican liberties, and with them, the power of the United States." His party, he told the assembled audience, was "in a word, . . . the people of the United States." The speech, as printed in the *Post,* was larded with bracketed laudatory phrases: "[Loud cheering]," "[Continued cheering]," "[Hear, hear, and loud applause]," "[Deafening cheers]," "[Cheers]," and "[Enthusiastic cheers]"; given the mostly Irish makeup of his audience, the night no doubt had been filled with the shouts of unbridled enthusiasm for Meagher.[42]

Dimsdale, of course, had taken notice of Meagher's conspicuous connection with the Fenians, whose operations in Montana were out in the open as they were almost everywhere in the United States. Now that the Fenians were no longer a totally secret organization, the public in Montana and elsewhere was becoming well aware of their military aims against the British.[43] Dimsdale and his *Post* reported to Montana citizens on October 28: "The Fenian movement is the great excitement at present. . . . Twenty millions of Irish are outside of Erin they say, and are preparing to get inside."[44] One faction of the Fenian Brotherhood planned to invade Canada and wrest it from the British so it could be bartered for freedom for Ireland. As an Englishman, Dimsdale did not view this goal kindly, and in the November 4 edition of the *Post* he questioned Irish patriotism, pointing to the alacrity with which the Irish had "voluntarily forsaken their country." He then proposed continued immigration as a solution to the Irish problem, suggesting that the remaining Irish in Ireland "could soon migrate" to Canada "without great inconvenience."[45]

It was easy for Dimsdale as an Englishman to say that the Irish should simply abandon Ireland, but inflammatory for Meagher and the Irish in Montana. Meagher, who called Irish emigration a "calamity" even as he recognized its painful necessity, must have been beside himself when he read those lines, which forever alienated him from Dimsdale.[46] The little English editor followed up three weeks later with a less demeaning article in which he acknowledged the Fenian Brotherhood's struggle for freedom from England, while at the same time throwing a jab at Meagher: "We are told the Irish revolution of '98, and the movement of '48, were failures."[47] This was a matter that Meagher himself would have freely acknowledged, but as a principal leader of the '48 revolution he certainly did not want to hear it from an Englishman. Besides editing the *Montana Post,* Dimsdale had set down the exploits of the vigilantes in a manuscript, which became *The Vigilantes of Montana.* This effort took him away from his full-time duties dealing with a rival, the *Montana Democrat,* and an opposing political viewpoint. In late August 1866 Dimsdale left Virginia City for the country to rest for a few weeks in an effort to recover from pulmonary problems and nervous exhaustion, but it was to no avail. He died on September 22, at the age of thirty-five. At his bedside was Wilbur F. Sanders, his friend, fellow Mason, and political collaborator. Dimsdale received an impressive Masonic burial on September 24, 1866.[48]

Dimsdale and Meagher also clashed on a religious front. While Meagher had arranged for a Catholic mass to be said in Virginia City on Christmas 1865, Dimsdale, acting as a lay reader, conducted the first Episcopal service there. Episcopal bishop Daniel Tuttle noted that Dimsdale had been a good lay reader but that his small congregation had been amused when he read from the English Prayer Book: he "prayed most loyally for the Queen, and entirely ignored the President." Tuttle claimed that Dimsdale had fallen into "bad habits" and died from them. The *Montana Post,* in publishing his obituary, said only that Dimsdale "suffered for many weeks from a complication of disorders, which finally triumphed over his strong constitution."[49] Dimsdale left a legacy of attacking Meagher. Meagher's problems with the *Montana Post* were not lessened by Dimsdale's death, for Henry Blake took over the editorship. Blake was a Bostonian Yankee, a graduate of Harvard University, and a lawyer. After arriving in Virginia City in 1866, he had been gratuitously notified by the vigilantes that he had been elected a member. Blake, believing that Meagher was excessively vain and loved to see his name in print with a "halo of praise," would not treat him kindly.[50]

To fight Dimsdale, and then Blake, Meagher had only the support of the weak-penned John Bruce, editor of the *Montana Democrat.* While Bruce's editorials and articles generally supported the Democrats, he was not as skilled as the *Post* editors and did not have their political fervor, leaving a somewhat one-sided journalistic record of Meagher's accomplishments. Blake's attacks took on an even more personal note

Henry N. Blake, the *Montana Post* editor after Dimsdale. (Courtesy Montana Historical Society, Helena)

than Dimsdale's. A total abstainer from alcohol and tobacco, Blake would write: "I was acquainted with the reputation of Gen. Meagher and his associates in the army for sobriety, and under the circumstances set forth was prejudiced against him. He did not read high sounding encomiums from my pen and what I did write respecting him was too true." When an article by Blake finally agitated Meagher to the point of distraction and indiscretion, Meagher wrote a letter regarding "the scandalous article you wrote and published against me personally" and demanded that Blake publish "an ample apology" in the next issue of the paper. If Blake did not do that, Meagher threatened to make "immediate arrangements . . . for affording me that satisfaction, which from your recent association with gentlemen in military life, it is, I presume, entirely unnecessary for me to particularize." Blake published Meagher's letter and took great delight in replying in print that he regarded "a duelist as a murderer" and that the "miscalled code of honor is a relic of barbarism and ignorance." In a softer tone, he said that he "could not stultify myself by attempting to take the life of a man against whom I have no feelings of enmity." Blake's reply was published under the heading "Pistols and Coffee for Two." Nothing ever came of the challenge.[51]

The initial breach between Meagher and Dimsdale might have become more pitched except that Meagher was away from Bannack in the fall of 1865 when the articles were printed. He was receiving his initiation into a situation that nothing in his education or experience had prepared him for: a face-to-face meeting with the Blackfeet tribes to negotiate a treaty.

The task of negotiating Indian treaties lay primarily with the United States Department of the Interior. As acting governor, however, Meagher was also the territory's acting superintendent of Indian affairs. The duties of the latter position were not clearly defined but were not inconsequential, because peaceful relations with the Indians were paramount to effective settlement of the region. As superintendent, Meagher's territory included two regions naturally divided by the Rocky Mountains, each with its own federally appointed Indian agent. The eastern agent oversaw the Gros Ventres and various tribes of Blackfeet, including Piegans, Bloods, and Blackfeet proper; the western agent supervised the Flatheads, Pend d'Oreilles, and Kootenais. The agents were supposed to report to the governor regularly, but they had been remiss in doing so.[52]

Congress had authorized negotiations with the Confederated Blackfeet with the goal of obtaining Indian lands south of the Missouri and Teton Rivers in March 1865, long before Meagher had arrived in Montana. The Department of Interior selected Gad E. Upson, the Blackfeet agent in Fort Benton, as its negotiator.[53] Major

Upson, as he was known, had acquired his military title in a period of soldiering first in the Mexican War and then as part of a mercenary filibustering expedition against Cuba. Deciding on a quieter life, he had worked for a time for the Department of the Interior in Washington and had been sent to his agency position in Montana in late 1863. But that is not all that Upson did. During his two years in Montana he acquired gold-mining claims in the Virginia City area and formed the Clark and Upson Mining Company to process ore.[54] Upson also ran for election as the Montana territorial delegate on the Republican ticket in 1865, only to suffer defeat by the Democratic incumbent, Samuel McLean.[55]

Upson did not think highly of the Indians. He believed that encounters with white settlers "had a tendency to create in their ignorant minds a jealousy and prejudice against the whites, amounting in several instances to open hostilities, and resulting in bloodshed to both parties. . . . Not one spark of civilization appears to have dawned upon their ignorant minds, and their capacity for improvement, if they ever had any, seems to have risen and set in total darkness." He concluded that because of intertribal wars, disease, and moral decay, "but a few years will elapse before all but a remnant of what they once were will have passed to their last 'hunting lands,' to return no more forever."[56]

In early summer Upson had reported that the Piegans and the Gros Ventres were peaceful, but that the Bloods and Blackfeet were hostile and that troops should be sent immediately to quiet the situation. This would turn out to be just another request for troops to quell the Indians that went unheeded in Washington. Being instructed to go ahead with the negotiation anyway, Upson invited Governor Edgerton to attend in his role as superintendent for Indian affairs.[57] Before he left, Edgerton asked Meagher to take his place. Meagher was eager to go; his long trip across the plains had given him a sense of the settlers' fear of the Indian tribes. Resolving to attend and contribute to the negotiations, he recruited a party of interested and knowledgeable people to go with him: Judge Lyman E. Munson, a prominent Republican with whom he had not yet parted ways; George J. Wood, sheriff of Edgerton County; Cornelius Hedges, a young lawyer from Helena; and Malcolm Clarke, a former agent for the American Fur Company at Fort Benton, who had a Piegan wife and considerable experience trading with the Indians and who as a Catholic was "a sincere and active friend of the Jesuit Fathers."[58]

The group included both Democrats and Republicans, but politically the trip would spell an end to Meagher's nonpartisan fantasies. During the 130-mile journey Meagher and Munson, two of the best-educated men in Montana, would find that they had nothing in common but their forensic ability to level charges at each other. By the end of the trip their mutual disrespect foreshadowed Meagher's relationships with the entire Republican faction.

The trip also served as Meagher's initiation to Montana's rugged weather and terrain. The road from Helena to Fort Benton was the best in the territory except for a fifteen-mile stretch north of Helena. There the road wound through Prickly Pear Canyon, crossing Little Prickly Pear Creek more than twenty-five times. Once out of the canyon, the road struck off from the creek over Lyons and Medicine Rock Mountains, a difficult route in any season or weather.[59] The party left Helena before the middle of October, "on a mid-summer day on the threshold of the winter—a bride in her joy, her beauty, and her jewels, on the verge of the grave," according to a letter that Meagher wrote Father Pierre De Smet, with whom he had begun to correspond. The party soon ran into trouble, however. Stopping at the Clarke ranch on Little Prickly Pear Creek after their first day on the road, the weary travelers felt the cold bite of the wind signaling the coming of winter. On their second day a major storm had descended by the time they arrived at a way station on the Dearborn River, and they had to stay for the night.[60]

Attempting to go about twelve miles the next day, the party picked up an Indian guide who led them through the blinding snow to a camp called Bird's Tail. There they met Father Frances Xavier Kuppens, a Jesuit missionary who was himself snowbound. Meagher's group crowded into the smoke-choked atmosphere of the missionary's buffalo skin tepee. Kuppens, a Belgian priest who had established the St. Peter's Mission, welcomed the travelers, who added their own pipe smoke to the central fire's almost unbearable smoky haze. Nevertheless, according to Meagher, the blazing fire provided a "delightful contrast to the wind which fiercely beat without, the rent and raging sky, the swollen river, which swept by his door so cold and white, and the snow which already began to [fall] rapidly in heavy flakes."[61]

After a dinner of mountain-goat stew, Meagher stretched himself out on his buffalo robe and pulled his saddle up to serve as a pillow.

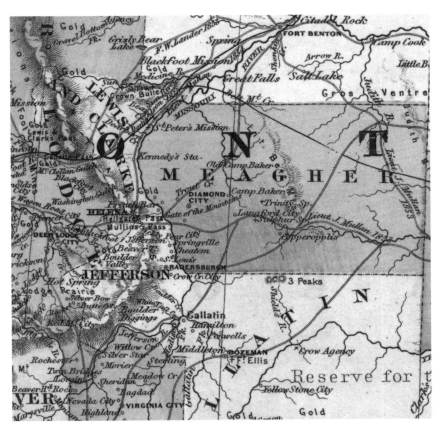

Portion of an early Montana map (by A. J. Johnson). This map of the western part of the Montana Territory was done in 1865 as a steel plate engraving. Some information on the map was added after that time, such as the name of Meagher County, created by the 1866 legislature and named after Thomas Francis Meagher. The map shows locations such as Virginia City, Helena, and Fort Benton and the Blackfeet Missions, with trails and wagon roads marked. (Courtesy Montana Historical Society, Helena)

While the others became engrossed in a game of cards, he opened a ragged copy of Shakespeare's plays and, he later remembered, "I . . . yielded myself in a luxurious rest to the visions and melodies of Shakespeare's 'Tempest' which glorious work of the world's greatest dramatist I turned to almost instinctively as the storm thickened round us."[62]

Meagher and his party stayed this way for two nights and two days until they ran out of food. Despite being warned of the danger of travel by a party of six gentlemen who had just arrived from Fort Benton, Meagher's group headed out into the storm toward the newly established St. Peter's

Mission, a distance of at most twelve miles but a daunting task in the driving snow. The travelers, wrapped in leathers and buffalo robes, mounted their horses and forded the Dearborn River single file, with their faces and eyes wreathed in ice and their beards crusted with snow. "The snow, in a word, had it all its own way," Meagher wrote. Finally, led by an Indian guide, the group arrived at the "new" St. Peter's mission, which "consisted, architecturally, of an Indian tent or tepee, capable of accommodating sixteen persons in Indian fashion," and a wall tent used for storage.[63]

As the snow continued, the party was delayed once again in a smoke-filled tent and once more ran out of food before Meagher and his companions decided to mount and move on. Their next destination was the "old" mission on the Missouri River, upstream a short distance from the confluence of the Sun River and another twenty-five miles toward Fort Benton. After a hard journey through the snow, the group finally made out the shapes of buildings, where they were welcomed by Father Anthony Ravalli and a lay brother, Francis DeKock. To Meagher's delight, he discovered that DeKock was originally from Tipperary. For a week the storm raged outside as the travelers accepted the hospitality of Father Ravalli, in whom Meagher's companions were "rather astonished to find so much true nobility of heart and mind under a threadbare and patched soutane."[64]

According to Clarke, the only other Catholic in the group besides Meagher, the Protestant members of the party were very uncomfortable: the "benighted travellers had never before shaken hands with a Jesuit, and, having preconceived anything but flattering ideas of the sons of Loyola," they stayed at the mission only out of necessity. But Meagher was ecstatic:

> In the sunny presence and cordial society of these dear, gentle, noble Fathers, many—very many—of the golden recollections of the cloudless and unembittered days of my boyhood and College life came crowding back to me, and thus, even in the midst of that storm, and after years of no very friendly experience of the world, was the spring-time of my life—with all its flowers and melodies, hopefulness and sprightliness—renewed.[65]

While the stay may have improved Meagher's spirits, it worsened his political situation by revealing his Catholicism and his collegiality with the priests to the staunchly Protestant Lyman Munson. The fiercely

Republican judge was undoubtedly doubly displeased to discover that Meagher now leaned politically toward the Democrats.

Meagher's party finally reached Fort Benton—and what a sight it was! Several thousand Indians dressed in tribal regalia and sporting painted faces assembled for the negotiation there. Meagher soon learned that this so-called negotiation was really not a bargaining session with the Indians at all. Rather, Indian treaties were almost always written out by the time the negotiations started; the goal of the negotiators was to get the Indian leaders to mark crosses next to their written names. Congress had appropriated $15,000 to pay the expenses of the negotiation, a large part of which was used to buy gifts for the Indian leaders, consistent with the government approach to the making of a treaty by "subsidizing" the chiefs and headmen.[66]

Arriving in Fort Benton, the delegation representing the United States proceeded to "negotiate" the treaty with the Gros Ventres, Piegans, Bloods, and Blackfeet. The first item of business was to hand out the goods that had been brought up the Missouri River for the Indians. The assembled tribes all occupied separate camps, so the distribution took three days.[67] The final treaty was signed on November 16, 1865, by Gad E. Upson, special commissioner, and Thomas Francis Meagher, acting governor of Montana and acting superintendent of Indian affairs for the United States; and by the chief, headmen, and delegates of the Blackfeet Nation and the Gros Ventre tribe, including over forty Indians. The treaty ceded to the United States all of the Indians' lands south of the Missouri and Teton Rivers. The territory between these streams and the Canadian boundary extending east from the Continental Divide to a line drawn north from the mouth of the Milk River would constitute an Indian reservation where no whites would be permitted to reside; but roads for whites could be constructed across the Indian lands.[68]

Most of the troubles at that time between the Indians and the white settlers had occurred around Fort Benton and along the stretch of the Mullan Trail extending to Helena, so it was thought that placing those lands in the hands of the United States government would eliminate the source of the conflict. Because the new reservation came only as far south as the mouth of the Marias River on the Missouri, the treaty left Fort Benton well outside of the contemplated reservation boundary.[69] The government agreed to expend $50,000 annually in "useful goods,

Judge Lyman Munson. (Courtesy Montana Historical Society, Helena)

provisions and other articles" at the president's discretion. The president could expend as much of the annual fund "as he shall deem proper" for "stock, animals, agricultural implements . . . providing necessary and proper medicines, medical attendance, care for and support of the aged, infirm or sick . . . for helpless orphans . . . and in other respect promoting their civilization, comfort and improvement." The principal Indian chiefs were to receive up to $250 a year so long as they kept the peace, with peace among the various tribes being an important point of the treaty.[70]

Almost immediately after Meagher and his party left to return home, however, trouble broke out in Fort Benton between two of the tribes. Meagher decided to return to Fort Benton, commandeering a small cannon along the way from an emigrant train. Back in Fort Benton the next morning, Meagher threatened to use it unless the some four hundred warriors dispersed, which they did before nightfall. The signed treaty was left with Gad Upson, who unfortunately became ill with tuberculosis and by mid-January 1866 was bedridden. Determined to get treatment on the East Coast, as well as to deliver the treaty to Washington, Upson left for California in February after transferring his mining claims in Virginia City. He planned to get a ship to Panama and another ship on the east side of the isthmus to get him to Washington. He died in California on March 28, 1866; when his body was discovered, the treaty was found in his baggage and forwarded to the secretary of the interior.[71] By that time it had become clear to officials in the Interior Department that neither whites nor Indians planned to respect the boundaries laid out by the treaty, and the document was never presented to the Senate for approval. The signing of the treaty had done nothing at all to solve the Indian problems, and misunderstanding in Montana regarding its status would only cause problems for Meagher.[72]

Meagher had his own thoughts on the treaty. What appeared to him to be bribery of the Indian chiefs had been a strong reminder of the evils of the "place hunting" that he had so despised in Ireland. Despite his commitment to expanding settlement, Meagher—the Irishman who had started a revolution because his countrymen were not represented in legislative matters—was now disturbed because he felt the Indians were not fairly represented at Fort Benton. While the Blackfeet "nation" was fully represented, the Bloods and Blackfeet "tribes" were not. According to Meagher only a single chief representing the Blackfeet tribe attended the negotiations, and the "hostile" Bloods had no representatives at all, even though nine Blood "signatures" were on the treaty. The unrepresented tribes had already retreated across the Canadian border.[73]

Within days of returning to Virginia City on December 9, Meagher wrote to the Indian commissioner in Washington, detailing his view on the negotiations and giving recommendations on the future handling of Indian affairs in Montana. To assure the free passage of white settlers to Montana, he advised the commissioner of the need for a treaty with the Crows in eastern Montana that would cede the land south of the Missouri to the United States. Furthermore, the trip to Fort Benton, which had lasted almost two months, had brought home the difficulty of covering the hundreds of miles of the territory on horseback, and Meagher proposed a special superintendency for eastern Montana. He had not visited the Flathead agent, Augustus Chapman, but he also had thoughts about the Flathead agency in western Montana, whose supervision had recently been transferred to Idaho, although the agency was physically located in Montana Territory. Meagher argued that the Flathead agent should report to the Montana superintendent, but he suggested that the role of Indian superintendent for the territory be separated from the duties of governor due to the vastness of the region.[74]

Upson had schooled Meagher on the necessity of force to control the Indians, and Meagher had seen its necessity when he broke up intertribal hostilities after the Fort Benton negotiation. Relying on this impression, he also expressed his belief to the commissioner that only force would subdue the Sioux and noted that he had asked the secretary of state to obtain a competent cavalry from the War Department.[75] Thus Meagher would join others, both before and after his tenure, who asked for troops in Montana to help quell Indian opposition to settlement.

Back in Virginia City, Meagher also described the negotiations and the troubles that followed the treaty in a speech to Madison County's Democratic convention. He said that only Upson had been required to sign the treaty and that he, as superintendent of Indian affairs in the territory, had only signed it to dignify the occasion. Meagher then attacked the government's distribution of food and trinkets to the Indians to get them to sign a document that they never intended to honor, if they even understood it.[76]

In the meantime Fort Benton remained in a state of unrest between Indians and whites. Hiram D. Upham, a clerk at the Blackfeet agency, wrote twice to Gad Upson about the problems. On January 9 and again on February 2, 1866, Upham reported that the Indians were killing whites and stealing horses, both from whites and from each other.[77] At the same time Indians were also being killed by whites, both individuals and organized vigilante groups. Members of one such Fort Benton group wrote a letter on January 10, expressing their indignation at the activities of the Indians, even as the treaty negotiation was going on. They announced that some of the citizens of the area had "put themselves on a war footing" for mutual protection and that by the next summer they hoped to make it safe for any white man traveling or living on the prairie. The letter also announced the group's motto: to "wipe from existence the name of P[i]egan, Blood and Blackfoot." Vigilante justice was again at work, this time against the Indians.[78]

At the end of 1865 Meagher found himself astraddle the insoluble conflict between the Indians and whites in Montana, for which, however, he thought he had some solutions. His most sensible suggestion—that the superintendent of Indian affairs be made a separate position from the governorship—was never seriously considered; nor, probably, were his other recommendations. As the new year opened, however, Meagher was beset with problems of a different nature as he attempted to handle the legislative mess that the departed Sidney Edgerton had left behind him. And instead of the fair and hospitable place he had dreamed of, he would find Montana to be profoundly inhospitable, both to himself and to the other Irish who had come to the territory.

CHAPTER NINE

An Irishman Again

Here, in Montana, an Irishman is as much a man as any other citizen.

Montana Post

In Irish circles Thomas Francis Meagher's name had often been paired with that of General James Shields, an Irishman from Tyrone who served as a United States senator from both Illinois and Minnesota. Irish immigrants had made Shields's career, and Meagher saw no reason why he could not follow in the footsteps of Shields.[1] In fact, entering Congress was behind Meagher's initial petition for a territorial governorship. Although he arrived in Montana in the less prestigious post of secretary, he still harbored political hopes. His situation was complicated, however, by the territory's highly partisan politics, nascent anti-Irish sentiment, money problems, and his struggle with alcohol.

Among Meagher's most profound challenges in territorial government was the legislative mess that he inherited when he became acting governor. The problem was a legacy of the first territorial assembly, convened by Governor Sidney Edgerton in mid-December 1864 in Bannack's snow-covered rough log buildings. After a census and an apportionment by Edgerton and an election organized according to procedures set out in the Organic Act (the legislation passed by Congress to form the Montana Territory), Democrats controlled the thirteen-member house,

248

while Republicans (campaigning under the name "Unionists") controlled the seven-member council.[2]

Although partisanship was fierce, the assembly had copies of the recently passed Idaho statutes and adopted many of those laws for Montana with little argument. When it was all said and done, the laws, memorials, and resolutions of the first legislative session made up a bound volume of over seven hundred pages. In addition to the many public laws produced, around a hundred private laws also passed, giving exclusive rights for mining companies, ditch companies, railroads, townsites, toll bridges, ferries, and wagon roads. Governor Edgerton promptly signed them.[3]

As the practice of the "toll road legislature" became known, even the *Montana Post* under the Republican Dimsdale commented unfavorably: "Charters are the chief subject of the legislation, and the idea seems to prevail that no good thing shall be saved for the public, but given to some one who claims it." The *Post*'s "correspondent" from Bannack reported that "there are in this assembly, some of the most venal, corrupt, and shameless legislators in the world. . . . Men openly in the streets propose to sell votes for a given price."[4]

Amid the corruption, the first legislature did seem to have accomplished one positive thing: it passed a series of laws assuring the orderly selection of future legislatures in the territory. These laws provided for an annual election day and an opening date for future legislatures and set a residency requirement for candidates. They established systems for voting, for reporting the vote, and for breaking ties. They also set legislative salaries and addressed the possibility of absences and vacancies.[5] Thus the Bannack legislature passed a package of bills all directed at assuring future well-structured legislatures. But one important thing that the Organic Act required was missing: a law providing for territorial legislative reapportionment. The absence of this one law created much of the controversy that Meagher inherited.

Members of Montana's first legislature had, in fact, introduced bills in both the house and council calling for the new apportionment into council and representative districts and calling for the maximum number of legislators allowed by Congress: fourteen in the council and twenty-six in the house. This was too many for legislator A. E. Mayhew, a Democrat from Madison County, who, protesting the cost of expanding the legislature, made a motion to change the bill's title to "Grand Swindle." The bill passed anyway.[6] On the forty-seventh day of the forty-eight day session, however, Governor Edgerton vetoed the bill in the morning, on the grounds that there was already at least one legislator per thousand people. Increasing the number of legislators further, he argued, would incur unnecessary expense.[7] In the afternoon the house was unable to override the governor's veto by one vote, and the matter was dropped. The next day Edgerton adjourned the legislature without its having passed the vital apportionment bill.[8]

The structure of territorial government had another gaping defect caused by Governor Edgerton and the Bannack legislature. On Saturday, February 25, 1865, the *Montana Post* reported that on the last day of the Bannack legislative session Edgerton had sent nominations to the council for its required approval of men for the offices of territorial treasurer, auditor, and superintendent of public instruction. The council, however, refused to act. Thomas Dimsdale of the *Post* noted brightly: "Of course it was not essential they should and these gentlemen have, or will have, their commissions."[9] The superintendent of public instruction nominee was none other than Thomas Dimsdale himself. Nonetheless, Democrats of the territory were already being given reason to voice their strong dissatisfaction with the Republican Edgerton and his political nominees.

The *Montana Post* in Virginia City had somewhat regularly reported on the proceeding in Bannack, under the correspondent's pseudonym "Franklin." He had noted the failure of the council to approve Edgerton's nominees; however, he had nothing at all to say about the impending death of the legislative function by failure to pass an apportionment law. At the end of the session he made not the slightest mention of this in the *Post*. During the long interim after the Bannack legislature adjourned, Dimsdale realized the problems that these failures portended for the territory and proposed a unique solution. Montana citizens reading the article "Call for a Convention" in the *Montana Post* of July 8, 1865, were treated to Dimsdale's view that "an auspicious opportunity presents itself to . . . elect Delegates to attend a Territorial Convention . . . to place in nomination one candidate for Delegate to Congress, one candidate for Territorial Treasurer, one candidate for Territorial Auditor, one candidate for Superintendent of Public Instruction."[10] But therein lay the rub, because, according to the laws just passed by the Bannack legislature, territorial officers could not be appointed without the advice and consent of the council. If there was no future legislature, then there could be no approval of the required state officers. Even the *Post* sheepishly admitted this, while at the same time pleading for people to attend the delegate-nominating convention of what they were now calling the "Territorial" party.[11]

But Dimsdale's plan for a nonpartisan nominating convention never worked. From the outset he did not appear to have the support he needed for his convention; while he referred in the plural to the signers of the proposal for the party, a statement was appended to it: "The names attached to the call will be published when the[y] are all returned from the different counties."[12] Soon the Madison Union party met on its own and selected delegates to the Territorial Union party convention, announcing that Colonel W. F. Sanders and Justice Hezekiah L. Hosmer, along with attorney general E. B. Nealley, would address a public meeting of the party.[13]

Confusion continued to reign in Montana as to what elections should be held and for what positions. As the summer of 1865 wore on, conventions of both parties were held around the territory, with candidates for those house seats created by the original apportionment being nominated for the next legislative session. But, given the different understandings of the status of the territory's legislative function, there was no consistency. The "People's Ticket" of Madison County, which was now supported by Dimsdale, listed nominees for a delegate to congress and several county officials but did not contain the names of nominees for the territorial council or house. The Democratic convention meeting in Deer Lodge County on August 12 nominated candidates for both council and house. The Union convention in Edgerton County nominated four individuals for the legislature.[14]

An election was held on September 4, the date set for elections by the first legislature. On September 16 the *Montana Post* gave the results for Madison County, showing that Democrat Samuel McLean had won over Unionist Gad Upson for territorial delegate to Congress and that votes for the territorial offices of auditor, treasurer, and superintendent of public instruction had been tabulated, as well as votes for a single councilman and six representatives. The Democrats won handily. Dimsdale commented: "We editorially touch our hat to the gentlemen. . . . Nobody else will ever do it, seeing that the first three offices are non-elective, and the balance bogus." At the same time Dimsdale said, "We accept the result, because such is the law and the will of the majority, which is the only piece of pure democracy about it." Now that the Democrats had won, he began raising questions about the integrity of the process.[15]

It was at this precise point that Thomas Francis Meagher arrived in the territory. In one of his first public appearances—at which Governor Sidney Edgerton also announced his departure—Meagher confidently declared that he would soon call a legislature. "It is his intention to call together the Legislature at the earliest possible moment," the *Post* reported without comment. It was clear that the Unionists had not yet decided on a plan of action and that at the time of the almost simultaneous arrival of Meagher and departure of Edgerton they expected the governor would be back in only "a few months."[16] By December, when Meagher had returned from the Indian negotiation and could focus on calling a legislature, it had become evident that Edgerton would be gone from the territory for some time. The last thing the Republicans wanted was for Meagher to convene a majority Democratic legislature. At that point the Republicans adopted the position that a legislature could not be called because the legislative function had expired for want of apportionment.

When Meagher asked for Judge Lyman Munson's opinion on the validity of the legislature, Munson, a prominent Republican himself, espoused the party line. At first Meagher was inclined to agree with him. With his characteristic decisiveness, Meagher passed the advice he had received on to the public, for he had promised a legislature when he first arrived. His declaration was printed on December 23 in the *Montana Post*. "It is clearly my conviction that the Legislative functions of the Territory have temporarily lapsed," he said. "To revive these functions, I am as clearly of opinion that an Enabling Act of Congress, empowering the governor to re-district the territory, apportion the representatives and convene them for business, is essentially required, and that no other proceeding can legitimately restore them, strange and embarrassing as the circumstances are in which their suspension places us."[17] Meagher had played into the hands of the Republicans, who had gotten just what they wanted.

But then Meagher received a letter from James H. Shober of Helena, enclosing a petition signed mostly by miners. "The Miners and others in this vicinity are universally in favor of a meeting of the Legislature," Shober said, because they needed laws in addition to those passed by the Bannack legislature.[18] Their petition struck a cord. After all, Meagher had fought in Ireland for citizens' right to legislate for themselves, and he blanched at the possibility of living in a territory in which citizens no longer had that right. Meagher's commitment to self-governance combined nicely with his political realignment, for he had also begun to rethink his relationship with Munson and Dimsdale, both of whom he had come to perceive as anti-Irish and anti-Catholic. Nothing could have alienated Meagher more than Munson's obvious discomfort at the Jesuit Mission. Dimsdale had earned Meagher's distrust when he criticized the Fenian ambition of a free Ireland in the *Montana Post*.[19]

Shifting allegiances aside, there was clearly also a legitimate legal basis for calling a legislature. Meagher had recognized the issue of self-governance as a problem from the beginning. Even as he asserted that the legislative function had lapsed, he left an opening: "Show me to-day that I have the right and power to convene such a Legislature, and it shall be convened forthwith."[20] Two prominent Democrats, Charles Bagg, a member of the Bannack legislature, and John P. Bruce, the editor of the *Helena Democrat,* eagerly took up the challenge. According to the *Montana Post,* these gentlemen "worked upon" Meagher and "showed him the law" to convince him to convene the "bogus legislature."[21] Contrary to the *Post*'s innuendo that Meagher acted only on the persuasion of his friends, however, Bruce and Bagg may literally have shown him the law, for copies of the statutes passed by the first legislature were hard to come by. The laws had not yet been printed, and the official handwritten copy had been taken to New York by Republican Edward Neally, the territorial attorney general, for printing.[22] Until his conversations with Bruce and Bagg, Meagher was likely unaware of the great lengths to which the Bannack legislature had gone to pass laws to provide for succeeding legislatures, only failing to pass the required apportionment act.

The Organic Act contained a provision under Section 11 providing that "there shall be but one session of the legislative assembly annually, unless on an extraordinary occasion, the governor shall think proper to call the legislative assembly together." On February 1, 1866, it had become known that the territory was deeply in debt, which certainly would have constituted an "extraordinary occasion."[23] Meagher did not recite this provision, however, when he called the legislature. Instead he relied on provisions of the various acts passed at Bannack to show the clear intent of the legislature to continue the legislative function. In a public proclamation, he explained his legal reasoning before summoning the legislature to convene on March 5, in Virginia City. It was to consist of "members of the Legislative Council duly and properly elected on the fourth day of October, 1864, and the members of the House of Representatives, duly and properly elected on the fourth day of September, 1865."[24]

Meagher's decision to call the legislature permanently alienated him from the Republicans, whose response was predictably ferocious. In the February 3, 1866, edition of the *Montana Post,* Dimsdale condemned him for his inconsistency. Meagher fired back in a speech he gave at the Democratic Convention of Madison County: "the less of Federal officialism, and the more of popular liberty and democratic power there prevailed in the Republic at large, and in every portion of it, the healthier, the stronger, the nobler would the American nation be." Clearly remembering life in Ireland, he noted that without a legislature "Montana would be nothing more than a Government farm, parceled out among Federal overseers, tax-gatherers and bailiffs."[25]

The Republican Unionist party, now led by Wilbur Sanders, was deeply disturbed. On February 14 he wrote to James Fergus: "Of course, we will squelch the Legislature by the courts. Do not allow this to be neglected if I am away."[26] But the most fanatical Meagher-hater among them was Judge Munson, whose advice Meagher was now totally ignoring. Showing no judicial restraint at all, Munson publicly stated that any law passed by the new legislature would be invalid. Meagher had already made his position clear on the power of the judiciary in a speech to the Democratic party in which he said that, rather than allowing the judges to invalidate the laws, he planned to see that they respected them just as any other citizens did. Clearly Meagher simply intended to ignore any judicial holdings of the invalidity of the second legislature until Congress told him otherwise.

On March 5, 1866, the Second Montana Territorial Legislature convened in Virginia City and got off to a roaring start.[27] Neil Howie, who observed the legislature, wrote in his diary: "The Legislature met to day[;] . . . the Governor very drunk[,] Major Briggs crazy drunk[;] went around to the governor's office with a party & made the brandy and wine fly[;] the boys nearly all drunk. Parrit the fiddler crazy . . . drunk."[28]

Despite this distraction, Meagher did manage to address the assembly as the first order of business. In his address he once again worked to validate the legislature, explaining:

> The act of the 17th of January, 1865, relating to the elections, as well as a subsequent act, creating certain officers in the Territory of Montana, were unknown to me until within the last four weeks. Brought to my notice by gentlemen who had assisted in passing them, it was clear to me that a Legislature did legally exist, and that inasmuch as I was enjoined by the Constitution of the Territory faithfully to execute the laws thereof, it was my sworn duty to give effect to the laws just cited, and that to do this I must re-organize [*sic*] [recognize] the elections that had taken place, and practically declare their validity, which was to be done solely by the Proclamation calling the Legislature I have now the honor to address.[29]

Meagher was quick to point out, however, that he realized the people of Montana might not be equally represented and urged the legislature to provide for such representation as one of its first duties, with an early day for elections under an apportionment bill and an early meeting of the new legislature no later than October of that year.

Apportionment was not its only order of business. The legislature soon gleefully turned itself to passing laws, including some extraordinarily partisan measures aimed at punishing the territorial judges. The legislature turned down a recommendation by the Helena bar that the judges' salaries be increased and denied them the additional pay awarded by the Bannack legislature.[30] The *Montana Post* criticized the decision, saying that it was based on the "Russian principle, of totally insufficient salaries, with the privilege to starve or to steal."[31] The legislature took aim at the judges again when Judge Hosmer was presiding in the case of *Godbe v. McCormick* across the street from the lawmakers. After a dissatisfied defendant's attorneys ran to the legislature for help, a law was

The Legislative Hall, Virginia City. This early Virginia City photograph shows the place where Meagher had his governor's office. He convened the 1866 legislature in the upstairs of this building on the corner of Jackson and Wallace Streets. (Courtesy Montana Historical Society, Helena)

immediately passed requiring judges to transfer a case to another judge upon the filing of an affidavit of bias, regardless of the truth or falsity of the allegations against him. Less contentiously, the legislature also honored Meagher, naming a new county after him.[32]

Meagher did not accept all the bills that the legislature passed. He vetoed a series of private laws granting monopolies for bridges, highways, and irrigation projects—even those sponsored by his fellow Democrats and fellow Irishmen. When the legislature discussed giving Meagher the "balance due the executive office out of the extra pay voted the Governor," as passed by the Bannack legislature, he expressed his "earnest wish that such discussion should cease" and that "if there is anything legally due the executive office it shall be transferred to the Miners' Hospital at Helena."[33] A year later, when he was nearly without funds, he would change his mind about this.

On March 30 Meagher was able to even the score with the *Montana Post* when he wrote the council that he had appointed Thomas J. Favorite, the editor and publisher of Helena's *Montana Radiator,* as the public printer for the territory. Meagher had already settled a personal score with the *Post*'s editor, Thomas Dimsdale, when he informed the Territorial Council on March 20, 1866, that "I have appointed Mr. Peter Ronan, of this city, Superintendent of Public Instruction, Mr. Dimsdale, having been relieved by me from that office, for having failed to make a report in compliance with the request of the Executive for the information of the Legislature."[34]

Although dismissing Dimsdale was clearly in part a partisan measure, Meagher did have a positive concern for education. He vetoed an education bill because the salary for the superintendent of public instruction was too low, calling the job "one of the most important duties which a public officer can be called upon to perform." Moreover, Meagher found that the bill did not "authorize the Superintendent of Public Instruction to exclude from the Public Schools of this Territory any *Sectarian* tracts, . . . having a tendency to excite discord upon religious subjects."[35] Keeping religion out of the public schools was a significant issue among Catholics of the day. Like most Catholics, Meagher embraced the Catholic parochial school system but emphatically objected to Protestants teaching their religion in the public schools.

Overall, Meagher's speeches and writings provide ample evidence that he spent long hours at work during the legislature. He was "in reality the first Governor of the Territory," according to early sources, and for the most part he functioned well and fully in that role.[36] His correspondence was voluminous, and his involvement in the affairs of the territory was conspicuous and regular. Meagher seemed to be clear in his purpose, and he earned the praise of the body assembled at the close of their proceedings.

Nevertheless, it is also clear that Meagher engaged in bouts of excessive drinking during the same period. At a time when $3 bought a bottle of whiskey, Meagher ran up a bill of $274 at one establishment for "wet goods" ranging from beer to whiskey to fine claret. Neil Howie, who enjoyed a drink himself, again commented on Meagher's drinking during the session when he noted in his diary on Friday, March 9, 1866: "the Governor tight again to day." As Meagher's drinking became increasingly public, the Montana Post picked up on his habits, and his detractors had a field day. On February 3, 1866, the Post sarcastically reported that Governor Meagher had experienced "sudden domestic bereavement . . . in the loss of his venerable father," an event that in point of fact had not occurred. According to the Post, the news had caused Meagher "such a depression of spirits as totally to incapacitate him for the performance of any public duty." Word of Meagher's drinking also spread to Washington. William Chumasero, a Republican lawyer in the territory, wrote Senator Lyman Trumbull of Illinois in March 1866, complaining that Meagher put himself on the side of "Missouri bush-whackers and secessionists." His habits were "beastly and filthy in the extreme—on his first arrival in Virginia City he became intoxicated and remained so for a number of days in his room polluting his bed and person in the most indecent and disgusting manner—and has in fact been drunk nearly every day since he has been in the Territory."[37]

It was not only publicly that Meagher was being criticized. In a sinister letter dated February 14, 1866, Wilbur Sanders, the former vigilante prosecutor, wrote to James Fergus: "Among decent men of all parties, he is dead beyond hope of resurrection. . . . we must put a quietus on the doings of this pretender."[38]

On St. Patrick's Day, March 17, 1866, Meagher lashed back at his detractors, whose criticisms he took not merely as personal attacks but also as attacks on the Irish. And for good reason: the temperance movement had long had an anti-immigrant tinge to it. Thus, addressing an Irish gathering at the People's Theatre in Virginia City, Meagher lambasted the Protestant nativist Americans:

> It is the American who has no heart, who has no thought beyond the putting a mighty dollar out at mighty interest, . . . who hates the Irish for their generous qualities, their infallible religion, and their inveterate democracy. . . . it is he alone who regards with a codliver eye, a nutmeg nose, a Maine-Liquor-Law howl, and a Cromwellian depreciation, the love of Ireland which the Irishman brings with him to America. . . . Let the marrowless bigot, then, carp and deprecate; let the hungry Puritan with his nasal music importune the God of Blue Laws to save the Yankee nation from the witch-craft of St. Patrick's daughters and the deviltry of St. Patrick's sons.[39]

The enthusiastic crowd let out a roar that reverberated throughout the territory. With his vitriolic response to his American critics, Meagher had given voice to the anger that many of Montana's frustrated Irish felt at the disrespect they routinely encountered from American-born Protestants. The speech marked Meagher's public abandonment of any hope he ever had to be a popular leader of all the people while at the same time reasserting his standing among his Irish compatriots as their leading spokesman.

When Meagher gave this speech, he may still have believed that a political career remained open to him as a representative of the Irish. Montana had to become a state, however, before its citizens would be able to elect Meagher or anyone else to the Senate. When he initially called the legislature in February 1866, he announced that one of its purposes would be to "give Legislative sanction and validity to the Convention directed to assemble at Helena, on Monday, the 26th day of March next."[40] That constitutional convention would be the first step toward statehood. Meagher was not the only Montana politician to see the political benefits of statehood. As an early traveler to Montana Territory once said, "Congregate a hundred Americans anywhere beyond the settlements, and they immediately lay out a city, frame a

State constitution and apply for admission into the Union, while twenty-five of them become candidates for the United States Senate."[41] That exaggeration came close to characterizing Montana's situation. For their own political ambitions and for the good of the territory, men of both parties eagerly sought early admission to the Union.

The Republicans may have been first to propose a constitutional convention. Certainly Republican James Tufts, who had come to the territory before Meagher and succeeded him as secretary, advocated one in the fall of 1865, writing Thomas Dimsdale: "I presume Montana has already thought of the subject of a State government. A suggestion from me may be out of place; but I shall run the risk of venturing this opinion, that the sooner we have a State organization the better it will be for us. I . . . hope to see Montana represented by two Senators and a Representative by a year from next December, or certainly by the first of January, 1867."[42]

When the convention did finally meet in April, the *Post* attacked it with bitter humor as "[s]ired by the Acting-one, and damned by the people" but "finally born" anyway.[43] Although Meagher likely still had senatorial ambitions when he called for a constitutional convention, by the time it met he had come to accept the fact that only wealthy men became senators. In May 1866 he wrote his brother-in-law, Samuel Barlow, about the problems he saw in attaining high office. Barlow bluntly replied: "No man without a fortune, can afford to hold [public office]." But at the same time Barlow urged Meagher to continue his quest. Meagher replied: "You don't see why I shouldn't come into Congress with Montana. There is every reason why I shouldn't . . . unless, indeed, I hit upon a gold or silver mine within the next year or two, At-all-events, I'd infinitely prefer, any day, to have a splendid yacht, a box at the opera, and four-in-hand, than have a seat for six years in the Senate."[44]

It remained a theoretical discussion, for the constitutional convention was an utter disaster. Although it was originally called for March 1866, spring storms delayed its meeting until April 9. Even then the delegates endured arduous travel on the muddy roads and trails that crossed the territory before they were finally able to convene in Virginia City. Meeting for less than a week, the convention adjourned on April 14, after producing a handwritten constitution that was then supposedly sent out of state for printing. The plan was to submit the printed constitution to the people for ratification. The document did not survive, however; nor did any records of the proceedings.[45]

In the meantime the Republicans awaited an opportunity to attack Meagher's legislature. Soon a case involving one of its laws came before Judge Munson, and he ruefully ruled that the law was invalid because it was passed by an invalid legislature. But Munson's objective was to pour scorn on Meagher. In his decision he could not resist citing the Irishman's own words of December 15, 1865, when Meagher had still trusted Munson and had supported the Republican view that the legislative power had lapsed. Now calling it "the view of Acting Governor Meagher," the judge hammered home his point: "An apportionment bill having been vetoed by Governor Edgerton, and the Legislature having failed to pass it over his veto by the necessary two-thirds vote, it is clearly my conviction that the legislative functions of the Territory have temporarily lapsed." Munson chose not to address the clear intention of the Bannack legislature to perpetuate itself; nor did he cite Section 11 of the Organic Act, which would arguably have given at least some independent basis for the second legislature. Instead he elected to pretend that Meagher could not understand the Organic Act provision on apportionment. "The language used is not only explicit and direct in its terms, but mandatory in its precepts," Munson sneered, "and so plain that a child cannot mistake its meaning, or err in its construction."[46]

Back in Congress, a political battle started over the validity of the Montana legislature that Meagher had called. Samuel McLean, the Montana congressional delegate and a popularly elected Democrat, rose on the floor of the House on May 4 to plead for the preservation of the acts that the legislature had passed. "The Legislative Assembly [had been] called into existence by the proclamation of the acting Governor, who supposed he was executing his legal duty, while he knew he was carrying out the will of a great majority of the people of the Territory," McLean explained. Montana needed laws. Without them, they had "been compelled to give way to the vigilante system of condemnation and execution." This, combined with the need for mining laws, had made it essential for Meagher to call the legislative assembly. But McLean's arguments were ignored in the Congress.[47]

The Senate recessed for the summer of 1866 without further considering the matter. When the senators returned in the fall they would find that they had yet another session of the Montana legislature to deal with. When territorial governor Green Clay Smith arrived in Montana on the night of October 3, 1866, to succeed Sidney Edgerton, he immediately agreed with Meagher that the legislative function had not lapsed. Five days later he called a third session of the Montana legislature.[48] On March 2, 1867, however, the Congress had the last word, amending the Montana Organic Act to nullify "[a]ll acts passed at the two sessions of the so-called Legislative Assembly of the Territory of Montana, held in eighteen hundred and sixty-six." But the Congress stopped short of nullifying the private acts granting rights for toll roads, bridges, mining, and the like. These acts were saved by a "vested rights" provision, which allowed that the parties receiving them "would not be precluded from making and testing said claim in the courts of the territory." In a nod to the right of the people of Montana to pass their own laws, the Senate provided that the acts of the 1866 sessions could be reenacted.[49] With that, the second and third legislatures (called by Meagher and Green Clay Smith, respectively) were nullified.

In the matter of the legislative fight, history was unkind to Meagher. He alone received the blame for calling a "bogus" legislature. No one referred to the nullified third legislature as "bogus" or blamed Green Clay Smith for calling it, and no one ever criticized Sidney Edgerton for failing to keep the first legislature in session until an apportionment law was passed. Meagher's detractors—particularly Dimsdale and Munson—thoroughly disseminated their version of events, assuring that Meagher shouldered full responsibility for the crisis.

The legitimacy of the legislature was not the only fight that the embattled Meagher engaged in during his first term as acting governor. The most tragic involved the fate of James Daniels, an Irishman living in Helena, who killed a gambler named A. J. Gartley in a fight over a card game. According to Nathaniel Langford, Daniels was a hard character who had murdered a man in California before coming to Montana. Others objected to that characterization. They called Daniels a respectable businessman and said he killed Gartley in self-defense.[50]

Charged with first-degree murder, Daniels was tried in Judge Munson's court, with William Chumasero, a Helena Republican and Meagher hater, serving as prosecutor. After a fiercely contested proceeding, the jury convicted Daniels of manslaughter. Munson sentenced him to three years in the territorial prison in Virginia City and fined him a thousand dollars. The case was not over, however, for Daniels's attorney, William Pemberton, then circulated a petition requesting acting governor Meagher to intervene. A goodly number of citizens signed it, including several members of the jury that had just unanimously found Daniels guilty.[51]

As Meagher considered the petition, he knew very well that under the Montana Organic Act only the president of the United States could grant pardons. He also knew, however, that the territorial governor could "grant pardons and respites for offences against the laws of [Montana] territory, and reprieve for offences against the laws of the United States *until* the decision of the President of the United States can be made known thereon" (emphasis added).[52] Meagher had reason to believe from Pemberton's petition and from statements given after the Daniels trial that Gartley had provoked the struggle and Daniels had acted in self-defense.

Acting on his convictions that Daniels would ultimately be found innocent, Meagher issued an order to the sheriff in Virginia City to release Daniels immediately, stating that his sentence had been "reprieved . . . until the decision of the President of the United States is made known thereon."[53] Meagher never "pardoned" Daniels because he did not have the power to do so, and he knew it. To him it was simply a proper application of *habeas corpus* principles to release Daniels while his pardon was being considered. Meagher's detractors, of course, preferred to treat the "reprieve" as a full and final "pardon," totally ignoring the distinctions between the two, and they immediately assailed Meagher for acting outside his powers.[54]

Judge Lyman Munson, already beside himself over Meagher's calling of the legislature, became even more furious when he heard that Meagher had released Daniels. On March 1 Munson dashed off a letter to Meagher, denouncing his actions as "a power not delegated to the executive, unwarranted by law, and the sheriff should have disregarded the order."[55] As Munson interpreted the Organic Act, governors could only act in more serious capital cases, so Meagher did not have the power to release Daniels from prison. Munson's interpretation of the act was far-fetched, but that did not stop him from trying to set matters straight with Meagher. The *Post* announced on March 3, 1866, that "Judge Munson has arrived from Helena, whence the learned gentleman has come post haste, to investigate and take action on the discharge of

the murderer Daniels by Acting-Governor Meagher." According to the
Post, however, Munson found Meagher drunk ("still in his debauch"),
so he issued his own order to have the prisoner rearrested to await
presidential action.[56]

Several years later Munson himself remorselessly told the rest of the
Daniels story. "On being released from prison, the man went back to
Helena, swearing revenge upon the witnesses who had testified against
him," he said. "Arriving at Helena about 9 o'clock in the evening, he was
immediately surrounded by the Vigilantees [sic], and was hanged at 10
o'clock, with the pardon in his pocket."[57] The hanging sent shockwaves
through Montana. Some, including the prosecutor, William Chumasero,
supported the vigilante action. Writing to Wilbur Sanders, he said that
Daniels "has gone to Helena and it is very much to be hoped that the
Vigilantes have performed the last said [sic] offices for him—I know they
will if they get hold of him."[58] Others, even among those who originally
supported the vigilantes, believed, as vigilante leader Nathaniel Langford
said, that the men responsible for Daniels's death exceeded any concept
of right and justice and that they themselves were the violators of law
and propriety.[59]

The Democrats, who supported Meagher, criticized Munson's conduct during the affair, accusing him of having "descended from the bench
and played the part of a low, petty bailiff." At about that same time
Meagher's legislature repealed the act passed by the first legislature that
gave Munson and the other judges extra pay of $2,500 a year.[60] Members
of the vigilantes, however, targeted Meagher for "pardoning" Daniels.
Almost six months after the event the August 18 *Montana Post* reported
that vigilantes stopped Meagher on his way from Virginia City to Helena
and told him to leave the territory. Afterward he received a crude "drawing
of a man hanging to a tree, accompanied by a small hangman's knot
labelled 'General Meagher.'"[61] The *Post* made light of the sinister message
in an editorial that praised the vigilantes: "It is outlaws, murderers and
thieves that fear the Vigilantes. . . . When they cease to be wanted, they
will cease to act." Apparently responding to protests raised in the Irish
community over the vigilantes' actions, Dimsdale condescendingly continued: "It is a gross insult to Irishmen to address such twaddle to their
passions, and to ignore them as reasoning beings capable of appreciating

James Daniels hanging. Vigilantes seized Daniels and strung him up from Helena's famous hanging tree. (Courtesy Montana Historical Society, Helena)

fact and argument. Here, in Montana, an Irishman is as much a man as any other citizen."[62]

The Daniels affair hastened Meagher's retreat into the Irish community. In the summer of 1866 he started spending increasing amounts of time readying Montana for what he hoped would be a massive inflow of Irish immigrants. He also began to spend increasing amounts of time with his Fenian brothers, looking toward the day when Ireland would be free. That day, it seemed, could be soon coming, for Fenianism was on the march nationally. The Fenians were not in lock step, however. On the East Coast, under John O'Mahony, the Fenians had established the structure of an offshore Irish government, including a senate, a war department, a state department, and a treasury and financial department that sold war bonds. But a split occurred because O'Mahony wanted to invade Ireland directly, while the majority favored invading Canada instead and then negotiating a trade for Ireland. William Randall Roberts and Thomas R. Sweeny led the majority faction, and by February 1866 they had assumed enough power within the organization to begin making preparations to invade Canada. The June 2, 1866, invasion was a disaster, with only a thousand of the expected ten thousand soldiers participating.[63] The Fenians from the Rocky Mountains and the West Coast had their own western strategy to invade Canada. According to Sweeny, "On the 11th of February last, I ordered Col. P. F. Walsh to California, to make San Francisco his Headquarters and organize a military movement in that Department." Sweeny had given Walsh "sealed dispatches to certain prominent persons there, belonging to our organization, with instructions to organize that contingent to act simultaneously with our movement east of the Rocky Mountains." They were to "seize and occupy Victoria, in British America, from which place privateers could be sent out to prey upon British commerce in the Pacific."[64]

Amid this disorganized patchwork of grandiose plans, Meagher drew closer to his fellow Irishmen in Montana and closer to the Fenians. In late summer 1866 he traveled to Blackfoot City to meet with Fenian leaders there, including Andrew O'Connell, the Montana "head centre."[65] Meagher had been entrusted with a letter from O'Connell's nephew, Lieutenant Martin E. Hogan of the 13th U.S. Infantry. Meagher had recently visited his post at the mouth of the Judith River on the Missouri River. Full of fervor, Hogan's letter promised O'Connell that "when the contest commences in earnest I shall make it my business to be somewhere in that vicinity with a squadron of Irish Cavalry."[66]

Hogan's promise to O'Connell was neither fleeting nor insincere. In January 1867 Hogan joined the Brian Boru chapter of the Fenian Brotherhood in Helena. Every fiber of his patriotic spirit for Ireland awakened, and an invasion of Canada was in his plans for the future. Hogan wrote to O'Connell: "Let Ireland be armed to a man, and once a footing is gained in Canada, a three-months campaign . . . will again proudly establish old Ireland amongst the nations of the earth." Hogan made it clear that he was ready to join a Fenian invasion at any time. "When the time comes, Sir, . . . I will respond to the call. . . . I have often told brother officers that when that event took place, I would bid the mess goodbye."[67]

The nature of secret organizations makes it difficult to discern how closely Meagher was connected to the various Fenian plots, but circumstantial evidence suggests that he may have been even more involved than the meeting in Blackfoot suggests. In January 1867 he sent a strange letter to O'Connell:

My Dear O'Connell, I received, yesterday, a communication from the Patent Office, Washington. Walsh's patent, I should say, is safe—hurrah! But it is absolutely necessary that he should come on here, at once, and sign a petition that has been forwarded to me for his signature. So I have written him a line, begging him to come on at once. You, too, ought to be here, as it [is] necessary to have two witnesses to Walsh's signature, and you and I would be the most desirable parties to the transaction—the fewer people knowing anything about his visit, the better.[68]

Although on its face the letter appeared to deal with ordinary legal business, government records indicate that no patent was applied for in that time-frame by anyone with the surname Walsh.[69] Thus the letter may well have contained a cipher known only to Meagher and O'Connell about instructions from Fenian Col. Walsh.[70]

Other circumstantial evidence of Meagher's continuing association with Fenianism comes from an event that occurred years later. In 1872 W. R. Roberts, president of the Fenians at the time of the East Coast invasion, had become a New York congressman. That year Roberts sponsored the application of Meagher's son, Thomas Bennett Meagher, to West Point. Perhaps he owed Meagher a favor, or perhaps this was merely a gesture of respect. Either way, Meagher continued to have friends among certain Fenian factions, just as his connections in Montana show his continued commitment to the cause.[71]

Fenianism aside, Meagher also engaged in more conventional activities to serve the Irish. In particular, he turned his attention toward strengthening the Catholic Church in Montana to ready the region for Irish settlement. Archbishop Ireland of St. Paul had encouraged him "to go forward and become the great founder of the Church in Montana." And that is exactly what Meagher did with the help of his wife, Elizabeth, after she arrived in the territory in the late spring of 1866. Both Thomas and Elizabeth wrote eloquently to the archbishop of St. Louis, lobbying for the appointment of a bishop for Montana. The archbishop passed their letters on to the second plenary council of Baltimore, which responded by establishing a vicariate in Montana and nominating Father Ravoux as its bishop.[72]

In a 1912 letter Archbishop Ireland gave all the credit to Meagher. "It was the act of General Meagher that brought the attention of the council to Montana, and induced the council to erect it into a vicariate," he said. "The situation of the Church in Montana at the time was such that there was nothing in it to justify the erection of the vicariate, but, as Bishop Grace said on his return from Baltimore, confidence was put on the promises and representations of General Meagher." Ireland also remembered Meagher's plan to obtain priests from Ireland: "how far he carried out his plan in securing for Montana priests from the College of All Hallows, Dublin, I do not know for certain, although the talk among ourselves always was that he had in fact written to All Hallows and engaged there students for Montana."[73]

In addition Meagher had established good relations with the Jesuits earlier and continued to help them in any way he could. In his most successful effort, he arranged for the sale of their abandoned mission at Sun River to the military. The Blackfeet had not welcomed the Jesuits' presence, and one of the fathers had received a severe arrow wound when two Blackfeet attacked him. The Jesuits had just finished moving from Sun River across the mountains to St. Ignatius when Meagher wrote telling them about three steamboats coming up the Missouri River loaded with soldiers and equipment. The soldiers would be establishing a new fort along the Missouri. Both the army and the Catholic Church would profit, Meagher thought, if the army took over the Jesuits' abandoned missions for that purpose, paying fair compensation, of course.[74]

Overjoyed with the prospect, the Jesuits dispatched Father Kuppens to travel with Meagher to meet the soldiers. The boats bearing the soldiers and supplies were too large to make it past the Judith River, so the two decided to board a steamboat with their horses and head downstream to meet them. The trip itself was filled with mishaps. Their boat repeatedly became stranded on sandbars, the boiler suffered mechanical failure, and the steering gear froze. Meagher's bizarre sense of humor complicated matters by hinting that all the problems arose because Kuppens rode a white horse; the superstitious crew considered a priest on a white horse bad luck. When the boat finally became hopelessly stuck in the sand, the crew turned on the two men. Meagher tried to reassure the crew that he had only been joking but, as Kuppens remembered, "for once all his blarney, Irish wit and eloquence failed"; both priest and governor ended up going overboard with their horses. Nevertheless, all ended well. The pair swam the river to the dry bank and continued on their way to meet the soldiers. With Meagher's help, Kuppens succeeded in renting the mission buildings at Sun River to the military. It was a great day for the Jesuits, and a great day for Meagher, who had recognized an opportunity to aid the Catholic Church and had seen it through.[75]

Meagher and Kuppens made a happy trip back to Helena as fast friends and parted there, but not before Meagher "had staked off on the hill overlooking the gulch on the east side a piece of ground for a Catholic church." Kuppens stayed on to encourage the start of the church, which was under construction by the time he left a few weeks later. He soon returned to Helena to serve as the community's priest, and he and Meagher spoke frequently about where they could recruit other priests to come to Montana.[76]

Despite his work for the Catholic Church, Meagher's vision of an Irish haven remained nonsectarian, as letters to his Irish Protestant friend the Reverend George Pepper make clear. In December 1865 Meagher, who was searching for someone to accompany his wife, Elizabeth, to the territory, wrote Pepper, then serving as a Methodist minister in Ohio, urging him to immigrate. "You, my dear friend, would exult in being here. It is just the country for one of your temperament, your intellect, your heart and eloquence," enthused Meagher. Promising Pepper a place where the Irish were truly equal citizens, he continued: "Come out to Montana—take . . . my word for it, you will feel yourself a new man, and an American citizen in full." He wrote again a month later in a less optimistic mood. "Do come," he pleaded. "We have too great a preponderance of Yankee blood (not blood, but serum) out here. I want to see a strong infusion of the rich, red, generous royal Celtic blood, to counteract the acidity and poverty of the former."[77]

Even after his brother-in-law, Samuel Barlow, arranged another escort for Elizabeth, Meagher continued to urge Pepper to accompany the party. "She leaves St. Louis by the first boat starting thence for the Upper Missouri," he wrote in February 1866. "Confidently reckon on her being here the end of May. I shall be deeply disappointed if I do not find you with her. We shall have the happiest times in Montana together. I promise you golden harvests for your labors as a clergyman. Now, I entreat of you to come—nay, I insist upon it." Pepper declined Meagher's invitation. Their esteem was clearly mutual, however, because Pepper named his youngest son after Meagher.[78]

Elizabeth arrived in Fort Benton in late spring 1866, after nearly a year of separation from her husband. Meagher was there to meet her with a startling story to tell about his journey from Virginia City, for he had traveled with a wagon train that he and his fellow travelers believed had been threatened by Indians. According to Will H. Sutherlin, a fellow traveler on the train, Meagher had roused everyone on the train at three in the morning after hearing a single shot. "General Meagher got his fellow passengers out in line and marched them in regular soldier form around and round the big corral in which the mules were secured, . . . and his strong voice echoed for nearly three hours, as he gave commands to keep in line ready for action and protect the camp." By Sutherlin's account, Meagher's quick action saved the group from Indian attack.[79]

Elizabeth's trip had been less dramatic, and Meagher was pleased to learn that she had been in the company of Father De Smet on the upriver trip from St. Louis. She had also been watched over by the boat's pilot, Johnny Doran, an Irishman who knew Meagher by reputation and was

Virginia City, Montana Territory. This 1866 photograph shows the new town of Virginia City in Alder Gulch. (Courtesy Montana Historical Society, Helena)

more than anxious to assure that Elizabeth's trip was safe and comfortable. The couple traveled to Virginia City aboard a wagon lent them by De Smet, and the trip went well. But Elizabeth must have been shocked to see the small cabin on Idaho Street that was to be her new home. By her wealthy New York City standards the abode, which only a few months earlier had been used as a butcher shop, was primitive at best.[80]

Undismayed, Elizabeth set about being a proper governor's wife and proved to be an animated and charming first lady for the territory. She had always received high praise, and the Episcopal bishop, Daniel Tuttle, added to it when he called on her on July 27, 1867, less than four weeks after her husband's death. "She is one of the cleverest women, and most brilliant in conversation, that I have ever met," he wrote. "She is a fine looking woman too, with the blackest eyes and queenliest presence and prettiest face I've seen in the mountains."[81]

Others were less enchanted. Virginia City resident James Knox Polk Miller met Elizabeth at a wedding reception in 1867, where "the company assembled comprised the elite of the country, among them the always prominent Mrs. Genl. Meagher." Miller called her "a very good representative of the grand lady, a superb lady. Very much like an immense work. She is very good to be seen at the proper distance but too large and unwieldy for a life companion." Nevertheless, he added, "from others I hear that she is a highly educated, versatile, and very agreeable lady."[82] These qualities certainly helped Elizabeth navigate the difficult political situation in which she found herself.

Elizabeth's life changed again when territorial governor Green Clay Smith, appointed by President Johnson to replace Sidney Edgerton, arrived in October 1866. Smith's arrival eased some of Meagher's burdens. As the *Montana Post* noted, Meagher "now [had] a chance to enjoy the roses of the Secretaryship and not be annoyed by the thorns of the gubernatorial chair." To his delight, he found that he and Smith hit it off well. Soon after meeting the new governor in October, Meagher glowingly wrote to Samuel Barlow that "Green Clay Smith is in *complete accord* with me. . . . He is a genial, bright-hearted, high-minded young fellow, and I expect we shall be fast friends."[83]

The *Montana Post* also noted: "The Territory has had no official head since Governor Edgerton departed for his home in Ohio. The Secretary of State, General Thomas F. Meagher, who has claimed to act

Thomas Francis Meagher in Montana. This carte de visite was taken by photographer A. C. Carter in Virginia City, Montana Territory, probably in 1866 or early 1867. (Courtesy Montana Historical Society, Helena)

Elizabeth Meagher in Montana. This carte de visite was taken in Virginia City sometime during Elizabeth's stay there, probably at the same time as her husband's carte de visite by the same photographer. After Meagher died, Elizabeth endorsed the back of one of the cartes de visite as "the widow of Maj. Gen. T. F. Meagher," perpetuating the legend among some that Meagher was a major general, rather than a brigadier general. (Courtesy Montana Historical Society, Helena)

in that capacity, has forfeited the respect of all parties by his violation of
the laws of morality and decorum upon great and small occasions. . . .
General Meagher, who has brought disgrace upon himself, his race, the
Territory and country generally, has been superseded." The *Post* then
talked of "[t]he universal contempt with which . . . 'the great Irish
patriot,' is everywhere greeted."[84]

Smith's arrival also meant that Meagher was no longer in the limelight. The *Montana Post* gloated, noting that since Smith's arrival no one
had made any inquiries about Meagher. Even the *Democrat* had not
published any of his speeches. "General Meagher will find that he is
now the most unimportant member of the community, and the flattering
demagogues who made him think that they heard his footsteps echoing
in the vestibules of the Senate chamber in Washington, will pass by
him, and be interested in something upon the opposite side of the
street," predicted the *Post*.[85]

Although the *Post*'s scorn implied that Meagher remained ambitious,
he himself had realized that he had no political future in Montana.[86]
Rumors had circulated in late summer 1866 that Meagher would resign
when Green Clay Smith arrived. A petition was signed in August by
some ninety-five Montana citizens and forwarded to President Andrew
Johnson to request that "Major John P. Bruce be appointed and commissioned to fill the vacancy about to be occasioned by the resignation
of Genl T. F. Meagher." Meagher finally did submit a formal resignation,
and Johnson formally nominated Bruce to replace him. But as it turned
out, Bruce had a bad reputation in Washington for his unsuccessful efforts
to seat himself as a congressman from Missouri, which were rejected by
a congressional majority that included at the time Green Clay Smith.
Hearing about Bruce's nomination, the *Montana Post* suddenly came out
in favor of Meagher staying on, noting that he "enjoys the confidence
of the 'powers that be' in Washington, and there will be no vacancy for
our editorial brother to fill."[87]

On March 1 the Senate refused to "advise and consent" to Bruce's
nomination; and on March 21 President Johnson nominated James
Tufts to replace Meagher "in the place of John P. Bruce, rejected."[88] But
Tufts was on the East Coast and would need a long time to get to
Montana. In the meantime Green Clay Smith left the territory early in
the year to go back east, and Meagher once again had to shoulder the

heavy burden of acting governor of the territory without the support of either the eastern political establishment or the strong Republicans in Montana. It was a situation he no longer wanted. As fate would have it, he was relieved of his burden only a few days before he died.

In the hiatus between his two terms as acting governor Thomas Francis and Elizabeth Meagher took the opportunity in the late summer and fall of 1866 to travel together through the valleys west of the mountains, meeting with Montana Fenians and Jesuit fathers. They visited the missionary priest Father Anthony Ravalli at Stevensville and served as sponsors for Mrs. John Simms, whom Ravalli baptized in the little log church of St. Michael on October 1, 1866. They then traveled to St. Ignatius, where Meagher gave the two highest peaks of the Mission Range the name "Twin Sisters" and "christened" a "4,000 feet high" waterfall "Elizabeth."[89]

On this trip Meagher also began conducting research for a series of articles he had proposed to *Harper's New Monthly Magazine*. Several years earlier *Harper's* had published his articles on Costa Rica; searching for a way to earn some money, Meagher had contacted the magazine to offer a similar series, which he styled "Rides through Montana." To illustrate the series, he proposed an accomplished but unknown landscape artist named Peter Peterson Tofft, a Danish immigrant, who had come to Montana as a prospector.[90]

Along his way to Montana from the West, Tofft had stopped to sketch many scenes. After he suffered a debilitating injury in the fall of 1866 while prospecting, he supported himself with his sketchpad and easel. By November 1866 Tofft was in Virginia City, selling his work on a regular basis. Among his work was a watercolor of the Meaghers' residence on Idaho Street, grandly titled *Gubernatorial Mansion*. The work depicted the insignificant log cabin with a large United States flag flying from a mast on the roof that dwarfed the tiny abode, and Tofft had proudly presented it to Elizabeth with his compliments. Meagher thought that Tofft was fully capable of producing the sketches he wanted for his articles in *Harper's;* in addition, Tofft already had sketches from his trip across the western valleys.[91]

Meagher planned to tour the territory with Tofft in the summer of 1867; but in the meantime he arranged to use Tofft's sketches of the Clark Fork and western Montana to illustrate the only article in the

The Meagher residence in Virginia City. This copy is from an original watercolor done by Peter Peterson Tofft, a Danish immigrant, and presented to Elizabeth Meagher. He inscribed the work to "Mrs. T. F. Meagher from her friend P. Tofft." It shows the small cabin under the U.S. flag that served as the Meagher residence in Virginia City. (Author's collection)

series that he completed. Meagher was proud of his article. A little over two weeks before his death, in June 1867, he wrote his last letter to Samuel Barlow, telling him to look for the article in *Harper's*. According to Meagher, Elizabeth had accompanied him on his "Rides" as far as the mission at St. Ignatius, but he had gone alone on foot and discovered the "Alice Cascade," which "I had the delight of naming after your very beautiful and bounteously good-hearted wife. I claim to have been the first white man who saw it. You will have, in the article referred to, a very spirited sketch of it."[92]

Although their trip to western Montana ultimately bore fruit in the *Harper's Magazine* article, not all was tranquil with the Meaghers in the fall of 1866. They were experiencing discord when they stopped at John Owen's trading post in Stevensville, and Owen noted in his diary: "the Gen. & his Lady out of humour to day [*sic*]." If the note referred to the Meaghers, drink may have been the cause of the friction. On their way to Owen's trading post a month earlier, Elizabeth rode in a wagon, and her husband followed on horseback with Judge T. M. Pomeroy. Meagher soon fell behind; and Owen reported in his diary that the judge had arrived alone later in the evening and explained that "the Gen. Was unwell & Would pass the Night With Mr. Collins on Lo Los ford & c." "Unwell" or drinking, Meagher did not show up. That night Owen "[p]layed a few games of Back Gammon with Mrs. M. & was Nobly defeated." Meagher finally appeared the next afternoon.[93]

Uncertainty about the future probably also played a role in any tension in their relationship. Elizabeth undoubtedly had shared Meagher's dream of moving to Washington, D.C., where she could shine as a senator's wife. All hope for that future had evaporated by fall 1866. Money was an issue too. The *Harper's* articles offered some respite, but they would not have been sufficient for the long term. Although Meagher, like almost every sojourner in Montana Territory, had begun to dabble in gold mining, that did not offer a secure future either. Quartz mining required large amounts of capital, for which he turned, once again, to his brother-in-law, Samuel Barlow. "From what I know of this property, I am perfectly satisfied, that any interest you might purchase in it would prove splendidly productive," the optimistic Meagher wrote Barlow. "I am myself largely interested in it, and have no doubt but that my share will be a little fortune in itself."[94]

In fact, by the fall of 1866 Meagher was deeply in debt. At the height of his influence in the territory when he had convened a legislature, he had on principle turned down the extra money that the territorial legislature had approved for its governor and secretary. That had been a mistake; he now had to borrow small amounts from his friends, and he purchased on credit wherever he could. In a letter written on September 26, 1866, Meagher turned to an old friend, fellow Irishman and Fenian "Baron" Cornelius O'Keefe, for money: "If possible let me have a little 'gift' of $1,000." Meagher gave his reason for the request: "having . . . secured the 'public' triumph, I want to complete it by the 'private—'. I want to return to Virginia City a proud and independent Irish gentleman—having no one to insult, or even to give me the cold shoulder, because I owe him a miserable little bill of '50,' or '100,' dollars."[95]

Meagher was evidently being hounded for the money he owed and asked O'Keefe to help him out. It is not clear whether the money he was asking for was O'Keefe's or whether it was coming from funds that O'Keefe was holding for Irish advancement purposes and perhaps for the Fenians. Meagher's reasons for requesting the money certainly appealed to the cause of the Irish. "I want my countrymen to place me up and beyond the sneers of these 'blackguards'—who are, ever, so ready to run down an Irishman, whenever, and wherever they have a chance," he said. "It is my ambition—it is indeed, and in truth my heart's desire—to be the representative and champion of the Irish Race in the wild great mountains; and, to enable me to be such, I do not hesitate to ask you to see that (so far as the sum named, or $800 or $900) I go back to resume my duties, proudly and independently, like a true brave Irishman, as you yourself are." Meagher closed his letter with characteristic humor: "and with the most enthusiastic wishes for the success and prosperity of Castle O'Keefe."[96]

There is good reason to think that O'Keefe did in fact lend him money, and Meagher may have tried to pay him back by crediting him as the author of the *Harper's* article. That article, published after Meagher's death in July 1867, listed "Colonel Cornelius O'Keefe, Late of the Irish Brigade" as its author, although O'Keefe never had served in the brigade. Meagher might have listed O'Keefe as the author because O'Keefe's travels actually matched Tofft's sketches of western Montana better than Meagher's own journey did. *Harper's* only offered the explanation that O'Keefe was a *nom de plume,* used by Meagher so he could "speak with a freedom which would hardly comport with the official dignity which would have seemed proper had he written directly in his own name." But this made no sense, because Meagher had already resigned his secretary-ship at the time he delivered the article. A plausible explanation is that he was indebted in some way to O'Keefe and naming him as author was the only way to pay him back.[97]

Whatever the case, by the winter of 1866–67 Meagher was clearly floundering. His agreement with *Harper's* aside, his finances remained in disarray; he did not even have the money to pay his doctor and druggist bills for treatment he received in February for what may have been a severe burn. His condition required daily and sometimes twice daily treatment by Dr. John W. Reins of Helena. In addition to the treatment he received at the doctor's office, Meagher was supplied medicines and drugs from Weir & Pope druggists, including powders and solutions for the injury; citrate of magnesium and various patent medicines; and several boxes of "soothing" pills, including opium tablets.[98] Both claimed payment from Meagher's estate after his death six months later.

Through it all, however, Meagher still managed to dazzle the public with his oratory. Early in 1867 he gave a benefit lecture for the Helena Catholic church titled "Reminiscences of the War," which Kuppen's described as "one anecdote after another, breezy, witty, humourous, ludicrous, . . . that kept the house spellbound for near three hours." Kuppen's praise for Meagher's skill was generous: "Sometimes he would be pathetic and brought tears to the bronzed faces of the miners, and then again he would launch into flights of oratory that brought his audience of over a thousand to their feet, standing, mouth open, stretching their necks, oblivious to all around, drinking in every word of the speaker. Never have I heard such oratory." Even a Republican adversary, Judge Hezekiah Hosmer, admitted it was a "brilliant lecture."[99]

That ability to speak had always served Meagher well. As he looked at his options for making a living, he toyed once again with rejoining the lecture circuit. Rumors circulated that Meagher had received an offer "from some Irish Organization at San Francisco" to lecture for their benefit for $5,000 a year and that he had taken them up on it. It was partially true; Meagher did receive an invitation to give at least one lecture to the Fenians in California. He had to decline the Fenians' invitation, however, writing: "I fear greatly that I cannot be with you.

Governor Smith won't be here till the middle of July, and it is uncertain when Secretary Tufts will arrive. I can't leave till either comes, the organic act not providing for any one taking my place in their absence; hence I am detained here, much to my vexation. God speed the Irish nation to liberty and power!"[100] Thus Meagher remained in Montana politics against his wishes. Having again shouldered the burden of acting governor, he would soon find himself the chief scapegoat in one of the most criticized Indian wars in the West.

CHAPTER TEN

Stampede

I believe you are stampeded until I hear of some fight in which you
whip the Indians or they whip you.

William Tecumseh Sherman to Meagher

Conflict with Montana's Native inhabitants caused settlers anxiety from
the early days of the gold rush. As white settlers crowded into the region
and wagon trains cut across prime Indian hunting grounds, Indians
responded in a variety of ways, some of which were violent. Rumors
flew, and any attacks on settlers—true or imagined—caused panic among
the rest. With each attack, white Montanans saw their situation as increasingly tenuous and clamored for federal protection. The military, however,
tended toward skepticism. Although they shared the goal of making the
West safe for white settlers by confining the tribes to reservations, the
military commanders questioned citizens' panicky calls for troops. A
history of settler overreaction and frontier profiteering at the expense
of the federal government made the military naturally wary. Nonetheless,
political pressure and the possibility of actual threat could force them into
action. During his second term as acting governor, Meagher responded
to settler fears—including his own—with demands for troops. Urged to
act, even by his political rivals, he formed the Montana militia to fight
what turned out to be a relatively bloodless, likely unnecessary, but very

expensive Indian war. Meagher died on July 1, 1867, before the war was over, and his death made it convenient for his enemies to assign him full blame for the "stampede."

Relations between whites and the tribes in Montana and the West had been uneasy since the beginning. General William Tecumseh Sherman, now in charge of military operations in the West, believed that the conflict would end only with the Indians' submission. "This conflict of authority will exist as long as the Indians exist, for their ways are different from our ways, and either they or we must be masters on the Plains," he wrote. "I have no doubt our people have committed grievous wrong to the Indians and I wish we could punish them but it is impracticable but both races cannot use this country in common, and one or the other must withdraw."[1]

Meagher's initial understanding of Indian affairs came from Blackfeet Indian agent Gad Upson, who shared Sherman's view and believed that the Indians as a people would soon be annihilated. Meagher's contacts with the Jesuits ultimately moderated his view. As he wrote his father, in the midst of his campaign to protect the Gallatin Valley from what he saw as a likely invasion by the Sioux, "the Indians on the west of the Mountains—all of whom are Catholics, and subject to the immediate control of the good Jesuit Fathers—are perfectly inoffensive, and we have no reason whatever to regard them otherwise than as friendly. Were they all Catholics on this side of the mountains, and subject to the same control, the Territory would have nothing to alarm it."[2]

Meagher's naive appreciation for the Jesuits' work did not change his underlying obsession with the independence of the Irish, of course. His only real interest in social justice was to bring the Irish even with the English; and he, like governors both before and after him, believed his primary responsibility was to protect white settlers from attack. This understanding provided common ground for those who otherwise disagreed politically. Territorial governor Sidney Edgerton, for example, issued a proclamation in 1865 calling for five hundred volunteers to protect the new immigrants arriving at Fort Benton and traveling to the mines. "I have just received reliable information of serious Indian difficulties near Fort Benton. Ten men were massacred 25th instant by the Bloods [and] Blackfeet. The danger to emigration now *en route* up the Missouri River is imminent. Am fitting out an expedition of 500 militia. We need troops; can you let us have two regiments?" he wrote to secretary of war Edwin Stanton.[3]

Edgerton continued to lobby for federal troops even after he left Montana, reporting to secretary of state William Seward that Indian depredations occurred almost daily within the territory.[4] Seward sent the report to secretary of the interior James Harlan, who in turn referred it to Dennis N. Cooley, commissioner of Indian affairs. Cooley's response would have disheartened Meagher had he heard of it. "According to public reports," Cooley stated in early spring 1866, acting governor Meagher "has not acted prudently towards the Indians, . . . which may result in large expense to the Government."[5]

Indeed, Meagher did act extraordinarily rashly in early 1866, before correcting his course later in the spring. On February 8, 1866, he issued a general order as commander-in-chief, attempting to raise a territorial militia. Colonel Neil Howie was directed to take charge of those who volunteered, with the "main and immediate object of the expedition being the relief of our fellow-citizens at Fort Benton, from the state of siege in which they have been vexatiously and cruelly detained for several weeks." Howie was further commanded to go to the Piegan camp and demand horses and other property, which, Meagher said, had been stolen from Fort Benton's residents. The troops were also to demand that the Piegans turn over Eagle Bird and the son of Little Dog; "after careful enquiry and full deliberation" of their case, they were to be executed by hanging in the presence of the Indian camp. Meagher decorated this vindictive sentence with words of fairness, but in addition to being unjust his proposed solution to the Blackfeet raids at Fort Benton was tailor-made to incite an all-out Indian war. Luckily, Meagher did not have the funds to execute the order, and nothing ever came of it.[6]

At the same time Meagher also requested that regular army troops be dispatched to the territory to quell the Indians, but it soon became clear that he would not get much help from the regular army. On February 17, 1866, he received a letter from his old antagonist in the Union Army, General Sherman, who bluntly stated:

You ask for a Regiment of Cavalry. I now have one Regiment of Regular Cavalry, the 2nd, for Montana, Dacotah, Nebraska, Colorado, Kansas, and New Mexico, so you see it is idle to expect all my Cavalry in one remote Territory. . . . And a still more important question is now under debate, whether to the Hostile Indians, we are to add all the white people of the South as permanent enemies to be watched and kept in subjection by Military Force. As soon as those are determined, we can arrive at the approximate estimate of what troops can be shared for Montana. Your people may safely count on the Missouri River and Platte Route to Laramie Fort Reno &c. to Montana, and that is about all we can attempt now. We cannot for months, if this year, promise to place any cavalry in Montana.[7]

With receipt of this letter, Meagher came to the painful realization that he would have to deal with the Indian situation without federal assistance for some time to come. Nevertheless, he doggedly kept up his pressure on Washington for troops. On April 20, 1866, a totally frustrated Meagher wrote to the Indian commissioner: "There is . . . no hope whatever to be entertained that such outrages will cease until the presence of a military force in the Territory." He had modified his hard line, however, and now suggested that the troops, "judiciously distributed and posted, shall, by intimidation, coerce these intractable savages to do what no treaty, however liberal, and no amount of annuities will, in my opinion, induce them to do."[8]

Despite this aggressive stance, Meagher also took his work as superintendent of Indian affairs seriously and investigated the existence of Indian tribes in southwestern Montana. He was able to advise that the Shoshones or Snakes and the Bannacks were in the area in force and, so far as he knew, had never been recognized by the government. Meagher recommended that Nathaniel T. Hall be appointed as agent for the tribes, which he described as living in misery and filth "exceeded only by the huts of the Terra del Fuegans" that he had seen as he rounded the southern tip of South America on his escape from Tasmania. Of the Bannacks he would say: "Unrecognized, unprotected, and outlawed, . . . as they now are, they are indeed a revolting reproach to our civilization."[9]

In the summer of 1866 the treaty that Meagher had signed in Fort Benton finally came unraveled completely. Hiram D. Upham, who was temporarily serving in place of the deceased Gad Upson, wrote the Indian commissioner about repeated attacks by the Bloods, Blackfeet, and a portion of the Piegans, both on white settlers and on each other. Upham described these tribes as being all one nation, speaking the common Blackfeet language, and intermarrying. The Blackfeet, Bloods, and the Northern Piegans lived mostly in Canada, crossing the border only to travel to Fort Benton to receive their annuity goods. Only the Gros Ventres, who were of a different nation, had lived up to the bargain. They had kept their part of the treaty but were at war with the Blackfeet, Bloods, and Piegans, because they had to fight their way through the others' territory to come to Fort Benton for their government annuity goods. He recommended that a separate agency be established for the Gros Ventres and the Crows, who were friendly to each other.[10]

Meanwhile conflict between Indians and settlers continued, not only around Fort Benton but also to the south and west. A primary source of settler anxiety was a series of concerted attacks in 1866 along the Bozeman Trail. The cutoff from the Platte River Road to the Virginia City goldfields traversed the last great Northern Plains Indian hunting area, then controlled by the Sioux, who were determined to close the trail. As part of the beginning of what became known as Red Cloud's War, Sioux attacks against emigrants using the cutoff left at least twenty-four civilian travelers and soldiers dead in a single week in July 1866.[11]

Montana settlers cared little for the reasons behind those attacks. At the beginning of 1867 the *Helena Herald* looked back on the previous year as a time in which "the roadways and trails of the unoffending pioneer and emigrant were continuously marked by more fresh-made graves—the victims of the tomahawk and scalping knife in the hands of merciless savages."[12] This grisly picture took on an even more desperate tinge after news reached Montana that Sioux warriors had killed ninety-three men under Captain William Fetterman's command along the Bozeman Trail at Fort Phil Kearny. To make matters worse, in a letter notifying the territorial governor of the Sioux attack, Captain Nathaniel Coates Kinney warned of a possible uprising brewing among the Crows as well.[13] In the absence of Governor Green Clay Smith, who had already left the territory to lobby in Washington for increased protection, Meagher received the letter and had to disclose its grim contents to the citizens.

In the meantime Smith presented his case that Montana desperately needed troops to General Ulysses S. Grant, then commander of the army.

Around noon on February 20, 1867, Grant telegraphed Lieutenant General William Tecumseh Sherman, commander of the Division of the Mississippi, which included the Department of Missouri, of which Montana was a part: "What do you think of giving to the Governor of Montana 2500 stand arms to enable him to organize Citizens for defence against Indians." Sherman responded that evening: "I think very well of your proposition to let the governor of Montana have twenty five hundred 2500 stand of arms to arm the Militia of the Territory. There is a good class of people in Montana & if they can protect themselves it relieves us to that extent."[14]

Even after Sherman's assent, several anxious weeks passed before Governor Smith received reason to hope. Finally, on April 2, General Sherman promised that two companies of the 13th U.S. Infantry and some recruits would be on their way up the Missouri to Montana as soon as the river opened. Two days later Sherman telegraphed more good news to Smith, who was still in Lexington, Kentucky: he had just received orders to send the muskets, guns, and ammunition to Montana and was only awaiting assignment of a boat that carried troops to bring the supplies upriver. But this information was not passed on to Meagher in Montana, who was starting to bear the brunt of the citizens calling for arms and troops to protect them.[15]

Despite his initial support for supplying arms for a Montana militia, Sherman was generally skeptical of the overall severity of the threat—and for good reason. Many of the reports of Indian depredations proved, on further investigation, to be highly exaggerated. Among the articles to reach Sherman's desk, for example, was one that ran in the *Yankton Union and Dakotaian* on March 20, 1867, reporting the "massacre" of the entire garrison at Fort Buford at the confluence of the Missouri and Yellowstone Rivers. Soon that report was completely discredited. About two months later the *Union and Dakotaian* corrected another false report: the story circulated by the *Council Bluffs Nonpareil* that Indians had scalped and killed the entire crew and all passengers on the steamboat *Miner* was also untrue.[16]

While Sherman may have had reason to doubt, settlers in the Montana Territory were more than willing to believe every sensationalized report published. They placed increasing pressure on acting governor Meagher to take action against the Indians. On March 25, 1867, the renowned John Bozeman wrote to Meagher from Bozeman City in the Gallatin Valley: "We have reliable reports here that we are in imminent danger of hostile Indians, and if there is not something done to protect this valley soon, there will be but a few men and no families left."[17]

When Henry Blake of the *Montana Post* became aware of Bozeman's fear, he at once issued an inflammatory alarm, saying the Indians must be stopped in the Gallatin; otherwise "it uncovers both our cities and we would probably have to fight the savages on our own door sills. . . . Let [the Indians] once be successful, and all the fiends will inspire them to massacre and rapine." He then assailed members of the Montana Democratic party and John Bruce, editor of the rival *Montana Democrat,* for quibbling about political matters in the presence of the Indian threat: "There is a most surprising lethargy exhibited in this matter, beside which our local political issues are minor considerations."[18]

"TURN OUT! TURN OUT!" was the ringing headline in the *Montana Post* as it announced an April 8, 1867, meeting in Virginia City for the purpose of organizing a defense against possible Indian attacks. The meeting sponsors included longtime Meagher antagonists Judge Hezekiah Hosmer and *Montana Post* editor Henry Blake, who were now more than willing to cooperate with Meagher to form a militia. Meagher did not attend the meeting, for he had left Virginia City for the Gallatin Valley on April 7, to gather information on the "true condition of affairs there."[19]

The citizens who did attend acted decisively and adopted a formal resolution to "organize one or more volunteer companies and immediately place them on as good a war footing as possible, to be held in readiness to march, and when called upon to the aid those threatened in any portion of our Territory." They also authorized Meagher to "telegraph the War Department for authority to raise and equip a Regiment of Volunteers, to serve against hostile Indians, in the Territory of Montana, until relieved by the regular forces of the United States."[20]

Meagher heeded the directive, bypassed Sherman, and telegraphed Grant, the commanding general of the U.S. Army, on April 9, stating that

> the greatest alarm reasonably prevails. . . . Danger is imminent & will overpower unless measures for defence are instantly taken. . . . We earnestly entreat permission from War Department to raise a force of one thousand 1000 Volunteers for menaced quarters to

be paid by general government while serving in field & to be rel[ie]ved by re[i]nforcements early in Summer. . . . People of territory will generously and bravely do their duty successfully defending themselves if priv[i]lege asked be granted."[21]

Meagher's telegram had an effect. On the following day Grant wrote to Secretary of War Stanton asking for more troops for the West and requesting that all military organizations west of the Mississippi be filled to the maximum authorized by law.[22] On Meagher's telegram he wrote: "Respectfully referred to the Sec. of War. If there is the danger which Governor Maher [sic] apprehends, and there wood [sic] seem to be, judging from all the information reaching us, the Citizens of Montana ought to have some organization to defend themselves until the troops of the United States can give them the required protection. I think however the Governor should know what self defense requires these Citizens to do." Grant then addressed the important question of how the volunteers would be paid, and his answer set the tone for the War Department's continuing equivocation over the matter. He proposed that "if the services rendered by them warrant it, they should, afterward, look to Congress for compensation." Grant clearly wanted a militia formed in Montana. Just as clearly, however, he did not want the War Department to have to pay for it, particularly if the situation proved to be a false alarm.[23]

On the same day that Meagher telegraphed Grant, he also sought regular army troops from Major William Clinton, who commanded the 1st Battalion, 13th Infantry, recently arrived at Camp Cooke, downriver from Fort Benton.[24] When Clinton refused to send troops to Bozeman from Fort Benton, his letter was read and "listened to with profound disgust" at a war meeting in Virginia City. At that same April 18 meeting, representatives from the Gallatin Valley came and "asserted that one half, and in some localities, two-thirds of the citizens had already left the valley." Then Colonel Thomas Thoroughman, a lawyer, took matters into hand and, "mounting a chair, called on all who were willing to accompany him to give in their names at once. In five minutes he had a full company." Before the meeting adjourned, "the other officers were instructed to commence operations in the morning."[25]

A week earlier Meagher had appointed Captain Martin Beem, described by the Post as "a thoroughly tried and gallant young officer of the war, to superintend the recruiting and organization of volunteers."[26] But despite the enthusiasm generated at the April 18 meeting, recruiting did not go well. According to United States Army inspector general James A. Hardie, who investigated the matter a few years later, "Upon the spur of the moment volunteers came forward; but, as merchants and others, finding little prospect of payment by the Federal authorities, and knowing the Territory could not pay, were unwilling to furnish supplies in sufficient quantities, some who had enlisted became discouraged and left, and recruiting was slack under the discouragement."[27]

Support for forming a militia—particularly one backed by federal dollars—did, however, manage to blur party lines. As warm weather began to open the mountain passes, the fear of an Indian attack became so great that friction between Meagher and the Unionists abated as he and chief justice Hezekiah Hosmer joined forces to telegraph Stanton, requesting authority to raise volunteers. Although they sent the joint request on April 27, it took until May 3 to receive a response from General Grant, who ignored Meagher and addressed only Hosmer: "There is no law authorizin[g] the calling out of Militia. The law of self defence will justify the Governor of the Territory in calling out troops for the protection of her citizens and Congress must be looked to afterwards for reimbursment [sic]." He continued: "In substance this same reply was made to Gn. Meaghr's [sic] first dispatch about three weeks since." Again Grant had stopped short of promising the government would pay.[28]

On May 3, 1867, Meagher received a telegram from Sherman, who told him that "General Augur will soon be among the Sioux and Crows on the Yellowstone, prepared to punish them." Christopher Augur, who commanded the army along the Platte, never arrived. Sherman also advised that "boats with twenty five hundred (2500) muskets and ammunition" were on their way to Montana. Sherman, who clearly distrusted Meagher's judgment, denied his request to raise troops. "There is no law to authorize enrolling troops in a Territory, subject to the governor, but you should meet these emergencies without a formal organization and muster into service of the United States, confining yourself to self protection."[29]

The alarmed citizens of Virginia City balked at Sherman's message, and Virginia City mayor John W. Castner sent his own telegram to the War Department, expressing fear of the Indian situation. He received a more favorable reply from Secretary of War Stanton:

Your telegram of yesterday's date has just been received. General Sherman, at St. Louis, has been authorized to call out, organize, arm, officer and equip local troops in Montana for its defense against Indians. A large supply of arms have been forwarded by the War Department, and General Sherman reports that he is in communication with General Smith, Governor of your Territory, and that General Augur is on the march against the Indians that threaten you. Your telegram to me has been forwarded to General Sherman for such action as circumstances may require, and you will promptly communicate with him at St. Louis, by telegraph, in respect to raising forces and such measures as you deem essential for the defense of your Territory, he having full power over the subject. This Department will do all in its power for your protection and relief.[30]

In the meantime Judge Hosmer had telegraphed again and also received a reply from the War Department dated May 4:

In answer to your telegrams of April 28 and May 2, in relation to Indian invasion, I am instructed by the Secretary of war to inform you that authority has been given by the Department to Lieut. Gen. Sherman to call out, organize, officer, arm and subsist such militia force in Montana Territory as he deems necessary for the protection of that Territory against hostile Indians. Any suggestions you may make to General Sherman at St. Louis on matters relating to this subject, will secure his attention. Please acknowledge receipt.

The telegrams received by Castner and Hosmer were soon published in the *Montana Post* under the bold heading: "THE GOVERNMENT AUTHORIZES THE ORGANIZING OF THE MILITIA—ON A SURE FOOTING AT LAST— DISPATCHES FROM THE SECRETARY OF WAR AND THE ADJUTANT GENERAL."[31]

An additional telegram to Castner from Sherman seemed to reinforce this view. According to the relieved editor of the *Post*, Sherman's telegram provided "sufficient authority for raising troops, and obviates, in a great measure, the difficulties of procuring equipments." Sherman's actual language was more cautious. Unlike Grant and Stanton, Sherman had his doubts, and he told Castner: "Your dispatch of May 4th to the Sec. of War is referred to me, our official reports from that quarter do not justify such extreme alarm, but if the inhabitants of Gallatin Valley be in such imminent danger from Indians, you may organize your people and go to their relief and defence under the general direction of your Governor."[32]

The standard for raising the troops was now set as "imminent danger." In addition, Sherman further advised that help was on the way: "Troops and arms are now coming towards the head of Yellowstone as fast as boats can ascend the Missouri river, or can march by land." Perhaps the most important part of the message, however, was Sherman's advice that "there is no necessity of mustering you in for three months. You should render this service in self defence & to help your neighbors without the formality of muster in or muster out." What Sherman apparently meant by this was that militia service should be voluntary. What the citizens of Virginia City saw in it was a confirmation of Grant and Stanton's promises that the government could be looked to for payment, albeit after service was rendered, and that the militia could be raised and sent to the field immediately without formal mustering into the army.[33]

With these telegrams flying, Sherman finally decided on May 7 to address Meagher directly. Sherman's and Grant's experiences with Meagher during the Civil War gave both of them good reasons to try to work around him. Meagher was acting governor, however, and they had reached a point where they could no longer avoid him. Thus Sherman wrote: "If Indians *enter* the Valley of the Gallatin, organize eight hundred (800) volunteers, and drive them out. Those troops should only be used till the Regulars reach Yellowstone" (emphasis added).[34]

The term "enter" turned out to be the key word of the telegram, although its presence there was disputed; Sherman later accused Meagher of circulating the telegram in Virginia City with "enter" changed to "threaten." It is doubtful that Meagher did so. In any case, it would not have mattered much. When read with the other messages, Sherman's telegram, no matter whether it used the word "enter" or "threaten," seemed to authorize Meagher to raise troops to stop Indians from coming into the Gallatin Valley.

Other telegrams from Sherman also seemed to support creation of a militia. When Sherman telegraphed Meagher, he also sent a telegram to chief justice Hezekiah Hosmer, directing him: "certainly raise as many regiments as you can & go to the help of your people until troops can reach you from the direction of Laramie. I have already telegraphed the same to your acting governor, for the purpose of self defense, you don't need to be mustered in by the United States, do that for yourselves."[35]

Nevertheless, Sherman remained skeptical about need, especially when dealing with Meagher. When Meagher requested cavalry from Utah, Sherman responded angrily on May 9: "I cannot and will not order cavalry, arms and equipments from Utah." He then ridiculed Meagher. "If the danger is so great that not an hour is to be lost, how can you wait for saddles from Utah?" Sherman also challenged Meagher to provide evidence of the necessity of raising a militia: "I believe you are stampeded until I hear of some fight in which you whip the Indians or they whip you. I won't believe it is anything more than a stampede." Finally, a frustrated and spiteful Sherman turned to pettiness: "I expect you to pay for dispatches at your end of the line."[36] Not long after, however, Sherman decided to dispatch Major W. H. Lewis from Utah to investigate the situation in Montana. Informing Lewis that "I hear of no facts that warrant a war in Montana," Sherman gave him strict instructions not to involve the army "in expense unless the safety of the settlements absolutely demands it." To emphasize his doubts, Sherman added: "A stampede now will be a public crime."[37]

Stampeded or not, Meagher's troops were in the field before Lewis arrived. A militia company had departed Virginia City in early May with fanfare reminiscent of the Irish Brigade's departure for the Civil War. The *Montana Post* reported that the troops formed a line in front of the Meaghers' residence on Idaho Street, where Elizabeth Meagher presented them a beautiful guidon. The captain gave Elizabeth his eloquent thanks, and the company gave "three rousing cheers for the fair donor." Then they were off to fight, if they must, the Indians in the Gallatin Valley.[38]

Lewis, for his part, arrived via stage from Salt Lake City around May 19 and immediately began his investigation. With him on the bumpy stage ride north had been Wilbur Fisk Sanders, who was returning to Montana after successfully petitioning Congress to invalidate Meagher's legislature.[39] Lewis undoubtedly heard a lot about Meagher from Sanders, and it would not have been good. Lewis also had special army intelligence, however, which led him to conclude the necessity of calling the militia. "I had received information, before I reached there, that an Indian campaign under General Augur was to take place by troops going north from Platte river," Lewis said when he later testified under oath about the matter. "I believed they would force the Indians into Gallatin Valley and that troops would be necessary to protect the settlers in that valley." Thus Lewis reported to both Sherman and Augur that "troops should be mustered in, and it was my intention to muster in a battalion of not to exceed four hundred men."[40]

On May 24 Sherman responded to Lewis's recommendation. "Muster in a battalion of eight hundred (800) men at once, at the cost of the United States for three months," Sherman directed. "Move quickly to the threatened point, when the danger will either disappear or be removed." As to arms and their mounts, he instructed: "Equip them as best you can till the arms *en route* reach Fort Benton. . . . Let the men furnish their own horses and arms at forty cents per day, and be rationed by contract. When the service is rendered I will order payment by the regular paymaster."[41]

With that, Lewis had all the authorization he needed to raise troops, with expenses paid by the government. Even then he had difficulty convincing the troops and the merchants who would supply them that Sherman had authorized the payments. Many in Montana were willing to provide goods and services to the war effort, but they knew the territory had no funds and wanted to be assured that the federal government would ultimately pay its bills.

Characteristic was the response of M. H. Insley, a merchant and freighter from Leavenworth in Virginia City with a load of flour that he had hauled to Montana on speculation. Insley sold the flour to Meagher's volunteers and transported it by six-mule teams "down to where they were in the service." But before agreeing to the transaction Insley asked for assurance that the government would pay, and he had seen the documents that stated it would. According to Insley in sworn testimony he gave in 1872 before Congress, Meagher "showed me the books in which they were copied—all this correspondence, with others; all that he had, the telegrams sent to Washington, with the replies." Insley had also seen the telegram that Lewis had received from Sherman. "Colonel [Major] Lewis exhibited his telegram, with others, to me, and had a copy of it tacked up in the banking-house of A. Hannan & Co., in Virginia City,"

Insley remembered. Lewis had also confirmed verbally that the telegram "was an answer sent by General Sherman to muster in these troops." In fact, Lewis had emphasized the matter to Insley and others. "There, gentlemen, is authority for you; that is sufficient," he had told them.[42] Only then was Insley willing to sell his flour.

Difficulty procuring supplies was only part of Lewis's problem. He also had trouble finding volunteers on his own, primarily because Meagher had already tapped many of the willing men for the Montana militia. Two things then occurred. First, Lewis reported to Sherman that the citizens had balked at furnishing their own horses and arms at only forty cents per day and requested that Sherman authorize him to move Major Clinton's forces of the regular army from their encampment at the mouth of the Judith into the Gallatin Valley. In response Sherman authorized Lewis to communicate directly with Clinton to ask for a portion of his troops, which were never sent.[43]

Second, Sherman reluctantly decided that since Meagher already had troops assembled the convenient thing to do would be to put Lewis in charge of them. On May 27, while still puzzling over the matter, Sherman wrote to Grant: "I hate to avail myself of the right to call for Volunteers, as it would stampede the whole country. In Montana we have no troops save at Camp Cooke and Sun River. The stampede there is further to the south and west, and to that point I have ordered from Utah a single officer, Major Lewis, and have authorized him to call for and use the battalion raised by Acting Governor Meagher, for two months only."[44] The same day Sherman telegraphed Grant once more: "Maj Lewis has reached Virginia City from Salt Lake & reports a great scarcity, I have authorized him to Employ for two (2) months a Battalion of Eight hundred (800) men to drive out of Montana the Sioux and open communication with Ft Benton. This will give time for the arrival of the arms for Governor Smith to reach his post & for Genl Augurs expedition to the Yellow Stone to produce its effect."[45]

Sherman had finally convinced himself that the threat was real and had devised a plan to deal with it. He also seems to have authorized payment for it. According to a later investigation by Inspector General James A. Hardie, "During the month of May, and especially toward its close, the correspondence between the governor, the Lieutenant General, and the War Department, . . . was assumed to exhibit the facts of the recognition on the part of the United States of the call for militia and of an engagement to pay the necessary expenses incurred therefor."[46]

That situation had changed by mid-June, when a Cheyenne attack on white settlements along the Pawnee River in Kansas convinced Sherman to cancel his plan to have General Augur advance against the Sioux, the maneuver that Lewis had feared would drive the Sioux into the Gallatin Valley. At the same time Sherman faced increasing requests for protection, not only from Montana but also from Minnesota, Dakota, Kansas, New Mexico, and Colorado. With the army stretched thin and inflamed citizens across the West calling for support, Sherman, Grant, and Stanton issued a formal policy on June 21—well after the Montana Militia had already been formed—explaining when and how such militias could be formed.[47] The policy set rates of pay, but it also declared that payment depended on congressional appropriations: "it must be clearly understood," the circular stated, "that it will require an appropriation by Congress to make the actual payment of everything, except rations, forage, and supplies." That was the bad news. There was no good news, other than the hope "but that Congress will so appropriate, there is little doubt, provided the necessity for the call be manifest, as evidenced by the judgment of the department commander, ratified by myself and the General-in-Chief."[48]

Meanwhile Sherman began an *ex post facto* implementation of the policy that required an immediate about-face on his part. On June 8 he telegraphed Grant: "Major Lewis who was sent to Montana reports 'that all the excitement here was founded on the murder of Boseman' [*sic*] I will not therefore accept any volunteers."[49] At best Sherman was displaying a convenient memory. At worst he was showing a blatant disregard for his previous authorizations to Meagher, Hosmer, and Castner and to his own officer, Lewis, as well as a disregard for Lewis's previous report that the territory needed troops. Although a change for Sherman, the new policy conformed to General Grant's more consistent view on funding the militia; but it was not what Sherman had communicated to Meagher, Lewis, and the citizens of Montana during the interim period.

In writing this mendacious telegram to Grant, Sherman was apparently under the misconception that Meagher wanted troops for his own personal gain. As Sherman said of the Indians, "They take no prisoners and always scalp the dead. It is this that enrages the People in . . . Montana

& else where [*sic*]. . . . They are clamorous for extermination which is easier said than done. . . . Like Meagher in Montana, and Hunt in Colorado they must use events of this kind as means to secure local popularity."[50]

Meagher would have laughed if he had known of Sherman's assessment of his motives, for by 1867 he wanted nothing more than to be relieved of his government post. With the people he confided in most freely, Meagher was unequivocal in his desire to leave government service. In a letter to Barlow written on June 15, 1867, he explained his predicament: "Governor Smith has not as yet relieved me. He is on the river, however, and expected at Fort Benton in another week or so. On his arrival, I shall be free—and right glad it will make me to be so, for I am downright sick of serving the Government in a civil capacity." Nor did Meagher any longer have political aspirations to be a territorial delegate or a senator. As he told Barlow: "I have been urged by many of the party to accept the nomination, but have obstinately declined. Not being rich enough, as yet, to support the grand responsibilities of the position." Physically ill and financially troubled, Meagher wanted only to move on—he was not completely sure where—in search of a better turn of luck.[51]

In the meantime, however, Sherman's latest advice was being heeded in Washington. On June 27, 1867, around noon, Grant telegraphed Sherman: "I do not think it advisable to call any Volunteers into service except such assistance becomes necessary for preservation of existing settlements and lines of travel." Sherman responded: "Despatch of today is rec'd Your conclusion is exactly right and I have called for no Volunteers at all." Thus Sherman had come full circle. Only six weeks earlier he had encouraged volunteers by promising that either the army paymaster would pay them or, at minimum, they would be able to apply to Congress for payment. Now Grant and Sherman were denying that they had ever given any authorization for a militia.[52]

By the time Grant and Sherman exchanged these words, of course, supplies had been purchased and the Montana volunteers were already in the field—and Sherman knew it. Nevertheless, he categorically denied that he had ever authorized troops and blamed the entire fiasco on Meagher, clearly stating that when Meagher assembled the Montana troops: "He had no authority from me, but such authority was emphatically withheld." Sherman was equally adamant that the "so-called troops were never mustered into the service of the United States, and no department of government is liable for the debts created or the vouchers issued."[53]

What Sherman failed to realize—or perhaps chose to ignore—was that many Montana citizens, entirely independently of Meagher, believed that the risk of Indian attack was great and that the United States government had agreed to come to their defense. One such citizen was Davis Willson of the Gallatin Valley, who had just welcomed back home his brother, Lester, a Civil War brevet brigadier general. Lester Willson had ridden up to Virginia City in the same stagecoach with Wilbur Sanders and Major Lewis. He had heard much from Lewis during the trip, which he then reported to Davis. As Davis wrote in a letter to relatives back east, Lester had told him that "the United States government was now interested in the Indian troubles in Montana and would do something about it."[54]

Interestingly, in the same letter Davis Willson also reported rumors that some members of the army doubted the severity of the problem. "We did not know how our Indian troubles were regarded by those in authority—but find that many are in doubt about it and are inclined to think it was got up for the purpose of making money." But Lester's recent encounter with Lewis reassured him. "We are made to feel easy about this however from the fact that Gen. Sherman has taken interest enough in us to send us a man to inquire into the actual state of things, and are assured now that we will get the required support." Based on this intelligence, Willson decided to remain in the Gallatin Valley instead of moving back east.[55]

Another Montana citizen who feared an all-out Indian attack was the venerable Granville Stuart, one of the territory's earliest pioneers. "The news of recent murders together with the report from a Bannack chief that the Bloods, Blackfeet, and Piegans had sent their squaws and children across the British line and were prepared to attack the Gallatin valley created the wildest excitement," according to Stuart. As Sherman had suspected, however, the excitement had little basis, and the war turned out to be both bloodless and a bit of a fiasco. Meagher's troops spent their time riding through the passes and valleys of the territory.

Desertion from the militia was common, and discipline was lacking. At one point, a soldier reportedly pointed a gun to Meagher's head when he tried to lecture the troops on discipline.[56]

Meagher, however, felt that the militia had achieved its aim and that their patrols had deterred Indians from making an attack. He wrote his father on June 15, reporting on his long patrols: "I have, however, for the last six weeks been constantly on horseback, and taking long rides on horseback to distant points of our Territory—it having become necessary to adopt precautions and defensive measures against the Indians on the line of our Eastern settlements." The Indians, he wrote, "have for some months displayed a very hostile spirit, and serious apprehensions were entertained early in April, that Montana would be threatened by them in formidable force. But I am satisfied that having acted promptly, . . . no mischief will accrue to the Territory from the spirit that animates the savages on our borders."[57] His friend Father Kuppens agreed. The Jesuit missionary had asked Meagher to order his troops not to fire the first shot, and he believed that the general had in fact issued such orders. According to Kuppens, Meagher had maintained the peace without resorting to violence by riding up and down Montana's valleys as a deterrent.[58]

Governor Green Clay Smith also continued to insist that the call-up had been necessary, as did the majority of the members of the Montana legislature, who wrote in a memorial on December 11, 1867, that "so imminent was the danger that many of the residents of Gallatin county, the most prosperous agricultural region of the Territory, were compelled to abandon their farms and flee for protection to the cities in the interior." Of course, the memorial was to Congress, asking for payment of the debts incurred in raising the Montana volunteers, so it could hardly be considered a disinterested statement.[59]

The more widely accepted view of the campaign, after the fact at any rate, was that the venture had been "Got up for A speculation," as William J. Snavely of Helena later put it in a letter to Grant. According to Snavely, some of the new arrivals to the territory wound up broke and jobless, so the merchants decided to "Get up an Indian Excitement and Let the Goverment [sic] pay the Bill." They prevailed on Governor Meagher to issue a proclamation to raise volunteers, and then General Sherman gave him an order to raise five hundred volunteers to protect the citizens of the Gallatin Valley. Snavely said that there was no apprehension about Indian attack and the whole thing was "a speculation . . . to swindel the Goverment [sic]" by "Pap Prices Armey [sic]," by which he meant ex-Confederate Missourians who had served under Confederate general Sterling Price. By Snavely's account, troops were sold very poor uniforms at high prices. After spending some time hanging around the Yellowstone River, over a hundred of the troops took their horses, guns, and whatever else they needed and headed for parts unknown. According to Snavely, the rest returned to Helena and Virginia City and sold their vouchers for fifteen to twenty-five cents on the dollar.[60]

Augustus Chapman also blamed Meagher for an unnecessary war. "Acting Governor Meagher's Indian war in Montana is the biggest humbug of the age, got up to advance his political interest, and to enable a lot of bummers who surround and hang on to him to make a big raid on the United States treasury," Chapman reported on July 5, 1867, after he had left the territory.[61] He was hardly a disinterested party, however; Meagher had removed the former Flathead Indian agent from his post because he suspected him of stealing from his charges. As one source indicates: "Chapman made numerous appeals to the Indian office for money for the Indians and apparently during the entire period was stealing from the agency." In fact Chapman's enmity was so strong that one of the many rumors surrounding Meagher's death named Chapman as a possible murderer.[62]

Henry Blake, editor of the *Montana Post*, retrospectively also came to believe that corruption surrounded the affair, though he continued to maintain that the original threat had been real—and well he should have. Stories in the *Post* had been instrumental in creating a climate of fear, and he had readily accepted a commission in the militia from Meagher. Nevertheless, by October 1867 Blake had come to believe that profiteering was rampant and wrote U.S. senator Henry Wilson of his home state of Massachusetts to tell him so. "An attempt will be made by certain parties to procure the passage of a bill by Congress appropriating money to defray the expenses of an irregular organization termed the Montana militia, which was created by General Meagher and destroyed by Genl. Terry," Blake wrote. He continued:

> I respectfully protest against the passage of any bill relating to the subject until a thorough investigation has been made by an upright

commission duly authorized by Congress to scrutinize every item of alleged expenditure. . . . If a Commission is appointed by Congress I earnestly trust that Gov. G. Clay Smith and most of our Territorial officials will not be named. I have the best of reasons for saying that Smith and others are implicated in the rascality connected with the movement, and will profit enormously, if the vouchers are paid by the National Government.[63]

Significantly, given the censure later directed at Meagher, Blake's letter questions the integrity not of Meagher but of Green Clay Smith. By implicating Smith, Blake obliquely excused Meagher from much of the wrongdoing. In fact Blake still supported Meagher's initial decision to call for at least a few troops: "A small force was required near the confluence of Twenty-five Yard Creek and the Yellowstone River to prevent bands of thieving Indians from molesting the residents of Gallatin County." But he particularly questioned the number of officers mustered into the force, however, as he explained: "About 400 soldiers were recruited for this purpose and nearly 100 officers, embracing many Colonels, were commissioned to take charge of them. . . . A large number of so-called Colonels have drawn the rations allowed to those of corresponding rank in the regular army and also claim the same pay, while the size of the command never justified the appointment of one officer of this rank."[64]

Much of the troop buildup that Blake criticized came under Smith's watch, not Meagher's. In the painstaking government investigation that followed, which included a trip to Montana, Inspector General James A. Hardie determined that "there were not more than eighty men at the end of April. During May there were probably 150, and from that time until the middle of July the number probably was about 250." According to Hardie, "About the middle of July Governor Green Clay Smith arrived at the capital, and thereupon reorganized the troops, giving them a regimental organization. At the end of July the numbers reported present and absent were 32 officers and 481 men; aggregate, 513." At the end of July, Hardie said, Smith "issued a proclamation . . . calling for the service of 800 men for six months from the 1st of August, and inviting the old force to reenlist."[65]

After listening to testimony from Major Lewis in 1870, the Senate Committee on Territories ultimately concluded that the entire war was unnecessary. According to Lewis, the only white death that could be attributed to Indians was that of John Bozeman in the spring of 1867, and the committee speculated that Bozeman had provoked the attack. Nevertheless, claims for payment kept coming in. By February 4, 1871, more than three and a half years after Meagher's death, a total of $980,313.11 had been claimed by suppliers and militia for the expenses of the war; but secretary of war William W. Belknap recommended that Congress pay only $513,343 of the amount, based on Hardie's report. The following year Belknap submitted additional papers to the House of Representatives, most of them containing claims for payment from Montana citizens during the summer and fall of 1867 in the form of "vouchers" showing approval by Governor Green Clay Smith as "Governor and Commander in Chief." The vouchers, describing the services rendered and/or the goods purchased, were from the "Headquarters Territorial Volunteers." But they definitely indicated payment by the federal government in their headings: "The United States to [named payee]." Congress took until March 1873 to approve payment of $513,343 with a joint resolution of the House and Senate.[66]

The 1872 congressional hearings were disastrous for Meagher's reputation. The "constituted authorities," wrote the committee in its report, should have investigated the situation more thoroughly. "Instead of performing this obvious duty, they seem, in the language of General Sherman, to have been 'stampeded'—frightened out of their propriety—when, by a moment of self-possessed and calm inquiry that could have harmed no one, the panic would have been quieted and the occasion for troops would have vanished from their imagination."[67] The report suited Sherman, for he had always been ready to blame Meagher for the situation. Upon Meagher's death in July 1867, Sherman stated that because "Meagher is no longer there, and Governor Smith has reached his Post, I feel satisfied matters in that remote territory will be less threatening."[68]

Sherman's satisfaction was unjustified. Although it was convenient to blame Meagher for the expensive and unnecessary war, he was only one of many who had participated in raising the alarm. Smith clearly took part in raising troops and authorizing the purchase of supplies to a much greater extent than did Meagher. If *Montana Post* editor Henry Blake is to be believed, it was Smith who actually profited from the war. Meagher, who died in poverty, did not. He may have been "stampeded," but he did not benefit personally from the undertaking.

To be sure, Indian relations were not Meagher's strong suit. He had come to Montana focused on the positive future that he saw in the new territory for the Irish and for himself and was completely unprepared for the problems that already existed. He had no perspective on how to balance the competing interests of the white settlers and their almost paranoid fear against humane and proper treatment of the Indians whose lands were being taken from them. Nor did he have good guidance. Upson, from whom Meagher first learned about Indian relations, had seen only annihilation as the future of the Indians and had left the territory and died shortly after Meagher met him. For his part, Flathead Indian agent Augustus Chapman, before his removal by Meagher, had refused to report to him and instead issued all of his communications directly to the commissioner of Indian affairs.

George B. Wright, who replaced Gad Upson as Blackfeet agent, was no help either. Wright suffered from a lack of judgment and a quarrelsome disposition; even before he arrived at his post he had antagonized three out of four members of the Indian Peace Commission, a group appointed to negotiate treaties with a series of Indian tribes. The three men signed a "report to protest" Wright's appointment to the post of Blackfeet agent.[69] Wright deplored the traders who plied the Indians with liquor, and he proposed removing the Blackfeet agency to a remote location far from the dram shops and the docked steamboats at Fort Benton.[70] It was an idea to consider, but his perspective was so far removed from Meagher's and his manner so difficult that he had no influence on Meagher whatsoever. In fact the two developed such an antipathy that Wilbur Fisk Sanders suspected, although without any evidence, that Wright had something to do with Meagher's untimely death.

A final potential source of advice was the Jesuits. Father De Smet and his priests had been in the area since 1841, bringing Catholicism to the Flatheads. Later they had established St. Peter's Mission in Blackfeet territory but had always lived there with considerable apprehension. Meagher had learned from Father Kuppens during his stopover on his way to the Fort Benton treaty negotiations that two Piegans had attacked and severely wounded Kuppens the previous year. Yet, despite withdrawing from Blackfeet territory, the Jesuits continued in their efforts to save the tribe in the only manner they knew.[71] In the end Meagher subscribed to their philosophy. In fact there was no easy solution. If Meagher mishandled the situation, so would his successors, and conflict between whites and Indians would haunt Montana for years to come.

CHAPTER ELEVEN

"Would That He Had Died on the Battlefield"

And is the patriot Meagher dead?
Who, in his youthful glory, rose, a champion of his race.

Poem published in the *Irish American*

On July 1, 1867, Thomas Francis Meagher came to the top of the bluffs overlooking Fort Benton. A military entourage of about a dozen members of the Montana militia accompanied him. All of the men were weary from the long horseback ride from Sun River, where they had last encamped—but none more so than Meagher. Now in his forty-fourth year, he still had the bearing of a Civil War brigadier general; but years of drinking and the rigors of his chaotic life had taken their toll. In addition, he was suffering from dysentery and had been for the last few days.

Below Meagher was the Missouri River, swollen to the top of its banks by spring rains and melting snow from the mountains. Beside it was Fort Benton, the Missouri's head of navigation. Several steamboats lay anchored and tethered to the bank along the waterfront, across from the frontier town's few business blocks. Meagher intended to proceed by steamboat with his troops downriver to pick up a cache of 130 rifles at Camp Cooke, 120 miles below Fort Benton. Begrudgingly sent upstream by the commander of the U.S. Army in the West, Major General William Tecumseh Sherman, the rifles were needed in Helena to arm members of the Montana militia, and Meagher's last official duty was to deliver them.

As Meagher looked out over Fort Benton, he knew that this would be his last act as the outgoing secretary of Montana Territory. His term as acting governor had ended when he met Governor Green Clay Smith, just back from Washington, on the trail to Helena a few days before. Meagher's replacement as territorial secretary, James Tufts, was also on his way upriver.[1] After Meagher delivered the rifles and ammunition to Helena, no other government employment was in the offing.

Meagher had begun making plans, but he had no definite prospects. One option was to return to the lecture circuit. Another option, even less well formed, was to remain in the Rocky Mountains, which he had grown to love, and enter into an enterprise that somehow involved the Jesuits in the western part of the territory. "I shall . . . take to certain explorations, with the assistance of the Good Fathers from which some material advantage will probably eventuate," Meagher had written his father.[2] A third stopgap plan involved traveling across the territory with artist Peter Tofft and writing a series of articles for *Harper's Magazine*. Meagher had already submitted one article, which he had finished by campfire during the recent military campaign, and had promised the magazine several more.

None of the plans amounted to much, given Meagher's prominence and early potential. Drink, recklessness, and politics had seemingly brought him to a dead end. Yet it was not the first time that he seemed to have reached the end of the road, and every time before he had gotten back on his feet. This time, however, he would not have that opportunity. By late evening he would be dead—drowned in the Missouri River after falling from a docked steamboat. The actual cause of Meagher's death has been one of the mysteries of his life. Speculation has abounded, with some suspecting suicide and still others positing that he was murdered. Although no one will ever know with certainty, the most probable explanation is the least glamorous: Meagher probably fell overboard—the victim of a broken handrail and too much alcohol.

Those who theorize that Meagher committed suicide note that he was not well the day he arrived in Fort Benton. He was terribly sick with diarrhea, which may only have been symptomatic of a more serious disease or internal bleeding.[3] Reports from several sources also suggest that

Steamboat at Fort Benton. This 1867 photograph, taken from across the Missouri River, shows Fort Benton and two rear-wheel steamboats similar to the *G. A. Thompson,* from which Meagher fell on the night of July 1, 1867. (Courtesy Schwinden Library and Archives/Over-holser Historical Research Center)

he was delusional, which may have been attributable to his physical ailments and maybe even to the opium pills that he is known to have been taking for illness not too long before. Equally significant, he needed money. Out of work and in debt, he did not even have enough funds to subsist, much less to live in a manner that befitted his dignity. When Meagher had tried to pay his doctor, John W. Reins of Helena, with a bank draft, the doctor reported that it "had to be protested for non payment [*sic*]." According to Reins, "the General was here, just prior to his going to Benton—he called at my Office and promised to pay it the next day—but failed to call [back]."[4]

"I am utterly—utterly—out of funds and it is absolutely necessary, I should have same," Meagher wrote to territorial auditor John Ming after he had ridden down from the bluffs and reached the streets of Fort Benton. Several months before, as the gravity of his financial situation bore down upon him, Meagher had thrown aside the principles that had led him to decline the additional pay approved by the Bannack legislature for the territorial governor and secretary and had brought a formal action before Judge Hosmer to require Ming to pay him the back amounts. Hosmer had ruled for Meagher in the amount of $3,687.52, and Meagher knew that he had to obtain the money to continue to support himself and pay off his debts. He now implored Ming "as a personal favor which shall be most gratefully remembered that you will send me the amount due (in whatever amount of greenbacks you can obtain for it) and direct the enclosure to this great seaport (Irish that) for me, to the care of I. G. Baker Esq."[5] The money due sounded like a considerable sum, but it would be paid in territorial funds, which would give him only a minor portion of the amount in U.S. currency at the going rates—and his debts exceeded the amount in any event. Meagher did not know that Ming had already signed the territorial warrants for at least some of the amount due him on June 27. On July 5 Ming had the sad duty of forwarding Meagher's last letter to his widow, Elizabeth.[6]

As it turned out—when Meagher's estate was probated after his death—the Meaghers owned only a few things other than their personal effects. They had two horses with a value of about $40 each, various household goods including furniture, and three small heating stoves and a stove pipe valued at around $90. Meagher's estate also had the territorial warrants for his back pay as governor with a face value of $2,200, but their value in U.S. currency was only about a quarter of that. In total, they had only a little over $1,200 in assets.[7] Against this was a long list of debts; for more than three years claims continued to come in against the estate, even though the administrator had totaled $3,190.18 in claims by February 23, 1868, and announced that "the Estate is largely in debt and that but a small Dividend can be expected by the creditors thereof."[8] When the estate administrator attempted to procure from the Interior department an allowance for Meagher's services as superintendent of Indian affairs, the answer came back that the decedent was considered "a defaulter to the Government on account of his administration of the affairs of the Indian Dept. in Montana Territory and therefore no settlement could be had until such discrepancy in decedents accounts could be arranged."[9]

Thomas Francis Meagher had existed in Montana partly on the credit and goodwill of merchants around the territory, and he was in debt for things such as meals, lodging, wine, champagne, cigars, candles, sugar, blankets, a shirt, two blank books, a bottle of catsup, candles, sugar, a $100 draft, two weeks and three days' board for his servant, meat from a butcher shop, a $50 currency loan, kitchen hardware, pants, gloves, ropes, a cash advance, and a meerschaum pipe. Meagher had also sought to improve the small house in which he and Elizabeth resided, and there was a record of purchases for lumber and building materials including shingles, locks, hinges, sash, plastering, and carpentry as well as a personal debt for office rent. He owed attorney James Spratt $500 for serving as his attorney in the mandamus action against treasurer Ming. Much of the debt had been run up before Elizabeth Meagher joined him in Montana in June 1866.[10]

The Meaghers did not even own the house they lived in on Idaho Street. They did have a contract to purchase the dwelling from Word and Spratt, attorneys, but $650 was still owed before the property could be deeded to them. The probate court determined that the property was exempt from creditors' claims as the homestead of Elizabeth Meagher; the amount owed to Word and Spratt was ordered to be paid out of the estate, further reducing the amount available to the other creditors. When the house was finally paid off, Elizabeth received a deed to the "property formerly occupied by George Williams as a Butcher Shop and dwelling house and lately occupied by Thomas Francis Meagher."[11] In turn she deeded the property to Dr. L. Daems, a Virginia City physician. Daems had filed a claim against Meagher's estate for $554 for money "loaned for family use," which was disallowed; but Elizabeth ended up deeding him the property in 1868 for $500, presumably to satisfy the debt.[12]

Some speculate that Meagher's desperate financial condition—especially when combined with his ill health—drove him into such despair that he decided to end his life. The only real evidence supporting this theory comes from the barber of the *G. A. Thompson,* the steamboat on which Meagher was last seen in Fort Benton. After learning that Meagher had drowned, Wilbur Fisk Sanders interviewed the barber, who said that he had seen "a man [who] had let himself down from the upper to the lower deck and jumped into the river and gone on down stream."[13] Weighing against this theory is the fact that Meagher was a staunch Catholic. As Father L. B. Palladino, a Montana Jesuit, said later when writing about the matter, "The idea that General Meagher might have taken his own life by deliberately throwing himself into the river, is inconceivable. He was a man of deep faith, he had a firm belief in God and a hereafter, and such men do not commit suicide." But even Palladino had to admit the possibility when he qualified "except they be temporarily unbalanced."[14]

According to Lieutenant James H. Bradley of the 7th Infantry, who was later in Fort Benton, Meagher's death could not have been a suicide, because "[h]is despairing cries for the help that could not be offered, while he was struggling in the water precludes such an assumption for Gen. Meagher was not a man to have been freightened [sic] into such demonstrations had he personally courted a waters grave. His stateroom opened upon a narrow strip of deck without guards quite favorable for an accidental [sic] fall had he passed out in a fit of sleep walking, or in the state of unsteadiness induced by the evenings dissipation."[15]

When considering Meagher's death, even more people suspected foul play than suspected suicide. The busy port of Fort Benton was filled with the passions and resentments of frontier society, some involving Meagher. Apart from the deeply felt political antagonism between Democrats and Republicans, he was also in the center of several other disputes: the personal and political animosity of Indian agents Augustus Chapman and George Wright; vigilante hostility for the Daniels "pardon"; and the enmity between the Irish and the British.[16]

The recent shooting death of British army captain Wilfred Dakin Speer aboard the steamboat *Octavia* intensified the climate of fear and suspicion—particularly with regard to the Irish/English conflict. By July 1 the *Octavia* had already left on its return downriver; but when it had arrived at Fort Benton on June 20, it had brought news of the gruesome details of Speer's death. On a dark night, while the *Octavia* was still in the Dakota Territory, U.S. Army infantryman, Irishman, and Fenian William Barry had shot Speer point blank in the head. Reportedly an "English nobleman," Speer was coming to Montana on unknown business with over $25,000 in U.S. bank accounts, allegedly for the sole purpose of defraying his travel expenses.[17]

Although Speer family records indicate that he was a dedicated adventurer coming to Montana for his own purposes and enjoyment, western Fenians might have suspected him of being a British agent.[18] Speer had boarded the *Octavia* in Omaha, along with a number of Union troops under the command of Lieutenant Horrigan. The *Octavia*'s captain, Joseph LaBarge, later recalled that Speer had seemed to make a special point of traveling on the *Octavia,* even though numerous steamboats were scheduled to go upriver, many not loaded to capacity and not requiring reservations. LaBarge also later wrote of his other passengers: "The troops were mostly Irish Fenians, and the Lieutenant in charge was an Irishman, all intensely hostile to the English. This fact may in part explain what subsequently transpired." According to LaBarge, "Speer himself felt doubts for his safety, and one day remarked to me that he would be lucky if he got out of this scrape without accident."[19] Certainly animosity toward the British was running high among the Irish immigrant soldiers on the western frontier; Lieutenant Martin Hogan of the 13th Infantry, for example, dramatically wrote his uncle, Andrew O'Connell, Montana Territory's Fenian "head centre," in January 1867: "Oh England, a day of bloody retribution is near at hand."[20]

After Speer's death, LaBarge formed a group of passengers to conduct an inquest, including Green Clay Smith, the territory's returning governor, and Samuel McLean, the territory's returning congressional delegate. The inquest determined that Speer was murdered. Barry was arrested but immediately released by his commanding officer, Lieutenant Horrigan. It took three years to bring Barry to trial in Vermillion, Dakota Territory, where, to much surprise, he was acquitted on the basis of his claim that he was only obeying orders to shoot unauthorized boarders. Nevertheless, Speer's death at the hands of a U.S. soldier, particularly one who was Irish, attracted the attention of the British government, which sent another British officer to St. Louis to investigate the case.[21]

Speer's killing was also no small matter in Fort Benton. After the *Octavia* tied up on June 20, the town was buzzing with rumor, suspicion, and accusations. In one instance a "drunken Irishman . . . accused [a] passenger of the Octavia of robbing him." In the confusion about whether a robbery had actually occurred, Governor Green Clay Smith, who had helped conduct the inquest on board and who was known more for his diplomacy than for his belligerence, "grabbed up a sort of fence stake and struck the drunken Irishman over the head, knocked him down, and would have beat his brains out, but the governor's friends got his stick away from him."[22] Speer's murder incited Fenian passions and anti-Irish feelings alike, and these lingering feelings may have worried Meagher. According to several reports, he sought to arm himself with revolvers after overhearing men say, "There he goes," on the streets of Fort Benton.[23]

Other suspects in Meagher's death include both of Montana's Indian agents, Augustus Chapman and George Wright. Both were men of dubious character. Flathead Indian agent Augustus Chapman was married to Abraham Lincoln's stepsister, Harriet Hanks. He so lacked integrity that other family members charged him with simply pocketing money that Lincoln sent to care for his beloved stepmother, Sarah Bush Johnston Lincoln, leaving the old woman impoverished. After Lincoln's assassination, Chapman played on his family connections to pressure President Andrew Johnson into offering him a government position. In September 1865 Johnson appointed him Flathead Indian agent. Chapman set out for the Montana Territory, where, by many accounts, he proceeded to rob both the tribes and the government shamelessly.[24]

According to one account, "Rumors of his thievery became so loud that Acting Governor Meagher dispatched the U.S. Marshal, John X. Beidler, to investigate the charges." Beidler, accompanied by Meagher's former personal secretary and Helena lawyer Arthur Barret, arrived at the Flathead Indian Agency with papers to suspend and arrest Chapman for theft. The men ordered Chapman to Missoula, where he was held for seven or eight days. Finally, however, they released him after Barret determined that Meagher, in his capacity as Indian superintendent, had no authority to arrest an agent. Meagher's only recourse was to suspend Chapman from his duties, which he did.[25]

Beidler and Barret stayed in Missoula to take testimony from witnesses, all of whom were alleged by the *Montana Post* to be personal enemies of Chapman. Hostile to Meagher as usual, the *Post* concluded that the case against Chapman was based on pure malice and that he could set the matter straight when he reported to the Indian commissioner.[26] Less sure of Chapman's honesty, others believed he had been caught red handed and claimed that he left the Flathead reservation in deplorable financial and physical condition.[27]

So great was Chapman's animosity toward Meagher that his letter to the commissioner did not offer any defense against the allegations of theft. Instead, Chapman focused exclusively on Meagher and blamed the acting governor for all the Indian troubles in the territory. When the letter was written on July 5, 1867, ostensibly from Charleston, Illinois, Chapman stated that he had "just arrived home from the Flathead agency" that day, after traveling downriver on the *Yorktown*. Some have suspected that Chapman was actually in Fort Benton at the time of Meagher's death and that he had a hand in it.[28] But he could only have been there if he had sent his letter on down the Missouri to be mailed from Charleston or some other place.

As unlikely as that was, Thompson Hart Doughly claimed that Chapman was in Fort Benton on July 1. Doughly also claimed to have been with Meagher constantly in the last days of his life. In a letter written almost fifty years later to the son of Fenian military commander Thomas Sweeny, Doughly described with some accuracy Meagher's trouble with Augustus Chapman and the enmity "between the Flat Head Indians and their Agent." "While walking about on the streets of Fort Benton" on July 1, Doughly said, he "was told that the Indian Agent whom Gov. Meagher had discharged was in Fort Benton and was drinking and making threats of doing Gov. Meagher bodily harm, and also had been skulking about the Boat landing." He reported the threat to Meagher, who "treated it lightly and took no extra precautions for his own protection."[29]

Also quite hostile to Meagher, but for completely different reasons, was the Blackfeet Indian agent, George Wright. A man of strong principles and a quarrelsome disposition, Wright was particularly appalled by the effects of liquor on the tribes. In December 1866 he wrote Governor Green Clay Smith, suggesting that the Blackfeet agency be moved far away from Fort Benton, where Indians could easily, if illegally, purchase liquor.[30] In Smith's absence, the letter went to Meagher, who forwarded it to the Interior Department without comment. Receiving no response to his suggestion, Wright became frustrated and took it out on Meagher. On April 14, 1867, he demanded an immediate answer to his concern. According to Wright, three new "dram shops" were under construction in Fort Benton, to be completed for the spring and summer steamboating season, and these establishments would be in contravention of the law if Fort Benton was still on an Indian reservation. Wilbur Fisk Sanders, who wrote an account of the day Meagher died, said that the situation escalated. Trouble was brewing for Meagher in Fort Benton, due to a "contention between the Blackfeet Indian agent, George Wright, and the general as superintendent of Indian affairs, wherein the general directed the release of all the intoxicating liquors in the country which the agent had assumed to seize."[31]

The other perennial suspects in Meagher's death are the vigilantes, who had earlier threatened to kill him if he did not leave the territory. Building on this story was a dubious confession that coincided with none of the known events. In 1913 a man going by the name Frank "Diamond," or "Dimond," who claimed to have been an active member of the vigilantes, said the vigilantes had hired him for the sum of $8,000 to kill Meagher near Cow Island in the Missouri and hide the body in the river. David McMillan Billingsly, also known as Dave Mack, corroborated Diamond's story. Mack claimed that the vigilantes were angered by Meagher's pardon of Daniels about a year and a half before and that a committee of ten had followed him from Virginia City to Fort Benton, where they took him off the boat, murdered him, and buried the body. Frank Diamond was drunk when he bragged about murdering Meagher; when he sobered up and found himself possibly facing criminal charges, he quickly recanted and said he had never killed anybody.[32]

What is, in fact, known about Meagher's last day? Many of the details come from the account by Wilbur Fisk Sanders, who said he spent much of that day with Meagher, even though the two were political adversaries. Sanders and his family had gone east together toward the end of February, so that he could lobby Congress to invalidate Meagher's "bogus" legislature; Sanders had returned to Montana ahead of his wife, Harriet, and their young children and had come to Fort Benton to meet their steamboat. When Meagher descended the bluffs and arrived on the streets of Fort Benton, Sanders "greeted" him "and his military staff[,] . . . who had made a swift and dusty ride from Sun river." The two unlikely companions then spent the middle of the day "in social visits through the business portions of the town." Contrary to his usual habits, Sanders reported, Meagher refused all offers of liquor. Instead "he resolutely and undeviatingly declined that form of hospitality with which Fort Benton then abounded."[33]

The time spent with Sanders, who had succeeded in having the legislature declared invalid, could not have been pleasant for Meagher. He had denounced Sanders as "an unrelenting and unscrupulous extremist" and "the most vicious of my enemies."[34] But Meagher was no longer a territorial official, so the two were able to maintain a civil, if not friendly, companionship. Among their stops was a visit to I. G. Baker's store, where Baker offered Meagher a seat in a back room so he could quietly read the paper.[35] At another point in the day Meagher was invited by Major T. H. Eastman of the American Fur Company to "dine with him at 6:00 o'clock, which invitation the General accepted," according to Sanders. But Meagher did not attend.[36]

Tied up along the bank of the Missouri that day were "[s]ix or seven steamboats from St. Louis, or beyond," according to Sanders, and "among them was a somewhat cheap and rude old craft named the *G. A. Thompson,*" which had arrived on June 29. "It was a freight boat, but had cabins for perhaps a dozen persons," he said. In keeping with the usual design of steamboats of that era, on the upper deck was "the Main Cabin in the center and on the sides of which were located the state rooms. Each stateroom had two doors, one leading into the Main Cabin and the other opening onto the deck." Around the outer deck was "a light railing about 4 feet high running along the outer edge so as to prevent anyone walking along the deck from falling overboard." However, the *Thompson* had collided with the *Waverly* downriver on June 8, "smashing [its] cookhouse into small pieces," and apparently damaging its railing, according to a passenger.[37]

The *G. A. Thompson*'s pilot was Johnny Doran. The Sanders version of the day's events said that he introduced Doran to Meagher at I. G. Baker's store. Doran (later referred to by Sanders as "Dolan") asked Sanders if this was indeed "the famous Thomas Francis Meagher."[38] In fact Doran needed no introduction, for he had piloted the boat that brought Elizabeth Meagher to Montana. Meagher had greatly appreciated Doran's efforts to assure her comfort during the trip. Doran believed that "General Meagher attached undue importance to this, and ever after, though it would be presumption for me to say that we were friends, yet I had much reason to believe that he ever entertained the kindliest feeling towards me."[39]

Doran's version of the events of the day does not even mention Sanders. According to Doran, at the time Sanders later claimed to have introduced him to Meagher, he had already spoken with him. "I went to the provision store of J. G. Baker [*sic*], and in a back room of the establishment I discovered General Meagher reading a paper. Looking up and immediately recognizing me, he greeted me most warmly, and both seating ourselves, we engaged in a long conversation."[40]

Meagher and Doran discussed many topics, including Meagher's health, which was not good. He told Doran that "on his road into Benton he was very sick, at Sun River, for six days." Despite his illness Meagher expressed his determination to complete his mission to pick up the cache of rifles from Camp Cooke. The two men drifted onto the topic of Elizabeth Meagher, and Doran reported that Meagher "also spoke in the most tender and affectionate terms of his wife, residing at Helena, saying that in their mountain home they were 'as happy as two thrushes in a bush.'" Finally, "learning that he was stopping at no particular place," Doran "invited him down to the boat to dine." Nothing was said about any dinner plans that Meagher had with Major Eastman, which Sanders said he had arranged.[41]

According to Doran's version of the events, Meagher and Doran "walked through the town" after dining on the *Thompson* and were greeted by numerous friends. Some invited them "to partake of the hospitalities always urgently extended to strangers in this section of the country," but Meagher was resolute in his refusal to drink. Doran confirmed that "on each instance the General politely but firmly refused to accede to their request." Meagher's reason was that "his experience at Sun River had given him a distaste for such amusement."[42]

Although he remained sober, Meagher began exhibiting what appeared to be symptoms of delusion and paranoia, according to Sanders. He noticed Meagher's strange behavior when he ran into him sitting with a group of men in the late afternoon in front of the I. G. Baker & Co. store "about dusk." Sanders said that he suddenly heard

abnormally loud conversation, and as the party came nearer I saw that it came from General Meagher. As the party came to the place where I was, . . . it was apparent that he was deranged. He was loudly demanding a revolver to defend himself against the citizens of Fort Benton who, in his disturbed mental condition, he declared were hostile to him, and several who had then joined us sought to allay his fears and by all the means in our power to restore to sanity his disturbed mental condition.

As Sanders related, he and Doran, who was still with Meagher, discussed Meagher's condition, and Sanders suggested that Meagher be taken to his stateroom on the *Thompson*.[43]

According to Sanders, "three or four of us accompanied him," but Meagher "was still insistent that the people at Fort Benton were hostile to him and was importunate for a revolver." He finally calmed down enough to agree that he should retire to his berth, which Sanders said was "on the starboard side of the boat next to the bank." Sanders said that he remained aboard the *Thompson* for a while, hoping that Meagher would sleep, but finally Sanders and the others "went on shore, seeking to allay his [Meagher's] anxiety by the promise of getting him a revolver." Meagher appeared to be making preparations to sleep, having "removed his outer garments and lain down in his berth." Sanders, who by this point seems to have felt partially responsible for him, hesitated to leave the boat. He concluded, however, that Meagher's mental state was "the result of the hot and exhausting ride of the morning, which sleep would speedily correct." Professedly confident of Meagher's "immediate recovery," Sanders and his friends left Meagher in the stateroom. Nothing was further from their thoughts, Sanders claimed later, than the "denouement then impending."[44]

Johnny Doran said that he was finally able to calm Meagher down while they were still in town; "towards evening [we had] wended our way to the boat (Thompson) to take tea." Then Doran recited an appealing and perhaps convenient story. According to him, "the sun had just begun to go down as we took our chairs out on the guards of the boat, and as the weather was very pleasant, we lit our cigars and commenced reading." Doran lent Meagher a book he had with him, *Collegians* by Gerald Griffin, and "he seemed to peruse it with great attention for about half an hour." Suddenly closing the book, Meagher "said very excitedly, 'Johnny, they threaten my life in that town!'" When he asked if Doran was armed, Doran "immediately produced two navy revolvers . . . ; and he seeing that they were loaded and capped, [Meagher] handed them back."[45]

"By this time it was pitch-dark, the hour being about half-past nine." According to Doran, Meagher became emotionally distraught: "He begged me not to leave him." After assuring Meagher that he would be gone only a few minutes, Doran said that he "fixed the clothes about him, locked the door of the state-room, and went down on the lower deck." A brief time later—maybe only a matter of minutes—Meagher plunged into the Missouri River and was never seen again. "I was with him constantly on the day of the sad occurrence, and was the last man that spoke to him on earth," Doran concluded.[46]

What Doran failed to reveal was that Meagher went to the boat's salon. Despite his earlier attempt at maintaining sobriety, he, Doran, and others engaged in a drinking bout and quickly became drunk.[47] An eyewitness to the occasion was the seventeen-year-old wife of James Wright; while checking on her husband, she saw Meagher, Doran, her husband, and James Woods, the captain of the *Thompson,* drinking together. As it turned out, the party was not confined solely to the boat; Meagher and Doran were also seen coming back to the *Thompson* after dark by John Leaman (or Lehman), a watchman on another boat.[48]

The omnipresent I. G. Baker had two different versions of the evening. The one given around the time of Meagher's death had him drinking. The other, given many years later, proclaimed Meagher sober. Meagher had known Baker for some time and owed him a small amount of money. On the day Meagher arrived in Fort Benton, they had visited. "When Meagher talked with me he was in excellent spirits but didn't seem to be in the best of health," Baker said in his later statement. He believed that Meagher had "got on a bender" in Sun River on his way to Fort Benton and was staying sober so as not to repeat the trauma of the event. "I am prepared to swear that he was stone sober," Baker said in an article published in 1901. According to that statement, Meagher left Baker's place at "about 6 or 7 o'clock" and returned to the *Thompson.*[49]

But that was not the story Baker told Lieutenant James H. Bradley. At that time he said that he saw Meagher drinking later in the evening. As recounted by Bradley, Baker told him the evening was passed "in a convivial manner," with Meagher drinking heavily and becoming intoxicated. Bradley also learned that Meagher became offended by some "meaningless remark" that angered him and that he accused some of the men present of wanting to take his life. The party finally broke up, and Meagher retired, laboring under the effects of the evening's dissipation.[50]

Indeed, it may have been the well-meaning Baker who unwittingly started Meagher on a last bender. During the afternoon Baker offered Meagher several glasses of blackberry wine, a common remedy for "summer complaint," to cure his diarrhea. According to the sentry on the *Thompson,* Meagher "went ashore on the levee and struggled to the . . . trading post, where he was accommodated with a seat . . . by the proprietor." Frequently he had "to hasten . . . to the woods" when "the violence of the disorder assailed him. The proprietor, learning his distress, urged him to take the only remedy in his power to offer, a glass of blackberry wine. This was repeated three times during his long and weakning [*sic*] agony . . . after which, toward nightfall he was conducted to the boat and retired to . . . the pilot's stateroom which was kindly given to him." For a drinker of Meagher's predilections, the three glasses could have been enough for him to lose any resolve about not drinking that evening.[51]

It was after dark when Johnny Doran finally managed to get Meagher into his cabin. A short time later, thinking Meagher was in bed and asleep, Doran left him and proceeded to the lower deck; soon he heard "a splash in the dark waters below, immediately followed by the cry of 'man overboard.'" Doran "rushed towards the water," when an engineer on the *Thompson* appeared and exclaimed: "Johnny, it's your friend." For a moment the stunned Doran considered jumping into the river in an attempt to rescue Meagher, but he decided it "would not only have been useless but almost certain death, as the river there was about twelve feet deep, and with a current rushing at the rate of nine miles an hour; and . . . it was so dark that no object could be discerned." Running downstream toward the *Guidon,* Doran heard "two agonizing cries from the man, the first one very short, the last prolonged, and of the most heart-rending description." Doran and others "rushed into the wheel of the steamer and lowered [themselves] hip-deep in the water." As they clung to the wheel looking for Meagher, "others threw out ropes and boards," but to no avail. Meagher was gone.[52]

Another person aboard the *Thompson* witnessed what Doran heard and saw. Mrs. A. B. Nichols said that between nine and ten o'clock in the evening she heard deckhands cry out that a man was overboard. One of the deckhands saw Meagher near the end of the boat, and then he was never seen again. She believed that Meagher had been put to bed in the cabin of Captain Woods, the outside door of which faced the water. Dressed only in his underclothes, Meagher went onto the deck, stumbled on a rope or other litter, and fell over the low rail. Mrs.

Nichols blamed Meagher's escort, Doran, for not locking the outside door to the cabin.[53]

At least three other people saw Meagher fall from the boat that night. John Lehman later told his story to Dennis Nolan of Butte, who wrote up the account. Sitting on the pile of freight he was guarding as a watchman on that "exceptionally bright moonlight night," Lehman observed Doran and a stranger return to the boat. "The two men walked along the star-board side to the bow and entered their state-roomes [sic]. About 10 minutes later the stranger reappeared dressed only in his underwear and walked along to the stern of the boat where he stopped and leaned over the rail as if to vomit." Lehman saw him suddenly fall overboard and sounded the alarm, but not until the next day did he learn that the man overboard was Meagher.[54]

Another man also witnessed the event. Described only as a "negro boatman," he was a sentry on the *Thompson* on duty that night. He heard a noise toward the stern and "saw somebody moving in white clothing (underclothes) toward the left rear," where the temporary toilet was. The sentry "heard a shout and then a splash," and he himself shouted "man overboard." The man who took the sentry's affidavit theorized that the crude style of the accommodations required an individual to perform "acrobatic feats" to keep his sea legs under him.[55]

A third man who saw Meagher fall was Ferd Roosevelt, who was a Wells Fargo agent at Fort Benton at the time of Meagher's death. In 1923 Roosevelt said that he saw Meagher fall overboard; he reported that there was no attacker, and no suicide, and that the acting governor had been drinking heavily.[56]

Thompson Hart Doughly slept through much of the commotion on the *G. A. Thompson* and was not awakened until about two in the morning, but he still laid claim to "hearing hurried steps outside my statesroom on the deck side and hearing men shouting 'A man overboard.'" According to his account, Doughly soon "learned that one of the watchmen had seen a mans [sic] body falling from the Cabin deck into the River and had then give[n] the alarm." Doughly "rushed to [Meagher's] Stateroom and found the door opening onto the deck was open but the General was not in the room, his clothing with the exception of his trousers were [sic] still in the room proving that he had left the room suddenly." He then noticed that the railing opposite the stateroom "for some reason or other had been removed." This, Doughly believed, was the reason Meagher fell from the deck: "The consequence of this neglect was that on a dark night anyone . . . coming on this deck from the Staterooms would not notice that the railing was missing and not appreciating the fact m[a]y walk overboard." Doughly also noted that there was "no lantern hung on the side to light this deck."[57]

By this time the entire riverfront was in frantic activity, and the commotion drew the attention of Wilbur Fisk Sanders, who was across the street from the riverbank where the *Thompson* was moored. In fact, he was in the office of George Wright, the Blackfeet Indian agent with whom Meagher had argued about the propriety of selling liquor in Fort Benton. Sanders was conscious of the time, because the letter he was writing had to be dispatched in the outgoing mail to Helena, "which left at 11 o'clock." Suddenly, he "heard Capt. James Gorman, the stage agent of C. C. Huntley, excitedly exclaim: 'General Meagher is drowned!'" Shocked by the news, Sanders dropped his pen. He could not believe what he had heard, because it had been less than an hour since he had left Meagher on the boat.

Sanders "hastened out the door and rushed across the gang plank and across the lower deck of the steamer." There he interrogated a "colored man" who was the boat's barber and was told that "a man had let himself down from the upper to the lower deck and jumped into the river and gone down stream." Sanders then "ran down the river bank, repeating the alarm until I reached one of the lower steamers, the *Guidon*, I believe, where I went across the boat to the river side to watch for the general." According to Sanders, "Boats were instantly lowered and manned, and many anxious eyes were peering in the darkness at the swift rolling waters of the great river, that never seemed so wicked as then."[58]

According to Sanders, he was horrified at what had happened. He had last seen Meagher safely aboard the *G. A. Thompson* in the hands of his fellow Irishman, Johnny Doran. Yet Sanders knew that Meagher was neither physically nor mentally well, and he felt that he had failed in his assumed responsibility to look after him. As the weight of the event bore down upon him, Sanders realized that it was now his task "to fulfill the sad duty of advising Mrs. Meagher of the overwhelming calamity which had befallen her and us all." Despite the approaching deadline for a mail dispatch—11:00 P.M. according to Sanders—he was able to send a letter that night to Dr. James Gibson, the postmaster at Virginia City. Sanders regarded him as "an accomplished gentleman and a fast friend of Mrs. Meagher."[59]

Sanders said that he left to Gibson's "discretion the manner in which he should break to her the melancholy news" but that he reported in the letter that Meagher's delusional state had caused his death. Sanders may have been implying that Meagher's drinking caused the delusions. The next day, when Sanders told Meagher's grim staff about the message he had sent, they reacted strongly and insisted that he must say that Meagher "fell from the boat accidentally and must not mention the mental aberration nor attribute it to that." Meagher's companions clearly did not want to be accused of neglecting to care for him while he was in such deplorable condition and also did not want it known that the cause of Meagher's death could have been inebriation, out of concern for Elizabeth. Pressured to change his conclusion, Sanders supplied the excuse that they all needed by explaining that the delusions he had written about could be justified, "if eager devotion to his duties in hand had brought upon him so great an affliction."[60]

When Sanders finally published his explanation of events many years later, he bolstered the story, claiming that "[t]hose who were with him on that last day of his life will join me I know in denying his death could be attributed to any convivial habit. I was with him most of the afternoon, and he was as resolutely abstemious as the most devout anchorite, and it is cruelly unjust to repeat such an accusation." His statement was cautiously worded, however, to say that his personal observations took place only in the "afternoon"; he did not say that he had seen Meagher in the evening, after he apparently had become inebriated. Even though Sanders's statement was somewhat disingenuous, he was not as deceptive as Johnny Doran, who drank heavily with Meagher in the evening and yet adamantly claimed that Meagher was sober at the time of his death. Doran's version was set down while he was in St. Louis in 1869 and was published in 1886, while the Sanders version may not have been published until 1902, which may explain their general consistency (except for the introduction of Doran to Meagher).[61]

According to Doughly, "Every possible effort was made that night and the following day to find the body, as owing to the water being at full height and the current running at [a] rate of 6 or 8 miles an hour we all know it would have been impossible even for an expert swimmer to save his life and as Gov. Meagher could not swim at all he had no chance whatsoever. Thus Gov. Meagher died."[62] Doughly would have received strong argument from a man named Foreman, who claimed that he witnessed the event. Foreman said: "The Governor was an expert swimmer, and battled with the rushing current a for a long time."[63] Whether Meagher was a swimmer or not, P. J. Condon, a Fenian and one-time president of the Irish Brigade Officers' Association who investigated Meagher's death in 1892, said that a search was commenced immediately with floating lifebuoys, boats, and lights, but the body was never found.[64]

Marie Louise Daems, the wife of Dr. Levinius Daems of Virginia City, wrote on June 13, 1899: "My brother John [Valtsin] came from Mexico to Mont. The Missouri River up in 1867. My husband and General Meagher went to meat [sic] him my Brother drowned when the Steamer Little rock landed at fort Benton the same night the General drowned my Brother had with him 3000 . . . and they never came on shore." This interesting account may not have been entirely correct, because according to a reliable source the *Little Rock* did not arrive at Fort Benton until July 14 and Valtsin had already drowned on June 5.[65]

News of Meagher's death spread quickly, and he was mourned widely, although even in death he remained controversial. Governor Green Clay Smith issued a memorial on July 3, 1867: "It is but due to the memory of our deceased friend and fellow-officer, that we should hold him in fond remembrance. He was a man of high social qualities, great urbanity, a high order of intellect, a brave soldier, a true gentleman, and an honor to his Territory and Government. This sad bereavement will be felt by every one who had the pleasure of his acquaintance throughout the Territory and the Nation."[66]

The Helena bar eulogized Meagher in a resolution as "a man who stood among his fellow men an intellectual giant, a loved and respected member of the Bar, a sympathizer with the oppressed of all nations, a genial companion, and a universal friend of mankind; . . . a brilliant orator, whose classic and glowing eloquence will live while literary mind is admired or the English language spoken." After passing the resolution, the members of the bar were invited to express their feelings about

Meagher's death. No one rose, however. After a few uncomfortable moments Judge Munson, Meagher's bitter antagonist in life, finally broke the silence: "it seems to be more in harmony with our sense of bereavement to sit in silence and ponder over the lessons of the hour, and, if possible, gather wisdom to ourselves out of this sad, mysterious dispensation." After reciting some of Meagher's accomplishments, Munson adjourned the court.[67]

Judge Hosmer, who had supported Meagher in his last days, convened a meeting of citizens at the Virginia City city hall to eulogize him: "Gentlemen:—In rising to announce the object of this meeting, I am oppressed with a sense of gloom that I find it difficult to overcome. Gen. Thomas Francis Meagher is no more." He then suggested a resolution to testify to their great loss. Upon a motion from John Bruce, Hosmer appointed Samuel Word, Captain J. H. Mills, and Judge William Y. Lovell to produce a resolution. A short time later the men returned with a statement that included the following words:

That in his official capacity as Secretary and Acting-Governor of this Territory, he has ever shown a zealous desire and untiring energy in advancing the material interests of Montana and won the gratitude of all by his able and unremitting efforts to protect our frontiers from the ravages of the hostile foe. That in the record of his life we read from his earliest days a daring spirit of liberty that flashed forth in his native mountains and beamed with renewed lustre on the battlefields of this Republic, endearing him to the American people, as a worthy, brave and trusty patriot.

Unlike the silent Helena meeting, a number of those present in Virginia City expressed their sorrow before the meeting adjourned.[68]

Meagher's death affected many others. The General Meagher Circle of the Fenian Brotherhood in Red Mountain City, Montana Territory, passed a series of resolutions mourning his death. A copy of them was delivered to Elizabeth Meagher in Virginia City on July 26 by Montana "head centre" Andrew O'Connell. In Colorado Territory the executive office was "draped in mourning as a token of respect." The Emmet Circle of the Fenian Brotherhood of Nevada City and the officers of the

Montana militia at a meeting at Camp Ida Thoroughman also passed resolutions of mourning in the week following Meagher's death.[69]

The *New York Times* published Meagher's obituary. Although word of his death had already spread, the *Irish American* announced it for the first time on July 13, 1867: "It is sad to think that one so gifted and so highly esteemed by thousands of his fellow-citizens, should be, in an instant, swept out of existence by an unforeseen casualty, and, after escaping all the vicissitudes of exile and tattle, should perish in a manner so sudden and unexpected. May God rest his soul." Meagher's unexpected death became a theme among the Irish. How could someone so brave and noble perish by a careless accident? Heroes like Meagher should not die that way.[70] One commemorative poem asked:

> And is the patriot, Meagher, dead?
> Who, in his youthful glory, rose,
> A champion of his race, and led
> His country 'gainst her foes,
> Who prized the sword 'bove "moral force,"
> When tyranny to dotage ran,
> And waked in tyrants a remorse
> For slavery in man.[71]

Soon New York was inundated with efforts to memorialize Meagher. The Knights of St. Patrick and the Irish Brigade cooperatively commemorated him in late July. On August 3, 1867, the *Irish American* published a reprint of the account of Meagher's death, taken from the *Montana Post.* On August 10, 1867, the *Irish American* reported on an event held on July 31 in which the Grand Army of the Republic lamented Meagher's death and passed a resolution attesting to his greatness.[72]

The tributes continued. The officers of the 69th Regiment adopted a resolution proclaiming that they had lost one who as "once a comrade in arms, added lustre to our name, not only by the aid of his distinguished name, but by his bravery in the field." And on September 14, 1867, the Friendly Sons of Ireland of Jersey City passed a resolution eulogizing Meagher as one whose "virtue and patriotism adorn the history of Ireland."[73] The *American* also published a final verse:

To thee, great heart, that 'neath the dark blue waters lies,
I'll only say farewell;
My country's pride, my father's guest, in days gone by,
Farewell, farewell!
Thy spring is past, thy summer glory fled,
We can but now in silence mourn the dead—
A last farewell![74]

In Dublin, the *Nation,* the paper that had nurtured Meagher in his early days in Ireland, also commemorated his death, recounting his career in glowing terms and eulogizing: "Sad that such a brain as his, one of the rarest gifts to humanity, should have its light quenched of a sudden in the heedless waters. But it is useless now to repine for the irreparable."[75]

Despite these tributes, Meagher did not leave the public memory without controversy, as sadly reported in an article that appeared on September 18, 1867, in the *New York Times:*

Though the old rule, "*de mortuis nil nisi bonum*," is doubtless followed often too far, sometimes to the extent of suppressing truths which, for the good of the living should be known, the contrary is only too often the case and the dead are abused, who can speak no word in their own defence. The meanest exhibition of this latter feeling that has come under our notice was given at the Fenian Congress at Cleveland last week. The report says: "A resolution of respect for the memory of THOS. FRANCIS MEAGHER created a heated discussion, there being a wide difference of opinion as to his merits, and the services he had rendered the Fenian cause. Applause and hisses greeted every repetition of his name."

Whatever may have been the faults of THOMAS FRANCIS MEAGHER, he was one of the most brilliant and talented Irishmen who have made this country their home. He ever commanded the respect and admiration of a large circle of friends, and was always most enthusiastic in his love for his native land. It was a melancholy display of unmanly spite for a "Congress" of Irishmen, assembled ostensibly for the benefit of Ireland, to hiss the name of a dead man, who had suffered so much for his devotion to her, as had THOMAS FRANCIS MEAGHER.

Despite widespread and well-deserved respect, Meagher had failed to restore his reputation completely among the Irish revolutionaries of the world.[76]

Elizabeth Meagher did not stay long in Montana after her husband's death. While it has been a popular myth that she walked the banks of the Missouri for months in search of his body, it appears that she was actually occupied in legal matters. Within two weeks of Meagher's death it became known that Judge Lovell would probate his estate. This required Elizabeth to remain in Virginia City for several weeks to sign papers. On August 10 she filed a document with the court claiming the family Bible and other books that had belonged to Thomas Francis Meagher as well as the stoves and household goods, which were awarded to her as her property under law. But there was no reason for her to stay any longer. A freighter bound for Fort Benton loaded these items on his wagon shortly after August 17. Elizabeth had already departed for Helena on August 12, and after staying there for most of two weeks, she left for Fort Benton, arriving there on the 29th. She headed downriver on the *Gallatin* on September 2.[77]

Elizabeth returned to her father's house in New York. By 1870 she was living comfortably with him and a number of servants in Orange County, New York. The Townsends also had a residence in New York City. Peter Townsend died in September 1885. It seems that he never forgave Elizabeth for marrying Thomas Francis Meagher. Elizabeth's widowed sister, Mrs. Crawford, and her five children also moved in with Townsend, then a widower. When he died, his will gave his residence and all furnishings to Mrs. Crawford and her children and divided the income from the remainder of his estate into thirty-seconds, giving Mrs. Crawford nineteen thirty-seconds, Mrs. Samuel Barlow eight thirty-seconds, and Elizabeth Townsend Meagher only five thirty-seconds.[78]

Despite her father's disapproval and despite being left solely dependent on her family for support, Elizabeth remained loyal to her husband's memory. She was immediately challenged to defend his reputation. The *Irish American* cited a letter from her shortly after Meagher's death, denying "*in toto* the rumor that had been circulated attributing the General's death to intoxication." Elizabeth also continued to support the Irish cause and remained in touch with Montana Fenian "head centre" Andrew O'Connell. She visited him on a trip to Yellowstone National Park in 1887 and told him in a letter in 1902 that she had named her home in Rye, New York, "after the old home of the O'Meaghers in Tipperary." Just as Elizabeth continued to stand by the Irish, Meagher's former comrades also continued to stand by her. Colonel Robert Nugent, who served under Meagher in the 69th, helped Elizabeth get a Civil War widow's pension in 1887, for example.[79]

In addition, Elizabeth remained in touch with Meagher's family in Ireland. When she could be of help to the fatherless Thomas Bennett Meagher, she stepped up to list herself first as his mother when he applied for admission to the United States Military Academy at West Point (which was denied for failure to pass an entrance examination) and then as his stepmother on a subsequent application for admission, which was accepted. Thomas Bennett, who emigrated to the United States when he was eighteen, received his nomination to West Point from congressman William Randall Roberts, the former head of the Fenian Brotherhood at the time of their invasion of Canada.[80] In a letter dated June 29, 1872, to W. W. Belknap, secretary of war, Roberts asked for permission to renominate Bennett and noted that "numerous friends of his father . . . are convinced that the chief cause of his failure, is to be attributed to the fact, that his studies were of a different character from those which would enable him to pass a successful examination." Roberts suggested that "an exception could very well be made in favor of the only son of a general, who rendered such distinguished service to the Union, it would be at once a tribute to his memory, & that of the brave men, who fell fighting under his command."[81] Unfortunately, the academy dismissed Thomas Bennett Meagher for academic failure in January 1873. He later sought the help of Samuel Barlow to seek a job in the New York state government, and then he dropped out of sight.[82]

In a final act of respect, Elizabeth tried to ensure that Meagher's memory lived on. In what was called an "adoption" by the wife of a grandson of Thomas Francis Meagher, Elizabeth made Thomas Meagher Durkin the executor of her will. He had changed his name from Thomas Durkin to Thomas Meagher Durkin in 1902 according to Westchester County records in New York. Mrs. Thomas F. Meagher III said: "But, it was knowen [sic] that he railroaded her is how he came into all Elizabeth['s] property & estate."[83]

Others, too, worked to keep Meagher's memory alive. Two years after his death Captain W. F. Lyons began working on a celebratory biography, which was ultimately published in 1886. Lyons, the editor of the *New York Herald,* was well qualified to write such a book. He had served under Meagher in the Civil War. As the title *Brigadier-General Thomas Francis Meagher: His Political and Military Career* indicates, the Lyons book focuses more on Meagher's military exploits in the United States than on his revolutionism in Ireland. A second laudatory biography, *Memoirs of Gen. Thomas Francis Meagher,* was published in 1892 by Michael Cavanagh, former secretary to John O'Mahony, the Fenian leader.

Not much was done in Ireland to honor Meagher. A new group of Irish revolutionaries had been at work there since his exile, and perhaps his memory had become temporarily eclipsed. Cavanagh noted twenty-five years after Meagher's death that no monument had been erected to him in his hometown of Waterford; the only memorabilia were "his portrait and the other mementoes of his fame which adorn their Municipal hall—and which are the gifts of his noble American-born widow."[84] Despite the lack of Irish biographies during the decades following his death, however, Meagher's name and memory were perpetuated with the other Young Irelanders in numerous anthologies and histories in Ireland. It was not until Arthur Griffith was looking for an anti-British propagandist in 1915 that he chose Meagher as "the National Orator" of his century.[85] Griffith, the founder of Sinn Fein and later one of the first leaders of independent Irish government, published Meagher's speeches and writings in a seminal book, *Meagher of the Sword,* in 1916. In Griffith's view, Meagher was the most accomplished Irish orator in the nineteenth century—even better than O'Connell.[86] With Griffith's publication, Meagher's name became legend in Ireland.

Meagher remained a source of Irish pride in Montana, and loyalty to his memory grew. In the face of ongoing prejudice, Montana's Irish needed a hero—and the Irish revolutionary Civil War general and territorial governor fit the bill. Just as Meagher had hoped, Irish immigrants flocked to Montana, though not as he had hoped as homesteaders and independent entrepreneurs and not at the time he wanted. Instead, toward the end of the nineteenth century, they were lured by jobs in Butte, which boasted the most productive copper mines in the world. By 1900 Butte had become home to over eight thousand Irish—over one-quarter of the city's population—the highest concentration of Irish in any city in America. The Catholic immigrants still faced hostility; mean-spirited jokes echoed from the stages of Butte playhouses, and the anti-Catholic American Protective Association had active chapters in Montana. Ethnic politics even became mixed up in the fight over where to situate the state capital: in Anaconda, as many Irish partisans preferred, or in Helena, the choice of the "Americans." Advocates for Helena won out, but the Butte Irish had the last word. Butte's two largest Irish organizations, the Ancient Order of Hibernians and the Robert Emmet Literary Association (a successor to the Fenians), joined together to erect a statue of Thomas Francis Meagher on the grounds of the new Capitol.[87]

No public funds went for the statue. Before the capital fight the Emmets and Hibernians had hoped to situate it on the banks of the Missouri River at Fort Benton. In 1898 the two organizations established a formal Meagher Monument Association to raise $20,000 for the project, declaring that they would accept contributions from any source except Meagher's antagonist Wilbur Fisk Sanders.[88] Sanders, incidentally, had also been a vocal supporter of Helena in the capital fight. Butte miners contributed the lion's share of the money. When they were still short of funds, the Emmets sought a loan of $300 from the national Emmet Revolutionary Fund, only to be instructed by the national headquarters to withdraw from the Meagher Memorial Association and devote their resources to the cause of Ireland. Yet the funds were finally raised, and the equestrian statue was installed in 1905.[89] Every inch the Irish general, Meagher remains there still, with his sword raised, an unlikely memorial to Irish Montana.

In more recent times Meagher has continued to be lionized. President John F. Kennedy honored Meagher and the Irish Brigade in a 1963 address to the Irish Parliament, in which he presented to the Irish people a flag that the brigade carried in the Civil War.[90] Even today Meagher's Civil War command is still honored when the Irish Brigade Association of New York City marches in the annual St. Patrick's Day Parade.[91] And at long last, in his native Ireland an impressive equestrian statute of Meagher has been erected in a place of honor on the Mall in Waterford.

Meagher's reputation has lived on, nurtured by laudatory biographies, Griffith's publication of his speeches and writings, and the need for an Irish American hero in the face of anti-Irish prejudice. But because heroes must be purer than life, the manner of his death continues to create dissension. Meagher was a great man, so his public wants him to

The Meagher statue in Waterford. Waterford, Ireland, now has a statue of its favorite son, erected in 2004. (Courtesy Catherine E. Greene)

have died a great death. This is suggested by eulogies like the one given by his friend and fellow Young Irelander Richard O'Gorman: "'Would that he had died on the battlefield.' I think I hear some friend say— Would that he had fallen there, with the flag he loved waving over him and the shout of triumph ringing in his ears; would that his grave were on some Irish hill-side, with the green turf above him."[92] As Meagher's reputation as a hero continued to grow, the manner of his death became increasingly important. The idea that he fell from the G. A. *Thompson* and drowned under the influence of alcohol does not sit well with the public's image of a great man—even a great man who drank too much. Rumors that Meagher was murdered persist.

In fact, too much weight has been placed on the manner of Meagher's death. It is Meagher's great courage, brilliant oratory, widespread influence, and world renown that should dominate the memory of the man, not his accidental death or his struggles with alcohol. Even as he wished for a nobler end for Meagher, Richard O'Gorman recognized this fact as well in the eulogy he gave at a requiem mass at the church of St. Francis on August 14, 1867. "His faults lie gently on him," O'Gorman said, while acknowledging that Meagher's memory would be clouded by the "evil tongues that respect not the majesty of death." "What matter to him now whether men praise or blame?" he queried. "The whole world's censure could not hurt him now."[93]

According to O'Gorman, Meagher's real greatness rested in his life-long devotion to Ireland. This overrode any mistakes that he made, including the harsh words that he uttered about the New York Irish establishment at the height of the Civil War. "Some things he did say from time to time that I did not agree with, that seemed to me hasty, passionate, unjust." But, O'Gorman continued, "When men speak much and often they cannot help sometimes speaking wrong." And Meagher's heart always lay with Ireland. "He never said a word that was not meant to help her and raise her," O'Gorman said, thus recognizing Meagher as Meagher himself no doubt would most like to have been remembered.[94]

Notes

ABBREVIATIONS

ANBA	Antietam National Battlefield Archives Antietam, Virginia
BSA	Butte Silver Bow Public Archives, Butte, Montana
CUL	Columbia University Libraries, New York
GU	Georgetown University, Washington, D.C.
HL	Huntington Library, San Marino, California
HSP	Historical Society of Pennsylvania, Philadelphia
LoC	Library of Congress, Washington, D.C.
MCC	Madison County Courthouse, Virginia City, Montana
MHS	Montana Historical Society, Helena
MNHS	Minnesota Historical Society, St. Paul
MSUSC	Montana State University Special Collections, Bozeman
NA	National Archives, Washington, D.C.
NARA	National Archives and Records Administration, Washington, D.C.
NLI	National Library of Ireland, Dublin
NYPL	New York Public Library, New York
NYSL	New York State Library, Albany
OR	U.S. War Department, *The War of the Rebellion: A Compilation of the Official Records of the Union and Confederate Armies*
OR (Navies)	Official Records of the Union and Confederate Navies in the War of the Rebellion
UMI	William L. Clements Library, University of Michigan, Ann Arbor
UMM	University of Montana, Missoula
UNDA	University of Notre Dame Archives, Notre Dame, Indiana
USMAL	United States Military Academy Library, West Point, New York
VHS	Virginia Historical Society, Richmond

INTRODUCTION

1. Bancroft, *History of Washington, Idaho, and Montana*, 651.
2. Bowers, *The Irish Orators*, 372.

CHAPTER 1

1. Meagher, *Speeches on the Legislative Independence of Ireland*, 219.
2. Cavanagh, *Memoirs of Gen. Thomas Francis Meagher*, 14–15.
3. Ibid., 16–17. From a speech given in St. Paul, Minnesota.
4. Foster, ed., *The Oxford History of Ireland*, 47–51; Costigan, *A History of Modern Ireland, with a Sketch of Earlier Times*, 36–39; Meagher, *Speeches on the Legislative Independence of Ireland*, 225–26 (quotation).
5. Costigan, *A History of Modern Ireland*, 41, 42.
6. Foster, *Modern Ireland, 1600–1972*, 23–24.
7. Ibid., 602; MacManus, *The Story of the Irish Race*, 496–98.
8. Foster, *Modern Ireland*, 11–14.
9. Willson, *A History of England*, 326–34.
10. Foster, *Modern Ireland*, 36–78; Costigan, *History of Modern Ireland*, 64–65.
11. Foster, *Modern Ireland*, 101–103.
12. Edmund Burke, *Letters, Speeches, and Tracts on Irish Affairs* (1881), quoted in MacManus, *The Story of the Irish Race*, 454–55, see also 456–69; Costigan, *History of Modern Ireland*, 90–96.
13. Lecky, *Leaders of Public Opinion in Ireland*, 11–21; Costigan, *History of Modern Ireland*, 90–96; MacManus, *The Story of the Irish Race*, 458–60; Foster, *Modern Ireland*, 154, 206–207.
14. George Berkeley, *The Querist* (1735–37), quoted in Costigan, *History of Modern Ireland*, 99–106.
15. Woodham-Smith, *The Great Hunger*, 27–28. The punishments were savagely inflicted. The wrongdoers' cattle were driven off the edge of cliffs, horses were hamstrung, burning stables became the pyres of the animals within, and dogs were clubbed to death.
16. Lecky, *History of Modern Ireland in the Eighteenth Century*, vol. 1, 148–49; MacManus, *The Story of the Irish Race*, 461–62.
17. *The Life and Times of Thomas Francis Meagher* (exhibition catalogue). The Meagher family later moved to another location. Meagher's father finally moved to Bray, where he lived at the time of his son's death in Fort Benton. Waterford Heritage Services, private report to the author, August 16, 2000. The records of the parish church in Waterford where the couple was married on October 12, 1820, indicate that a dispensation from publication of the banns of marriage was obtained. Bianconi and Watson, *Bianconi*, 71–72. An alternate spelling "Cummins" is used in the book. A copy of an aquatint of the hotel appears between pages 74 and 75.
18. Costigan, *History of Modern Ireland*, 113–15; Lecky, *Leaders of Public Opinion in Ireland*, 135–43; Meagher, *Speeches on the Legislative Independence of Ireland*, 226.
19. Meagher, *Speeches on the Legislative Independence of Ireland*, 224.
20. Costigan, *History of Modern Ireland*, 115.
21. Meagher, *Speeches on the Legislative Independence of Ireland*, 228–29.
22. O'Leary, *Recollections of Fenians and Fenianism*, vol. 1, 5–6; Meagher to unknown correspondent, November 8, 1848, NLI. Meagher was president of the Grattan Club at the

time when he was incarcerated in Kilmainham Gaol. Later, in the United States, Meagher's circumstances made him see differently the American version of patronage in a democracy.

23. Foster, *The Oxford History of Ireland*, 151–53; Costigan, *History of Modern Ireland*, 116–20.

24. Costigan, *History of Modern Ireland*, 121–22; MacManus, *The Story of the Irish Race*, 509–11.

25. Meagher, *Speeches on the Legislative Independence of Ireland*, 220–21.

26. Costigan, *History of Modern Ireland*, 124–31.

27. Quoted in ibid., 133–36 (quotation on 136).

28. Griffith, *Meagher of the Sword*, 144.

29. Moley, *Daniel O'Connell*, xi–xv; Costigan, *History of Modern Ireland*, 144–46; MacManus, *The Story of the Irish Race*, 467. Unable to obtain an adequate education for him in Ireland, O'Connell's family had sent him to the Irish College at St. Omer in France. He later went to England, completed his education, and studied law at Lincoln's Inn. The Grattan Parliament's Catholic Relief Act of 1793 had permitted Catholics to become members of the bar. After being called to the bar, O'Connell returned to Ireland to practice law in Dublin. By 1815 he had become a well-known and wealthy figure through his skill as a barrister. Costigan, *History of Modern Ireland*, 144–46.

30. Killeen, *A Short History of Ireland*, 44–45; Lecky, *Leaders of Public Opinion in Ireland*, vol. 2, 204–205.

31. Lecky, *Leaders of Public Opinion in Ireland*, vol. 2, 204–205.

32. Waterford Heritage Services, private report to the author, August 16, 2000.

33. *The Life and Times of Thomas Francis Meagher*. As the Meagher family members passed away over the years, they were buried in Faithlegg cemetery, about five miles from Waterford, which now contains the graves of grandfather Thomas Meagher, the Newfoundland businessman, and his Newfoundlander wife, Mary Crotty Meagher, who returned to Ireland with him. Also buried at Faithlegg is Thomas Francis Meagher's brother Henry Meagher, who returned to Ireland after years of service in the Papal Guard in Rome, serving Pope Pius IX; his mother, Alicia Quan; an older brother who died in infancy, also named Thomas Meagher; two sisters who died young, Mary Josephine and Alicia; and his tragic first wife, Catherine Bennett Meagher, who died at twenty-two. Thomas Francis Meagher, Sr., is buried in Glasnevin Cemetery.

34. Atkinson, *Mary Aikenhead*, 283–93; Cavanagh, *Memoirs*, 19 (quotation).

35. Griffith, *Meagher of the Sword*, 268–70; Corcoran, *The Clongowes Record, 1814 to 1932*, 52–59, 60–63.

36. Corcoran, *The Clongowes Record, 1814 to 1932*, 66.

37. Griffith, *Meagher of the Sword*, 273–79 (quotations on 278).

38. Savage is quoted in Cavanagh, *Memoirs*, 19. Savage also pointed out that "in English composition and rhetoric he was above all competitors, and already became remarkable for that elegant enthusiasm which afterwards, in so short a space of time, placed his name on the list of the recognized orators who have contributed so largely to make the history and literature of his country" (19).

39. Griffith, *Meagher of the Sword*, 272.

40. Cavanagh, *Memoirs*, 24–27 (quotation on 26).

41. Corcoran, *The Story of Clongowes Wood, A.D. 1450–1900*, 26–27.

42. Costigan, *History of Modern Ireland*, 54. Trinity was in part established to counteract the Catholic colleges on the continent, such as St. Omer's, where young Irish students

from wealthy families were sent; Gruggen and Keating, *Stonyhurst,* 1–8, 236, 246; Henderson, *The Stone Phoenix,* 17–20.

43. David Knight, archivist, Stonyhurst College, correspondence with the author, February 21, 2005. Meagher arrived at Stonyhurst on October 17, 1839, and left on August 17, 1843.

44. Gruggen and Keating, *Stonyhurst,* 176; Bowers, *The Irish Orators,* 331, 332.

45. Cavanagh, *Memoirs,* 29.

46. Ibid., 29–30; Athearn, *Thomas Francis Meagher,* 2.

47. Cavanagh, *Memoirs,* 31, 32.

48. David Knight, archivist, Stonyhurst College, correspondence with the author, February 21, 2005. Don Ramon Páez attended Stonyhurst from December 27, 1840, to December 17, 1841. See Graham, *José Antonio Páez,* 102n, 273–77.

49. Foster, *Modern Ireland,* 299–300; Somerset Fry and Somerset Fry, *A History of Ireland,* 219–20; Griffith, *Meagher of the Sword,* 292–96.

50. Griffith, *Meagher of the Sword,* 292–96.

51. Ibid., 296.

52. To provide a venue for speeches in support of his cause, O'Connell would have Conciliation Hall built in Dublin, which became the place where serious opinions against the English were expressed. Among them was O'Connell's own: he coined the motto "Ireland for the Irish—God save the Queen." Savage, *'98 and '48,* 255–56.

53. Lecky, *Leaders of Public Opinion in Ireland,* vol. 2, 193, 194, 238–52.

54. Ibid., 235–39, 252; Costigan, *History of Modern Ireland,* 7–8, 156.

55. MacIntyre, *The Liberator,* 267.

56. Griffith, *Meagher of the Sword,* 280.

57. Ibid., 286–87 (quotation on 287).

58. Ibid., 299.

59. Ibid., 300.

60. Ibid., 307.

61. Ibid., 298.

62. Cavanagh, *Memoirs,* 33–34; Savage, *'98 and '48,* 257; Costigan, *History of Modern Ireland,* 192–95.

63. Handwritten account from Stephan Thelen Co. with entries in 1845 and 1846, MS 7410, NLI. Meagher's penchant for keeping a large correspondence was also in evidence, and his account with Thelen included large supplies of paper and envelopes.

64. Griffith, *Meagher of the Sword,* 271.

65. Duffy, *Four Years of Irish History, 1845–1849,* 59. The Library of Ireland was issued monthly, according to John Savage, "and ran to twenty two volumes." No volumes were located. Savage, *'98 and '48,* 258.

66. Costigan, *History of Modern Ireland,* 155. There is no agreement as to the origin of the name "Young Ireland."

67. Touhill, *William Smith O'Brien and His Irish Revolutionary Companions in Penal Exile,* 7–10; Griffith, *Meagher of the Sword,* 345; Pigott, *Personal Recollections of an Irish National Journalist,* 9.

68. Griffith, *Meagher of the Sword,* 338–49.

69. Elgee to unknown correspondent, University of Reading, quoted in Melville, *Mother of Oscar,* 28. In her poetry Speranza also penned the following descriptions of Meagher: "In his

beauty and his youth" and "So he stood before us then, one of God's eternal men, / Flashing eye, and hero mould of stature." Willett, ed., "Poems (1871?)."

70. Keneally, *The Great Shame and the Triumph of the Irish in the English-Speaking World,* 120.

71. Cavanagh, *Memoirs,* 133.

72. Duffy, *Four Years of Irish History,* 434.

CHAPTER 2

1. Meagher, *Speeches on the Legislative Independence of Ireland,* xvi; Costigan, *History of Modern Ireland,* 151–57; Somerville-Large, *Dublin,* 230–31.

2. Griffith, *Meagher of the Sword,* vi; Costigan, *History of Modern Ireland,* 151–52.

3. Meagher, *Speeches on the Legislative Independence of Ireland,* xvi.

4. Griffith, *Meagher of the Sword,* vi.

5. Ibid., 1–15.

6. Ibid., 6–8. Meagher, who still had not reached his twenty-third birthday, revealed his youth again when he said: "I tell you candidly, if my father was in parliament, and had up to this period refused to join the Association, . . . I would be the first to vote against him. It is better that the hearts of a few should be pained, than that the great heart of the nation should be broken." Ibid., 14.

7. Ibid., 18.

8. Ibid., v–vi.

9. Ibid., 89; Duffy, *Four Years of Irish History,* 9–10.

10. Griffith, *Meagher of the Sword,* 19.

11. Trench, *The Great Dan,* 304–305.

12. Griffith, *Meagher of the Sword,* 21–26 (quotation on 22).

13. Ibid., 25–26 (quotation on 26).

14. Ibid., 27–37 (quotation on 35).

15. Ibid., 32–33.

16. Ibid., 35.

17. Ibid., 36–37.

18. Duffy, *Four Years of Irish History,* 236.

19. Ibid., 9, 161–62 (first quotation on page 9; second quotation on pages 161–62).

20. Ibid., 9.

21. Griffith, *Meagher of the Sword,* 285–92 (quotation on 288). In the end Meagher would learn that Nash had died somewhere in Ireland, in utter poverty, without companions and perhaps nameless. Yet Nash had been conspicuous in Waterford politics for twenty years during the initiation of the Catholic rent, the Stuart election, and the election of Meagher's own father, Thomas Meagher, Sr., to the English Parliament in July 1847. Ibid., 289, 304.

22. Duffy, *Four Years of Irish History,* 351.

23. Kee, *The Most Distressful Country,* 170–78.

24. Ibid.

25. Ibid., 175–77; Foster, *Modern Ireland,* 320–22; Costigan, *History of Modern Ireland,* 168–69. When the Irish population rose (from about 5 million people in 1800 to 6.8 million in the country's first real census in 1821 and to 8.2 million by 1841), the cultivated acreage

in Ireland actually decreased over this period. At the same time, mass-produced foreign goods were ruining Ireland's industries. Costigan, *History of Modern Ireland,* 167–68.

26. Kee, *The Most Distressful Country,* 173–75.

27. O'Grada, *Black '47 and Beyond,* 41.

28. Woodham-Smith, *The Great Hunger,* 283.

29. As quoted in Costigan, *History of Modern Ireland,* 169; Thackeray, *The Irish Sketch Book,* 110.

30. Duffy, *Four Years of Irish History,* 353.

31. Costigan, *History of Modern Ireland,* 174; Duffy, *Four Years of Irish History,* 353–55.

32. Duffy, *Four Years of Irish History,* 355–56.

33. Ibid., 358–65.

34. Griffith, *Meagher of the Sword,* 53–66, speech on January 13, 1847, to the Irish Confederation. The full passage is as follows:

> Sir, in what year, since the enactment of the Union, will the disciples of William Pitt find the fulfillment of that promise? In 1801, when the English parliament visited this country with an Insurrection Act? In 1803, when that parliament imposed a martial law? In 1807, when the Insurrection Act of 1801 is renewed, continuing in force until 1810? In 1814, when for a third time, the Insurrection Act of 1801 is renewed, and inflicted up to 1824? In 1836, when the Lord High Chancellor of England spurns you as aliens in language, in religion, and in blood? In 1839, when you claimed equal franchises with the people of England, and are denied them by the Whig Secretary for Ireland? In 1843, when a minister of the crown declares that concession has reached its limits, and an assassin proclamation proscribes your right of petition? In 1846, when the Coercion Bill is levelled against your liberties, and the Arms' Act is re-introduced by the Whigs? Tell me— is it fulfilled in 1847, when the Treasury confiscates the Island, and famine piles upon it a pyramid of coffins? A lie! exclaims the broken manufacturer. A lie! protests the swindled landlord. A lie! A lie! shrieks the skeleton from the putrid hovels of Skibbereen. (Ibid., 55–56)

35. Costigan, *History of Modern Ireland,* 162.

36. Woodham-Smith, *The Great Hunger,* 300.

37. Pepper, "Personal Recollections of General Thomas Francis Meagher," 532. When Meagher mounted the platform, Pepper observed that "he was fairly tall and possessed an attractive presence; he was young and lithe, with curling brown hair, light blue eyes and a very radiant expression."

38. Duffy, *Four Years of Irish History,* 523–26; Cavanagh, *Memoirs,* 89–96.

39. Cavanagh, *Memoirs,* 101–109 (quotation on 109).

40. Ibid., 118–19.

41. Duffy, *Four Years of Irish History,* 562–63; Cavanagh, *Memoirs,* 119–22. By this time the delegation also included Martin MacDermott, Richard O'Gorman, and Eugene O'Reilly.

42. Cavanagh, *Memoirs,* 160–64 (quotation on 164).

43. Ibid., 150–51.

44. Ibid., 170–73.

45. Ibid., 174–80, 194.

46. Ibid., 185. Cavanagh also notes that there was an honest Protestant on the jury, which would have made the vote ten to two for conviction.

47. "A Review of the Last Session," 283.

48. *Irish American,* December 3, 1853, reprinted from the *Nation,* June 5, 1848. When asked for an apology, Meagher stated firmly that he had none. In an attempt to avoid an embarrassing showdown, the judge said that he would accept an apology at any time during the sitting of the court; however, Meagher stood resolute. Finally, John Dillon, seeing his predicament and recognizing that Meagher was more valuable working for the confederation on a major insurrection rather than spending his time in jail on a senseless matter, stood and said that in expressing his sympathy for the prisoner Meagher did not intend any disrespect for the court. The judge persisted in requesting an apology, however, which Meagher would not give. In the hands of the police in the courtroom, not wanting to back down, Meagher attempted to find a middle ground by saying that he could not retract anything but did not mean any disrespect or contempt toward the court. Being pressed to say that he was excited at the time of the applause, Meagher would say only that he meant no contempt. At that point he was discharged by the judge, who did not wish to escalate the matter further.

49. Cavanagh, *Memoirs,* 208.

50. Duffy, *Four Years of Irish History,* 610–12. When the vote was counted for the new council, Thomas Francis Meagher had thirty-one votes, as did Father Kenyon. William Smith O'Brien, Charles Gavan Duffy, John Dillon, and Richard O'Gorman had thirty votes each; and a number of others, including P. J. Smyth with twenty-eight votes, were also elected.

51. Cavanagh, *Memoirs,* 207–209 (quotation on 208).

52. Duffy, *Four Years of Irish History,* 608–11.

53. Ibid., 625; Cavanagh, *Memoirs,* 223–27.

54. Duffy, *Four Years of Irish History,* 623, 625–26; Cavanagh, *Memoirs,* 227–30. In the meantime Duffy had also been arrested in July for publishing articles, including one entitled "Mr. Meagher and the Clubs." In the end Duffy was tried five times; but no jury would convict him, and he walked out of prison after the last trial as a free man. Despite the new arrests, Young Ireland kept on berating the British. The *Nation* continued to publish articles against the government, even while Duffy was in prison, until the paper was finally suppressed on July 29. Cavanagh, *Memoirs,* 218–19.

55. Cavanagh, *Memoirs,* 236–40 (quotation on 239).

56. Ibid., 241.

57. Griffith, *Meagher of the Sword,* 173–74 (quotation on 174).

58. Gwynn, *Young Ireland and 1848,* 239.

59. Griffith, *Meagher of the Sword,* 182–88.

60. Ibid., 187.

61. Ibid., 193.

62. Ibid., 199–203.

63. Ibid., 203.

64. Ibid., 212–13.

65. Ibid., 212–15.

66. Ibid., 224–27 (quotation on 227). This was not the last time that Meagher had contact with O'Mahoney, who eventually made his way to New York and was head of the Fenian Brotherhood in America.

67. Ibid., 227–28.

68. Ibid., 229–31 (quotation on 231).

69. Ibid., 230–32. Opposed to this ill-equipped and untrained group were the troops of a garrison that consisted of a thousand infantry with two units of cavalry and some small amount of ordnance, behind walls ten feet high and fitted to resist an attack from three thousand or four thousand enemy infantry. The huge error soon became apparent to O'Brien, Dillon, and Meagher, who attempted to reconsider their strategy. Dillon offered to take the garrison if five hundred armed men could be obtained, and Meagher offered to leave immediately for Waterford to return in the morning with one hundred more. Though gallant, this idea was soon discarded; Dillon and Meagher favored immediate attack. Smith O'Brien perhaps had the more effective approach; he believed, as in one of their earlier proposed strategies, that one or all of them should be arrested and then rescued to arouse the sympathies and the passions of the people, after which they would lead the attack. Once again the idea was rejected, and the revolution went forward. Ibid., 232–34.

70. Duffy, Four Years of Irish History, 669–71.

71. Ibid., 670–71; Cavanagh, Memoirs, 273.

72. Duffy, Four Years of Irish History, 684–89. The wounded man, John Kavanagh, survived to fight again, this time in the American Civil War against the South, where he served with credit and met his death.

73. Ibid., 681–92; Cavanagh, Memoirs, 288–89. After John Blake Dillon and Terence Bellew MacManus had both left Ireland, MacManus sent Dillon a narrative of the final days of the uprising, describing the confusion of the hour.

74. Griffith, Meagher of the Sword, 300.

75. Duffy, Four Years of Irish History, 697–99.

76. According to the anti-Catholic Blackwood's Edinburgh Magazine, "the unconstitutional fostering of the Roman Catholic Church" had contributed to the rebellion. "A Review of the Last Session," 261.

77. This ancient punishment for treason dated back to at least 1352, when the Statute of Treasons was passed. It made disloyalty to the Crown a special crime, ranking above normal felonies and deserving of special and cruel punishments. Clark, "Capital Punishment U.K.: Hanging, Drawing and Quartering."

78. Cavanagh, Memoirs, 291.

79. Ibid., 291–92.

80. (London) Times, October 24, 1848, and October 25, 1848, Mitchel, Jail Journal, 83; Duffy, Four Years of Irish History, 717–18.

81. (London) Times, October 11, 1848, October 24, 1848, and October 25, 1848; O'Leary, Recollections of Fenians and Fenianism, vol. 1, 19; Athearn, Thomas Francis Meagher, 13, (quotation).

82. Cavanagh, Memoirs, 293–94.

83. Pepper, "Personal Recollections of General Thomas Francis Meagher," 533.

84. Mitchel, Jail Journal, 83, entry for November 21, 1848.

85. "The State Trials—Writ of Error," Illustrated London News, January 20, 1849.

86. Mitchel, Jail Journal, 120.

87. New Ireland, vol. 1, 202, quoted in Atkinson, Mary Aikenhead, 355n1.

88. Gwynn, Young Ireland and 1848, 38–39; Meagher to "Johnny," November 9, 1848, NLI.

89. Griffith, Meagher of the Sword, xvi; Duffy, Four Years of Irish History, 713–14. Although a shorter sentence of transportation for fourteen years had been given to John Mitchel under

the Treason Felony Act, the four of them found guilty of high treason (Meagher, O'Brien, MacManus, and O'Donoghue) were being banished from their homeland forever.

90. Cavanagh, *Memoirs,* 284–85.

91. Ibid., 285.

92. Meagher to Elizabeth Townsend, January 2, 1855, MHS.

93. Handwritten bill from Henry FitzGibbon, Woolen Draper & Clothier, Dublin, June 9, 1849, MS 7410, NLI. Meagher received a bill of £19.1 for these items, which was paid on June 9, a month before his departure for Tasmania. The bill was marked "Settled per stamp receipt—Henry FitzGibbon."

94. "Valuable Book of Thomas Meagher Found in Ontario," unidentified newspaper clipping bearing notation "3-12-1932," Thomas Francis Meagher vertical file, MHS. The book was found in a "collection of uncatalogued books" in the University of Western Ontario library near London, Ontario. The date of the inscription was June 23, 1849.

95. *Montana Post,* September 7, 1867. This news item was published after Meagher's death and was supposedly referred to in a speech by "Collector Russell" at Faneuil Hall in Boston.

96. "Valuable Book of Thomas Meagher Found in Ontario," MHS; Meagher to O'Doherty, n.d., Thomas F. Madigan Papers, NYPL. The two names, Miss Cooper and Miss O'Ryan, could have been fictitious and possibly may have been the same person, given the secrecy of the engagement and the lack of any available information on these women.

97. Davis, *William Smith O'Brien,* 25–26.

98. Mitchel, *Jail Journal,* 152–53, entry for July 26, 1849.

CHAPTER 3

1. Cavanagh, *Memoirs,* 298–300.

2. Keneally, *The Great Shame and the Triumph of the Irish,* 194.

3. Touhill, *William Smith O'Brien,* 27, 28; Adam-Smith, *Heart of Exile,* 192–93.

4. Touhill, *William Smith O'Brien,* 28–34, 182.

5. Log entry of the *Swift,* No. 13, MS 13610, NLI.

6. Touhill, *William Smith O'Brien,* 13. The letter was written on June 5, 1849. See also Hopkins, *The Convict Era,* 19.

7. Touhill, *William Smith O'Brien,* 13–14.

8. Mitchel, *Jail Journal,* 201–202 (quotation on 201), entry for February 10, 1850.

9. Touhill, *William Smith O'Brien,* 39.

10. Meagher to Colman O'Loghlen, August 27, 1851, NLI.

11. Mitchel, *Jail Journal,* 203, entry for February 13, 1850.

12. Meagher to Kellon, November 14, 1849, MS 8237, NLI.

13. Meagher to O'Loghlen, August 27, 1851, NLI.

14. Ibid.

15. Bruce, *Lectures of Gov. Thomas Francis Meagher,* 21.

16. Meagher to O'Loghlen, August 27, 1851, NLI.

17. Ibid.

18. Touhill, *William Smith O'Brien,* 68–69.

19. Mitchel, *Jail Journal,* 216.

20. Ibid., 218.

21. Ibid., 219.

22. Ryan, *The Fenian Chief*, 102; Adam-Smith, *Heart of Exile*, 233–38; Meagher to Smith O'Brien, October 9, 1852, MS 445, O'Brien Papers, NLI; Meagher to O'Loghlen, August 27, 1851 (quotation), NLI. According to Meagher, he had been able to raise £522.15, with £450 coming from "T. F. O'Meagher, Esq." and £35 directly from Smith O'Brien and another £37.10 from O'Brien through William Reeves and received from W. Dunne. With these funds, Meagher had purchased one-half of the cutter *Victoria* for £200 and rented the other half for a year for £88.4. With the remaining money he had paid off "Fine and costs" of £120.9 and "lawyer's bills" of £9.9, leaving Young Ireland with nothing for its investment other than the possible payoff of lawyer's fees to Colman O'Loghlen. Handwritten account by Meagher, August 1852, MS 2825, NLI. O'Brien had felt compelled to assume the loss as his own and was setting aside any money that was coming to him from Ireland for its repayment. In the fall of 1851 Meagher set out to settle his account with Colman O'Loghlen, who had represented him in his trials in Ireland. On August 27 Meagher wrote to him, forwarding his long overdue fee. It was an awkward moment, because the sum had been due for more than two years, and required his amends: "I am painfully annoyed when I think of this debt having been delayed so long." Meagher to O'Loghlen, August 27, 1851, NLI.

23. Touhill, *William Smith O'Brien*, 93.

24. Kiernan, *The Irish Exiles in Australia*, 99–100; Meagher, Sr., quoted in Touhill, *William Smith O'Brien*, 118.

25. Meagher to Kevin O'Doherty, n.d., Thomas F. Madigan Papers, NYPL.

26. Ibid.

27. Cullen, *Young Ireland in Exile*, 76–78; Adam-Smith, *Heart of Exile*, 231–32. Not much is known about Bryan Bennett, but Meagher was almost certainly being sanguine when he later described him as "an honest, pious, venerable, poor old man, who, years before, had journeyed from Ireland to that distant land, and there built up, with thrifty and courageous industry, a sweet though humble home for the children who made the evening of his life vocal with the song, and crowned his grey hairs with the flowers, of hope." Meagher to Elizabeth Townsend, January 2, 1855, MHS.

28. Cullen, *Young Ireland in Exile*, 76–78; Meagher to Townsend, January 2, 1855, MHS (quotation).

29. Marriage Permission Search Results, Archives Office of Tasmania.

30. Letter from Smith O'Brien to Meagher, n.d., and letter from Mitchel to O'Doherty, n.d., both quoted in Adam-Smith, *Heart of Exile*, 231.

31. Meagher to Kevin O'Doherty, n.d., Thomas F. Madigan Papers, NYPL.

32. Ibid.

33. Adam-Smith, *Heart of Exile*, 261; Meagher to Colman O'Loghlen, August 27, 1851, NLI; Touhill, *William Smith O'Brien*, 98 (quotation).

34. Adam-Smith, *Heart of Exile*, 261–63, 231.

35. Ibid., 232.

36. Ibid.

37. Meagher to Stephen Curtis, October 20, 1851, NLI.

38. Meagher to Dick Sargeant, August 27, 1851, NLI.

39. Meagher to O'Loghlen, August 27, 1851, NLI; "Personal Recollections: Christmas Eve in Tasmania—the Lady of the Lake," *Irish News*, December 27, 1856.

40. Meagher to Townsend, January 2, 1855, MHS.

41. Handwritten statement of P. J. Smyth regarding the escape of T. F. Meagher, March 8, 1884, MS 8216/2, NLI.

42. Cavanagh, *Memoirs,* 307.

43. Ibid.

44. Ibid.

45. Ibid., 308.

46. Adam-Smith, *Heart of Exile,* 267–68. P. J. Smyth, who conducted an investigation of the matter many years later, visited Meagher's former home "in company with a young colonist who had been Meagher's companion on the occasion." Smyth said: "The distance which separated the parties when the above colloquy took place was about 15 paces. I asked my friend if the constables would have fired? He said, 'Most certainly—had he waited two seconds more they would either have taken him down, or shot his horse under him. They had him under cover from the moment he hailed them. Only for me he would have been shot or captured. I seized the rein & turned the horse into the bush there through that opening'" (Statement of P. J. Smyth, March 8, 1884, NLI).

47. Adam-Smith, *Heart of Exile,* 269–71.

48. Athearn, *Thomas Francis Meagher,* 25–27; Adam-Smith, *Heart of Exile,* 269–71; "General Meagher in Boston," *Irish American,* May 14, 1864.

49. Catherine Meagher to unknown correspondent, January 11, 1852, quoted in Adam-Smith, *Heart of Exile,* 273.

50. Touhill, *William Smith O'Brien,* 142.

51. Cavanagh, *Memoirs,* 305–306.

52. Martin to O'Doherty, January 18, 1852, quoted in Touhill, *William Smith O'Brien,* 143.

53. Touhill, *William Smith O'Brien,* 160.

54. Ibid., 142–43; Watson, *The Life and Times of Thomas Francis Meagher,* 53–54.

55. Meagher to the editor of the *New York Daily Times,* June 5, 1852, quoted in Cavanagh, *Memoirs,* 306–307; Statement of P. J. Smyth, March 8, 1884, NLI.

56. "A New Song, on the Escape of Thomas Francis Meagher, the Irish Exile," in *America Singing: Nineteenth-Century Song Sheets.*

57. Mitchel, *Jail Journal,* 252, entry for January 1, 1853.

58. Ibid., 276–77, entry for June 12, 1853; Touhill, *William Smith O'Brien,* 162–65, 172–73.

59. Touhill, *William Smith O'Brien,* 189–94.

CHAPTER 4

1. *Boston Pilot,* May 15, 1852, quoted in Athearn, *Thomas Francis Meagher,* 26.

2. "Electric Telegraphic Dispatches," *(London) Times,* April 24, 1852.

3. Athearn, *Thomas Francis Meagher,* 28.

4. Meagher, "Ireland and the Holy Alliance," 10.

5. Athearn, *Thomas Francis Meagher,* 31–33.

6. Ibid., 31–39.

7. *New York Herald,* May 31, 1852, quoted in Athearn, *Thomas Francis Meagher,* 29.

8. Handwritten note, August 1852, MS 2825, NLI. In August 1852 Meagher copied in his own hand the declaration he had made: "T. F. Meagher has made a final declaration of

his intention of becoming a citizen of the United States. He declared to renounce forever all allegiance & fidelity to any foreign Prince, potentate or sovereignty whatever, & particularly to the Queen of G. B. & Ireland, of whom I am now a subject."

9. Athearn, *Thomas Francis Meagher,* 36–38.

10. Meagher to "My Dear Eva," September 25, 1854, Thomas F. Madigan Papers, NYPL; see Meagher, *Speeches on the Legislative Independence of Ireland.*

11. Adam-Smith, *Heart of Exile,* 273; *Waterford Mail,* June 18, 1853.

12. Adam-Smith, *Heart of Exile,* 273.

13. *Waterford Mail,* July 6, 1853.

14. "Mrs. Thomas F. Meagher: Her Reception in Waterford," *Irish American,* July 30, 1853, quoting the *Waterford Chronicle,* July 9, 1953.

15. Before Catherine left, the welcoming committee members had attempted to procure a casket (jewelry box) similar to the one given to another respected lady; however, upon learning that it would require some months to prepare, they selected a bracelet, a brooch, and a card case, all of which were presented to Mrs. Meagher at the home of her father-in-law. "The Presentation of Ornaments to Mrs. Meagher," *Waterford Mail,* July 9, 1853.

16. *The Irish American,* August 6, 1853, with excerpts from the "*Dublin Nation,*" undated.

17. "Thomas Francis Meagher," *Irish American,* July 16, 1853; "Arrival of Mrs. Thomas Francis Meagher and Thomas Meagher, Esq., M.P., in New York," *Irish American,* July 30, 1853. See also Port of New York Passenger Lists, for the ship *Arctic,* July 25, 1853, listing as passengers Mr. Thomas Meagher, age 58 [*sic*], occupation lawyer, and Mrs. T. F. Meagher, age 21. Although the *Irish American* indicated an arrival date in the city of July 23, the more reliable date, given in the Port of New York Passenger Lists, would be July 25.

18. "Arrival of Mrs. Thomas Francis Meagher and Thomas Meagher, Esq., M.P., in New York," *Irish American,* July 30, 1853.

19. MacManus, ed., *Thomas Davis and Young Ireland,* 73.

20. "Remarks" and reprinted letter from Thomas Meagher, Sr., August 1, *Irish American,* August 13, 1853.

21. Cavanagh, *Memoirs,* 341.

22. Adam-Smith, *Heart of Exile,* 274.

23. "Remarks," *Irish American,* August 13, 1853.

24. Cavanagh, *Memoirs,* 341.

25. Thomas Bennett Meagher was baptized in the Waterford parish cathedral on March 30, 1854, with the sponsors being listed as Meagher's brother Henry and aunt Hannah Quan. Catherine was buried at the graveyard of Faithlegg, four miles east of Waterford. Waterford Heritage Services, private report to the author, August 16, 2000.

26. "Cadets Admitted in 1872," in *Official Register of the Officers and Cadets of the U.S. Military Academy, West Point, New-York,* 23. Catherine reached New York on July 23, 1853. See the *Irish American,* July 30, 1853, for the date of her arrival in the United States.

27. Thomas Bennett Meagher to the Honorable Secretary of War, May 26, 1872, RG 94, entry 214, box 25, folder 8, USMAL; Waterford Heritage Services, private report to the author, August 16, 2000.

28. Mitchel, *Jail Journal,* 270, entry of January 13, 1853.

29. Duffy, *Four Years of Irish History,* 692; Cavanagh, *Memoirs,* 285.

30. "The Meagher Banquet," *Irish American,* August 13, 1853.

31. "'Suppression' of the Irish-American," *Irish American,* October 1, 1853.

32. "Meagher in San Francisco: Lecture on Irish Republicanism," *Irish American*, April 8, 1854.

33. Cavanagh, *Memoirs*, 341.

34. "The Citizen," *Irish American*, December 17, 1853.

35. Shaw, *Dagger John*, 302–303 (Mitchel quotation on 303).

36. Ibid.

37. Ibid., 235–38; Slattery, *The Assassination of D'Arcy McGee*, 26–27.

38. Slattery, *The Assassination of D'Arcy McGee*, 34–36.

39. "Death of Patrick O'Donoghue," *Irish American*, January 28, 1854, and eulogy in the *Citizen*, as quoted in Adam-Smith, *Heart of Exile*, 266. Michael Doheny and John O'Mahony were mentioned as pallbearers.

40. Keneally, *The Great Shame and the Triumph of the Irish*, 272.

41. "Street Encounter: Affray between Thomas Francis Meagher and J. A. McMaster," *New-York Daily Times*, July 19, 1854, citing a McMaster article reproduced from the *Freeman's Journal*, Saturday, July 15, 1854.

42. Ibid.; Athearn, *Thomas Francis Meagher*, 48.

43. Meagher to Elizabeth Townsend, January 2, 1855, MHS.

44. Ibid.

45. "A Fifth-Avenue Romance," *New-York Daily Times*, November 3, 1855.

46. "In the matter of the estate of Peter Townsend deceased: Brief for objecting legatees," n.d., Surrogates Court, Orange County, N.J., Samuel Latham Mitchell Barlow Files, HL. Elizabeth Meagher and Alice Barlow filed a contest to the distribution under the will. The outcome of their petition is not known.

47. Cavanagh, *Memoirs*, 345; Meagher to Smith O'Brien, August 8, 1856, MS 2920, NLI.

48. Meagher to Smith O'Brien, August 8, 1856, NLI.

49. Meagher, "Personal Recollections: Christmas Eve in Tasmania—the Lady of the Lake," *Irish News*, December 27, 1856.

50. Meagher to Smith O'Brien, August 8, 1856, NLI.

51. The *Irish News* had ten or more pages per edition, with substantial advertising appearing on the front page and news and editorials inside, including both world and local news.

52. Meagher to Smith O'Brien, August 8, 1856, MS 2920, NLI.

53. "Answers to Correspondents," *Irish News*, April 12, 1856.

54. "Military News: The Sixty-ninth Regiments at the Academy of Music," *Irish News*, April 19, 1856.

55. "Military Memoirs: Meagher Guard, Charleston, S.C.," *Irish News*, May 3, 1856.

56. "Our Second Volume," *Irish News*, October 11, 1856.

57. Meagher to Smith O'Brien, August 8, 1856, MS 2920, NLI.

58. "Glimpses of the South (From the back pages of a Reporter's Note-Book)," *Irish News*, October 18, 1856.

59. Ibid.

60. Rice, *American Catholic Opinion in the Slavery Controversy*, 120–21.

61. The letters had originally been sent years earlier to John Forsyth, then secretary of state of the United States. They attempted to explain the Catholics' view on slavery.

62. "Bishop England on American Slavery," *Irish News*, October 25, 1856. England's letters purported to refute the notion that Pope Gregory XVI had outlawed slavery. Rather, Bishop England would argue, the pope had only prohibited "slave-trade," a practice that

was then also illegal in the United States. The pope had not urged the abolition of slavery as it then existed in the southern states.

63. *New-York Daily Tribune*, August 27, 1856, quoted in Athearn, *Thomas Francis Meagher*, 51. In support of Bishop England's views on slavery, the *Irish News* also published a column that had appeared in the *United States Catholic Miscellany* on December 9, 1843, in which the editors stated that "there is no danger—no possibility, on our principles—that Catholic theology should ever be tinctured with the fanaticism of abolition." "Bishop England on Southern Slavery," *Irish News,* October 18, 1856.

64. Meagher to Smith O'Brien, March 6, 1857, MS 2945, NLI.

65. "The President and the Press," *Irish News,* March 28, 1857.

66. Meagher to Buchanan, January 28, 1857, Historical Society of Pennsylvania, quoted in Athearn, *Thomas Francis Meagher*, 62–66.

67. Athearn, *Thomas Francis Meagher*, 62–66.

68. Crowther, *The Romance and Rise of the American Tropics*, 101–28. The trouble lasted until the United States and Great Britain signed the Clayton-Bulwer Treaty, under which both countries agreed not to claim exclusive power over a future canal in Central America or gain exclusive control over any part of the region. The contract was signed on August 26, 1849.

69. Ibid.; Bancroft, *History of Central America,* 327–28, 328n6, 336.

70. Crowther, *The Romance and Rise of the American Tropics,* 101–28; Bancroft, *History of Central America,* 350, 353n27.

71. "Nicaragua," *Irish News,* May 10, 1856. Later in the Year Meagher expressed his thoughts on the future of his fellow Irish in Nicaragua:

> I break through the silence I have heretofore observed, and assert that I represent thousands upon thousands of Irishmen in America, and I and they are with the gallant fellows who thus might vindicate with steel and fire the supremacy of American laws, interests, enterprise, and manhood—and their political predominance on the Nicaraguan Isthmus—a predominance on which depends the commercial consequence and territorial inviolability of these United States. ("Letter from Thomas Francis Meagher," *Irish News*, December 27, 1856)

72. Keneally, *The Great Shame and the Triumph of the Irish,* 305.

73. Crowther, *The Romance and Rise of the American Tropics,* 127–28.

74. Port of New York Passenger Lists, for the bark *Ariel*, August 21, 1860, and for the steamship *Empire City,* June 28, 1858.

75. *Irish News,* March 13, 1858, quoted in Athearn, *Thomas Francis Meagher,* 70.

76. Graham, *José Antonio Páez,* 293; Athearn, *Thomas Francis Meagher,* 71.

77. Graham, *José Antonio Páez,* 280; Athearn, *Thomas Francis Meagher,* 71.

78. Port of New York Passenger Lists, for the ship *Persia,* June 23, 1858.

79. Hershkowitz, "The Irish and the Emerging City," 20–21.

80. "Irish Aid Society: New-York," *Irish News,* July 5, 1856.

81. Ibid. Meagher's fuller comments were as follows:

> One of the saddest misfortunes which happens to our countrymen on their arrival in America, is that of their being unable to get out of the city in which

they first set foot. It is perhaps, the most grievous misfortune which befals [*sic*] them, for, in many instances, it is the cause of every other evil which overtakes them. . . . Industry, ingenuity, daring—all bringing floods of health and heart, manly beauty and bright morality with them—will supply at a little cost out there what it takes days of aching drudgery to purchase on the seaboard.

82. Athearn, *Thomas Francis Meagher,* 75.

83. Bancroft, *History of Central America,* 592–94. The new colonization law was passed on April 23, 1858.

84. Athearn, *Thomas Francis Meagher,* 75. In the same letter he also expressed his gratitude to Mrs. Daly for somehow providing the means for him "to step into a new field of life, discernment, and exposition and for having made me independent of the capricious favors of Government." Professor Athearn believed, as I do, that Meagher's reference was to President Buchanan, who did not give Meagher the courtesy of a reply to his request for a diplomatic position in Central or South America.

85. Ibid., 85–87. Ambrose W. Thompson headed the Chiriqui Improvement Company, which owned land in Panama, and proposed to supply the U.S. government with coal mined there by colonized freedmen. The Lincoln administration at one time backed the plan and entered into a provisional contract with Thompson in September 1862, but it was never implemented. See also Ambrose W. Thompson to Abraham Lincoln, March 28, 1863; and Buel Conklin to Lincoln and Congress, December 1, 1863, Abraham Lincoln Papers, LoC.

86. Port of New York Passenger Lists, for the ship *Ariel,* January 25, 1861.

87. *Irish News,* May 10, 1856. The ad also read that the practice would include "conveyancing, [and] practice in all the courts of the state of New-York and of the United States, and general collecting business in all parts of the world. Particular attention will be given to the prosecution of claims against the United States in the Court of Claims."

88. "Topics of the Day," *Irish News,* February 7, 1857.

89. "Speech of T. F. Meagher, in Defense of Colonel Fabens, the Director-General of Emigration to Nicaragua, before the United States Commissioner," *Irish News,* February 28, 1857.

90. Athearn, *Thomas Francis Meagher,* 58–62.

91. Brandt, *The Congressman Who Got Away with Murder,* 23; Swanberg, *Sickles the Incredible,* 229–30. The case involved a claim to land in California, which gave Sickles a pecuniary interest in the matter.

92. Fontaine, *DeWitt's "Special Report,"* 42. After considerable argument between counsel and the court, extending into the ninth day of trial, the judge ruled the writing inadmissible as the declaration of a wife either for or against her husband.

93. Brandt, *The Congressman Who Got Away with Murder,* 153.

94. *Harper's Magazine,* April 16, 1859, and diary entry for May 26, 1859, both quoted in Brandt, *The Congressman Who Got Away with Murder,* 155, 237.

95. Fontaine, *DeWitt's "Special Report,"* 41, 99–100.

96. Ibid., 99–100.

97. Swanberg, *Sickles the Incredible,* 66, 223; Brandt, *The Congressman Who Got Away with Murder,* 184 (quotation).

98. Meagher to Smith O'Brien, March 6, 1857, MS 2945, NLI.

99. Ryan, *The Fenian Chief,* xxii–xxiii, 114.

100. Ibid., 53–54, quoted at 54*n*10.

101. *Weekly Freeman,* October 13, 1882, quoted in Kee, *The Bold Fenian Men,* 8; *Weekly Freeman,* November 3, 1883, quoted in ibid., 9.

102. Kee, *The Bold Fenian Men,* 12–13 (quotation on 12).

103. Ryan, *Fenian Chief,* 51; Comerford, *The Fenians in Context,* 47–48; Moody, *The Fenian Movement,* 17. Theoretically, each level would have nine captains, nine sergeants reporting to each captain, and nine privates reporting to each sergeant.

104. Ryan, *Fenian Chief,* 112.

105. Ibid.

106. Ibid., 102–103.

107. Ibid., 110–12, 117 (quotations on 110 and 117).

108. Ibid., 114–15.

109. Ibid., 115; Costigan, *History of Modern Ireland,* 129–32.

110. Ryan, *Fenian Chief,* 119–20. McGee would deliver an anti-Fenian lecture in Canada in 1865. He was assassinated in 1868, three months after Lord Mayo had praised his advocacy of British rule.

111. Ibid., 121–22.

112. Ibid., 126–27.

113. Ibid., 127, 131–32. The letters were written to Judge O'Connor, Judge Robert Emmet, Richard O'Gorman, Horace Greeley, and Meagher.

114. Ibid., 154–55. John O'Leary, who was with Stephens on the trip, would later rebuke Meagher for his weakness of will in withdrawing, blaming Meagher's action on afterthoughts when he learned that Mitchel did not support the Fenian scheme. Stephens left the United States with nothing good to say about the Young Irelanders, and he would imbue this attitude in the Fenian organization. O'Leary, *Recollections of Fenians and Fenianism,* vol. 1, 95–96.

115. Ryan, *Fenian Chief,* 156; D'Arcy, *The Fenian Movement in the United States,* 26.

116. Comerford, *The Fenians in Context,* 51; D'Arcy, *The Fenian Movement in the United States, 1858–1886,* 12.

117. D'Arcy, *The Fenian Movement in the United States,* 13, 13–14*n*35.

118. Cavanagh, *Memoirs,* 489.

119. Ibid., 364–66, 417–25.

120. Rafferty, *The Church, the State, and the Fenian Threat, 1861–75,* 25–31; O'Sullivan, *The Young Irelanders,* 208–209; O'Leary, *Recollections of Fenians and Fenianism,* vol. 1, 164.

121. Athearn, *Thomas Francis Meagher,* 90–91.

CHAPTER 5

1. Cavanagh, *Memoirs,* 367–69.

2. In an April 7, 1847, speech, for example, Meagher said:

I think that, in a free state, an aristocracy is a wise—an ennobling institution. . . . It is the graceful and pictured architrave of the great temple, sacred to law and freedom, of which the people are the enduring foundations and the sustaining pillars. Whilst the peasant tills the land, . . . let the noble—residing amongst those who enrich his inheritance by their toil . . . be the patron of those pursuits in which the purer genius of a nation lives—pursuits which chasten and expand a nation's soul. (Griffith, *Meagher of the Sword,* 89)

3. *Irish News,* October 18, 1856, as cited in Athearn, *Thomas Francis Meagher,* 55.

4. Cavanagh, *Memoirs,* 368.

5. Rice, *American Catholic Opinion in the Slavery Controversy,* 122–23.

6. Lane, "Colonel Michael Corcoran, Fighting Irishman," 13–19; Cavanagh, *Memoirs,* 370.

7. Jones, *The Irish Brigade,* 16–18. According to Jones, the regiment grew to an amazing sixty-five hundred volunteers, as reported by the *New York Tribune.*

8. Cavanagh, *Memoirs,* 362.

9. *Irish American,* April 20, 1861, quoted in Jones, *The Irish Brigade,* 53–54.

10. Cavanagh, *Memoirs,* 369. Michael Cavanagh was later a biographer of Meagher.

11. Jones, *The Irish Brigade,* 18.

12. Ibid., 35, as the advertisement appeared in the *New-York Daily Tribune,* April 23, 1861.

13. Wright, *The Irish Brigade,* 2. See also Pritchard, *The Irish Brigade,* 25–26.

14. Villard, *Memoirs of Henry Villard,* 173–75. Villard said that it was his duty to look up the Irish units, but that he "performed it reluctantly and as rarely as possible."

15. Ibid., 183–84.

16. Cavanagh, *Memoirs,* 378–79.

17. Quoted in Jones, *The Irish Brigade,* 16–17.

18. McPherson, *Battle Cry of Freedom,* 333.

19. Corcoran to Daly, July 8, 1861, Charles P. Daly Papers, NYPL. Daly knew Meagher, and it is likely that he would have recognized his hand.

20. Lane, "Colonel Michael Corcoran, Fighting Irishman," 21–23.

21. Sherman, *Memoirs,* ix–x, 13, 166. The 29th New York did not proceed into battle, being left behind in charge of the forts and camps.

22. "Report of Kelly," July 24, 1861, in *OR,* series 1, vol. 2, 371–72.

23. Bilby, *The Irish Brigade in the Civil War,* 11.

24. "Report of Kelly," July 24, 1861, in *OR,* series 1, vol. 2, 371–72.

25. Ibid.; "The 69th in Virginia: Incidents of the Campaign," *Irish American,* August 17, 1861 (quotation); Burton, *Melting Pot Soldiers,* 115.

26. "Report of Kelly," July 24, 1861, in *OR,* series 1, vol. 2, 372.

27. Wright, *The Irish Brigade,* 1, quoting a letter published in the *New York Leader.*

28. Thomas Francis Meagher, "The Last Days of the 69th in Virginia: A Narrative in Three Parts: Part the Third," *Irish American,* August 17, 1861.

29. Hammond, *Diary of a Union Lady,* 40; Bilby, *The Irish Brigade in the Civil War,* 15–17; Costigan, *History of Modern Ireland,* 108. Almost one hundred years later a leading Irish revolutionary, Thomas Davis, commemorated the victory of the Irish Brigade at Fontenoy with a poem: "On Fontenoy, on Fontenoy, hark to that fierce huzzah, Revenge! remember Limerick! dash down the Sasanach!" The term "Sasanach" or "Sasanech" was sometimes used by the Irish and Scots to refer to the English or Saxons.

30. Hammond, *Diary of a Union Lady,* 41.

31. *New-York Daily Tribune,* July 25, 1861, cited by Athearn, *Thomas Francis Meagher,* 97. Russell's own diary entry of August 3, 1861, seems to indicate that he had some responsibility for the *Tribune* article, although he later acknowledged that the *Tribune* had quoted something like that and that he might get in trouble for it. Russell's diary entry for August 26 says: "Wrote to the Tribune in reference to the 69th and T. F. Meagher"; and the entry on November 22 says: "It appears that Meagher expresses very friendly feelings towards me . . . I have been looking thro' my mind & find I like Meagher personally." Whatever Russell said or did not

say, he was generally blamed for reporting the Civil War in favor of the South, which earned him the name of "Bull Run Russell." Crawford, *William Howard Russell's Civil War,* 98, 111, 183; Hammond, *Diary of a Union Lady,* 63n108.

32. O'Reilly to Daly, September 4, 1861, Charles P. Daly Papers, NYPL; see also Hammond, *Diary of a Union Lady,* 63, for Maria Daly's comments on the letter.

33. Perry, *A Bohemian Brigade,* 39. The reporter was Edmund Clarence Stedman of the *New York World,* who watched the battle from a nearby hill.

34. Sherman, *Memoirs,* 168–74.

35. Ibid., 166–67.

36. Ibid., 174–75.

37. Ibid.

38. Ibid., 175–76. Lincoln's correspondence does not contain notes of the incident; nor does the report of his remarks that appeared in the *New York Herald* on July 24. As the *Herald* would report, Lincoln and Seward visited Camp Corcoran, where they were received with enthusiasm by the 69th. When asked if they intended to reenlist, the reply was "they would if the President desired it." Basler, ed., *The Collected Works of Abraham Lincoln,* vol. 4, 458.

39. Meagher, "The Last Days of the 69th in Virginia: A Narrative in Two Parts," *Irish American,* August 31, 1861.

40. "Meagher to Cameron," September 7, 1861, in *OR,* series 3, vol. 1, 491; "Cameron to Meagher," September 7, 1861, in ibid.; "Morgan to Cameron," September 10, 1861, in ibid., 497.

41. "Curtin to Cameron," September 18, 1861, in *OR,* series 3, vol. 1, 526–27.

42. "Hayes to Davis," January 6, 1864, in *OR,* series 4, vol. 3, 4–6. At the time this letter was written, Hayes was at the Register's Office, Richmond House, Richmond, Virginia.

43. Shaw, *Dagger John,* 344.

44. Hammond, *Diary of a Union Lady,* 64.

45. Ibid., xxxii–xxxiv. In 1872 Daly took on William M. "Boss" Tweed and Tammany Hall during the impeachment trial of Mayor Abraham Oakey Hall. During his career Daly amassed an almost endless list of achievements and public acclaim. In his civic duties he welcomed dignitaries, dedicated monuments, presided over public meetings, and led movements for public reform. He also supported the cause of Jews, authored the *History of Jews in North America,* and helped found the Jewish Orphan's Home in New York City.

46. Athearn, *Thomas Francis Meagher,* 75. The Dalys were longtime supporters of an all-Irish Brigade and of Michael Corcoran, who they thought should be its leader. So supportive was Judge Daly of the efforts of Corcoran and the Irish that he armed himself with a revolver and followed Corcoran's regiment to Camp Seward in Arlington Heights during the first battle of Bull Run and helped to guard the ramparts when there was a threat of attack. Hammond, *Diary of a Union Lady,* xv–xvi.

47. Hammond, *Diary of a Union Lady,* 41, 63–64, 68–69, 75, 101.

48. Spann, "Union Green," 198–99.

49. Basler, *The Collected Works of Abraham Lincoln,* vol. 4, 418. James W. Denver was a breveted major general in the Mexican War, who had served under President Buchanan as governor of Kansas and commissioner of Indian Affairs; Milton S. Latham was a senator from California. Michael Corcoran was recommended by Roman Catholic archbishop John Hughes and was appointed brigadier general of volunteers.

50. Shields had come to the United States from Ireland at an early age and, after studying law, became an Illinois legislator in 1836 and an Illinois Supreme Court judge in 1843. He served in the Mexican War, where he became a major general and survived a serious

wound. Afterward he was appointed governor of the Oregon Territory and was elected United States senator from the state of Minnesota and then from Illinois. Leaving the Senate, he had pursued mining ventures in Mexico and was there when the Civil War started. Finally, on August 19, 1861, he was made a brigadier general of Union volunteers and led his brigade into battle at Winchester and the Shenandoah Valley; he was defeated at Port Republic in June 1862. Disappointed, he resigned his commission in 1863 and proceeded to California as a civilian, where he pursued a minor political career until he died there. Hammond, *Diary of a Union Lady*, xxvii–xxviii.

51. Lyons, *Brigadier-General Thomas Francis Meagher*, 126.

52. Conyngham, *The Irish Brigade and Its Campaigns*, 49.

53. "Thomas F. Meagher, January 1862 (Recommendation)." The document is designated "January 1862"; because of the reference to the coming new year as a proximate event, however, it was likely submitted to Lincoln in the latter part of 1861, before he authorized Cameron to appoint Meagher a brigadier general.

54. Ibid.

55. Ibid.

56. Shaw, *Dagger John*, 346–47, 390, citing an unpublished letter to Dublin's *Freeman's Journal*, December 1, 1861.

57. Shaw, *Dagger John*, 351–53.

58. Basler, *The Collected Works of Abraham Lincoln*, vol. 5, 76.

59. Ibid. The appointees included Joseph McCoy of the Fifth Cavalry for Meagher's assistant adjutant general and Dr. Francis Reynolds as his brigade surgeon. McCoy was credited with saving Meagher's life at the Battle of Bull Run. Dr. Reynolds was an Irish physician and a fellow of the Royal College of Surgeons in Dublin and had served with the Irish Brigade recruited in Ireland for the Crimean War. Ibid., 79. On November 16, 1861, Lincoln had honored Meagher and the Irish Brigade's requests when he ordered Simon Cameron to appoint W. W. Leland as brigade commissary. Ibid., 25.

60. "Thomas to Meagher," February 18, 1862, in *OR*, series 3, vol. 122, 895.

CHAPTER 6

1. "Our Camps in Virginia: How St. Patrick's Day Was Spent in Them: The Irish Brigade," *Irish American*, April 11, 1863.

2. Corby, *Memoirs of Chaplain Life*, 29.

3. Ibid., 28–29.

4. Ibid., 21–23. Camp California was named in honor of the Division Commander, Major General Edwin Sumner, recently in command of regular troops in California.

5. Bilby, *The Irish Brigade in the Civil War*, 33.

6. Meagher to Barlow, March 4, 1862, HL.

7. Bilby, *The Irish Brigade in the Civil War*, 33; Corby, *Memoirs of Chaplain Life*, 31; Hammond, *Diary of a Union Lady*, 187–88.

8. Beller, *Never Were Men So Brave*, 32.

9. Eicher, *The Longest Night*, 268–79.

10. Conyngham, *The Irish Brigade and Its Campaigns*, 144–51. The Battle of Fair Oaks is also referred to as the Battle of Seven Pines. The two locations are within about a mile of each other. The Union Army generally called it the Battle of Fair Oaks. See McPherson, *Battle Cry of Freedom*, 461–62, 465 (map).

11. "Report of Meagher," June 4, 1862, in *OR,* series 1, vol. 11, pt. 1, 775–76.

12. Conyngham, *The Irish Brigade and Its Campaigns,* 149–51; "Report of Meagher," June 4, 1862, in *OR,* series 1, vol. 11, pt. 1, 778–79.

13. "Report of Meagher," 776.

14. Corby, *Memoirs of Chaplain Life,* 62–63.

15. "Report of Meagher," June 4, 1862, in *OR,* series 1, vol. 11, pt. 1, 777–78.

16. Conyngham, *The Irish Brigade and Its Campaigns,* 154. David Power Conyngham was attached to the Irish Brigade after the Battle of Fredericksburg for a short time and was an aide in General Meagher's staff during the Battle of Chancellorsville. Ibid., xix–xx. Conyngham signed a letter written to Meagher on May 20, 1863, along with the other officers of the brigade, as "D. P. Conyngham, Captain, Acting Aide-de-Camp." Ibid., 408–409.

17. "Report of Richardson," June 6, 1862, in *OR,* series 1, vol. 11, pt. 1, 766.

18. Darby to "Miss E. Marie," June 25, 1862, Darby Papers, VHS.

19. "Report of Meagher," June 4, 1862, in *OR,* series 1, vol. 11, pt. 1, 778–79.

20. Conyngham, *The Irish Brigade and Its Campaigns,* 158.

21. "Report of Meagher," June 4, 1862, in *OR,* series 1, vol. 11, pt. 1, 779.

22. Meagher to Notch, June 21, 1862, Schoff Civil War Collection, Letters and Documents, William L. Clements Library, UMI.

23. See Currier and Ives, *Genl. Meagher at the Battle Of Fair Oaks VA, June 1st, 1862* (lithograph).

24. George W. Barr to Vinnie Barr, June 7, 1862, George W. Barr Papers, Schoff Civil War Collection, Soldiers' Letters 32:49, William L. Clements Library, UMI.

25. Samito, *Commanding Boston's Irish Ninth,* 191–92n44; Bilby, *The Irish Brigade in the Civil War,* 205.

26. Darby to Connelly, January 4, 1863, Thomas Darby Papers, VHS.

27. "Report of Meagher," July 6, 1862, in *OR,* series 1, vol. 11, pt. 2, 70.

28. Ibid. Meagher reported that the crossing of the Chickahominy was made on "Woodbury's (or Alexander's) Bridge."

29. "Report of McClellan," August 4, 1863, in *OR,* series 1, vol. 11, pt. 1, 56–57.

30. Ibid. Not everyone agreed with McClellan's report. In February 1864 Brigadier General Philip St. George Cooke of the Fifth Cavalry, whose charge General Porter and General McClellan said was unsuccessful, complained that their reports were false and that French's brigade had been fired into by "a battery belong[ing] to or with said brigade." Cooke to Adjutant-General, February 6, 1864, in *OR,* series 1, vol. 11, pt. 2, 43.

31. "Report of Hill," July 3, 1863 [*sic:* should be 1862], in *OR,* series 1, vol. 11, pt. 2, 626.

32. "Report of McClellan," August 4, 1863, in *OR,* series 1, vol. 11, pt. 1, 57; "Report of Meagher," July 6, 1862, in *OR,* series 1, vol. 11, pt. 2, 70–71.

33. "Report of French," July 5, 1862, in *OR,* series 1, vol. 11, pt. 2, 75–76.

34. "Report of McClellan," August 4, 1863, in *OR,* series 1, vol. 11, pt. 1, 57; "Report of Meagher," July 6, 1862, in *OR,* series 1, vol. 11, pt. 2, 70–71; "Report of French," July 5, 1862, in *OR,* series 1, vol. 11, pt. 2, 75–76 (quotation).

35. Meagher to Turner, August 10, 1863, Turner Papers, NYSL.

36. Heintzelman to McClellan, June 29, 1862, McClellan Papers, LoC.

37. "Report of Meagher," July 6, 1862, in *OR,* series 1, vol. 11, pt. 2, 71. Command of the Irish Brigade was taken over by Colonel Nugent of the 88th while Meagher was under arrest.

38. Burton, *Extraordinary Circumstances,* 215–16. I am indebted to Professor Burton for supplying important information on Meagher's arrest.

39. "Report of Meagher," July 6, 1862, in *OR,* series 1, vol. 11, pt. 2, 71; Cavanagh, *Memoirs,* 449–50.

40. "Report of Sumner," July 4, 1862, in *OR,* series 1, vol. 11, pt. 2, 49–51; "Report of Richardson," July 6, 1862, in *OR,* series 1, vol. 11, pt. 2, 55.

41. "Report of Richardson," July 6, 1862, in *OR,* series 1, vol. 11, pt. 2, 55.

42. "Report of King," July 6, 1862, in *OR,* series 1, vol. 11, pt. 2, 57–60; Bilby, *The Irish Brigade in the Civil War,* 42–43.

43. "Report of Meagher," July 2, 1862, in *OR,* series 1, vol. 11, pt. 2, 72.

44. Cavanagh, *Memoirs,* 450–51.

45. "Report of Meagher," July 2, 1862, in *OR,* series 1, vol. 11, pt. 2, 73–74.

46. Ibid., 74; Corby, *Memoirs of Chaplain Life,* 287–90.

47. "Report of Meagher," July 6, 1862, in *OR,* series 1, vol. 11, pt. 2, 70–72.

48. Fox, *Regimental Losses in the American Civil War,* 204.

49. "Special Orders, No. 205," July 16, 1862, in *OR,* series 1, vol. 11, 325. Orders signed on July 16, 1862, from Camp near Harrison's Landing, Virginia, by Assistant Adjutant-General S. Williams.

50. Jones, *The Irish Brigade,* 127–36.

51. Conyngham, *The Irish Brigade and Its Campaigns,* 278.

52. "McClellan to Halleck," August 29, 1862, in *OR,* series 1, vol. 11, pt. 1, 97–98; "McClellan to Halleck," ALS (telegram sent), Records of the Office of the Secretary of War, RG 107 (M-504:65), NA, as cited in Sears, *The Civil War Papers of George B. McClellan,* 415.

53. Conyngham, *The Irish Brigade and Its Campaigns,* 276–85; "Biggs to Burnside," August 27, 1862, in *OR,* series 1, vol. 12, pt. 3, 701.

54. "General T. F. Meagher," *Irish American,* August 2, 1862; "The Irish Brigade: General Meagher's Reception in New York," *Irish American,* August 9, 1862 (quotations).

55. "McClellan to Barlow," July 30, 1862, ALS, Barlow Papers, HL, as cited in Sears, *The Civil War Papers of George B. McClellan,* 376–77.

56. Meagher to Abraham Lincoln, July 30, 1862, Abraham Lincoln Papers, LoC. Despite Meagher's urging, Shields would not be renominated.

57. Jones, *The Irish Brigade,* 132–34; Burton, *Melting Pot Soldiers,* 55.

58. "The Irish Brigade," *Irish American,* August 23, 1862.

59. "Report of Halleck," November 25, 1862, in *OR,* series 1, vol. 19, pt. 1, 4–7.

60. "Report of Meagher," September 30, 1862, in *OR,* series 1, vol. 19, pt. 2, 293.

61. Ibid.

62. James J. Smith to J. C. Sterns and Gen. H. Heth, April 10, 1893, typescript copy, 69th New York Volunteer Infantry Regiment File and "Carman Union" II Corps, 1 Div., 2 Brig., Meagher File, ANBA.

63. "Report of Meagher," September 30, 1862, in *OR,* series 1, vol. 19, pt. 1, 293.

64. Ibid., 293–94.

65. Leander M. Vaughan, "History of My Life during the Civil War," typed notebook (copy), marked "Dec = 1917," 29th Mass. VIR 15th–35th File, ANBA. Vaughan, who spells "Antietam" as "Antidum," seemingly misstates several facts, including his statements that the battle lasted for three days and that the Irish Brigade defended the right flank, rather than the left.

66. "Report of Meagher," September 30, 1862, in *OR*, series 1, vol. 19, pt. 1, 293–94.

67. Ibid., 294.

68. Robbins to anonymous, September 21, 1862, typescript copy, Mass. 29th Volunteer Infantry Regiment File, ANBA.

69. Dillon to "Sir," n.d., typescript copy, 63rd N.Y. Volunteer Infantry Regiment File, ANBA.

70. "Report of Meagher," September 30, 1862, in *OR*, series 1, vol. 19, pt. 1, 294–95.

71. Ibid.; Eby, *A Virginia Yankee in the Civil War*, 109–11.

72. Eby, *A Virginia Yankee in the Civil War*, 113; Burton, *Melting Pot Soldiers*, 123. Most notably, when Strother worked from his diary several years later to produce a series of articles, he devoted nineteen pages to describing the battle of Antietam, without mentioning Meagher or his Irish Brigade. Strother, "Personal Recollections of the War by a Virginian," 273–91.

73. "Report of Hancock," September 29, 1862, in *OR*, series 1, vol. 19, pt. 1, 279; "Report of McClellan," October 15, 1862, in *OR*, series 1, vol. 19, pt. 1, 58–59.

74. "Report of Sumner," October 1, 1862, in *OR*, series 1, vol. 19, pt. 1, 276.

75. Andrews, *The North Reports the Civil War*, 284; Smart, ed., *A Radical View*, vol. 1, 229. Reid was a good journalist, but his career had already included a vicious and unfounded attack on William Tecumseh Sherman, following the lead of others in the profession who had accused Sherman of being insane. Reid reported from his personal observations that Sherman "was the victim of hallucinations and appears clearly to have been gradually sinking into his present mournful condition" and further that Sherman was "either a self absorbed military enthusiast or a monomaniac." Perry, *A Bohemian Brigade*, 118–19.

76. Hitchcock, *War from the Inside*, 63–64.

77. T. C. Grey to S. H. Gay, June 2, 1863, Sydney Howard Gay Collection, CUL.

78. See Murfin, *The Gleam of Bayonets*, 255; and Priest, *Antietam*, 206.

79. William McCarter, "My Life in the Army," December 1875, vol. 4, 43–46, HSP; O'Brien, ed., *My Life in the Irish Brigade*, 16, 69–71. McCarter was an able writer and had joined Meagher's staff.

80. Hitchcock, *War from the Inside*, 228; Sears, *Chancellorsville*, 504–505; Smith, *Ulysses S. Grant*, 83–89, 172–73.

81. Hedrick and Davis, eds. and comps., *I'm Surrounded by Methodists*, 14–16, 57.

82. Bilby, *The Irish Brigade in the Civil War*, 60.

83. Pryor, *Reminiscences of Peace and War*, 194–95.

84. "Report of Hancock," September 29, 1862, in *OR*, series 1, vol. 19, pt. 1, 277–80. While there is no record on the Confederate side of any encounter between Meagher and Pryor, it was recorded that Pryor ventured beyond Union lines at the Battle of Manassas and was detained for a while until he escaped. See "Report of Pryor," October 5, 1862, in *OR*, series 1, vol. 12, pt. 2, 601–602; "Pryor to Beauregard," December 4, 1962, in *OR*, series 1, vol. 18, 790.

85. Alfred R. Waud, drawing, LoC, reproduced in Ronald H. Bailey, *The Bloodiest Day: The Battle of Antietam* (Alexandria, Va.: Time-Life Books, 1984), 152.

86. Conyngham, *The Irish Brigade and Its Campaigns*, 316–19; Corby, *Memoirs of Chaplain Life*, 118.

87. Meagher, General Order No. 9 and General Orders No. 1 and 3, November 9, 1862, Barlow File, HL.

88. Corby, *Memoirs of Chaplain Life*, 128–30.

89. Ibid., 130–32.

90. Stacy to "Father," December 22, 1862, Stacy Files, VHS.

91. "Report of Meagher," December 20, 1862, in *OR,* series 1, vol. 21, 240.

92. O'Brien, *My Life in the Irish Brigade,* 154–56.

93. Ibid., 161, 163–64.

94. Ibid., 163–67.

95. "Report of Meagher," December 20, 1862, in *OR,* series 1, vol. 21, 241.

96. McCarter, "My Life in the Army," December 1875, vol. 9, 24, HSP; O'Brien, *My Life in the Irish Brigade,* 171–72.

97. McCarter, "My Life in the Army," December 1875, vol. 9, 25, 34–35, HSP.

98. Ibid., 33, 36.

99. Swinton, *Army of the Potomac,* 250–51; Corby, *Memoirs of Chaplain Life,* 132.

100. "Report of Meagher," December 20, 1862, in *OR,* series 1, vol. 21, 241–42.

101. "Kelly to Hart," December 20, 1862, in *OR,* series 1, vol. 21, 251–52.

102. "Report of Condon," December 24, 1862, in *OR,* series 1, vol. 21, 250.

103. Bilby, *The Irish Brigade in the Civil War,* 66–67.

104. O'Reilly, *The Fredericksburg Campaign,* 315–16; Kohl and Cosse Richard, eds., *Irish Green and Union Blue,* 42–43.

105. "Kelly to Hart," December 20, 1862, in *OR,* series 1, vol. 21, 252.

106. McCarter, "My Life in the Army," vol. 9, 38–40, HSP.

107. Bilby, *The Irish Brigade in the Civil War,* 66; "Report of Hancock," December 25, 1862, in *OR,* series 1, vol. 21, 228–29.

108. "Report of Hancock," December 25, 1862, in *OR,* series 1, vol. 21, 228; "Report of Meagher," December 20, 1862, in *OR,* series 1, vol. 21, 242–43.

109. "Report of Meagher," December 20, 1862, in *OR,* series 1, vol. 21, 242–43.

110. Ibid.; "Report of Hancock," December 25, 1862, in *OR,* series 1, vol. 21, 228.

111. "Report of Hancock," December 25, 1862, in *OR,* series 1, vol. 21, 228; "Report of Meagher," December 20, 1862, in *OR,* series 1, vol. 21, 242–43.

112. Moore, *The Rebellion Record,* "London 'Times' Narrative: Headquarters of General Lee, near Fredericksburg, December 12, 1862," doc. 25, 107, 111.

113. Stager to Stanton, December 13, 1862, Abraham Lincoln Papers, LoC, http://memory.loc.gov/cgi-bin/query/r?ammam/mal:@field(DOCID+@lit(d2016900)) (accessed December 26, 2005). Stager was the general superintendent of the Western Union Telegraph Company.

114. Cavanagh, *Memoirs,* 471–73.

115. Ibid., 473, 477, 478*n.*

116. Mulholland, *The Story of the 116th Regiment, Pennsylvania Volunteers, in the War of the Rebellion,* 60–61.

117. Cavanagh, *Memoirs,* 467*n,* quoting letter from Thomas to Elizabeth Meagher, December 17, 1862.

118. Barlow to Meagher, December 18, 1862, Barlow Papers, HL.

119. Cavanagh, *Memoirs,* 473–74.

CHAPTER 7

1. Basler, *The Collected Works of Abraham Lincoln,* vol. 6, 101. Patrick Kelly was killed in action on June 16, 1864, still a colonel. Robert Nugent was finally breveted a brigadier general on March 13, 1865, as the war was ending. See Dyer, *A Compendium of the War of the Rebellion,* pt. 1, 288.

2. Medical Certificate, (signed) F. Reynolds, December 15, 1862; and, Medical Certificate, signed Wm. F. Edgar, January 11, 1863; and, "Form of a Medical Certificate (Form 20)," signed Wm. F. Edgar, February 3, 1863, Thomas Francis Meagher, M-1064 Roll #187, Letters Received by the Commission Branch of the Adjutant General's Office, 1865, NARA.

3. Meagher to "Adjutant General," February 3, 1863, with attachment "Form of a Medical Certificate (Form 20)," signed by Wm. F. Edgar, February 3, 1863, Thomas Francis Meagher, M-1064 Roll #187, Letters Received by the Commission Branch of the Adjutant General's Office, 1865, NARA.

4. Meagher to Stanton, February 19, 1863, quoted in Cavanagh, *Memoirs,* app. 23–26.

5. Cavanagh, *Memoirs,* 477.

6. "Application for leave of absence for the purpose of visiting Wash'n to facilitate the removal of his Brigade from the Army of the Potomac," and Meagher to the Assistant Adjutant-General, Hancock's Division, February 26, 1863, Thomas Francis Meagher, M-1064 Roll #187, Letters Received by the Commission Branch of the Adjutant General's Office, 1865, NARA.

7. "By command of Major Genl. Hooker, S. Williams, Asst. Adjt. Genl., March 2d, 1865" (notation on file), M-1064 Roll #187, Letters received by the Commission Branch of the Adjutant General's Office, 1865, NARA.

8. Corby, *Memoirs of Chaplain Life,* 140–41.

9. Conyngham, *The Irish Brigade and Its Campaigns,* 380–81.

10. Athearn, *Thomas Francis Meagher,* 124–25.

11. "Meagher to Hancock," April 28, 1863, in *OR,* series 1, vol. 25, pt. 1, 326–27; Cavanagh, *Memoirs,* 482.

12. "Meagher to Hancock," April 28, 1863, in *OR,* series 1, vol. 25, pt. 1, 326–27.

13. Ibid.; Cavanagh, *Memoirs,* 482.

14. "Couch to Williams," May 9, 1863, in *OR,* series 1, vol. 25, pt. 1, 305–306.

15. "Hancock to Potter," May 19, 1863, in *OR,* series 1, vol. 25, pt. 1, 311–12.

16. Ibid. Colonel Orlando H. Morris, commander of the 66th New York, was on the battlefield from "about daylight" of May 2. "About 10 a.m. of the same day, this command was detached to take up position on the Fredericksburg road and throw up intrenchments [*sic*], connecting the line of works on the left of the Chancellor house, having the Eighty-eighth New York on our right," reported Morris. "Our position here was protected in front by a slight skirting of woods, and intended to secure a flank fire upon the enemy in case of an attack." "Morris to Faville," May 8, 1863, in *OR,* series 1, vol. 25, pt. 1, 331.

17. Mulholland, *The Story of the 116th Regiment,* 93–96; on the retreat of Howard's Eleventh Corps, see Sears, *Chancellorsville,* 272–81.

18. Mulholland, *The Story of the 116th Regiment,* 96–97.

19. "Hancock to Potter," May 19, 1863, in *OR,* series 1, vol. 25, pt. 1, 312–16.

20. "Pettit to Wainwright," May 8, 1863, in *OR,* series 1, vol. 25, pt. 1, 349.

21. "Mulholland to Wall," May 4, 1863, in *OR,* series 1, vol. 25, pt. 1, 328.

22. "Whiteford to Wall," May 3, 1863, in *OR,* series 1, vol. 25, pt. 1, 327.

23. Letters reproduced in Mulholland, *The Story of the 116th Regiment,* 106–107.

24. "Ellis to Franklin," May 7, 1983, in *OR,* series 1, vol. 25, pt. 1, 497.

25. Frank Henry to Abraham Lincoln, May 3, 1863, Abraham Lincoln Papers, LoC, http://memory.loc.gov/cgi-bin/query/r?ammem/mal:@field(DOCID+@lit(d2328900)) (accessed December 26, 2005).

26. Mulholland, *The Story of the 116th Regiment,* 102.

27. Kohl and Cosse Richard, *Irish Green and Union Blue,* 90–91, letter of May 7, 1863, to "My dear wife."

28. "Hancock to Potter," May 19, 1863, in *OR,* series 1, vol. 25, pt. 1, 315.

29. Addenda, in ibid., 316.

30. Cavanagh, *Memoirs,* app., 26–27.

31. T. C. Grey to S. H. Gay, June 2, 1863, Sydney Howard Gay Collection, CUL. Grey's letter also accused Meagher of having been carried off the field drunk at Antietam.

32. Cavanagh, *Memoirs,* 485–86.

33. "The Irish Brigade," *Irish American,* June 6, 1863.

34. Corby, *Memoirs of Chaplain Life,* 132.

35. "The Irish Brigade," *Irish American,* June 6, 1863.

36. Ibid.; "General T. F. Meagher," *Irish American,* June 13, 1863.

37. "The Irish Brigade," *Irish American,* June 6, 1863.

38. Meagher to Edwin M. Stanton, July 13, 1863, Thomas Francis Meagher, M-1064 Roll #187, Letters Received by the Commission Branch of the Adjutant General's Office, 1865, NARA.

39. "Lincoln to Meagher," June 16, 1863, in *OR,* series 3, vol. 3, 372.

40. "General Meagher and 'The Irish Brigade,'" *Irish American,* June 20, 1863; "Honors to General Meagher," *Irish American,* June 27, 1863.

41. "General Meagher and 'The Irish Brigade,'" *Irish American,* June 20, 1863; "Honors to General Meagher," *Irish American,* June 27, 1863.

42. Davis, *Don't Know Much about the Civil War,* 311–15. This amount was less than an average yearly wage of about $500 in those days. The effect of the law was to allow the wealthy to sit out the war.

43. John Hughes, *Complete Works of the Most Rev. John Hughes, D.D.,* ed. Lawrence Kehoe (New York: Catholic Publication House, 1864), vol. 2, 373, quoted in Shaw, *Dagger John,* 359.

44. "T. F. Meagher Literary Union," *Irish American,* July 4, 1863.

45. "General Meagher's Irish Brigade," *Irish American,* July 11, 1863.

46. Bernstein, *The New York City Draft Riots,* 18–26.

47. Ibid., 27–30; Burns and Sanders, *New York,* 122–24.

48. "Fry to Seymour," April 24, 1863, in *OR,* series 3, vol. 3, 166; "Colonel Robert Nugent," *Irish American,* May 9, 1863; *New York Herald,* July 18, 1863, quoted in Shaw, *Dagger John,* 365; Bernstein, *The New York City Draft Riots,* 39–40; "Nugent to Fry," July 15, 1863, in *OR,* series 1, vol. 27, pt. 2, 898–99. Nugent also reported that the object seemed to be to plunder rather than any real opposition to the draft.

49. Bernstein, *The New York City Draft Riots,* 52–53; "Nugent to Fry," July 18, 1863, in *OR,* series 1, vol. 44, 903–904.

50. *Irish American,* July 25, 1863.

51. McPherson, *Battle Cry of Freedom,* 591–92; Pepper, "Personal Recollections of General Thomas Francis Meagher," 536, quoting Meagher's letters to Pepper of August 11, 1863, and September 8, 1863. Meagher asked to be compensated for the trip, saying that in truth he could not dispense with it and lamenting that he wished he could do as he did in Ireland, where he "serve[d] the public interests without a cent of compensation." He also requested a formal invitation from the committee "so as to justify my visit, or at all events to divest it of an intrusive character."

52. "Letter of General Meagher to the 'Union Committee' of Ohio," *Irish American,* October 3, 1863. Meagher also denounced the "mutilation of the harmless and helpless negroes

of New York." A copy of the letter, dated September 23, 1863, as it appeared in *The Voice of the War Democracy* under the title "Patriotic Letters of Gen. John A. Dix and Gen. Thomas Francis Meagher," is available from the Western Reserve Historical Center, Cleveland, Ohio.

53. "General Meagher and the Ohio Election," *Irish American,* October 3, 1863. The paper pointed out that the *Tribune* was the first paper to "seize and propagate the lying accusation" that Meagher had been "recreant" at the first Battle of Bull Run, that the *New York Times* had attempted to show that the Irish Brigade had not shared in the victory at Gaines's Mill, and that the *Tribune* had only recently published the letter from General French in "vindication of the share the Irish Brigade had in the battle," which had been written a year earlier.

54. "So-Called 'Federal Enlistments' in Ireland," *Irish American,* May 16, 1863; "The Alleged Federal Enlistment in Ireland," *Irish American,* June 13, 1863.

55. "Benjamin to Mason," April 29, 1863, in *OR (Navies),* series 2, vol. 3, 753–74; "Mason to Benjamin," June 4, 1863, in ibid., 782–83; "Benjamin to Capston," July 3, 1863, in ibid., 828–29.

56. "Benjamin to Bannon," September 4, 1863, in ibid., 893–95; "Mann to Benjamin," November 14, 1863, in ibid., 952–55. Mann was accompanied by his private secretary, W. Grayson Mann.

57. Letter from Meagher to Charles F Donnelly, Esq., Boston, *Irish American,* September 26, 1863; "Our Correspondence from the Irish Brigade," *Irish American,* October 10, 1863 (quotations).

58. Sears, *George B. McClellan,* 371.

59. "Some Letters of General T. F. Meagher," 83–84, letter from Meagher to James R. O'Beirne, March 25, 1863.

60. Ibid., 84–85, letter from Meagher to James R. O'Beirne, October 9, 1863.

61. Ibid.

62. Meagher to James Turner, August 10, 1963, Turner Papers, NYSL.

63. Samito, *Commanding Boston's Irish Ninth,* xxx–xxxii; "General T. F. Meagher Once More," *Irish American,* October 15, 1864.

64. Samito, *Commanding Boston's Irish Ninth,* 225–28.

65. See Meagher, *Letters on Our National Struggle.*

66. Ibid., 6–15.

67. Ibid., 1–5.

68. Ibid., 6.

69. Meagher to Seward, October 5, 1863, Thomas Francis Meagher, M-1064 Roll #187, Letters Received by the Commission Branch of the Adjutant General's Office, 1865, NARA.

70. "Letter from Charles Graham Halpine to General George Cullum (November 26, 1863)," in *The Lincoln Log.* Halpine said that General Halleck was also at the meeting, although the log of Lincoln's visits that day does not mention Halleck.

71. "Thomas F Meagher" abstract, n.d. (filing mark May 5, 1886), indicating "Resign'n cancelled 23 Dec 63," Thomas Francis Meagher, M-1064 Roll #187, Letters Received by the Commission Branch of the Adjutant General's Office, 1865, NARA.

72. Corby, *Memoirs of Chaplain Life,* 213.

73. Athearn, *Thomas Francis Meagher,* 131–32.

74. Osborne, *The Civil War Diaries of Col. Theodore B. Gates, 20th New York State Militia,* xi–xv, 151–52.

75. Corby, *Memoirs of Chaplain Life,* 264–68.

76. Simon, ed., *The Papers of Ulysses S. Grant,* vol. 12, 149; "Special Orders, No. 303," September 13, 1864, in *OR,* series 1, vol. 39, pt. 2, 371; Thomas Francis Meagher, "The Last Days of the 69th in Virginia: A Narrative in Two Parts," *Irish American,* August 31, 1861.

77. "General T. F. Meagher Once More," *Irish American,* October 15, 1864. The letter was published in the October 9, 1864, *New York Times.*

78. *A Vigorous Prosecution of the War the Only Guaranty for an Honorable Peace!* (Boston: T. O. H. P. Burnham, 1864), 1. This 15-page pamphlet includes Meagher's letter along with writings by Generals Grant and Sherman, Governor Edward Everett, Alex Stephens, and George Sennott, Esq. The leading article is entitled "An Appeal to Intelligent Irishmen upon the Duty They Owe to the Country in the Present Canvass," by N. W. Coffin, Esq. Meagher's letter was published in the *New York Times* on October 9 and the latest speech in the campaign document is dated October 4, so it seems likely that the campaign document was published after the *Times* article.

79. Sullivan to Meehan, October 26, 1864, marked "Private," Thomas F. Meehan Papers, Special Collections, GU.

80. Pepper, "Personal Recollections of General Thomas Francis Meagher," 533.

81. Ibid.; Anbinder, *Five Points,* 297–98.

82. "Webster to Sherman," November 5, 1864, in *OR,* series 1, vol. 39, pt. 3, 640.

83. "Sherman to Webster," November 5, 1864, in *OR,* series 1, vol. 39, pt. 3, 641. Major General Thomas was commander of the U.S. Volunteers for the Department of the Cumberland.

84. "Special Field Orders, No. 122," November 11, 1864, in *OR,* series 1 vol. 39, pt. 3, 742; "Special Field Orders, No. 313," November 15, 1864, in *OR,* series 1 vol. 52, pt. 1, 660; "Thomas to Steedman," November 16, 1864, in *OR,* series 1, vol. 45, pt. 1, 914.

85. "Special Orders, No. 50," November 25, 1864, in *OR,* series 1, vol. 45, pt. 1, 1051.

86. "General and Special Orders, No. 1," December 3, 1864, in *OR,* series 1, vol. 45, pt. 1, 39–40; "General Thomas F. Meagher," *Irish American,* January 28, 1865.

87. "Steedman to Whipple," January 10, 1865, in *OR,* series 1, vol. 45, pt. 2, 564; Athearn, *Thomas Francis Meagher,* 135–36.

88. "Meagher to Steedman," January 14, 1865 (from Tullahoma), in *OR,* series 1, vol. 45, pt. 2, 591; "Meagher to Steedman," January 15, 1865 (from Murfreesborough), in ibid., 595; "Meagher to Steedman," January 17, 1865 (from Nashville), in ibid., 608.

89. "Halstead to Dana," January 29, 1865, War Department File H-363, Department of War, NA, cited in Athearn, *Thomas Francis Meagher,* 136.

90. "Parsons to McKim," January 30, 1865, in *OR,* series 1, vol. 47, pt. 2, 280–82; "Parsons to Dana," January 31, 1865, in *OR,* series 1, vol. 47, pt. 2, 192; "Meagher to Dana," February 3, 1865, War Department File H-363, Department of War, NA, cited in Athearn, *Thomas Francis Meagher,* 136.

91. "Cross to Halleck," January 24, 1865, in *OR,* series 1, vol. 47, pt. 2, 127; "Halleck to Grant," January 23, 1865, in ibid., 116; "Grant to Halleck," January 23, 1865, in ibid.; "Halleck to Meagher," January 23, 1865, in ibid., 119.

92. "Meagher to Halleck," January 23, 1865, in ibid., 126.

93. "Grant to Halleck," January 24, 1865, in ibid., 121.

94. "Cross to Halleck," January 24, 1865, in ibid., 127; "Halleck to Schofield," January 25, 1865, in ibid., 131; "Schofield to Grant," January 31, 1865, in ibid., 191; "Grant to Schofield," January 31, 1865, in ibid.; "Halleck to Grant," January 31, 1865, in *OR,* series 1,

vol. 46, pt. 2, 313; "Halleck to Augur," January 31, 1865, in *OR,* series 1, vol. 47, pt. 2, 192; "Schofield to Meagher," February 1, 1865, in ibid., 204. The February 1 Schofield telegram addresses Meagher as "Brig. Gen. T. F. Meagher, Commanding Provisional Division, Armies of the Tennessee and Cumberland, Annapolis, Md."

95. "Scott to Halleck," February 2, 1865, in *OR,* series 1, vol. 47, pt. 2, 214. Scott also advised that they were experiencing great difficulty in coaling the vessels and supplying them with water.

96. Robert N. Scott to Meagher (telegram), February 4, 1865, Thomas Francis Meagher, M-1064 Roll #187, Letters Received by the Commission Branch of the Adjutant General's Office, 1865, NARA.

97. "Scott to Halleck," February 4, 1865, and February 2, 1865, in *OR,* series 1, vol. 47, pt. 2, 305–306; "Halleck to Scott," February 5, 1865, in ibid., 317; "Halleck to Grant," February 5, 1865, in ibid., 306.

98. Order from Robert N. Scott, Depot Quartermaster's Office, Annapolis, February 5, 1865, Thomas Francis Meagher, M-1064 Roll #187, Letters Received by the Commission Branch of the Adjutant General's Office, 1865, NARA.

99. Ibid.

100. "Scott to Halleck," February 6, 1865, in *OR,* series 1, vol. 47, pt. 2, 326–27; "Grant to Halleck," February 6, 1865, in ibid., 318.

101. Simon, *The Papers of Ulysses S. Grant,* vol. 13, 456–57n; General Papers and Records, Secretary of War, vol. IV, M344, National Archives, cited in Keneally, *The Great Shame and the Triumph of the Irish in the English-Speaking World,* 395.

102. "'4. Encls.' Relative to Brig. Genl T. F. Meagher," February 9, 1865, Thomas Francis Meagher, M-1064 Roll #187, Letters Received by the Commission Branch of the Adjutant General's Office, 1865, NARA.

103. Simon, *The Papers of Ulysses S. Grant,* vol. 13, 456–57n1; Smith, *Ulysses S. Grant,* 86–87. Even after Grant had rejoined the army in the Civil War, on one occasion Halleck, McClellan, and then Stanton all approved of an order to remove Grant from his command, based on alleged rumors that he had resumed drinking. Smith, *Ulysses S. Grant,* 172–73.

104. "Grant to Halleck," February 20, 1865, in *OR,* series 1, vol. 47, pt. 2, 501.

105. Simon, *Ulysses S. Grant,* vol. 13, 456–57n1.

106. Special Orders No. 3 [?], Major General Schofield, February 24 [?], 1865, Thomas Francis Meagher, M-1064 Roll #187, Letters Received by the Commission Branch of the Adjutant General's Office, 1865, NARA.

107. "Palmer to Sherman," February 13, 1865, in *OR,* series 1, vol. 47, pt. 2, 415–16; "Schofield to Grant," March 9, 1865, in ibid., 743–44.

108. Meagher to "Adjutant General, U.S.A.," March 10, 1865; Meagher to "Adjt Genl USA" (telegram); T. M. Vincent to Meagher (telegram), Thomas Francis Meagher, M-1064 Roll #187, Letters Received by the Commission Branch of the Adjutant General's Office, 1865, NARA.

109. "St. Patrick's Day in the Army: Irish Brigade Horse and Foot Races," *Irish American,* April 1, 1865.

110. Pepper, *Under Three Flags,* 332–33.

111. "Some Letters of General T. F. Meagher," 85–86, letter from Meagher to James R. O'Beirne, April 30, 1865.

112. Ibid. Meagher's behavior *could* have been the subject of a court-martial if it could be proved that he had abandoned his troops.

113. Athearn, *Thomas Francis Meagher,* 139.

114. Meagher to O'Beirne, with attachments, Thomas Francis Meagher, M-1064 Roll #187, Letters Received by the Commission Branch of the Adjutant General's Office, 1865, NARA.

115. "Thomas F. Meagher" abstract, n.d. (filing mark May 5, 1886), Thomas Francis Meagher, M-1064 Roll #187, Letters Received by the Commission Branch of the Adjutant General's Office, 1865, NARA. A undated document entitled "2nd Auditor—For Mil. history of Thos. Francis Meagher, late Brig. Genl Vols." in the same source reads: "by letter of Dec. 23, 1863, this office, . . . he was informed that by direction of the secretary of war, the letter from this office of May 14, 1863, acceptg his res'n. was cancelled and his resignation is to be taken as withdrawn. From January to Sept 13, 1864, he is reported as awaiting orders. Sept. 13, 1864, he was ordered to proceed to Nashville, Tenn., and report to Genl Sherman for assignment to duty."

116. See, for example, "Gen. Meagher on Negro Suffrage," *Irish American,* August 19, 1865.

117. John C. Foley to General L. Thomas, July 9, 1867, Thomas Francis Meagher, M-1064 Roll #187, Letters Received by the Commission Branch of the Adjutant General's Office, 1865, NARA.

CHAPTER 8

1. "Irish Aid Society—New-York," *Irish News,* July 5, 1856.

2. "Mr. Meagher's First Lecture," *San Francisco Daily Herald,* January 25, 1854.

3. "Reception of General T. F. Meagher at Virginia City," *Montana Post,* October 7, 1865. Meagher gave his reminiscences in a speech in Virginia City, Montana, on September 30, 1865.

4. Ibid.; "Mr. Meagher and the Dinner to Gen. Wool," *Irish American,* April 15, 1854; "Meagher in San Francisco: Lecture on Irish Republicanism," *Irish American,* April 8, 1854.

5. Traveler's Club invitation to hear J. L. Fisk, dated June 22, 1865, Fisk Files, MNHS.

6. Palladino, *Indian and White in the Northwest,* 30; Small, *Religion in Montana,* 48; Meagher to Meagher, Sr., July 17, 1865, NLI.

7. Meagher to Meagher, Sr., July 17, 1865, NLI.

8. Andrew Fisk Diary, entry of July 25, 1865, Fisk Files, MNHS.

9. Athearn, *Thomas Francis Meagher,* 144; Emmons, *The Butte Irish,* 61; Reardon, *The Catholic Church in the Diocese of St. Paul,* 160. Ultimately, of course, the Irish did come to Montana; in 1910 there were 10,000 Irish in Butte, compared to 3,000 Austrians, 2,500 Germans, 1,600 Italians, at least 1,500 Finns, and a good number of English. Emmons, *The Butte Irish,* 63.

10. Palladino, *Indian and White in the Northwest,* quoting from a letter from Ireland to Palladino, January 29, 1912, 291.

11. "The Relationship of Irish Immigrants to the United States: An Address by Gen. T. F. Meagher, before the Irish Immigration Society of St. Paul, Minn., Wednesday Evening, August 2d," *Irish American,* August 19, 1865.

12. "Gen. Meagher on Negro Suffrage," *Irish American,* August 19, 1865.

13. "Some Letters of General T. F. Meagher," 85–86, letter from Meagher to James R. O'Beirne, April 30, 1865.

14. "The City: Gen. Meagher," *St. Paul Press,* July 27, 1865.

15. Andrew Fisk Diary, entry for August 13, 1865, Fisk Files, MNHS.

16. Spence, *Territorial Politics and Government in Montana,* 18. Perhaps Coburn regretted his decision, because considerably later he was to accept a position as an associate justice in the Montana Territory. Ibid., *n*38.

17. "The Relationship of Irish Immigrants to the United States," *Irish American,* August 19, 1865.

18. Athearn, *Thomas Francis Meagher,* 146.

19. Thane, "An Ohio Abolitionist in the Far West," 152–53.

20. Ibid., 153; Thane, ed., *A Governor's Wife on the Mining Frontier,* 2.

21. First Legislative Assembly of the Territory of Montana, *Acts, Resolutions and Memorials* (Bannack, 1864–65), 31.

22. Wilbur Fisk Sanders, "Partial History of Early Montana," n.d., MC 53, box 4, folder 7, Wilbur Fisk Sanders Papers, MHS.

23. "The Arrival of General Meagher," *Montana Post,* September 30, 1865.

24. Spence, *Territorial Politics and Government in Montana,* 18–19.

25. "The Arrival of General Meagher," *Montana Post,* September 30, 1865; Graetz and Graetz, *Bannack,* 12; "A Journey to Benton," 47, letter from Meagher to Father De Smet, December 15, 1865.

26. Raymer, *Montana,* 214–18.

27. Ibid., 220–27.

28. Leeson, *History of Montana, 1739–1885,* 276–302.

29. "Helena Items," *Montana Post,* September 23, 1865; "Local Items" and "Diamond City Items," *Montana Post,* September 30, 1865; "Helena Items," *Montana Post,* October 7, 1865.

30. Dimsdale, *The Vigilantes of Montana,* 13.

31. "The Arrival of General Meagher," *Montana Post,* September 30, 1865; Deed from Edgerton to Joseph H. Millard, September 12, 1865, Madison County Recorder's Office.

32. Schwantes, *In Mountain Shadows,* 66–68; Spence, *Territorial Politics and Government in Montana, 1864–89,* 247 (quotation).

33. Jackson, "The Appointment and Removal of Sidney Edgerton, First Governor of Montana Territory," 297–98, letter from Edgerton to Seward, January 30, 1866.

34. Ibid., 303, letter from Harlan to Seward, April 11, 1866.

35. "Local Items," *Montana Post,* October 14, 1865.

36. Raymer, *Montana,* 237–38.

37. "Arrived," *Montana Post,* September 23, 1865.

38. "The Arrival of General Meagher," *Montana Post,* September 30, 1865.

39. "Biographical Sketch of Brevet Major-General Meagher," *Montana Post,* October 21, 1865.

40. Ibid.

41. "Reception of General T. F. Meagher at Virginia City," *Montana Post,* October 7, 1865.

42. Ibid.

43. "Proceedings of the First General Convention of the Fenian Brotherhood of Montana Territory," *Montana Post,* December 23, 1865. Andrew O'Connell was listed as territorial "centre," with sixteen named delegates from Virginia City, Nevada City, Washington Gulch, and Helena. Resolutions were passed, including one which "would urge the necessity of ALL who are friendly to the cause of freedom assisting, with their means, with their influence, and

if necessary, to give their lives, to raise once more that time-honored banner, the ancient ensign of the Harp and the Sunburst." A motion was passed to request publication of the proceedings in the Montana papers and also in the *Boston Pilot* and *Irish American*.

44. Editorial, *Montana Post*, October 28, 1865.

45. "The Progress of Fenianism—What Are Its Aims?—Our Duty of Neutrality," *Montana Post*, November 4, 1865.

46. "The Relationship of Irish Immigrants to the United States," *Irish American*, August 19, 1865.

47. "Another 'Irrepressible Conflict,'" *Montana Post*, November 25, 1865.

48. "Professor Thomas J. Dimsdale," *Montana Post*, September 29, 1866; Dimsdale, *The Vigilantes of Montana*.

49. "Professor Thomas J. Dimsdale," *Montana Post*, September 29, 1866; Tuttle, *Missionary to the Mountain West*, 130.

50. Paladin, "Henry N. Blake: Proper Bostonian, Purposeful Pioneer," 32–56.

51. Meagher to Blake, October 19, 1866; Blake to Meagher, October 19, 1866, as quoted in "Pistols and Coffee for Two," *Montana Post*, October 20, 1866; Paladin, "Henry N. Blake: Proper Bostonian, Purposeful Pioneer," 32–56.

52. U.S. Bureau of Indian Affairs, *Report of the Commissioner of Indian Affairs for the Year 1865*, 30–31. The numbers were as follows: about 1,800 Gros Ventres; and various tribes of Blackfeet Indians, including about 1,870 Piegans, 2,150 Bloods, and 2,450 Blackfeet proper; and a western group that included about 550 Flatheads, 900 Pend d'Oreilles, and 270 Kootenais.

53. Hamilton, *From Wilderness to Statehood*, 181.

54. Safford, *The Mechanics of Optimism*, 36–37.

55. "The County Election," *Montana Post*, September 16, 1865.

56. U.S. Bureau of Indian Affairs, *Report of the Commissioner of Indian Affairs for the Year 1865*, 510–15, letter from Upson to Cooley, October 2, 1865.

57. Ibid., 250–52, letter from Upson to Dole, July 12, 1865, letter from Dole to Upson, March 24, 1865.

58. "A Journey to Benton," 46–49, 48–49n3–6, letter from Meagher to Father De Smet, December 15, 1865.

59. "The Wagon Road to Benton," *Montana Radiator*, January 27, 1866. The Bannack legislature had granted Clarke the right to build a toll road through the canyon. He had in turn sold the charter to King and Gillette, a partnership of two enterprising townsmen of Helena, who proposed a road through a narrow pass that would overcome the ascent and descent and shorten the route several miles. Today this stream is called Little Prickly Pear Creek, which shares the crowded floor of Wolf Creek Canyon with Interstate Highway 15.

60. "A Journey to Benton," 48–50.

61. Ibid., 50–51.

62. Ibid., 51–52.

63. Ibid., 52–53.

64. Ibid., 57–58.

65. Ibid., 58.

66. Hamilton, *From Wilderness to Statehood*, 181.

67. Ibid., 183.

68. United States, "Treaty between the United States and the Blackfoot Nation of Indians, Etc., November 16, 1865," 1133–37; Hamilton, *From Wilderness to Statehood*, 182. The financial aspects of the treaty are apparently incorrect in Hamilton.

69. Hamilton, *From Wilderness to Statehood,* 182.

70. United States, "Treaty between the United States and the Blackfoot Nation of Indians," 1133–37.

71. Hamilton, *From Wilderness to Statehood,* 182–83; U.S. Bureau of Indian Affairs, *Report of the Commissioner of Indian Affairs for the Year 1866,* 197, letter from Upson to Cooley, April 6, 1866; Safford, *The Mechanics of Optimism,* 44.

72. Hamilton, *From Wilderness to Statehood,* 183.

73. U.S. Bureau of Indian Affairs, *Report of the Commissioner of Indian Affairs for the Year 1866,* 196, letter from Meagher to Cooley, December 14, 1865. The "hostile" Bloods, who were accused of murdering eleven whites in April, had departed immediately for the border and had not returned to the territory. When Upson dispatched messengers to try to bring in the Blackfeet from Canada, they were turned back by a tribe of Kootenai Indians.

74. Ibid., 196–97.

75. Ibid., 197.

76. Hamilton, *From Wilderness to Statehood,* 183.

77. U.S. Bureau of Indian Affairs, *Report of the Commissioner of Indian Affairs for the Year 1866,* 197–99, letters from Upham to Upson, January 9 and February 2, 1865. Upham told Upson that white men in Fort Benton had organized a vigilance committee for self-protection against both Indians and other whites. He also observed that Indian war parties were regularly stopping at Fort Benton on their way to their enemies' camps.

78. "Letter from Fort Benton: Indians on the War Path—Shocking Murders—Heavy Robberies of Stock—Determination on the Part of the Settlers to Kill the Last Indian," *Montana Post,* February 3, 1866. The letter was signed by H. A. Kennedy, Joseph Hill, George Steele, J. J. Healy, William T. Hamilton, and A. B. Hamilton. Hamilton was then the agent of the *Montana Post* in Fort Benton.

CHAPTER 9

1. "Catholic Encyclopedia: James Shields."

2. Spence, *Territorial Politics and Government in Montana, 1864–89,* 23–24.

3. See First Legislative Assembly of the Territory of Montana, *Acts, Resolutions and Memorials* (Bannack, 1864–65). The Idaho statutes had been obtained for them by David D. Chamberlain, who was reimbursed three hundred dollars. Ibid., 573.

4. "Bannack's Correspondence," *Montana Post,* January 21, 1865; "Bannack's Correspondence," *Montana Post,* February 4, 1865.

5. See First Legislative Assembly of the Territory of Montana, *Acts, Resolutions and Memorials.* On December 31, 1864, Edgerton signed into law an act that made the opening of the Legislative Assembly the first Monday of November of each year; on January 17, 1865, Edgerton signed an act providing for the election day to be the first Monday of September of each year. It was also made law that no one could run for the council or house unless he had been a resident of the territory for a year; the place of voting was set. A form was established for reporting the vote, and a system was set in place for breaking a tie between candidates for the council or the house. Another provision was passed for handling elections where a council or representative district comprised two or more counties. Salaries of legislators were set, and contingencies in the event of absences were put into effect.

6. First Legislative Assembly of the Territory of Montana, *House Journal of the First Session of the Legislative Assembly of the Territory of Montana* (Bannack, 1864–65), 178.

7. Ibid., 200. The council took up the matter first and passed Bill No. 74, which increased the number of members in the council and the house and reapportioned the territory into council and representative districts. This bill was then sent to the house, where it was amended and sent back to the council. The amendments were not approved; when a conference committee appointed the next day could not resolve the impasse, Bill No. 74 was shelved. On the forty-sixth day House Bill No. 131 was introduced for the same purpose and passed, but over the strong objection of Erasmus Leavitt of Beaverhead County, a Democrat who had voted for the bill but then made a motion for reconsideration after it had passed. First Legislative Assembly of the Territory of Montana, *Council Journal of the First Legislative Assembly of Montana Territory* (Bannack, 1864–65), 272.

8. First Legislative Assembly of the Territory of Montana, *House Journal of the First Session* (Bannack, 1864–65), 204.

9. "Local and Other Items," *Montana Post,* February 25, 1865.

10. "Call for a Convention," *Montana Post,* July 8, 1865. The announcement read in part:

Inasmuch as by the termination of the war, the political issues to which it gave rise have become things of the past, and it is desirable that all future political questions should be determined upon their merits, as they shall arise, it is the judgment of very many citizens of this Territory that an auspicious opportunity presents itself to consult their own immediate wants, and to act with reference thereto, and that in so doing they are obeying no less the impulse of patriotism than the voice of duty, and that any other course can only end in a perpetuation of the feuds, prejudices and passions, which the past has engendered, without any compensation whatever.

Acting in the light of these truths, the undersigned respectfully invite their fellow-citizens, without regard to past political differences, who cheerfully accept the inevitable logic of events, who desire to aid in developing the resources of the Territory, in supplying the wants of her people, and who seek to promote the peace, harmony and prosperity of the whole country, and lay the foundation of her material prosperity and social order on a stable footing, and who will co-operate in securing the accomplishment of such purposes—to meet in their respective counties, as below specified, on Saturday, the 29th day of July, 1865, at 3 o'clock P.M., to elect Delegates to attend a Territorial Convention, to be held at the City of Virginia, on Wednesday, the 9th day of August, 1865, at 12 o'clock noon, of said day, to place in nomination one candidate for Delegate to Congress, one candidate for Territorial Treasurer, one candidate for Territorial Auditor, one candidate for Superintendent of Public Instruction, to be supported at the ensuing election, and to transact such other business as may be brought before the Convention.

11. "The Mass Convention To-day" and "Territorial Offices," *Montana Post,* July 29, 1865. That edition of the *Post* also reported that the Democratic County Convention had been held five days earlier, nominating only county officers and adjourning until August 15 for other business. "Democratic County Convention," *Montana Post,* July 29, 1865.

12. "Call for Convention," *Montana Post,* July 8, 1865.

13. "Primary Union Meetings" and "Local Items: Public Meeting," *Montana Post,* August 5, 1865

14. "People's Ticket—Madison County," *Montana Post,* August 26, 1865; "Minutes of the Democratic Territorial Convention," *Montana Post,* August 12, 1865; "Miscellaneous Items," *Montana Post,* August 19, 1865.

15. "The County Election," *Montana Post,* September 16, 1865.

16. "The Arrival of General Meagher," *Montana Post,* September 30, 1865.

17. Spence, *Territorial Politics and Government in Montana,* 36–38; "Calling of the Legislature," *Montana Post,* December 23, 1865.

18. Shober to Meagher, December 16, 1865, SC 309, MHS.

19. "The Progress of Fenianism—What Are Its Aims?—Duty of Neutrality," *Montana Post,* November 4, 1865.

20. "Calling of the Legislature," *Montana Post,* December 23, 1865.

21. "Judge J. L. McCullough, Democratic Nominee for Sheriff," *Montana Post,* August 17, 1867. This was reported well over a year later.

22. Neally to Meagher, November 17, 1865, SC 309, MHS. In his letter Neally advised Meagher that it was the territorial secretary's duty to send the laws to Congress and asked Meagher to send him two signed transmittal letters so that he could forward them himself. Neally also said that he was on his way to New York to get the laws published.

23. First Legislative Assembly of the Territory of Montana, *Acts, Resolutions and Memorials,* 29. The federal government had provided little or no money. Goods and services for the territory were paid for by territorial warrants, with no treasury to back them up. At this time the first territorial auditor, John S. Lott, made his initial report on the financial standing of Montana. Most of the taxes had been collected from Madison County, where miners were present, and from Gallatin County, where serious agricultural operations were beginning. Against the over $65,000 of issued warrants, only a little under $34,000 had been received. See the Organic Act, in ibid.

24. "[Official] Proclamation," *Montana Post,* February 3, 1866.

25. "Calling the Legislature," *Montana Post,* February 3, 1866; Bruce, *Lectures of Gov. Thomas Francis Meagher,* 40–48.

26. Sanders to Fergus, February 14, 1866, typescript copy, SC-50, Fergus Papers, MHS.

27. "Abstract of Proceedings of the Legislature," *Montana Post,* March 17, 1866.

28. Neil Howie diary, entry for Monday, March 5, 1866, MHS.

29. Bruce, *Lectures of Gov. Thomas Francis Meagher,* 71.

30. Legislative Assembly of the Territory of Montana, *Council Journal,* 2nd sess. (1866), 139, 155–56; *Laws of the Territory of Montana,* 2nd sess. (1866), act of March 26, 1866, 3, cited in Spence, *Territorial Politics and Government in Montana,* 41.

31. *Montana Post,* March 10, 1866, quoted in Spence, *Territorial Politics and Government in Montana,* 41.

32. Raymer, *Montana,* 253; "An Act to divide the present County of Gallatin, and to create New Counties out of the same," *Laws of the Territory of Montana,* 11–12, approved March 26, 1866.

33. As quoted in Leeson, *History of Montana,* 247.

34. Meagher to the President of the Council, March 20 and March 30, 1866, Terr. 2, Territorial Papers, MHS.

35. Meagher to the Speaker of the House Representatives, April 10, 1866, Terr. 2, Territorial Papers, MHS.

36. Quotation from Leeson, *History of Montana,* 248.

37. Ledger for unidentified Virginia City establishment, 1866 [?], Probate Court files, MCC; see also West, "Thomas Francis Meagher's Bar Bill," 20; Neil Howie diary, entry for Friday, March 9, 1866, MHS; "Local Items: Disappointment," *Montana Post,* February 3, 1866; Chumasero to Sanders, March 4, 1866, Sanders Papers, MHS.

38. Sanders to Fergus, February 14, 1866, MSS10, James Fergus Papers, box 9, folder 47, K. Ross Toole Archives and Special Collections, UMM.

39. Bruce, *Lectures of Gov. Thomas Francis Meagher,* 28–29. Meagher also told the assembled group that George Washington had become a member of the Friendly Sons of St. Patrick of Philadelphia and "did not think it incompatible with his Americanism to . . . drown the Shamrock with that convivial Brotherhood, and do it honestly like a noble Virginian as he was." He also noted that "Henry Clay did not think it incompatible with his Americanism to wet his clay with the Irishmen of Kentucky." Ibid.

40. "[Official] Proclamation," *Montana Post,* February 3, 1866. There are three different proclamations by Meagher in this edition, each entitled "[Official] Proclamation."

41. Richardson, *Beyond the Mississippi,* 177.

42. "Letter from New York City," *Montana Post,* October 28, 1865.

43. *Montana Post,* April 14, 1866, quoted in Spence, *Territorial Politics and Government in Montana,* 292.

44. Barlow to Meagher, May 11, 1866, Barlow File, HL; Meagher to Barlow, October 26, 1866, Barlow File, HL.

45. Spence, *Territorial Politics and Government in Montana,* 293.

46. "Illegality of the Acts of the Legislature—Judge Munson's Decision," *Montana Post,* June 9, 1866. The case in which Munson declared the legislature invalid was *Townsend and Baker v. Amos T. Laird,* in which the defendant's lawyers raised the illegality of a new attachment law just passed by Meagher's legislature. Munson held the law invalid on the grounds that the legislature that had passed it had not been apportioned by the first territorial legislature. He went on to say in his opinion that only Congress had the power to validate the legislature and its work.

47. U.S. House of Representatives, *Appendix to the Congressional Globe,* "Remarks of Hon. S. McLean, of Montana, in the House of Representatives, May 4, 1866," 201–202.

48. "Governor Smith," *Montana Post,* October 6, 1866; "Proclamation," *Montana Post,* October 13, 1866.

49. United States, *Statutes at Large of the United States of America,* 39th Cong., 2nd sess., 426–27.

50. Mather and Boswell, *Vigilante Victims,* 154, citing an Idaho City editor who described Daniels as an upstanding citizen.

51. "When Governor Meagher and Judge Munson Clashed, Vigilantes Stepped In and Executed James B. Daniels," *Hardin Tribune,* April 11, 1919.

52. First Legislative Assembly of the Territory of Montana, *Acts, Resolutions and Memorials,* 22.

53. Daniels Pardon, February 22, 1866, MHS.

54. "When Governor Meagher and Judge Munson Clashed, Vigilantes Stepped In and Executed James B. Daniels," *Hardin Tribune,* April 11, 1919.

55. Munson to Meagher, March 1, 1866, typescript copy, Lyman E. Munson File, MHS.

56. "Local Items," *Montana Post,* March 3, 1866.

57. Munson, "Personal Recollections of Life, Scenes, and Incidents in the Early Settlement of Montana," Lyman E. Munson Papers, MHS. Munson stated: "This was the 9th specimen of kindred fruit that famous hang-man's tree at Helena had borne in so many months. They all went up with their boots on; and as death found them, so the grave gover[n]ed them." Years later it would be claimed that Alex Leggat, a curio collector in Butte, had obtained from a dealer in St. Louis the exact handwritten document that Daniels was claimed to have had in his pocket when he was hanged. At the time of its purchase the note had been in the hands of a resident of Quincy, Illinois, whose father was a railroad man and an admirer of Meagher. "Documental Reprieve Given Victim of Crude Vigilante Justice Owned by Butte Man," *Butte Daily Post,* September 25, 1931.

58. Chumasero to Sanders, March 4, 1866, Sanders Papers, MHS.

59. Langford, *Vigilante Days and Ways,* 296.

60. "Extra Compensation," *Montana Democrat,* March 29, 1866.

61. "We Understand: Left the Country," *Montana Post,* August 18, 1866. The source of this information was the *Idaho World* of July 28. The *Post* did not subscribe to either the report or the vigilante action and scolded the editor of the paper from which it came. It countered that Daniels was hanged not because he was pardoned but rather because he had a record of homicides and threatened to commit them again.

62. Ibid.

63. U.S. House of Representatives, *The Counter Case of Great Britain as Laid before the Tribunal of Arbitration, Convened at Geneva,* 60–64; Denieffe, *A Personal Narrative of the Irish Revolutionary Brotherhood,* 139–40n1, 260. These various branches of the Fenian "government" served to take away O'Mahony's effective power, and finally he was deposed in favor of William R. Roberts as the head of the organization. Ibid., 260.

64. Denieffe, *A Personal Narrative of the Irish Revolutionary Brotherhood,* 261.

65. Meagher to O'Connell, August 8, 1866, Meagher File, UNDA. Meagher wrote: "My Dear Andrew O'Connell, I find I cannot be with you until next Saturday—will then be with you positively. Ever yours truly T. F. Meagher."

66. Hogan to O'Connell, July 21, 1866, MHS.

67. Hogan to O'Connell, January 6, 1867, MHS. Hogan was in Helena for the purpose of establishing a mail route to the mouth of the Judith. He formed numerous "agreeable acquaintances" there, among them, John Kingsly, "centre" of the Brian Boru circle of the Fenian Brotherhood.

68. Meagher to O'Connell, January 15, 1867, MHS.

69. Moreover, the records of Madison County do not indicate that a land patent was issued to anyone named Walsh.

70. Denieffe, *A Personal Narrative of the Irish Revolutionary Brotherhood,* 207. On November 24, 1865, Colonel Walsh, as inspector general of the Fenian Brotherhood, had been ordered on a tour of inspection of all circles in the states. While the Fenian organization was now out in the open, the communications and individuals within the organization were often still secret. Many measures were still in place to assure secrecy, and assumed names were frequently used. For example, Colonel Thomas Kelly used the name "T. J. French" as well as several other aliases. Members of the Fenian Brotherhood also often wrote to each other in an official code published by the Fenian headquarters, consisting of numerals and various geometric shapes that stood for letters of the alphabet. That policy of secrecy might explain this somewhat strange letter written by Meagher. Ibid., 191.

71. Roberts to the Secretary of War, May 16, 1872, RG 94, entry 214, box 25, USMAL.

72. Palladino, *Indian and White in the Northwest,* 501–502.

73. Ibid.

74. "A Journey to Benton," 57; Palladino, *Indian and White in the Northwest,* 319.

75. Kuppens, "Thomas Francis Meagher, Montana Pioneer," 131–35.

76. Palladino, *Indian and White in the Northwest,* 318–20.

77. Pepper, "Personal Recollections of General Thomas Francis Meagher," 536–37, letters from Meagher to Pepper, December 17, 1865, and January 20, 1866.

78. Ibid., 537–38, letter from Meagher to Pepper, February 7, 1866.

79. Vaughan, *Then and Now,* 106–109. From a letter from Will H. Sutherlin (White Sulphur Springs, Montana, November 12, 1899).

80. Lyons, *Brigadier-General Thomas Francis Meagher,* 351–52.

81. Tuttle, *Missionary to the Mountain West,* 135.

82. Rolle, *The Road to Virginia City,* 103–104.

83. "Miscellaneous Items," *Montana Post,* October 6, 1866; Meagher to Barlow, October 26, 1866, HL.

84. "Governor Smith," *Montana Post,* October 6, 1866.

85. "Miscellaneous Items," *Montana Post,* October 6, 1866.

86. Athearn, *Thomas Francis Meagher,* 155.

87. Petition to President Andrew Johnson from Anson L. Potter et al., August 1866, SC 309, MHS; Miscellaneous Items, *Montana Post,* October 13, 1866; *House Journal,* 38th Cong., 1st sess., December 10, 1863, and April 8, May 6, and May 10, 1864, http://memory .loc.gov/ammem/amlaw/lwhj.html. After several weeks of consideration, the House voted that he was not entitled to the seat; however, they did approve of his expenses incurred while he was contesting the matter. *House Journal,* 38th Cong., 1st sess., May 11 and May 13, 1864. While Bruce did obtain the presidential nomination as secretary, the Senate Committee on Territories "reported adversely thereon." *Senate Executive Journal,* 39th Cong., 2nd sess., February 23, 1867, http://memory.loc.gov/ammem/amlaw/lwej.html.

88. *Senate Executive Journal,* 40th Cong., 1st sess., March 21, 1867, http://memory .loc.gov/ammem/amlaw/lwej.html.

89. Evans, *Good Samaritan of the Northwest,* 191; Palladino, *Indian and White in the Northwest,* 92–93.

90. O'Keefe [Meagher], "Rides through Montana," 568*n.* Tofft had come to Montana in late 1865 from the West, up the Clark Fork River, finally arriving at Fort Owen in the Bitterroot Valley in late December. Staying there until mid-February 1866, he then set out to Elk Creek in what is now Deer Lodge County to mine for gold. Bigart and Woodcock, "Peter Peterson Tofft," 9.

91. Bigart and Woodcock, "Peter Peterson Tofft," 2, 9. Years later, in 1882, Tofft would renew his acquaintance with the widowed Elizabeth Meagher in New York, where she would attempt unsuccessfully to interest some of her friends in buying his art work. Ibid., 14.

92. Meagher to Barlow, June 15, 1867, HL. It appears, however, that if it was Tofft's sketch then Meagher could not have been the first white man to see the falls.

93. Dunbar, *The Journals and Letters of Major John Owen,* 29, 36.

94. Meagher to Barlow, January 30, 1867, HL.

95. Meagher to O'Keefe, September 26, 1866, Meagher File, MHS.

96. Ibid.

97. O'Keefe [Meagher], "Rides through Montana," 568.

98. Bill of Weir & Pope, n.d., Probate Court files, MCC; Bill of Dr. Reins, n.d., Probate Court files, MCC. According to pioneer medicine expert Volney W. Steele, M.D., of Bozeman, Montana, the opium pills could have been used to stop diarrhea caused by intestinal bleeding.

99. Kuppens, "Thomas Francis Meagher, Montana Pioneer," 137–38; see also Hosmer to Sanders, January 24, 1867, Sanders Papers, MHS.

100. Hosmer to Sanders, January 24, 1867; "The Late General Meagher," *Irish American*, August 10, 1867.

CHAPTER 10

1. Simon, *The Papers of Ulysses S. Grant,* vol. 17, 174, Sherman to Grant, June 10, 1867.

2. Meagher to Meagher, Sr., June 15, 1867, NLI.

3. Bancroft, *The Works of Hubert Howe Bancroft,* 694; "Edgerton to Stanton," May 30, 1865, in *OR,* series 1, vol. 48, pt. 3, 690.

4. Edgerton to Seward, January 30, 1866, Montana Territorial Papers, NA, cited in Jackson, "The Appointment and Removal of Sidney Edgerton, First Governor of Montana Territory," 297–98.

5. Cooley to Harlan, April 10, 1866, Montana Territorial Papers, NA, cited in Jackson, "The Appointment and Removal of Sidney Edgerton, First Governor of Montana Territory," 302.

6. "General Order No. 1," *Montana Post,* February 17, 1866.

7. Sherman to Meagher, February 16, 1866, Terr. 2, Montana Territorial Papers, MHS. The letter was addressed to Meagher as "Secretary of Montana," even though he was acting governor at the time.

8. U.S. Bureau of Indian Affairs, *Report of the Commissioner of Indian Affairs for the Year 1866,* 199–200, Meagher to the Commissioner, April 20, 1866.

9. Ibid.

10. Ibid., 202–203, Upham to Cooley, July 25, 1866.

11. Doyle, *Journeys to the Land of Gold,* vol. 1, 7–8.

12. "Indian Affairs," *Helena Herald,* January 17, 1867.

13. Nathaniel Coates Kinney to His Excellency the Governor of Montana, February 8, 1867 (but marked as "resd Jan. 7, 1867"), MHS. Kinney warned that the Crows would attack if the obligations of the Fort Union treaty were not met.

14. Simon, *The Papers of Ulysses S. Grant,* vol. 17, 54.

15. Sherman to Smith, April 2, 1867, Territorial Governor File, MHS; Sherman to Smith, April 4, 1867 [?], Territorial Governor File, MHS.

16. "Reported Massacre of the Garrison at Fort Buford," *Union and Dakotaian,* March 20, 1867; "Fort Buford No. 2—Council Bluffs in the 'Massacre' Business," *Union and Dakotaian,* May 13, 1867.

17. "Shall We Aid or Abandon?" *Montana Post,* April 6, 1867.

18. Ibid.

19. "TURN OUT! TURN OUT!" *Montana Post,* April 6, 1867.

20. "The War Meeting," *Montana Post,* April 13, 1867.

21. Simon, *The Papers of Ulysses S. Grant,* vol. 17, 106.

22. Ibid., 104–105. Grant forwarded Stanton several reports by military officers in the West; the most important was the dispatch he had received from Meagher that day and the repeated dispatches from the governor of Texas and its citizens.

23. Ibid., 106–107.

24. Reprint of letter, *Montana Post,* April 13, 1867, Meagher to Clinton, April 9, 1867.

25. "Our Country's Defenders" and "The Indian War," *Montana Post,* April 27, 1867, reprinted letter from Clinton to Meagher, April 17, 1867. Clinton declined, saying that he was not authorized and furthermore that he had no desire to split his command and be "whipped in detail, as was done at Fort Phil. Kearney."

26. "Recruiting," *Montana Post,* April 13, 1867.

27. U.S. House of Representatives, *Report upon the Montana Indian War Claims of 1867,* 41st Cong., 3rd sess., 8.

28. Simon, *The Papers of Ulysses S. Grant,* vol. 17, 107.

29. Sherman to Meagher, May 3, 1867, Territorial Governor File, MHS. A day later, on May 4, the following telegram was sent to Meagher by G. S. Townsend of the War Department: "In answer to your telegram of April (28) twenty eight in relation to Indian invasion, I am instructed by the Sec'y. of War to inform you that authority has been given by this department to Lieut. Genl. Sherman, to call out, organize, officer, arm and subsist such militia force in Montana Territory as he deems necessary for the protection of that Territory, against hostile Indians. Any suggestion you may make to Genl. Sherman at St. Louis on matter relating to this subject, will receive his attention. Acknowledge receipt." Townsend to Meagher, May 4, 1867, Territorial Governor File, MHS.

30. "The Government Authorizes the Organizing of the Militia—On a Sure Footing at Last—Dispatches from the Secretary of War and the Adjutant General," *Montana Post,* May 11, 1867, reprinted letter from Stanton to Castner, May 5, 1867.

31. Ibid., reprinted letter from Townsend to Hosmer, May 4, 1867.

32. "The Indian Movement," *Montana Post,* May 11, 1867.

33. Sherman to Castner, May 6, 1867, Territorial Governor File, MHS.

34. Sherman to Meagher, May 7, 1867, Territorial Governor File, MHS.

35. Sherman to Hosmer, May 7, 1867, Territorial Governor File, MHS.

36. Sherman to Meagher, May 9, 1867, Territorial Governor File, MHS.

37. Sherman to Lewis, May 29, 1867, Territorial Governor File, MHS.

38. "Gone to the Front," *Montana Post,* May 18, 1867.

39. U.S. Senate, *Report to Accompany Bill S. 519;* Davis Willson to "Folks at Home," May 29, 1867, 1407, Willson Collection, MSUSC.

40. U.S. Senate, *Report to Accompany Bill S. 519,* 2.

41. U.S. House of Representatives, *Report to Accompany H. Res. 23,* 13. Whether the telegram actually said "three months" or "two months" became a subject of debate in congressional hearings held later. In the Montana War-Claim hearings conducted by the House of Representatives in 1872, five years after the fact, M. H. Insley, a freighter, testified that he had supplied goods and services, upon being shown the telegram by Meagher. At the congressional hearing Insley was also shown the second version of the telegram, which read: "Muster in a battalion of eight hundred men at once, at the cost of the United States for three months. Equip them as best you can till the arms *en route* reach Fort Benton. Move quickly to the threatened point, when the danger will either disappear or be removed. Let the men furnish their own horses and arms at forty cents per day, and be rationed by contract. When the service is rendered I will order payment by the regular paymaster. W. T. Sherman, Lieutenant General, Commanding." Insley testified that this too was the telegram furnished to him by the governor. "There might be the difference of a word or two, but the purport was the same." He said that he had gone to the telegraph office to

determine if the telegram was authentic and that he had kept a copy for a long time but had misplaced it. Insley said further that he had seen the original copy of the telegram that Colonel Lewis had and that Lewis had furnished the governor with a copy. Ibid., 26–27.

42. Ibid., 25–27. When Insley delivered the flour to Fort Parker, where the troops were camped about "one hundred and twenty-five miles" from Virginia City, he "saw three men brought in who were shot to pieces. . . . The only men I saw killed were these three. I saw them brought in from across the Yellowstone."

43. U.S. Senate, *Report to Accompany Bill S. 519,* 2–3. Lewis also testified before Congress that he had received the May 24 dispatch from Sherman but had replied that he could not raise troops. Lewis did not receive Major Clinton's response to his request for troops until after he had returned to Salt Lake City.

44. Simon, *The Papers of Ulysses S. Grant,* vol. 17, 159–60. Sherman also told Grant:

> If Major Lewis had enough men to feel out to Gallatin Valley I doubt if he would use the Volunteers at all, and I regard this as experimental only. I expect we shall be all summer fighting with little bands of horse-stealing Indians, and doubt if we can prevent them; but increased emigration to Montana and increased population along the Platte and Smoky Hill will divide the northern and southern Indians permanently, when we can take them in detail. I will write to General Dodge and have him keep his people at work, at all events this side of Fort Sanders.

45. Ibid., 160.

46. U.S. House of Representatives, *Report upon the Montana Indian War Claims of 1867,* 41st Cong., 3rd sess., 8.

47. Athearn, *William Tecumseh Sherman and the Settlement of the West,* 163–64.

48. Circular issued by Sherman, Headquarters Military Division of the Missouri, St. Louis, June 21, 1867, MHS.

49. Simon, *The Papers of Ulysses S. Grant,* vol. 17, 173. On June 10 Grant endorsed a copy of this telegram to Stanton. On June 10 Sherman also telegraphed to Grant again: "Major Lewis reports from Montana that all the trouble reports sent by the governor and others had no other foundation than the murder of Boseman [*sic*]. He will not therefore accept any more Volunteers there." On the same day Sherman wrote to Grant, advising that the Spencer carbines and the Colt pistols supplied the Indians by their agents were being skillfully used in "riding down the Overland Stages." Sherman asked that arms be distributed only by the military, using "ordinary prudence and safety"; at the same time he was in agreement that the treaty annuities should go to the Indians. "This conflict of authority will exist as long as the Indians exist, for their ways are different from our ways, and either they or we must be masters on the Plains. I have no doubt our people have committed grievous wrong to the Indians and I wish we could punish them but it is impracticable but both races cannot use this country in common, and one or the other must withdraw." Ibid., 174.

50. Ibid., 176–77.

51. Meagher to Barlow, June 15, 1867, HL.

52. Simon, *The Papers of Ulysses S. Grant,* vol. 17, 179.

53. U.S. Senate, *Report to Accompany Bill S. 519,* 2.

54. Davis Willson to "Folks at Home," May 29, 1867, 1407, Willson Collection, MSUSC.

55. Ibid.

56. Phillips, *Forty Years on the Frontier,* vol. 2, 64; Thomas H. LeForge, *Memoirs of a White Crow Indian,* 17.

57. Meagher to Meagher, Sr., June 15, 1867, NLI.

58. Kuppens, "Thomas Francis Meagher, Montana Pioneer," 138–39.

59. *Memorial of the Legislature of Montana Asking an Appropriation for Paying Debts Created in Raising Montana Volunteers,* 40th Cong., 2nd session, Misc. Doc. No. 125, 1.

60. Snavely to Grant, March 1, 1870, quoted in Simon, *The Papers of Ulysses S. Grant,* vol. 17, 151–52.

61. U.S. House of Representatives, *Message of the President of the United States and Accompanying Documents,* Chapman to Taylor, July 5, 1867.

62. Haines, *Flouring Mills of Montana Territory,* 88; Doughly to William M. Sweeny, August 30, 1915, SW 135, HL.

63. Blake to Wilson, October 15, 1867, quoted in Simon, *The Papers of Ulysses S. Grant,* vol. 17, 150–51.

64. Ibid.

65. U.S. House of Representatives, *Report upon the Montana Indian War Claims of 1867,* 41st Cong., 3rd sess., 8.

66. Ibid., 1; U.S. Senate, *Report to Accompany Bill S. 519;* U.S. House of Representatives, *Report upon the Montana Indian War Claims of 1867,* 42nd Cong., 2nd sess., 7–8; *1867 Indian War Claims,* May–October 1867, RS 162, MHS; U.S. House of Representatives, *House Journal,* 42nd Cong., 3rd sess., 550.

67. U.S. Senate, *Report to Accompany Bill S. 519,* 4.

68. Sherman to Grant, July 19, 1867, quoted in Simon, *The Papers of Ulysses S. Grant,* vol. 17, 241.

69. Wright to Smith, July 5, 1867, quoted in U.S. House of Representatives, *Report on Indian Affairs by the Acting Commissioner for the Year 1867,* 253–59.

70. Ibid.

71. Palladino, *Indian and White in the Northwest,* 202.

CHAPTER 11

1. "Secretary of Montana," *Union and Dakotaian,* March 20, 1867.

2. Meagher to Meagher, Sr., June 15, 1867, Meagher File, MHS.

3. Volney W. Steele, M.D., interview by author, June 16, 2003. Dr. Steele of Bozeman, Montana, is a pathologist and medical historian.

4. John W. Reins to James Gibson, July 11, 1867, Probate Court Files, MCC.

5. Meagher to Ming, July 1, 1867, written from Benton City [Fort Benton], Montana, MHS.

6. "Estate of T. F. Meagher Dec'd: Report, Petition and Decree," February 23, 1868, Probate Court Files, MCC; Warrants, June 27, 1867, Territorial Auditor's File, MHS; Ming to Elizabeth Meagher, July 5, 1867, MHS.

7. "T. F. Meagher's Estate: Appraisement," August 8, 1867, Probate Court Files, MCC. This appraisal was filed by F. C. Deimling, O. P. Thomas, and J. T. Conner. The most valuable items were $2,200 in territorial warrants, which the appraisers valued at twenty-five cents on the dollar for a total of $798 in U.S. currency. The territorial warrants were later sold at forty-five cents on the dollar. "Report of James Gibson Administrator of the Estate of

Thomas Francis Meagher to the Probate Court of Madison County, Montana," August 18, 1868, Probate Court Files, MCC.

8. "Estate of T. F. Meagher Dec'd: Report, Petition and Decree," February 23, 1868, Probate Court Files, MCC. The claims were in U.S. dollars.

9. "In the Matter of the Estate of Thomas Francis Meagher dec'd: The report of F. C. Deimling Adm. de bonis nom of said Estate," October 13, 1870, Probate Court Files, MCC.

10. "Jas G. Spratt vs Est of T. F. Meagher," February 19, 1868, Probate Court Files, MCC. The claim indicated that as surety for the payment of his fees Spratt held territorial warrants amounting to $860 in face value.

11. "In the Matter of the Estate of T. F. Meagher: Petition for Removal of Administrator," March 23, 1868, Book 37, 430, Probate Court Files, MCC; "Samuel Ward and James G. Spratt Deed to E M J Meagher," May 15, 1868, Madison County Recorder's Office, MCC.

12. "Elizabeth M J Meagher Deed to L Daems M.D.," May 30, 1870, Book Q, 402, Madison County Recorder's Office, MCC; "In the Matter of the Estate of T. F. Meagher: Petition for Removal of Administrator," March 23, 1868, Book 37, 430, Probate Court Files, MCC.

13. "How Gen. Meagher Met His Death," *Butte Inter Mountain,* March 15, 1902. The Sanders report included the statement: "No person, so far as I know, save the colored man, saw the general go into the river, and he related to me the circumstances as I have told." See also Sanders, *A History of Montana,* 338–41, where substantially the same story is given and the author states that this "statement of the tragedy, prepared at that time by W. F. Sanders, is the most comprehensive one in existence."

14. Palladino, *Indian and White in the Northwest,* 303.

15. "Bradley Manuscript—Book II: Account of the Drowning of Gen. Thomas Francis Meagher," 132.

16. Overholser, *Fort Benton,* 384.

17. Ibid., 62–63; "Tragedy on Board the Steamer Octavia!: Shooting of an English Nobleman!" *Helena Herald Supplement,* June 26, 1867.

18. Private Speer family history manuscript in the author's collection. Some say that many of Meagher's friends believed that he had been assassinated by British agents. Thompson, "The Death of Thomas Francis Meagher Revisited," 2.

19. Affidavit of Joseph LaBarge, Report of Committee of Inquest, n.d., MHS; Chittenden, *History of Early Steamboat Navigation on the Missouri River,* 409–12, as quoted therein; see also Andrew Fisk Diary, entry for Tuesday, June 25, 1867, MNHS.

20. Hogan to O'Connell, January 6, 1867, MHS.

21. Chittenden, *History of Early Steamboat Navigation on the Missouri River,* 412–15; private correspondence from a Speer family descendant containing a copy of a letter written on July 10, 1867, to the Speer family attorney Mr. William Trollope by M. S. Mepham of St. Louis, January 11, 2005. The killing of Speer drew the attention of the British government, and it was reported in the *New York Times* on July 26, 1867, that "Courtney F. Terry, of the British 68th Royal Rifles, a personal friend of Capt. Speer," was in Saint Louis investigating the case "under the instructions of the English Minister at Washington." "The Murder of a British Officer on the Missouri River," *New York Times,* July 26, 1867.

22. Reinhart, *The Golden Frontier,* 268.

23. Lyons, *Brigadier-General Thomas Francis Meagher,* app. 354, letter from Dolan to Lyons, December 16, 1869. Many of Meagher's friends believed that he had been assassinated by British agents.

24. John J. Hall to Lincoln, October 18, 1864, Abraham Lincoln Papers, Library of Congress, http://memory.loc.gov/cgi-bin/query/r.?ammem/mal:@field(DOCID+@lit(d3 736800)); Coleman, *Abraham Lincoln and Coles County, Illinois,* 152.

25. Haines, *Flouring Mills of Montana Territory,* 88; "From Missoula," *Montana Post,* May 11, 1867.

26. "From Missoula," *Montana Post,* May 11, 1867. While awaiting Chapman's arrival, Beidler had sent to Fort Owen for witnesses and a copy of a digest of U.S. laws. Barret employed learned counsel to conduct Chapman's examination. After the counsel had examined the U.S. laws he came to the conclusion that Meagher could not have Chapman arrested in his capacity as Indian superintendent.

27. Haines, *Flouring Mills of Montana Territory,* 88. Haines concluded: "Chapman made numerous appeals to the Indian office for money for the Indians and apparently during the entire period was stealing from the agency. Rumors of his thievery became so loud that Acting Governor Meagher dispatched the U.S. Marshal, John X. Beidler, to investigate the charges. Beidler spent March 4 through April 5, 1867 investigating and as a result of his findings Chapman was dismissed."

28. U.S. House of Representatives, *Annual Report on Indian Affairs, by the Acting Commissioner,* 259–60, Chapman to Taylor, July 5, 1867. After his return to his hometown Chapman apparently settled down there, first becoming an assistant assessor of internal revenue until 1871 and later being appointed circuit clerk. He became a special agent for a railroad company and then a traveling freight agent until his death on September 11, 1898, followed by burial in Charleston. "Biographical Sketches of Charter Members and Masters of Wabash Lodge, No. 179, A.F. and A.M. Coles County, IL."

29. Doughly to Sweeny, August 30, 1915, SW 135, HL. Doughly had the date of Meagher's dismissal of Chapman "about the middle of June 1867." Doughly's letter was to William Sweeny, the son of the Fenian military commander Thomas Sweeny; its purpose is not known. Doughly may have been a pseudonym. There is no conspicuous record of Doughly in the Montana newspapers or in the rolls of the Montana Militia. Yet he maintained in 1915, when he wrote this letter from his home in Brooklyn, that he was a major in the Montana Militia in 1867 and on the staff of General Meagher.

30. U.S. House of Representatives, *Report on Indian Affairs by the Acting Commissioner for the Year 1867,* 253–59; "From Benton: Mr. Wright's Vindication of His Action in the Agency Affair—The Reverse View of the Question," *Montana Post,* May 25, 1867.

31. "From Benton: Mr. Wright's Vindication of His Action in the Agency Affair—The Reverse View of the Question," *Montana Post,* May 25, 1867; "Late Col. W. F. Sanders Described in Detail the Death of General Meagher," *Butte Miner,* June 10, 1913.

32. Hunt, "Thomas Francis Meagher," 24–28; "General Meagher Executed by Vigilantes, Dave Mack Says," *Anaconda Standard,* June 2, 1913.

33. "How Gen. Meagher Met His Death," *Butte Inter Mountain,* March 15, 1902; "Late Col. W. F. Sanders Described in Detail the Death of General Meagher," *Butte Miner,* June 10, 1913. Sanders did not recall the members of Meagher's militia detachment who were with him, other than "Captain William Boyce, afterward a resident of Butte."

34. Meagher to Johnson, January 29, 1866, Johnson Papers, Division of Manuscripts, LoC, quoted in Spence, *Territorial Politics and Government in Montana,* 37–38.

35. Lyons, *Brigadier-General Thomas Francis Meagher,* 353.

36. "Late Col. W. F. Sanders Described in Detail the Death of General Meagher," *Butte Miner,* June 10, 1913. According to Sanders, Eastman's "dinners were veritable feasts of Lucullus and scarce a day passed that a choice lot of merry guests did not surround his hospitable board."

37. Ibid.; Doughly to Sweeny, August 30, 1915, SW 135, HL; Rolle, *The Road to Virginia City*, 119, 124–25.

38. Lyons, *Brigadier-General Thomas Francis Meagher*, 353; "Late Col. W. F. Sanders Described in Detail the Death of General Meagher," *Butte Miner*, June 10, 1913.

39. Lyons, *Brigadier-General Thomas Francis Meagher*, 352.

40. Ibid., 353.

41. Ibid., 353–54.

42. Ibid., 354.

43. "Late Col. W. F. Sanders Described in Detail the Death of General Meagher," *Butte Miner*, June 10, 1913.

44. Ibid.

45. Lyons, *Brigadier-General Thomas Francis Meagher*, 354–55.

46. Ibid., 351–52, 355.

47. "Bradley Manuscript—Book II," 131.

48. Hunt, "Thomas Francis Meagher," 33; Dennis Nolan to Hon. D. H. Kelly, June 4, 1913, Attorney General Files, MHS. Leaman's name was apparently really Lehman, and both he and Dennis Nolan are listed in a Lewistown history book, which states that John Lehman was one of the first two people admitted to the new St. Joseph's Hospital when it opened in 1908. Nolan is listed as a council officer of the Lewistown chapter of the Knights of Columbus when it was chartered in 1911. Dissly, *History of Lewistown*, 42, 223. The letter was written to the Montana attorney general and advised that Lehman had a "reputation for being truthfull [*sic*] and honest to a fault." The letter also said that Lehman was working on the *John D. Lee;* however, no mention of the arrival of the *John D. Lee* at Fort Benton has been found either in Overholser, *Fort Benton,* or in the early Montana newspapers; nor have any boats with similar names been found. It would be unusual for a passenger and freight boat arrival not to be noted.

49. *Anaconda Standard,* September 19, 1901, quoted in "Baker Tells Of Death of Gen. Meagher," unidentified newspaper clipping, June 20, 1943, MHS.

50. "Bradley Manuscript—Book II," 131.

51. Hunt, "Thomas Francis Meagher," 32; Cavanagh, *Memoirs,* app. 12.

52. Lyons, *Brigadier-General Thomas Francis Meagher,* 355–56.

53. Hunt, "Thomas Francis Meagher," 33. "Woman Refutes Diamond Story," *Montana Daily Record,* June 4, 1913. The article is based on items taken from the *Missoulian.* After reading the story of a confession of Meagher's murder in 1913, Mrs. Nichols informed the *Missoulian* of her observations.

54. Nolan to Kelly, June 4, 1913, Attorney General Files, MHS.

55. Cavanagh, *Memoirs,* app. 12–13. In 1892 P. J. Condon, a former member of the Irish Brigade, was the president of the Irish Brigade Officers' Association and a Fenian leader. In a letter to Michael Cavanagh, Condon advised that he had been in Omaha in the fall of 1868 when he formed the acquaintance of the "soldier" who was on sentry duty on the boat from which Meagher fell. Soon afterward Condon visited with "the proprietor of the Indian trading post at Benton." Later Condon visited with "the captain of the vessel and the pilot who accompanied Gen. Meagher to his stateroom on the boat." Condon forwarded the report he had prepared on these meetings to Captain W. F. Lyons, who was then editor of the *New York Herald* and was at the time writing a book on Meagher.

56. Overholser, *Fort Benton,* 63.

57. Doughly to Sweeny, August 30, 1915, SW 135, Barlow Files, HL. Richard O'Gorman said: "There was no railing on the guards opposite his stateroom door, it having

been broken off in some way. About ten o'clock at night he went on the guards. Here, it is supposed, he stumbled on a coil of rope, lost his balance, and was precipitated over the side of the boat." Cavanagh, *Memoirs,* app. 10. Several people believed that the handrail opposite Meagher's cabin was missing or broken. See Palladino, *Indian and White in the Northwest,* 304. Steamboats often collided with one another as they literally raced each other upstream, and it would not be unusual for railings on the boats to be broken. See Harriet Sanders diary, Sanders File, MHS.

58. "How Gen. Meagher Met His Death," *Butte Inter Mountain,* March 15, 1902; "Late Col. W. F. Sanders Described in Detail the Death of General Meagher," *Butte Miner,* June 10, 1913. Sanders's report included the statement: "No person, so far as I know, save the colored man, saw General Meagher go into the river, and he related to me the circumstances as I have told."

59. "How Gen. Meagher Met His Death," *Butte Inter Mountain,* March 15, 1902.

60. Ibid. According to Sanders, "As there was no telegraph, the news of the event went by mail that night."

61. See Lyons, *Brigadier-General Thomas Francis Meagher,* app. 354–57, letter from Dolan to Lyons, December 16, 1869; "How Gen. Meagher Met His Death," *Butte Inter Mountain,* March 15, 1902. Historian Helen Fitzgerald Sanders, daughter-in-law of Wilbur Sanders, published his version of the events that day in Sanders, *History of Montana,* 338–41. She claims that his version was taken from notes at the time of Meagher's death.

62. Doughly to Sweeny, August 30, 1915, SW 135, HL. Doughly said: "The writer took the first boat down the river after the accident with the hopes of find[ing] the Generals [*sic*] body but although a careful watch was kept no body was found either floating in the river or on its banks."

63. "Death of General Meagher," *Bunker Hill [Illinois] Union Gazette,* August 8, 1867.

64. Cavanagh, *Memoirs,* app. 12.

65. "Daems, Marie L. to Sanders, James U.," letter dated October 17, 1901, copy provided to the author by Donna Daems, Bozeman, Montana. Marie L. Daems was born in Belgium. "Benton and Missouri River News," *Montana Post,* June 19, 1867.

66. "The Late Gen. Meagher—Particulars of His Death," *New York Times,* July 29, 1867; "Proclamation by the Governor," *Virginia Tri-Weekly Post,* July 11, 1867.

67. "Resolutions of the Helena Bar," *Virginia Tri-Weekly Post,* July 11, 1867.

68. "Meeting in Virginia," *Virginia Tri-Weekly Post,* July 11, 1867.

69. "Resolutions of Sympathy" and "Our Neighbors," *Montana Post,* July 27, 1867; "The Emmett [*sic*] Circle" and "Resolutions of the Military," *Montana Post,* July 13, 1867.

70. *New York Times,* July 8, 1867; "Death of Gen. Meagher," *Irish American,* July 13, 1867.

71. "Thomas Francis Meagher: Died, July 1st, 1867," *Irish American,* July 20, 1867.

72. "The Death of Gen. Meagher," *Irish American,* July 27, 1867; "Gen. Thomas F. Meagher," *Irish American,* August 3, 1867; "The Late Gen. Meagher," *Irish American,* August 10, 1867.

73. "The Late Gen. Meagher," *Irish American,* August 31, 1867; "The Late Gen. Meagher," *Irish American,* September 14, 1867.

74. "Gen. T. F. Meagher (From the *London Universal News*)," *Irish American,* October 12, 1867.

75. "The Late Gen. Meagher," *Irish American,* August 17, 1867, quoting the *Dublin Nation* of July 27, 1867.

76. "Miscellaneous," *New York Times,* September 18, 1867.

77. "In Re Estate of Thos Francis Meagher: Claims of Widow," August 10, 1867, Probate Court File, MCC; Reinhart, *The Golden Frontier,* 269. *Montana Post,* August 17, 1867, and September 28, 1867; *Montana Post Tri-Weekly,* August 31, 1867; and *Helena Herald Weekly,* August 21, 1867.

78. 1870 United States Federal Census, Monroe, Orange County, N.Y., June 25, 1870; "In the matter of the estate of Peter Townsend deceased: Brief for objecting legatees," n.d., Surrogates Court, Orange County, N.J., Barlow Files, HL. Elizabeth Meagher and Alice Barlow filed a contest to the distribution under the will. The outcome of their petition is not known.

79. "The Late Gen. Meagher: His Obsequies in New York," *Irish American,* August 24, 1867; Elizabeth Meagher to Andrew O'Connell, November 12, 1902, MHS; *Report to Accompany Bill H. R. 8463,* 2, letter from Nugent to Brady, May 17, 1886.

80. Thomas Bennett Meagher to the Honorable Secretary of War, May 26, 1872, Thomas Bennett Meagher to the Honorable Secretary of War, August 13, 1872, and Hon. William R. Roberts to the Secretary of War, May 16, 1872, RG 94 entry 214, box 25, folder 8, USMAL. At the semiannual examinations held the next January, Cadet Meagher was found deficient in both mathematics and French and was discharged from the academy, after which little is known. Roberts first nominated Bennett on May 16, listing his age at eighteen years and zero months. On May 26 Bennett acknowledged the receipt for his contemplated appointment from West Point and certified "on honor" that he was eighteen years and one month of age, in which case he probably would have been born in late April or early May 1854. In Roberts's second nomination on July 18 Meagher was listed again as eighteen years and zero months; acknowledging receipt of the contemplated appointment on August 13, Bennett said that he was eighteen years and three months old, again indicating that he had been born in late April or early May 1854. When he was declared "deficient" in January 1873, however, his age was listed as nineteen years and zero months, indicating that he had been born in January 1854. Official records of the U.S. Military Academy indicate that Thomas Bennett Meagher was eighteen years and eight months on September 1 and nineteen years and zero months in January 1873. Young Meagher's aptitude was listed as "very little"; he was also listed as "very studious" and under "discipline" as "not attentive." "Report of the Cadets of the U.S. Military Academy who at the Examination in January, 1873, were 'declared deficient' 4th Class only," January 9, 1873, RG 94, entry 235, box 1, USMAL; Hon. William R. Roberts to the Secretary of War, May 16, 1872, Thomas Bennett Meagher to the Honorable Secretary of War, May 26, 1872, Hon. William R. Roberts to the Secretary of War, July 18, 1872, and Thomas Bennett Meagher to the Honorable Secretary of War, August 13, 1872, RG 94, entry 214, box 25, folder 8, USMAL; "Cadets Admitted in 1872," in *Official Register of the Officers and Cadets of the U.S. Military Academy, West Point, New-York,* 23.

81. William R. Roberts to Hon. W. W. Belknap, June 29, 1872, RG 94, entry 214, box 25, folder 8, USMAL.

82. T. Bennett Meagher to Barlow, November 22, 1874 [?], and December 8, 1874, Barlow Files, HL. The November 22 letter has no year date, but from the context it appears that it was 1874. Both letters list 137 Broadway as Bennett Meagher's address.

83. "Westchester County Miscellaneous Records 1840–1916, A–L"; Mrs. Thomas Meagher III to Robert Athearn, July 17, 1946, MHS. In the letter Mrs. Meagher also says that her husband's father was "Thomas Meagher II" and that he died in Manila. Apparently the family had come to refer to Thomas Bennett Meagher as Thomas Francis Meagher II.

84. Cavanagh, *Memoirs,* 495–96. In 2004 Waterford finally made plans to erect an equestrian statue of Meagher.

85. Gwynn, *Thomas Francis Meagher,* 2; Griffith, *Meagher of the Sword,* xviii.

86. Costigan, *History of Modern Ireland,* 202.

87. Emmons, *The Butte Irish,* 13, 19, 23, 118.

88. "Proceedings at the meeting of the joint committee representing Camps No. 233 and No. 90 held at Butte, Mont. On Jany. 23, 1898 to organize a movement with the object in view of erecting a monument to the memory of Thomas Francis Meagher," AOH File, BSA.

89. Emmons, *The Butte Irish,* 119.

90. "Address before the Irish Parliament, Dublin, June 28, 1963."

91. Charles Laverty, president of the Irish Brigade Association, phone interview by author, October 24, 2000.

92. Cavanagh, *Memoirs,* app. 10.

93. Ibid.

94. Ibid.

Bibliography

ARCHIVAL COLLECTIONS

Abraham Lincoln Papers, Division of Manuscripts, Library of Congress, Washington, D.C.
Antietam National Battlefield Archives, Antietam, Va.
Attorney General Files, Montana Historical Society, Helena.
Butte Silver Bow Public Archives, Butte, Mont.
Darby Papers, Virginia Historical Society, Richmond.
Fisk Files, Minnesota Historical Society, St. Paul.
Gettysburg College Special Collections, Gettysburg
James Fergus Papers, Montana Historical Society, Helena.
Johnson Papers, Division of Manuscripts, Library of Congress, Washington, D.C.
K. Ross Toole Archives and Special Collections, University of Montana, Missoula.
Lyman E. Munson Papers, Montana Historical Society, Helena.
McCarter Papers, Historical Society of Pennsylvania, Harrisburg.
McClellan Papers, Division of Manuscripts, Library of Congress, Washington, D.C.
Meagher File, University of Notre Dame Archives, Notre Dame, Ind.
Meagher Files, Montana Historical Society, Helena.
Montana Territorial Papers, National Archives, Washington, D.C.
O'Brien Papers, National Library of Ireland, Dublin.
Probate Court Files, Madison County Courthouse, Virginia City, Mont.
Samuel Latham Mitchell Barlow Files, Huntington Library, San Marino, Calif.
Schoff Civil War Collection, William L. Clements Library, University of Michigan, Ann Arbor.
Stacy Family Papers, Virginia Historical Society, Richmond.
Sydney Howard Gay Collection, Manuscript Collections, Columbia University Libraries, New York.
Territorial Auditor's File, Montana Historical Society, Helena.
Territorial Governor's File, Montana Historical Society, Helena.
Territorial Papers, Montana Historical Society, Helena.

Thomas F. Madigan Papers, New York Public Library, New York.
Thomas Francis Meagher Files, National Archives and Records Administration, Washington, D.C.
Thomas F. Meehan Papers, Special Collections, Georgetown University, Washington, D.C.
Turner Papers, New York State Library, Albany.
United States Military Academy Library, West Point, N.Y.
Wilbur Fisk Sanders Papers, Montana Historical Society, Helena.
Willson Collection, Montana State University Special Collections, Bozeman.

GOVERNMENT PUBLICATIONS

First Legislative Assembly of the Territory of Montana. *Acts, Resolutions and Memorials, of the Territory of Montana, Passed by the First Legislative Assembly.* Virginia City, Mont.: D. W. Tilton & Co., 1865.
———. *Council Journal of the First Legislative Assembly of Montana Territory.* Virginia City, Mont.: D. W. Tilton & Co., 1865.
———. *House Journal of the First Session of the Legislative Assembly of the Territory of Montana.* Virginia City, Mont.: D. W. Tilton & Co., 1865.
Laws of the Territory of Montana Passed at the Second Session of the Legislature, 1866. Virginia City, Mont.: D. W. Tilton & Co., 1866.
Legislative Assembly of the Territory of Montana. *Council Journal of the First Legislative Assembly of Montana Territory.* 2nd sess. Virginia City, Mont.: D. W. Tilton & Co., 1866.
United States. Naval War Records Office. *Official Records of the Union and Confederate Navies in the War of the Rebellion.* Washington, D.C.: Government Printing Office, 1894–1922.
———. *Statutes at Large of the United States of America.* 39th Cong., 2nd sess. Washington, D.C.: Government Printing Office, 1867.
———. "Treaty between the United States and the Blackfoot Nation of Indians, Etc., November 16, 1865." In *Indian Affairs: Laws and Treaties.* Vol. 4, pt. 4. Washington, D.C.: Government Printing Office, 1866.
U.S. Bureau of Indian Affairs. *Report of the Commissioner of Indian Affairs for the Year 1865.* Washington, D.C.: Government Printing Office, 1866.
———. *Report of the Commissioner of Indian Affairs for the Year 1866.* Washington, D.C.: Government Printing Office, 1867.
U.S. House of Representatives. *Appendix to the Congressional Globe.* "Remarks of Hon. S. McLean, of Montana, in the House of Representatives, May 4, 1866." 39th Cong., 1st sess. Washington, D.C.: Government Printing Office, 1866.
———. *The Counter Case of Great Britain as Laid before the Tribunal of Arbitration, Convened at Geneva.* 42nd Cong., 2nd sess., Ex. Doc. No. 324. Washington, D.C.: Government Printing Office, 1872.
———. *House Journal.* 38th Cong., 1st sess. Washington, D.C.: Government Printing Office, 1864.
———. *House Journal.* 42nd Cong., 3rd sess. Washington, D.C: Government Printing Office, 1873.
———. *Message of the President of the United States and Accompanying Documents.* 40th Cong., 2nd sess. Washington, D.C.: Government Printing Office, 1868.
———. *Report on Indian Affairs, by the Acting Commissioner.* 40th Cong., 2nd sess., Ex. Doc. No. 1. In *Message of the President of the United States and Accompanying Documents, to the*

Two Houses of Congress at the Commencement of the 2nd Session of the 40th Congress. Washington, D.C.: Government Printing Office, 1868.

———. *Report to Accompany H. Res. 23.* 42nd Cong., 2nd sess., Report No. 82. Washington, D.C.: Government Printing Office, 1872.

———. *Report to Accompany Bill H. R. 8463.* 49th Cong., 2nd sess., Report No. 1731. Washington, D.C.: Government Printing Office, 1887.

———. *Report upon the Montana Indian War Claims of 1867.* 41st Cong., 3rd sess., Ex. Doc. No. 98. Washington, D.C.: Government Printing Office, 1871.

———. *Report upon the Montana Indian War Claims of 1867.* 42nd Cong., 2nd sess., Report No. 82. Washington, D.C.: Government Printing Office, 1872.

U.S. Senate. *Memorial of the Legislature of Montana Asking an Appropriation for Paying Debts Created in Raising Montana Volunteers.* 40th Cong., 2nd sess., Misc. Doc. No. 125. Washington, D.C.: Government Printing Office, 1868.

———. *Report to Accompany Bill S. 519.* 41st Cong, 2nd sess., Report No. 31. Washington, D.C.: Government Printing Office, 1870.

———. *Senate Executive Journal.* 39th Cong., 2nd sess. Washington, D.C.: Government Printing Office, 1867.

———. *Senate Executive Journal.* 40th Cong., 1st sess. Washington, D.C.: Government Printing Office, 1867.

U.S. War Department. *The War of the Rebellion: A Compilation of the Official Records of the Union and Confederate Armies.* 70 vols. in 128. Washington, D.C.: Government Printing Office, 1880–1901.

BOOKS, PAMPHLETS, AND PERIODICALS

Adam-Smith, Patsy. *Heart of Exile: Ireland, 1848, and the Seven Patriots Banished; Their Adventures, Loneliness and Loves in Three Continents as They Search for Refuge.* Melbourne: Nelson Publishers, 1986.

Anbinder, Tyler. *Five Points.* New York: Plume/Penguin Putnam, 2002.

Andrews, J. Cutler. *The North Reports the Civil War.* Reprint. Pittsburgh: University of Pittsburgh Press, 1985.

Athearn, Robert G. *Thomas Francis Meagher: An Irish Revolutionary in America.* Boulder: University of Colorado Press, 1949.

———. *William Tecumseh Sherman and the Settlement of the West.* Norman: University of Oklahoma Press, 1956.

Atkinson, Sarah Gaynor. *Mary Aikenhead: Her Life, Her Work, and Her Friends, Giving a History of the Foundation of the Congregation of the Irish Sisters of Charity.* Dublin: M. H. Gill & Son, 1879.

Bancroft, Hubert Howe. *History of Central America.* San Francisco: History Co., 1887.

———. *History of Washington, Idaho, and Montana.* San Francisco: History Co., 1890.

———. *The Works of Hubert Howe Bancroft.* Vol. 31. New York: Arno Press, n.d.

Basler, Roy P., ed. *The Collected Works of Abraham Lincoln.* 9 vols. and 2 supplements. The Abraham Lincoln Association, Springfield, Illinois. New Brunswick, N.J.: Rutgers University Press, 1953–55, 1990.

Bayor, Ronald H., and Timothy J. Meagher, eds. *The New York Irish.* Baltimore: John Hopkins University Press, 1966.

Beller, Susan Provost. *Never Were Men So Brave: The Irish Brigade during the Civil War.* New York: Margaret K. McElderry Books, 1998.

Bernstein, Iver. *The New York City Draft Riots: Their Significance for American Society and Politics in the Age of the Civil War.* New York: Oxford University Press, 1990.

Bianconi, M. O'C., and S. J. Watson. *Bianconi: King of the Irish Roads.* Dublin: Allen Figgis, 1962.

Bigart, R., and C. Woodcock. "Peter Peterson Tofft: Painter in the Wilderness." *Montana, the Magazine of Western History* (October 1975).

Bilby, Joseph G. *The Irish Brigade in the Civil War: The 69th New York and Other Irish Regiments of the Army of the Potomac.* Hightstown, N.J.: Longstreet House/Conshohocken, Pa.: Combined Publishing, 1998.

Bowers, Claude G. *The Irish Orators.* Indianapolis: Bobbs-Merrill, 1916.

"Bradley Manuscript—Book II: Account of the Drowning of Gen. Thomas Francis Meagher." *Contributions to the Historical Society of Montana* 8 (1917).

Brandt, Nat. *The Congressman Who Got Away with Murder.* Syracuse: Syracuse University Press, 1991.

Bruce, John P., ed. *Lectures of Gov. Thomas Francis Meagher, in Montana, Together with His Messages, Speeches, Etc.* Virginia City, Montana Territory: Bruce & Wright Printers, 1867.

Burns, Ric, and James Sanders. *New York: An Illustrated History.* New York: Alfred A. Knopf, 1999.

Burton, Brian K. *Extraordinary Circumstances: The Seven Days Battles.* Bloomington: Indiana University Press, 2001.

Burton, W. L. *Melting Pot Soldiers.* Ames: Iowa State University Press, 1988.

Callaway, Llewellyn L. *Montana's Righteous Hangmen: The Vigilantes in Action.* Norman: University of Oklahoma Press, 1982.

Cavanagh, Michael. *Memoirs of Gen. Thomas Francis Meagher.* Worchester, Mass.: Messenger Press, 1892.

Chittenden, Hiram Martin. *History of Early Steamboat Navigation on the Missouri River: Life and Adventures of Joseph LaBarge.* New York: Francis P. Harper, 1903.

Chittenden, Hiram Martin, and Alfred Talbot Richardson, eds. *Life, Letters, and Travels of Father Pierre-Jean De Smet, S.J., 1801–1873.* New York: Francis P. Harper, 1905.

Cole, J. A. *Prince of Spies: Henri Le Caron.* London: Faber & Faber, 1984.

Coleman, Charles H. *Abraham Lincoln and Coles County, Illinois.* New Brunswick, N.J.: Scarecrow, 1955.

Comerford, R. V. *The Fenians in Context: Irish Politics and Society, 1848–82.* Dublin: Wolfhound, 1985.

Conyngham, David Power. *The Irish Brigade and Its Campaigns, with Some Account of the Corcoran Legion, and Sketches of the Principal Officers.* New York: Fordham University Press, 1981.

Corby, William. *Memoirs of Chaplain Life: Three Years with the Irish Brigade in the Army of the Potomac.* New York: Fordham University Press, 1992.

Corcoran, T. *The Clongowes Record, 1814 to 1932; with Introductory Chapters on Irish Jesuit Educators, 1564 to 1813.* Dublin: Browne & Nolan, 1932.

———. *The Story of Clongowes Wood, A.D. 1450–1900.* Dublin: Catholic Truth Society of Ireland, 1900.

Costigan, Giovanni. *A History of Modern Ireland, with a Sketch of Earlier Times.* New York: Pegasus, 1969.

Crawford, Martin, ed. *William Howard Russell's Civil War: Private Diary and Letters, 1861–1862.* Athens: University of Georgia Press, 1992.

Crowther, Samuel. *The Romance and Rise of the American Tropics.* Garden City, N.Y.: Double-day, Doran & Co., 1929.

Cullen, J. H. *Young Ireland in Exile: The Story of the Men of '48 in Tasmania.* Dublin: Talbot, 1928.

D'Arcy, William. *The Fenian Movement in the United States, 1858–1886.* Washington, D.C.: Catholic University of America Press, 1947.

Davies, Norman. *The Isles: A History.* Oxford: Oxford University Press, 1999.

Davis, Kenneth C. *Don't Know Much about the Civil War.* New York: William Morrow & Co., 1996.

Davis, Richard P. *William Smith O'Brien: Ireland—1848—Tasmania.* Dublin: Geography Publications, 1989.

Denieffe, Joseph. *A Personal Narrative of the Irish Revolutionary Brotherhood.* Shannon, Ireland: Irish University Press, 1969.

DePew, Chauncy M., et al., eds. *The Library of Oratory, Ancient and Modern, with Critical Studies of the World's Great Orators by Eminent Essayists.* Vol. 10. New York: Globe Publishing, 1902.

Dimsdale, Thomas J. *The Vigilantes of Montana or Popular Justice in the Rocky Mountains.* Norman: University of Oklahoma Press, 1953. Rpt. Guilford, Conn.: Globe Pequot, 2003.

Dissly, Robert, ed. *History of Lewistown.* Lewistown, Mont.: News-Argus Printing, 1984.

Donnelly, James S., Jr., ed. *Encyclopedia of Irish History and Culture.* 2 vols. Farmington Hills, Mich.: Macmillan Reference USA, 2004.

Doyle, Susan Badger, ed. *Journeys to the Land of Gold: Emigrant Diaries from the Bozeman Trail, 1863–66.* 2 vols. Helena: Montana Historical Society Press, 2000.

Duffy, Charles Gavan. *A Bird's-Eye View of Irish History.* Dublin: James Duffy & Co., 1882.

———. *Four Years of Irish History, 1845–1849.* Melbourne: George Robertson, 1883.

———. *Young Ireland: A Fragment of Irish History, 1840–1850.* New York: G. Munro, 1880.

Dunbar, Seymour. *The Journals and Letters of Major John Owen, Pioneer of the Northwest, 1850–1871.* New York: Edward Eberstadt, 1927.

Dyer, Frederick H. *A Compendium of the War of the Rebellion, Compiled and Arranged from Official Records of the Federal and Confederate Armies, Reports of the Adjutant Generals of the Several States, the Army Registers, and Other Reliable Documents and Sources.* 3 vols. Des Moines: Dyer, 1908.

Eby, Cecil D., Jr., ed. *A Virginia Yankee in the Civil War: The Diaries of David Hunter Strother.* Chapel Hill: North Carolina University Press, 1961.

Edwards, R. Dudley. *Daniel O'Connell and His World.* London: Thames & Hudson, 1975.

Eicher, David J. *The Longest Night: A Military History of the Civil War.* New York: Simon & Schuster, 2001.

Emmons, David M. *The Butte Irish: Class and Ethnicity in an American Mining Town, 1875–1925.* Urbana: University of Illinois Press, 1990.

Evans, Lucylle H. *Good Samaritan of the Northwest: Anthony Ravalli, S.J., 1812–1884.* Stevensville: Montana Creative Consultants, 1981.

Fontaine, Felix G. *DeWitt's "Special Report": Trial of the Hon. Daniel E. Sickles for Shooting Philip Barton Key, Esq., U.S. District Attorney, of Washington, D.C.* New York: R. M. DeWitt, 1859.

Foster, R. F., ed. *Modern Ireland, 1600–1972.* London: Allen Lane/Penguin Press, 1988.

———. *The Oxford History of Ireland.* Oxford: Oxford University Press, 1989.

Fox, William Freeman. *Regimental Losses in the American Civil War: 1861–1865.* Albany: Albany Publishing Co., 1889.

Garrison, Webb B. *Friendly Fire in the Civil War: More Than 100 True Stories of Comrade Killing Comrade.* Nashville: Rutledge Hill Press, 1999.

Golway, Terry. *Irish Rebel: John Devoy and America's Fight for Ireland's Freedom.* New York: St. Martin's Press, 1998.

Graetz, Rick, and Susie Graetz. *Bannack: Foundation of Montana.* Helena: Montana Fish, Wildlife & Parks, 2004.

Graham, R. B. Cunninghame. *José Antonio Páez* (1929). New York: Cooper Square Publishers, 1970.

Griffith, Arthur, ed. *Meagher of the Sword: Speeches of Thomas Francis Meagher in Ireland, 1846–1848.* Dublin: M. H. Gill & Son, 1916.

Gruggen, George, and Joseph Keating. *Stonyhurst: Its Past History and Life in the Present.* London: K. Paul, Trench, Trubner & Co., 1901.

Guice, John D. W. *The Rocky Mountain Bench: The Territorial Supreme Courts of Colorado, Montana, and Wyoming, 1861–1890.* New Haven: Yale University Press, 1972.

Gwynn, Denis. *Thomas Francis Meagher: O'Donnell Lecture Delivered at University College, July 17th, 1961.* Dublin: National University of Ireland, 1961.

———. *Young Ireland and 1848.* Cork: Cork University Press, 1949.

Haines, Tom. *Flouring Mills of Montana Territory.* Missoula: Friends of the University of Montana Library, 1984.

Hamilton, James McClellan. *From Wilderness to Statehood: A History of Montana, 1805–1900.* Portland, Ore.: Binfords & Mort, 1957.

Hammond, Harold Earl. *A Commoner's Judge: The Life and Times of Charles P. Daly.* Introduction by Allan Nevins. Boston: Christopher Publishing House, 1954.

———, ed. *Diary of a Union Lady: 1861–1865.* New York: Funk & Wagnalls, 1962.

Hassard, Albert R. *Famous Canadian Trials.* Toronto: Carswell Co., 1924.

Hedrick, David T., and Gordon Barry Davis, Jr., eds. and comps. *I'm Surrounded by Methodists: Diary of John H. W. Stuckenberg, Chaplain of the 145th Pennsylvania Volunteer Infantry.* Gettysburg, Pa.: Thomas, 1995.

Henderson, Andrew. *The Stone Phoenix: Stonyhurst College 1794–1894.* Worthing, England: Churchman Publishing, 1986.

Hereward, Senior. *The Fenians and Canada.* Toronto: Macmillan of Canada, 1978.

Hershkowitz, Leo. "The Irish and the Emerging City: Settlement to 1844." In Bayor and Meagher, *The New York Irish,* 11–34.

Hirshson, Stanley P. *The White Tecumseh: A Biography of General William T. Sherman.* New York: J. Wiley, 1997.

Hitchcock, Frederick L. *War from the Inside: The Story of the 132nd Regiment Pennsylvania Volunteer Infantry in the War for the Suppression of the Rebellion, 1862–1863.* Philadelphia: J. B. Lippincott, 1904. Rpt. Alexandria, Va.: Time-Life Books, 1985. Page references are to the 1904 edition.

Hopkins, David, comp. *The Convict Era: Transported beyond the Seas.* Devenport, Tasmania: Taswegia, 1993.

Hunt, Lewis W. "Thomas Francis Meagher: The 1913 Hoax." *Montana, the Magazine of Western History* (Winter 1962).

Hynes, Daniel. *A Short History of Dublin.* Killeen, Ireland: Killeen Books, 1996.

Jackson, W. Turrentine. "The Appointment and Removal of Sidney Edgerton, First Governor of Montana Territory." *Pacific Northwest Quarterly* (July 1943).

Johnson, Dorothy M. *The Bloody Bozeman: The Perilous Trail to Montana's Gold.* Missoula: Mountain Press, 1983.

Jones, Paul. *The Irish Brigade.* Washington, D.C.: R. B. Luce, 1969.

"A Journey to Benton." *Montana, the Magazine of Western History* 1:4 (October 1951).

Kee, Robert. *The Bold Fenian Men.* Vol. 2 of *The Green Flag.* London: Penguin Books, 1972.

————. *The Most Distressful Country.* Vol. 1 of *The Green Flag.* London: Penguin Books, 1972.

Keneally, Thomas. *The Great Shame and the Triumph of the Irish in the English-Speaking World.* New York: Nan A. Talese/Doubleday, 2000.

Kiernan, T. J. *The Irish Exiles in Australia.* Melbourne and London: Buirns & Oates, 1954.

Killeen, Richard. *A Short History of Ireland.* Surrey, England: CIB Publishing, 1994.

Knappen, M. M. *Constitutional and Legal History of England.* Hamden, Conn.: Archon Books, 1964.

Kohl, Lawrence Frederick, and Margaret Cosse Richard, eds. *Irish Green and Union Blue: The Civil War Letters of Peter Welsh, Color Sergeant, 28th Regiment, Massachusetts Volunteers.* New York: Fordham University Press, 1986.

Kuppens, Francis Xavier. "Thomas Francis Meagher, Montana Pioneer." *Mid-America: An Historical Review* 14:3 (1931–32).

Lane, Phyllis. "Colonel Michael Corcoran, Fighting Irishman." In Seagrave, ed., *The History of the Irish Brigade.*

Langford, Nathaniel Pitt. *Vigilante Days and Ways.* Helena, Mont.: American & World Geographic Publishing, 1996.

Lecky, William Edward Hartpole. *A History of Ireland in the Eighteenth Century.* New impression. Vol. 1. London: Longmans, Green & Co., 1913.

————. *Leaders of Public Opinion in Ireland.* Vol. 2. London: Longmans, Green & Co., 1903.

Leeson, Michael A. *History of Montana, 1739–1885.* Chicago: Warner, Beers & Co., 1885.

LeForge, Thomas H. *Memoirs of a White Crow Indian.* Lincoln: University of Nebraska Press, 1974.

Lepley, John G. *Packets to Paradise: Steamboating to Fort Benton.* Missoula: Pictorial Histories Publishing, 2001.

Leyburn, James Graham. *The Scotch-Irish: A Social History.* Chapel Hill: University of North Carolina Press, 1962.

The Life and Times of Thomas Francis Meagher. Waterford: Reginald's Tower, 1982 (an exhibition catalogue).

Lonn, Ella. *Desertion during the Civil War.* Lincoln: University of Nebraska Press, 1998.

Lyons, W. F. *Brigadier-General Thomas Francis Meagher: His Political and Military Career; with Reflections from His Speeches and Writings.* New York: D. & J. Sadlier & Co., 1886.

MacIntyre, Angus. *The Liberator: Daniel O'Connell and the Irish Party, 1830–1847.* New York: Macmillan, 1965.

MacManus, M. J., ed. *Thomas Davis and Young Ireland.* Dublin: Stationery Office, 1945.

MacManus, Seumas. *The Story of the Irish Race: A Popular History of Ireland.* New York: Irish Publishing, 1921.

Malone, Michael P. *The Battle for Butte: Mining and Politics on the Northern Frontier, 1864–1906.* Seattle: University of Washington Press, 1981.

Mather, R. E., and F. E. Boswell. *Vigilante Victims: Montana's 1864 Hanging Spree.* San Jose: History West Publishing, 1991.

McPherson, James M. *Battle Cry of Freedom: The Civil War Era.* New York: Ballantine Books, 1988.

Meagher, Thomas Francis. "Ireland and the Holy Alliance." *United States Democratic Review* 31:168 (July 1852).

————. *Letters on Our National Struggle.* New York: Loyal Publication Society, 1863.

————. *Speeches on the Legislative Independence of Ireland.* New York: Redfield, 1853.

Melville, Joy. *Mother of Oscar: The Life of Jane Francesca Wilde.* London: John Murray, 1994.

Miller, Robert Ryal. *Shamrock and Sword: The Saint Patrick's Battalion in the U.S.-Mexican War.* Norman: University of Oklahoma Press, 1989.

Mitchel, John. *Jail Journal; or, Five Years in British Prisons.* Author's edition. Glasgow: Cameron & Ferguson, n.d.

Moley, Raymond. *Daniel O'Connell: Nationalism without Violence.* New York: Fordham University Press, 1974.

Moody, T. W. *The Fenian Movement.* Dublin: Mercer Press, 1978.

Moore, Frank, ed. *The Rebellion Record: A Diary of American Events* (1863). Vol. 6. New York: Arno, 1977.

Mulholland, St. Clair. *The Story of the 116th Regiment, Pennsylvania Volunteers in the War of the Rebellion.* Philadelphia: F. McManus, Jr. & Co., 1903. Rpt. Lawrence F. Kohl, ed. New York: Fordham University Press, 1996. References are to the 1996 edition.

Murfin, James V. *The Gleam of Bayonets: The Battle of Antietam and Robert E. Lee's Maryland Campaign, September 1862.* Baton Rouge: Louisiana State University Press, 1965.

Myers, Rex C., ed. *Lizzie: The Letters of Elizabeth Chester Fisk, 1864–1893.* Missoula: Mountain Press, 1989.

O'Brien, Kevin E., ed. *My Life in the Irish Brigade: The Civil War Memoirs of Private William McCarter, 116th Pennsylvania Infantry.* Campbell, Calif.: Savas Publishing Co., 1996.

————. "Sprig of Green: The Irish Brigade, Chapter III." In Seagrave, *The History of the Irish Brigade.*

O'Broin, Leon. *Fenian Fever: An Anglo-American Dilemma.* New York: New York University Press, 1971.

O'Ferrall, Fergus. *Daniel O'Connell.* Dublin: Gill & Macmillan, 1981.

Official Register of the Officers and Cadets of the U.S. Military Academy, West Point, New-York. West Point, N.Y.: Headquarters, Military Academy, 1873.

O'Grada, Cormac. *Black '47 and Beyond: The Great Irish Famine in History, Economy, and Memory.* Princeton: Princeton University Press, 1999.

O'Keefe, Colonel Cornelius [Thomas Francis Meagher]. "Rides through Montana." *Harper's New Monthly Magazine* (October 1867).

O'Leary, John. *Recollections of Fenians and Fenianism.* 2 vols. London: Downey & Co., 1896.

O'Reilly, Francis Augustín. *The Fredericksburg Campaign: Winter War on the Rappahannock.* Baton Rouge: Louisiana State University Press, 2003.

Osborne, Seward R., ed. *The Civil War Diaries of Col. Theodore B. Gates, 20th New York State Militia.* Highstown, N.J.: Longstreet House, 1991.

O'Sullivan, Thomas F. *The Young Irelanders.* Tralee, Ireland: Kerryman Ltd., 1945.

Overholser, Joel. *Fort Benton: World's Innermost Port.* Fort Benton, Mont.: Joel Overholser, 1987.

Paladin, Vivian A. "Henry N. Blake: Proper Bostonian, Purposeful Pioneer." *Montana, the Magazine of Western History* 14:4 (Autumn 1964).

Palladino, L. B. *Indian and White in the Northwest: A History of Catholicity in Montana, 1831 to 1891.* Lancaster, Pa.: Wickersham Publishing Co., 1922.

Pepper, George W. "Personal Recollections of General Thomas Francis Meagher." *Donahoe's Magazine* 41 (May 1899).

————. *Under Three Flags; or, The Story of My Life as Preacher, Captain in the Army, Chaplain, Consul, with Speeches and Interviews.* Cincinnati: Curts & Jennings, 1899.

Perry, James M. *A Bohemian Brigade: The Civil War Correspondents, Mostly Rough, Sometimes Ready.* New York: Wiley, 2000.

Phillips, Paul C. *Forty Years on the Frontier, as Seen in the Journals and Reminiscences of Granville Stuart, Gold-Miner, Trader, Merchant, Rancher and Politician.* Vols. 1 and 2. Cleveland: Arthur H. Clark, 1925.

Pigott, Richard. *Personal Recollections of an Irish National Journalist.* London: Hodges, Figgis & Co., 1882.

Priest, John Michael. *Antietam: The Soldiers' Battle.* New York: Oxford University Press, 1993.

Pritchard, Russ A. *The Irish Brigade: A Pictorial History of the Famed Civil War Fighters.* Philadelphia: Courage Books, 2004.

Pryor, Mrs. Roger A. [Sara Agnes Rice]. *Reminiscences of Peace and War.* New York: Macmillan, 1905.

Rafferty, Oliver P. *The Church, the State, and the Fenian Threat, 1861–75.* London: Macmillan Press/New York: St. Martin's Press, 1999.

Raymer, Robert George. *Montana: The Land and the People.* Vol. 1. Chicago: Lewis Publishing, 1930.

Reardon, James Michael. *The Catholic Church in the Diocese of St. Paul, from Earliest Origin to Centennial Achievement: A Factual Narrative.* St. Paul, Minn.: North Central Publishing, 1952.

Reinhart, Herman Francis. *The Golden Frontier: The Recollections of Herman Francis Reinhart, 1851–1869.* Ed. Doyce B. Nunis, Jr. Austin: University of Texas Press, 1962.

"A Review of the Last Session." *Blackwood's Edinburgh Magazine* (September 1848).

Rice, Madeleine Hooke. *American Catholic Opinion in the Slavery Controversy.* Gloucester, Mass.: Peter Smith, 1964.

Richardson, Albert D. *Beyond the Mississippi.* Hartford: American Publishing Co., 1867.

Rolle, Andrew. *The Road to Virginia City: The Diary of James Knox Polk Miller.* Norman: University of Oklahoma Press, 1960.

Ronan, Margaret. *Girl from the Gulches: The Story of Mary Ronan.* Helena: Montana Historical Society Press, 2003.

Ryan, Desmond. *The Fenian Chief: A Biography of James Stephens.* Coral Gables: University of Miami Press, 1967.

Safford, Jeffrey J. *The Mechanics of Optimism: Mining Companies, Technology, and the Hot Spring Gold Rush, Montana Territory 1864–1868.* Boulder: University Press of Colorado, 2004.

Samito, Christian G., ed. *Commanding Boston's Irish Ninth: The Civil War Letters of Colonel Patrick R. Guiney, Ninth Massachusetts Volunteer Infantry.* New York: Fordham University Press, 1998.

Sanders, Helen Fitzgerald. *A History of Montana.* Chicago: Lewis Publishing Co., 1913.

Sanders, W. F., II, and Robert T. Taylor. *Biscuits and Badmen: The Sanders' Story in Their Own Words.* Butte, Mont.: Editorial Review Press, 1983.

Savage, John. *'98 and '48: The Modern Revolutionary History and Literature of Ireland.* Redfield, Ireland: Redfield, 1856.

Schwantes, Carlos A. *In Mountain Shadows: A History of Idaho.* Lincoln: University of Nebraska Press, 1991.

Seagrave, Pia Seija, ed. *The History of the Irish Brigade: A Collection of Historical Essays.* Fredericksburg, Va.: Sergeant Kirkland's Museum & Historical Society, 1997.

Sears, Stephen W. *Chancellorsville.* Boston: Houghton-Mifflin, 1996.

————, ed. *The Civil War Papers of George B. McClellan: Selected Correspondence, 1860–1865.* New York: Da Capo, 1992.

————. *George B. McClellan: The Young Napoleon.* New York: Ticknor & Fields, 1988.

————. *Landscape Turned Red: The Battle of Antietam.* Norwalk, Conn.: Easton Press, 1983.

Shaw, Richard. *Dagger John: The Unquiet Life and Times of Archbishop John Hughes of New York.* New York: Paulist, 1977.

Sherman, William Tecumseh. *Memoirs.* New York: Penguin, 2000.

Simon, John Y., ed. *The Papers of Ulysses S. Grant.* Vols. 12, 13, and 17. Carbondale: Southern Illinois University Press, 2003.

Slattery, T. P. *The Assassination of D'Arcy McGee.* Toronto: Doubleday & Co., 1968.

————. *"They Got to Fine Mee Guilty Yet."* Toronto: Doubleday Canada, 1972.

Small, Lawrence F. *Religion in Montana: Pathways to the Present.* Billings: Rocky Mountain College, 1995.

Small, Stephen. *Irish Century from the Famine.* London: Barnes & Noble Books, 1998.

Smart, James G., ed. *A Radical View: The "Agate" Dispatches of Whitelaw Reid, 1861–1865.* 2 vols. Memphis: Memphis State University Press, 1976.

Smith, Jean Edward. *Ulysses S. Grant.* New York: Simon & Schuster, 2001.

"Some Letters of General T. F. Meagher." *Journal of the American Irish Historical Society* 30 (1932).

Somerset Fry, Peter, and Fiona Somerset Fry. *A History of Ireland.* New York: Routledge, 1988. Rpt. New York: Barnes & Noble, 1993.

Somerville-Large, Peter. *Dublin.* London: Hamish Hamilton, 1979.

Spann, Edward K. "Union Green: The Irish Community and the Civil War." In Bayor and Meagher, *The New York Irish,* 193–212.

Spence, Clark C. *Montana: A Bicentennial History.* New York: Norton, 1978.

————. *Territorial Politics and Government in Montana, 1864–89.* Urbana: University of Illinois Press, 1975.

Strother, David H. "Personal Recollections of the War by a Virginian." *Harper's New Monthly Magazine* 36 (December 1867–May 1868).

Stuart, Granville. *Diary and Sketchbook of a Journey to "America" in 1866, and Return Trip up the Missouri River to Fort Benton, Montana.* Los Angeles: Dawson's Book Shop, 1963.

Swanberg, W. A. *Sickles the Incredible.* Gettysburg: Stan Clark Military Books, 1991.

Swinton, William. *Army of the Potomac.* New York: Smithmark, 1995.

Thackeray, William Makepeace. *The Irish Sketch Book.* Dover, N.H.: Blackstaff, 1985.

Thane, James L., Jr., ed. *A Governor's Wife on the Mining Frontier.* Salt Lake City: Tanner Trust Fund, 1976.

————. "An Ohio Abolitionist in the Far West: Sidney Edgerton and the Opening of Montana, 1863–1866." *Pacific Northwest Quarterly* (October 1976).

Thompson, Angela Faye. "The Death of Thomas Francis Meagher Revisited." Master's thesis, University of Montana, 1998.

Touhill, Blanche M. *William Smith O'Brien and His Irish Revolutionary Companions in Penal Exile.* Columbia, Mo.: University of Missouri Press, 1981.

Trefousse, Hans Louis. *Andrew Johnson: A Biography.* New York: Norton, 1989.

Trench, Charles Chenevix. *The Great Dan: A Biography of Daniel O'Connell.* London: Jonathan Cape, 1984.

Tucker, Phillip Thomas. "Celtic Warriors in Blue." In Seagrave, *The History of the Irish Brigade.*

Tuttle, Daniel Sylvester. *Missionary to the Mountain West: Reminiscences of Episcopal Bishop Daniel S. Tuttle, 1866–1886.* Salt Lake City: University of Utah Press, 1987.

Vaughan, Robert. *Then and Now; or, Thirty-six Years in the Rockies.* Helena, Mont.: Farcountry, 2001.

Villard, Henry. *Memoirs of Henry Villard: Journalist and Financier, 1835–1900.* Vol. 1. New York: Da Capo, 1969.

Walker, Mabel Gregory. *The Fenian Movement.* Colorado Springs: Ralph Myles, 1969.

Watson, Reg. A. *The Life and Times of Thomas Francis Meagher, Irish Exile to Van Diemen's Land.* Lindisfarne: Anglo-Saxon-Celtic Society, 1989.

Way, Frederick Jr. *Way's Packet Directory, 1848–1994: Passenger Steamboats of the Mississippi River System since the Advent of Photography in Mid-Continent America.* Athens: Ohio University, 1994.

West, Elliott. "Thomas Francis Meagher's Bar Bill." *Montana, the Magazine of Western History* 35 (Winter 1985).

Willson, David Harris. *A History of England.* New York: Holt, Rinehart & Winston, 1967.

Wischmann, Lesley. *Frontier Diplomats: The Life and Times of Alexander Culbertson and Natoyist-Siksina'.* Spokane: Arthur H. Clark Co., 2000.

Woodham-Smith, Cecil. *The Great Hunger: Ireland 1845–1849.* London: Penguin Books, 1962.

Wright, Steven J. *The Irish Brigade.* Springfield, Pa.: Steven Wright Publishing, 1992.

Ye Galleon. *Old Fort Benton, Montana.* Fairfield, Wash.: Ye Galleon Press, 1997.

WEBSITES

"Address before the Irish Parliament, Dublin, June 28, 1963." *John F. Kennedy Library and Museum.* http://www.cs.umb.edu/~rwhealan/jfk/j062863.htm (accessed September 27, 1999).

"Biographical Sketches of Charter Members and Masters of Wabash Lodge, No. 179, A.F. and A.M. Coles County, IL." *Illinois Trails History & Genealogy.* http://genealogytrails .com/ill/coles/masonbios.html (accessed January 10, 2005).

"Catholic Encyclopedia: James Shields." *New Advent.* http://www.newadvent.org/cathen/ 13758a.htm (accessed January 10, 2005).

"Catholic Encyclopedia: Secret Societies." *New Advent.* http://www.newadvent.org/ cathen/14071b.htm (accessed July 10, 2002).

Clark, Richard. "Capital Punishment U.K.: Hanging, Drawing and Quartering." http:// www.richard.clark32.btinternet.co.uk/hdq.html (accessed November 14, 2004).

"Letter from Charles Graham Halpine to General George Cullum (November 26, 1863)." Early American Fiction Collection, University of Virginia Library. http://etext.virginia .edu/etcbin/eafbin2/toccer-eaf?id=Hp63k26&data=/www/data/eaf2/private/texts& tag=public&part=1&division=div (accessed November 19, 2006).

The Lincoln Log: A Daily Chronology of the Life of Abraham Lincoln. http://www.stg.brown .edu/projects/lincoln/ (accessed March 12, 2006).

Marriage Permission Search Results. Archives Office of Tasmania. http://resources.archives .tas.gov.au./archmarriage/ (accessed February 2, 2004).

"A New Song, on the Escape of Thomas Francis Meagher, the Irish Exile." *America Singing: Nineteenth-Century Song Sheets.* Digital ID sb30363a. American Songs and Ballads, Rare Book and Special Collections Division, Library of Congress. http://memory.loc.gov/ ammem/amsshtml/amsshome.html (accessed December 4, 2006).

Plante, Trevor K. "The Shady Side of the Family Tree: Civil War Union Court-Martial Case Files." *National Archives and Records Administration.* http://www.archives.gov/publications/prologue/1998/winter/union-court-martials.html (accessed September 22, 2000).

Port of New York Passenger Lists. *Ancestry.com.* http://landing.ancestry.com/immigration/ny/ (accessed February 4, 2006).

"Thomas F. Meagher, January 1862 (Recommendation)." *The Abraham Lincoln Papers at the Library of Congress.* Series 1, General Correspondence 1833–1916. http://memory.loc.gov/cgi-bin/query/P?mal:1:./temp/~ammem_l1vD:: (accessed December 4, 2006).

"Westchester County Miscellaneous Records 1840–1916, A–L." *Westchester County Archives.* http://www.westchestergov.com/wcarchives/Online_Indexes/PersonalNameIndexes miscellaneousrecords/misc_records_A_L.htm (accessed December 4, 2006).

Willett, Perry, ed. "Poems (1871?): A Machine-Readable Transcription." *Victorian Women Writers Project: An Electronic Collection.* http://www.indiana.edu/~letrs/vwwp/wilde/speranza.html (accessed January 25, 2000).

Index

Hardie, James A., 294–95, 300

Harlan, James, 232, 283

Harper's Magazine, 106, 275, 277–79, 305

Harper's Weekly, 168

Hayes, S. C., 134

Hedges, Cornelius, 239

Heenan, Dennis, 174

Heintzelman, Samuel, 155

Helena, Mont.: Constitutional Convention, 259–60; James Daniel's hanging, 262–66; Meagher statue in, 3–4, 8, 328–29; as territory capitol, 329

Helena Democrat, 236, 253

Helena Herald, 285

Henry, Frank, 189

Henry II (King of England), 13

Henry VIII (King of England), 13

Hill, Daniel H., 153

History of Invention (Beckford), 30

History of Ireland (Keating), 115

History of Jews in North America (Daly), 350n45

Hogan, Martin E., 266–67, 310

Holmes, Robert, 49–50

Holywood, Edward, 47

Hood, John Bell, 234

Hooker, Joseph, 142, 161, 167, 183–84, 190

Horgan, William, 174, 179

Horrigan (Lieutenant), 310

Hosmer, Hezekiah L., 229, 231, 251, 255, 279, 287–91, 307, 323

Howard, Jack, 231

Howard, Oliver, 186

Howie, Neil, 254–55, 258, 283

Hughes, John J., 90, 93, 97, 101, 105, 115, 134, 137–39, 196, 198

Humboldt, Alexander von, 30

Humboldt's Cosmos (Humboldt), 30

Huntley, C. C., 320

Idaho Territory, 219–20, 226–27, 248–49, 364n3

Indian Wars, western migration and, 281–84

Ingoldsby, Felix, 83

Insley, M. H., 293–94, 371n41

Ireland: Act of Union of 1800, 19–20; English invasion and rule of, 12–16; Great Famine of 1847, 42–44; historical figures of, 8–10; Meagher death and legacy in, 328–31; Meagher loyalty to, 86–87, 94, 109–10, 118; politics and resistance, 17–19, 26–28; rebellion of 1798, 113; rebellion of 1803, 110; Revolution of 1798, 18–19, 62, 112–13, 235–36; Revolution of 1848, 3–5, 52–57, 110, 235–36; U. S. militia recruitment in, 138–39; "Young Ireland" group, 3, 31–33

Ireland, John, 224, 268

Irish Aid Society of New York, 105, 221

Irish American, 90, 92, 119, 191–93, 199, 208–09, 225–26, 324

Irish Brigade: battle losses, 149, 158, 168, 177, 181–82, 190; Battle of Antietam, 160–69, 353n65; Battle of Bull Run, 208, 350n46, 358n53; Battle of Chancellorsville, 166, 184–90; Battle of Fair Oaks, 145–50, 351n10; Battle of Fredericksburg, 170–79, 217; Battle of Gaines's Mill, 152–55, 358n53; Battle of Malvern Hill, 145; Battle of Savage Station, 155–56; battles of the Peninsula campaign, 5, 145–52, 158, 161; Civil War engagements of, 145; "Death Feast," 178–79, 183; formation of, 137; Meagher as commander, 137–41; Meagher as member of, 3–7; Meagher death and legacy, 324, 329; Meagher resignation, 190–92; pre-battle camp life, 142–45; rebuilding the, 193–94, 197, 200–201; recruitment of, 134, 136, 150, 158–60; Seven Days battles, 152; St. Patrick's Day celebrations, 142–43, 184, 201, 216–17, 329. *See also* 69th New York State Militia; Civil War

Irish Brigade Association, 9–10, 322, 329

Irish Confederation, *41*, 45–55, 338n34

Irish Free State, 328